MEDICAL ASSISTANT
Digestive System, Nutrition, Financial Management, and First Aid
Module C

MEDICAL ASSISTANT
Digestive System, Nutrition, Financial Management, and First Aid
Module C

Material Selected from:

Mastering Healthcare Terminology
Second Edition
by
Betsy J. Shiland, MS, RHIA, CPHQ, CTR

Saunders Textbook of Medical Assisting
(textbook and workbook)
by
Diane M. Klieger, RN, MBA, CMA

Medical Transcription: Techniques and Procedures
Sixth Edition
by
Marcy O. Diehl, BVE, CMA-A, CMT, FAAMT

SAUNDERS

ELSEVIER

11830 Westline Industrial Drive
St. Louis, Missouri 63146

DIGESTIVE SYSTEM, NUTRITION, FINANCIAL MANAGEMENT,   ISBN: 978-1-4377-0342-9
AND FIRST AID—MODULE C

Chapter 1 from Shiland BJ: *Mastering healthcare terminology,* ed 2, St Louis, 2006, Mosby.

Chapters 2, 3, 4, and 5 from Klieger DM: *Saunders textbook of medical assisting,* St Louis.
Copyright © 2005, Elsevier.

Chapter 6 by Cathy A. Flite, M.Ed.,RHIA, Assistant Professor, Department of Health
Information Management, Temple University, Philadelphia, Pennsylvania.
Copyright © 2010, Elsevier.

Chapter 7 from Diehl MO: *Medical transcription: techniques and procedures,* ed 6, St Louis.
Copyright © 2007, Saunders.

Appendixes A and B from Klieger DM: *Workbook to accompany Saunders textbook of medical
assisting,* St Louis.
Copyright © 2005, Elsevier.

Portions of Appendixes A and B copyright © 2010 by Corinthian Colleges, Inc.

Notice

Knowledge and best practice in this field are constantly changing. As new research and
experience broaden our knowledge, changes in practice, treatment and drug therapy may
become necessary or appropriate. Readers are advised to check the most current
information provided (i) on procedures featured or (ii) by the manufacturer of each
product to be administered, to verify the recommended dose or formula, the method and
duration of administration, and contraindications. It is the responsibility of the
practitioner, relying on their own experience and knowledge of the patient, to make
diagnoses, to determine dosages and the best treatment for each individual patient, and to
take all appropriate safety precautions. To the fullest extent of the law, neither the
Publisher nor the Authors assume any liability for any injury and/or damage to persons or
property arising out of or related to any use of the material contained in this book.

The Publisher

ISBN: 978-1-4377-0342-9

Printed in the United States of America

Last digit is the print number: 9 8 7 6 5 4 3 2

ACKNOWLEDGMENTS

Thank you to our advisory board members and the CCi Medical Assisting Program community for your dedication, teamwork, and support over the years.

HOW TO USE THIS BOOK

This textbook has been designed for your success. Each feature has been chosen to help you learn medical assisting quickly and effectively. Colorful boxes, tables, and illustrations will visually spark your interest, add to your knowledge, and aid in your retention of the material. Most chapters end with a review that asks you to apply the terms and concepts you have learned.

USE ALL THE FEATURES IN THE CHAPTER

Key Terms

The key terms list provides you with a quick overview of the terms you will encounter as you work your way through the chapter. You can also use this page to help you review for tests.

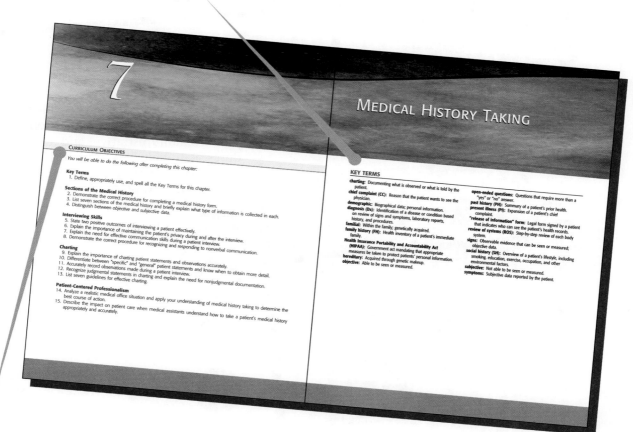

Objectives

Each objective is a goal for you. You should refer to these objectives before you study the chapter to see what your goals are and then again at the end of the chapter to see if you have accomplished them.

Exercises

Some chapters have exercises located after passages of information. Make sure you do these exercises to help you retain your new knowledge. Your instructor can check your work.

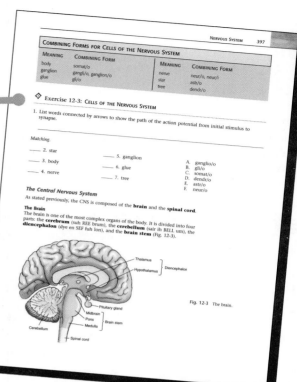

Procedures

Many chapters will contain illustrated step-by-step procedures showing you how to perform administrative and clinical procedures. Rationales for most steps explain why the step is important, and icons let you know which standard precautions to follow:

 Handwashing

 Gloving

 Personal Protective Equipment

 Biohazardous Waste Disposal

 Sharps Disposal

Plus, sample documentation shows you how to chart clinical procedures.

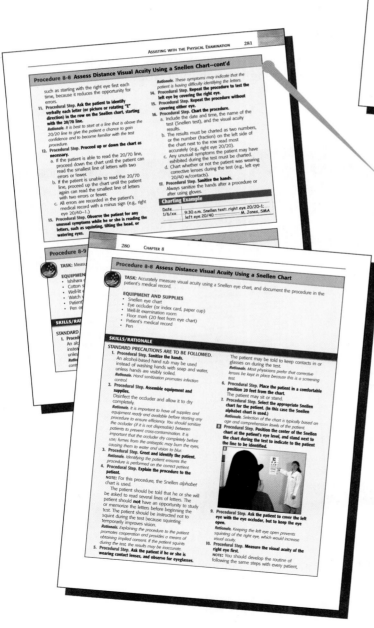

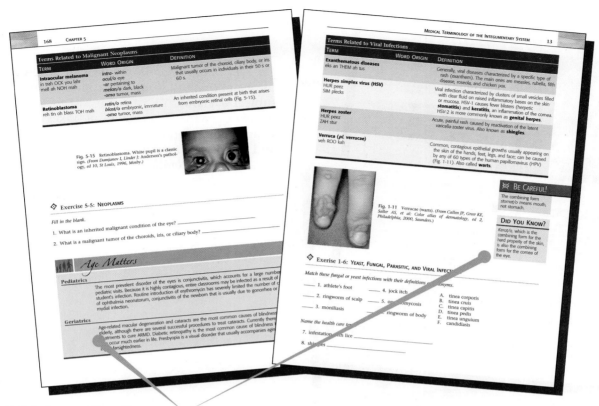

Special Information Boxes

Special information boxes that offer interesting facts or cautions are scattered throughout each chapter.
- *Did You Know?* boxes highlight the fascinating, sometimes strange history that underlies the origins of health care terms.
- *Be Careful!* boxes point out common pitfalls that you might experience when health care terms and word parts are spelled similarly but have different meanings.
- *Age Matters* boxes highlight important concepts and terminology for both pediatric and geriatric patients.

- *Careers* boxes are intended to give you more information about the job outlook, tasks, and educational requirements for the other members of the health care team.

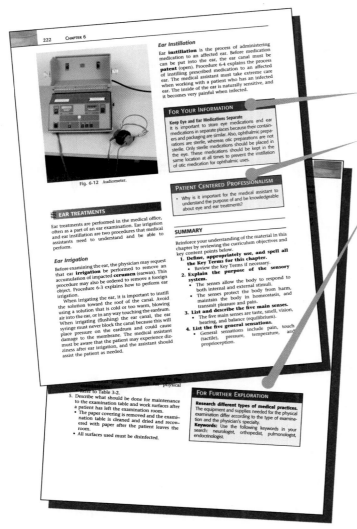

- *For Your Information* boxes provide interesting informational "tid-bits" on topics related to the subject at hand.
- *Patient-Centered Professionalism* boxes prompt you to think about the patient's perspective and encourage empathy.
- *For Further Exploration* boxes suggest topics for further Internet research to expand your comprehension of concepts and inspire you to "learn beyond the text."

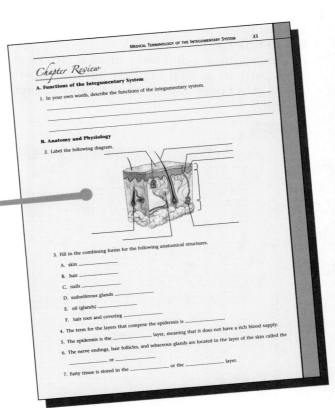

Chapter Review

A variety of exercises, including reviews of chapter terminology, theory, and critical-thinking, are included at the end of each chapter to help you test your knowledge. Most chapter reviews also include case studies to give you the opportunity to apply your recently gained knowledge to real-life situations. Your instructor can check your work on the chapter review section.

514 APPENDIX A

Student Name _____   Date _____

CHECKLIST: PERFORM PROPER HANDWASHING FOR MEDICAL ASEPSIS

TASK: Prevent the spread of pathogens by aseptically washing hands, following Standard Precautions.

CONDITIONS: Given the proper equipment and supplies, the student will be required to demonstrate the proper method of performing handwashing for medical asepsis.

EQUIPMENT AND SUPPLIES
- Liquid antibacterial soap
- Nailbrush or orange stick
- Paper towels
- Warm running water
- Regular waste container

STANDARDS: Complete the procedure within _____ minutes and achieve a minimum score of _____%.

Time began _____ Time ended _____

Steps	Possible Points	First Attempt	Second Attempt
1. Assemble all supplies and equipment.	5		
2. Remove rings and watch or push the watch up on the forearm.	5		
3. Stand close to the sink, without allowing clothing to touch the sink.	5		
4. Turn on the faucets, using a paper towel.	5		
5. Adjust the water temperature to warm—not hot or cold. Explain why proper water temperature is important.	10		
6. Discard the paper towel in the proper waste container.	5		
7. Wet hands and wrists under running water, and apply liquid antibacterial soap. Hands must be held lower than the elbows at all times. Hands must not touch the inside of the sink.	10		
8. Work soap into a lather by rubbing the palms together using a circular motion.	10		
9. Clean the fingernails with a nailbrush or an orange stick.	5		
10. Rinse hands thoroughly under running water, holding them in a downward position and allowing soap and water to run off the fingertips.	10		
11. Repeat the procedure if hands are grossly contaminated.	10		
12. Dry the hands gently and thoroughly using a clean paper towel. Discard the paper towel in proper waste container.	10		
13. Using a dry paper towel, turn the faucets off, clean the area around the sink, and discard the towel in regular waste container.	10		
Total Points Possible	100		

Comments: Total Points Earned _____   Instructor's Signature _____

Appendixes

Appendixes include competency checklists. They are organized into two groups. There are Core Competency Checklists for core skills, such as taking vital signs, giving injections, and assigning insurance codes, that you will be practicing in every module. The Core Competency Checklists are followed by the Procedure Competency Checklists, which are unique to the topics you are learning in this module. Each group of checklists has a Grade Sheet to summarize your performance scores when demonstrating your competencies to your instructor.

CONTENTS

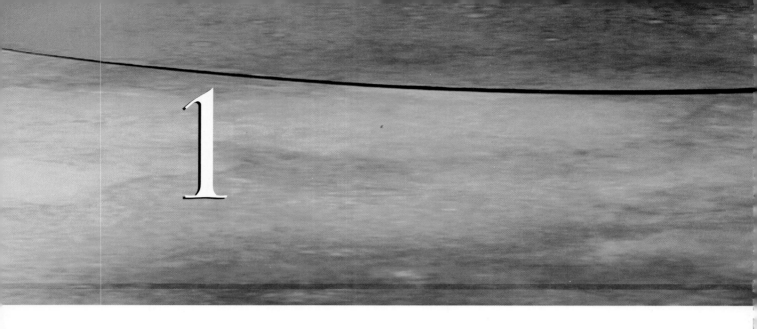

1

"Anybody who believes that the way to a man's heart is through his stomach flunked geography."
—Robert Byrne

OBJECTIVES

1. Recognize and use terms related to the anatomy and physiology of the digestive system.
2. Recognize and use terms related to the pathology of the digestive system.
3. Recognize and use terms related to the diagnostic procedures for the digestive system.
4. Recognize and use terms related to the therapeutic interventions for the digestive system.

MEDICAL TERMINOLOGY OF THE DIGESTIVE SYSTEM

CHAPTER AT A GLANCE

ANATOMY AND PHYSIOLOGY

alimentary canal	deglutition	large intestine	pylorus	stomach
anus	digestion	liver	peristalsis	
appendix	esophagus	mastication	rectum	
cecum	gallbladder	oral cavity	sigmoid colon	
colon	ingestion	pancreas	small intestine	

KEY WORD PARTS

PREFIXES	SUFFIXES	COMBINING FORMS
a-	-ectomy	append/o, appendic/o
dys-	-emesis	cholecyst/o
hyper-	-pepsia	col/o, colon/o
par-	-rrhea	dent/i, odont/o
peri-	-scopy	enter/o
sub-	-stalsis	esophag/o
	-stomy	gastr/o
	-tresia	hepat/o
		or/o
		pancreat/o
		proct/o

KEY TERMS

anastomosis	dyspepsia	hematochezia	inguinal hernia
appendicitis	dysphagia	hemoccult test	melena
barium enema	endoscopy	hemorrhoid	periodontal disease
cholecystitis	esophageal atresia	hepatitis	polyp
colonoscopy	gastroenteritis	herniorrhaphy	pyloric stenosis
colostomy	gastroesophageal reflux disease (GERD)	ileus	
diarrhea	hematemesis		
diverticulosis			

FUNCTIONS OF THE DIGESTIVE SYSTEM

The digestive system (Fig. 1-1) provides the nutrients needed for cells to replicate themselves continually and build new tissue. This is done through several distinct processes: **ingestion**, the intake of food; **digestion**, the breakdown of food; **absorption**, the process of extracting nutrients; and **elimination**, the excretion of any waste products. Other names for the system are the **gastrointestinal (GI) tract**, which refers to the two main parts of the system, and the **alimentary** (al ih MEN tair ee) **canal**, which refers to the tubelike nature of the digestive system, starting at the mouth and continuing in varying diameters to the anus.

The health care term for the process of chewing is **mastication** (mass tih KAY shun); the term for swallowing is **deglutition** (deh gloo TIH shun). The wavelike movement that propels food through the alimentary canal is known as **peristalsis** (pair ih STALL sis). The combining form *phag/o* means to *eat* or *to swallow*; hence, difficulty with deglutition could be termed **dysphagia** (dis FAY zsa). The term **hyperalimentation** (hye pur al ih men TAY shun) refers to the process of taking in more nutrients than the body optimally needs.

COMBINING FORMS FOR THE DIGESTIVE SYSTEM

MEANING	COMBINING FORM
eat or swallow	phag/o
intestines	intestin/o
nutrition	aliment/o
stomach	gastr/o

PREFIXES AND SUFFIXES FOR THE DIGESTIVE SYSTEM

PREFIX/SUFFIX	MEANING
dys-	difficult
hyper-	excessive
peri-	surrounding
-stalsis	contraction

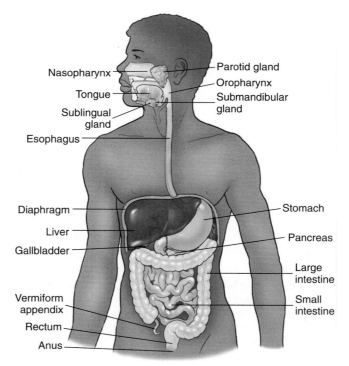

Fig. 1-1   The gastrointestinal system.

◆ Exercise 1-1: FUNCTIONS OF THE DIGESTIVE SYSTEM

Fill in the blanks.

1. Alternative terms for the digestive system are the ___alimentary___ canal and ___gastrointestinal___ tract.

2. The digestive system provides ___nutrient___ needed for ___cells___ to replicate themselves and build new tissue.

Identify the GI function described using one of the following terms.

absorption, ingestion, elimination, digestion

3. If the body were not able to break down food mechanically or chemically, it would not be able to

   accomplish which process of the GI system? ___digestion___.

4. Problems with taking nutrients into the body's cells *after* food has been broken down within the

   digestive tract have to do with the process of ___absorption___.

5. A patient who has difficulty getting rid of the waste products of the digestive process has problems

   with which function of the GI system? ___elimination___.

6. The process of taking in food is called ___ingestion___.

Matching.

___C___ 7. deglutition   ___B___ 10. alimentary canal   A. process of chewing
                                                               B. GI tract
___D___ 8. peristalsis   ___A___ 11. mastication   C. process of swallowing
                                                               D. wavelike movement through the GI system
___F___ 9. dysphagia   ___E___ 12. hyperalimentation   E. excessive nutrient intake
                                                               F. difficulty swallowing

ANATOMY AND PHYSIOLOGY

Oral Cavity

Food normally enters the body through the mouth, or **oral cavity** (Fig. 1-2, A). The function of this cavity is initially to break down the food mechanically by chewing (mastication) and lubricate the food to ease in swallowing (deglutition).

The oral cavity begins at the **lips**, the two fleshy structures surrounding its opening. The inside of the mouth is bounded by the **cheeks**; the **tongue** at the floor; and an anterior **hard palate** (PAL it) and posterior **soft palate**, which form the roof. The upper and lower jaws hold 32 permanent **teeth** that are set in the flesh of the **gums**. The **uvula** (YOO vyoo lah) is the tag of flesh that hangs down from the medial surface of the soft palate. The three pairs of **salivary** (SAL ih vair ee) **glands** provide **saliva**, a substance that moistens the oral cavity, initiates the digestion of starches, and aids in chewing and swallowing. The glands are named for their locations: **parotid** (pair AH tid), near the ear; **submandibular** (sub man DIB yoo lur), under the lower jaw; and **sublingual** (sub LEENG gwul), under the tongue.

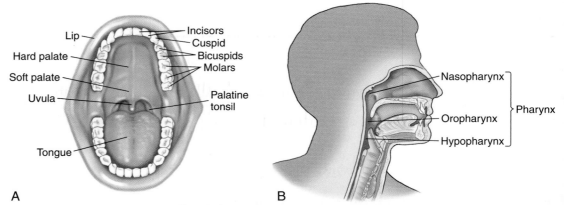

Fig. 1-2 **A,** The oral cavity. **B,** The pharynx.

Throat

The throat, or **pharynx** (FAIR inks), is a tube that connects the oral cavity with the esophagus. It can be divided into three main parts: the nasopharynx, the oropharynx, and the hypopharynx. The **nasopharynx** (nay soh FAIR inks) is the most superior part of the pharynx, located behind the nasal cavity. The **oropharynx** (oh roh FAIR inks) is the part of the throat directly adjacent to the oral cavity, and the **hypopharynx** (hye poh FAIR inks) is the part of the throat directly below the oropharynx (Fig. 1-2, *B*).

Esophagus

The **esophagus** (eh SAH fah gus) is a muscular, mucus-lined tube that extends from the throat to the stomach. It carries a masticated lump of food, a **bolus** (BOH lus), from the oral cavity to the stomach by means of peristalsis. The glands in the lining of the esophagus produce mucus, which aids in lubricating and easing the passage of the bolus to the stomach. The muscle that must relax before the food enters the stomach is known by three names: the lower **esophageal** (eh sah fah JEE ul) **sphincter** (SFINK tur) **(LES)**; the **gastroesophageal sphincter**; or the **cardiac sphincter**, which gets its name because of its proximity to the heart.

DID YOU KNOW?

A *sphincter* is a ringlike muscle; sphincters appear in other parts of the body as well (e.g., in the urinary system and the eye.).

COMBINING FORMS FOR THE ORAL CAVITY, THROAT, AND ESOPHAGUS

MEANING	COMBINING FORM	MEANING	COMBINING FORM
cheek	bucc/o	nose	nas/o
ear	ot/o	oral cavity	or/o
esophagus	esophag/o	pharynx	pharyng/o
gums	gingiv/o	saliva	sial/o
hard and soft palates	palat/o	salivary glands	sialaden/o
heart	cardi/o	teeth	dent/i, odont/o
jaw bone (lower)	mandibul/o	throat	pharyng/o
jaw bone (upper)	maxill/o	tongue	lingu/o, gloss/o
lips	labi/o, cheil/o	uvula	uvul/o
mouth	or/o, stom/o, stomat/o		

PREFIXES FOR ANATOMY AND PHYSIOLOGY

PREFIX	MEANING
hypo-	below
par-	near, beside
sub-	below

◇ Exercise 1-2: ORAL CAVITY, THROAT, AND ESOPHAGUS

Match the combining forms with the following definitions. There may be more than one combining form for a given definition.

M 1. teeth   B 7. cheek

H 2. gums   O 8. salivary gland

BF 3 roof of mouth   J 9. saliva

E 4. tongue   N 10. uvula

K 5. mouth   L 11. throat

G 6. lips   A 12. esophagus

A. esophag/o
B. bucc/o
C. cheil/o
D. or/o
E. lingu/o
F. palat/o
G. labi/o
H. gingiv/o
I. gloss/o
J. sial/o
K. stomat/o
L. pharyng/o
M. dent/i, odont/o
N. uvul/o
O. sialaden/o

Fill in the blanks with the following choices.

sphincter, esophagus, hypopharynx, bolus, nasopharynx, oropharynx, pharynx

13. What is the general term for the throat? _pharynx_

14. What is the term for the part of the throat that is behind the mouth?

oropharynx

15. What is the part of the throat that is behind the nasal cavity? _nasopharynx_

16. What is the name for the section of the throat that is *below* the oral cavity?

hypopharynx

17. What is the name of the tube that extends from the throat to the stomach?

esophagus

18. What is the term for a ringlike muscle? _sphincter_

19. What is the name for a chewed mass of food that is swallowed? _masticated lump_

Name the salivary gland.

20. The one that is "near the ear": _parotid_

21. The one that is "under the tongue": _sublingual_

22. The one that is "under the lower jaw bone": _submandibular_

List the three names for the ringlike muscle between the esophagus and the stomach.

23. <u>esophageal sphincter</u>   24. <u>gastroesophageal</u>   25. <u>cardiac sphincter</u>

Stomach

The stomach, an expandable vessel, is divided into three sections: the **fundus** (FUN dus), the **body**, and the **pylorus** (pye LORE us) (Fig. 1-3). The portion of the stomach that surrounds the esophagogastric connection is the fundus (*pl.* fundi), which is also referred to as the **cardia** (KAR dee ah), or cardiac region. This section of the stomach has no acid-producing cells, unlike the remainder of the stomach. The body is the central part of the stomach, and the pylorus (*pl.* pylori) is at the distal end of the stomach, where the small intestine begins. A small muscle, the **pyloric sphincter**, regulates the gentle release of food from the stomach into the small intestine. When the stomach is empty, it has an appearance of being lined with many ridges. These ridges, or wrinkles, are called **rugae** (ROO jee) (*sing.* ruga).

The function of the stomach is to temporarily store the chewed food that it receives from the esophagus. This food is mixed with gastric juices and hydrochloric acid to further the digestive process chemically. This mixture is called **chyme** (kyme). The smooth muscles of the stomach contract to aid in the mechanical digestion of the food. A continual coating of mucus protects the stomach and the rest of the digestive system from the acidic nature of the gastric juices.

Small Intestine

Once the chyme has been formed in the stomach, the pyloric sphincter relaxes a bit at a time to release portions of it into the first part of the **small intestine**, called the **duodenum** (doo AH deh num). The small intestine gets its name not because of its length (it is about 20 feet long) but because of the diameter of its **lumen** (LOO mun) (a tubular cavity within the body). The remaining two sections of the small intestine are the **jejunum** (jeh JOO num) and **ileum** (ILL ee um).

Multiple circular folds in the small intestines, called **plicae** (PLY see), contain thousands of tiny projections called **villi** (VILL eye) (*sing.* villus), which contain blood capillaries that absorb the products of carbohydrate and protein digestion. The villi also contain lymphatic vessels, known as **lacteals** (LACK tee uls), that absorb **lipid** (LIH pid) substances from the chyme.

Large Intestine

In contrast to the small intestine, the **large intestine** (Fig. 1-4) is only about 5 feet long, but it is much wider in diameter. The primary function of the large intestine is the elimination of the waste products from the body. Some synthesis of vitamins occurs in the large intestine, but unlike the small intestine, the large intestine has no villi and is not well suited for absorption of nutrients. The **ileocecal** (ILL ee oh SEE kul) valve is the exit from the small intestine and entrance to the colon. The first part of the large intestine, the **cecum** (SEE kum), has a wormlike appendage, called the **vermiform appendix** (VUR mih form ah PEN dicks) (*pl.* appendices), dangling from it. Although this organ does not seem to have any direct function related to the digestive system, it is thought to have a possible immunological defense mechanism.

No longer called chyme, whatever has not been absorbed by the small intestines is now called **feces** (FEE sees). The feces pass from the cecum to the **ascending colon** (KOH lin), through the **transverse colon**, the **descending colon**, the **sigmoid colon**, and on to the **rectum**, where they are held until released from the body completely through the anal sphincter. The process of releasing feces from the body is called **defecation**.

DID YOU KNOW?

The suffix *-ase* is used to form the name of an enzyme. It is added to the name of the substance upon which the enzyme acts: for example, *lipase*, which acts on lipids, or *amylase*, which acts on starches. *-ose* is a chemical suffix indicating that a substance is a carbohydrate, such as *glucose*.

✖ BE CAREFUL!

Don't confuse the term *ilium*, meaning part of the hip bone, with *ileum*, meaning part of the small intestine.

✖ BE CAREFUL!

The combining form *gastr/o* refers only to the stomach. The combining forms *abdomin/o*, *lapar/o*, and *celi/o* refer to the abdomen.

✖ BE CAREFUL!

Do not confuse *-cele*, the suffix meaning herniation, with *celi/o*, the combining form for abdomen.

✖ BE CAREFUL!

Do not confuse *an/o*, the combining form for anus; *ana-*, the prefix meaning up or apart; and *an-*, the prefix meaning no or not.

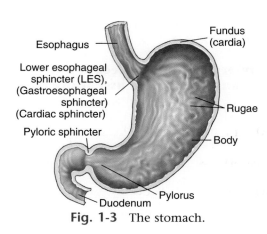

Fig. 1-3 The stomach.

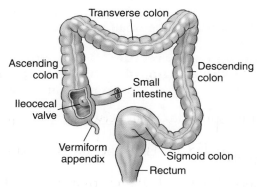

Fig. 1-4 The large intestine (colon).

COMBINING FORMS FOR THE STOMACH AND INTESTINES

MEANING	COMBINING FORM	MEANING	COMBINING FORM
abdomen	abdomin/o, celi/o, lapar/o	lipid (fat)	lip/o
anus	an/o	rectum	rect/o
appendix	append/o, appendic/o	rectum and anus	proct/o
cecum	cec/o	sigmoid colon	sigmoid/o
colon	col/o, colon/o	small intestines	enter/o
fold	plic/o	starch	amyl/o
ileum	ile/o	stomach	gastr/o
jejunum	jejun/o	sweet, sugar	gluc/o

◈ **Exercise 1-3: THE STOMACH, SMALL INTESTINE, AND LARGE INTESTINE**

Match the following combining forms and body parts with their terms.

J 1. fat

K 2. folds

O 3. colon

H 4. jejunum

P 5. ileum

I 6. starch

N 7. rectum

Q 8. anus

F 9. sugar

L 10. duodenum

G 11. stomach

b 12. cecum

R 13. sigmoid colon

E 14. tubular cavity

D 15. enter/o

M 16. pylorus

A 17. rectum and anus

C 18. appendix

A. proct/o
B. first part of large intestines
C. structure hanging from cecum
D. small intestines
E. lumen
F. gluc/o
G. gastr/o
H. second part of small intestines
I. amyl/o
J. lip/o
K. plicae
L. first part of small intestines
M. muscle between stomach and first part of small intestines
N. last straight part of colon
O. large intestines
P. distal part of small intestines
Q. final sphincter in GI tract
R. S-shaped part of large intestine

19. Place the following terms in anatomical order, starting with the small muscle between the stomach and the first part of the small intestine and going down the body.

descending colon, rectum, ileum, duodenum, pyloric sphincter, cecum and appendix, ileocecal valve, sigmoid colon, anal sphincter, transverse colon, ascending colon, jejunum

pyloric sphincter, duodenum → jejunum → ileum →
cecum ; appendix → ileocecal valve → ascending colon → transverse colon →
descending colon → sigmoid colon → rectum → fecal

Circle the correct answer.

20. When chewed food is mixed with gastric juices and hydrochloric acid in the stomach, it becomes *(rugae,* (chyme)*.* When this mixture enters the large intestine, it becomes *(urine,* (feces)*.*

21. The villi and plicae are structures that serve to (*absorb nutrients,* form waste products).

22. In which intestine are the majority of nutrients absorbed? *(large,* (small)*.*

Accessory Organs (Adnexa)

The accessory organs are the gallbladder, liver, and pancreas (Fig. 1-5). These organs secrete fluid into the GI tract but are not a direct part of the tube itself. Sometimes these structures are referred to as **adnexa** (ad NECK sah).

The two lobes that form the **liver** (LIH vur) virtually fill the right upper quadrant of the abdomen and extend partially into the left upper quadrant. The liver forms a substance called **bile**, which **emulsifies** (ee MUL sih fyez), or mechanically breaks down, fats into smaller particles so that they can be chemically digested. Bile is composed of **bilirubin** (BILL ee ROO bin), the waste product formed by the normal breakdown of hemoglobin in red blood cells at the end of their life spans, and **cholesterol** (koh LESS tur all), a fatty substance found only in animal tissues. **Bile ducts** in the liver merge into the **hepatic** (heh PAT ick) **duct**, which carries the bile out of the liver. The hepatic duct joins with the **cystic** (SISS tick) **duct** of the gallbladder, forming the **common bile duct**, which carries the bile to the duodenum. The bile is stored in the gallbladder (GALL blad ur), a small sac found on the underside of the right lobe of the liver. When fatty food enters the duodenum, a hormone called **cholecystokinin** (koh lee sis toh KYE nin) is secreted, causing a contraction of the gallbladder to move bile out into the cystic duct, then the common bile duct, and finally into the duodenum.

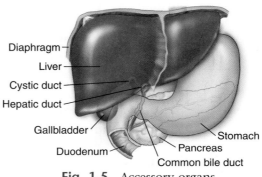

Diaphragm
Liver
Cystic duct
Hepatic duct
Gallbladder
Duodenum
Stomach
Pancreas
Common bile duct

Fig. 1-5 Accessory organs.

The **pancreas** (PAN kree us) is a gland located in the upper left quadrant. It is involved in the digestion of the three types of food molecules: carbohydrates, proteins, and lipids. The pancreatic enzymes are carried through the pancreatic duct that empties into the common bile duct. Pancreatic involvement in the food digestion is an **exocrine** (ECK soh krin) function.

COMBINING FORMS FOR THE ACCESSORY ORGANS

MEANING	COMBINING FORM	MEANING	COMBINING FORM
bile	chol/e, bil/i	liver	hepat/o
bile vessels	cholangi/o	lobe	lob/o
common bile duct	choledoch/o	pancreas	pancreat/o
gallbladder	cholecyst/o		

◈ Exercise 1-4: ACCESSORY ORGANS

Match the combining forms with their terms.

G 1. pancreas   B 5. bile

D 2. gallbladder   E 6. bile vessels

A 3. lobe   F 7. common bile duct

C 4. liver

A. lob/o
B. chol/e, bil/i
C. hepat/o
D. cholecyst/o
E. cholangi/o
F. choledoch/o
G. pancreat/o

8. Name the quadrants in which each of the accessory organs is located.

A. liver ___right upper quadrant partly extended to left quadrant___

B. gallbladder ___right lower quadrant___

C. pancreas ___upper left quadrant___

Fill in the blanks using the following terms.

emulsification, bilirubin, cholesterol, cholecystokinin, adnexa

9. Another word for GI accessory structures: ___adnexa___

10. The process of breaking down fats into smaller particles: ___emulsification___

11. The hormone that causes a contraction of the gallbladder to release bile:

   ___cholecystokinin___

12. The waste product left over from breakdown of red blood cells: ___bilirubin___

13. A fatty substance found in animal tissues: ___cholesterol___

Synergy Hospital
781 Magnolia Blvd.
Atlanta, GA 30311

OPERATIVE REPORT

SURGEON:	Alan Jerome, MD
ANESTHESIOLOGIST:	Kelley Hicks, MD
ANESTHESIA:	General
DATE:	07/20/xx
PREOPERATIVE DIAGNOSIS:	Rule out GI pathology
POSTOPERATIVE DIAGNOSIS:	See "Impression" below
OPERATION:	Upper GI endoscopy

Patient was brought into the endoscopy suite where continuous oximetry, blood pressure and ECG monitoring was placed. She was given 50 μg of fentanyl before procedure. The GIF Olympus 150 video endoscope was introduced through the pharynx without difficulty. Proximal portion of the esophagus appeared normal. At approximately mid esophagus there were noted streaks of erythema extending up into the esophagus. The squamocolumnar junction was 33 cm where there was a smooth concentric narrowing of the esophagus. There was mild friability of this tissue and distally was a moderate hiatal hernia. The scope was advanced through this into the gastric fundus which was visualized both in the forward and retroflexed manner. Mucosa appeared quite normal. Distally, there was a marked erythema of the antrum, particularly surrounding the pylorus. Biopsy was taken for *H. pylori*. The duodenum was difficult to intubate but appeared normal. Scope was withdrawn again to the level of the lower esophageal sphincter at 36 cm. Biopsies were taken from that area and circumferentially up to approximately 32 cm. There was minimal bleeding. Patient tolerated the procedure well.

IMPRESSION:

1. Reflux esophagitis with stricture at 33 cm

2. Moderate hiatal hernia

3. Probably Barrett esophagus

4. Diffuse antral gastritis, biopsy pending

Alan Jerome, MD

Exercise 1-5: OPERATIVE REPORT

Using the operative report on p. 10, answer the following questions.

1. What was the route of the endoscope? _Upper GI_

2. The portion of the esophagus that appeared normal was (close to/far from) the mouth. Circle one.

3. What is *H. pylori*, and why would a biopsy be done? _Helicobacter pylori / marked erythema of the antrum._

4. What are synonyms for the "lower esophageal sphincter"? _esophagus_

≋ PATHOLOGY

DID YOU KNOW?

Remember what onomatopoeia is? It means words such as "pop" or "fizz" that imitate sounds. The term *hiccup* is a health care example of a word that was created to imitate the sound of the act.

DID YOU KNOW?

Nausea derives its name from the Greek word for seasickness. Notice the similarity between the words *nausea* and *nautical.*

DID YOU KNOW?

Heartburn is a misnomer, although an understandable one. When one experiences this burning sensation, it is in the chest area near the heart.

Terms Related to Upper Gastrointestinal Complaints

TERM	WORD ORIGIN	DEFINITION
Dyspepsia dis PEP see ah	*dys-* abnormal, bad *-pepsia* digestion	Feeling of epigastric discomfort that occurs shortly after eating. The discomfort may range from a feeling of nausea, fullness, heartburn, and/or bloating. Also called **indigestion**.
Eructation ee ruck TAY shun		Release of air from the stomach through the mouth. Eructation may be caused by rapid eating or by intentionally or unintentionally swallowing air **(aerophagia)**. Also called **burping** or **belching**.
Halitosis hal ih TOH sis	*halit/o* breath *-osis* abnormal condition	Bad-smelling breath.
Heartburn	See **Did You Know?** box	Painful burning sensation in esophagus, usually caused by reflux of stomach contents, hyperactivity, or peptic ulcer. Also known as **pyrosis** (pye ROH sis).
Hiccup HICK up	See **Did You Know?** box	Involuntary contraction of the diaphragm, followed by a rapid closure of the glottis (which in turn causes the characteristic sound of a hiccup). Also known as **hiccough** or **singultus**.
Nausea NAH see ah	See **Did You Know?** box	Sensation that accompanies the urge to vomit but does not always lead to vomiting.
Regurgitation ree gur jih TAY shun		Return of swallowed food to the mouth. Regurgitation may, however, describe any backward flow in the body, not just that of a GI nature.
Vomiting VAH mih ting		Forcible or involuntary emptying of the stomach through the mouth. The material expelled is called **vomitus** or **emesis**. The vomiting of blood is called **hematemesis** (hee mah TEM eh sis).

Terms Related to Lower Gastrointestinal Complaints

TERM	WORD ORIGIN	DEFINITION
Constipation kon stih PAY shun		Infrequent, incomplete, or delayed bowel movements. **Obstipation** is extreme constipation or intestinal obstruction.
Diarrhea dye ah REE ah	*dia-* through, complete *-rrhea* discharge, flow	Abnormal discharge of watery, semisolid stools.
Flatus FLAY tus		Gas expelled through the anus. Also referred to as *flatulence*.
Hematochezia hee mat oh KEE zee ah	*hemat/o* blood *-chezia* condition of stools	Bright red, frank lower GI bleeding from the rectum that may originate in the distal colon. Passage of bloody stools.
Irritable bowel syndrome (IBS)		Abnormal increase in the activity of the small and large intestines, leading to diarrhea and flatus.
Melena mah LEE nah	*melan/o* black, dark	Black, tarry stools caused by the presence of partially digested blood.

◇ Exercise 1-6: UPPER AND LOWER GI COMPLAINTS

Matching.

H 1. diarrhea   J 6. IBS

J 2. obstipation   a 7. constipation

E 3. flatus   D 8. nausea

G 4. melena   A 9. hematochezia

B 5. halitosis   F 10. regurgitation

A. bloody stools
B. bad breath
C. delayed defecation
D. feeling of need to vomit
E. gas passed through the anus
F. backward flow
G. black, tarry stools
H. loose, watery stools
I. extremely delayed defecation
J. diarrhea/gas/constipation resulting from stress with no underlying disease

Match the synonyms.

D 11. indigestion   C 14. eructation

B 12. singultus   A 15. emesis

E 13. pyrosis

A. vomit
B. hiccup
C. burping
D. dyspepsia
E. heartburn

Terms Related to Congenital Disorders

TERM	WORD ORIGIN	DEFINITION
Cleft palate kleft PAL it		Failure of the palate to close during embryonic development, creating an opening in the roof of the mouth. Cleft palate is often accompanied by a cleft lip (Fig. 1-6).
Esophageal atresia eh soff uh JEE ul ah TREE zsa	*esophag/o* esophagus *-eal* pertaining to *a-* not, without *-tresia* condition of an opening	Esophagus that ends in a blind pouch and therefore lacks an opening into the stomach.
Hirschsprung disease HERSH sprung		Congenital absence of normal nervous function in part of the colon, which results in an absence of peristaltic movement, accumulation of feces, and an enlarged colon. Also called **congenital megacolon**.
Pyloric stenosis pye LORE ick sten OH sis	*pylor/o* pylorus *-ic* pertaining to	Condition in which the muscle between the stomach and the small intestine narrows or fails to open adequately to allow partially digested food into the duodenum (Fig. 1-7).

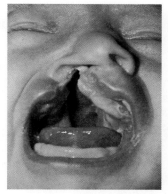

Fig. 1-6   Cleft palate and cleft lip. *(From Zitelli BJ, Davis HW: Atlas of pediatric physical diagnosis, ed 4, St Louis, 2002, Mosby.)*

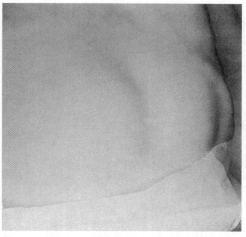

Fig. 1-7   Pyloric stenosis. The giant gastric waves are best seen just after a feeding. *(From Zitelli BJ, Davis HW: Atlas of pediatric physical diagnosis, ed 4, St Louis, 2002, Mosby.)*

  Exercise 1-7: CONGENITAL DISORDERS

Fill in the blank with the correct term.

pyloric stenosis, cleft palate, esophageal atresia, Hirschsprung disease, congenital megacolon

1. The term that refers to the lack of an opening in the tube that extends from the throat to the stomach is ___Esophageal atresia___.

2. A congenital fissure in the roof of the mouth is called ___Cleft palate___.

3. If the patient has a lack of normal nervous function in part of the large intestine, which results in an accumulation of feces, he or she may be diagnosed with *Hirschprung disease*.

4. Another name for the answer to question 3 is *Congenital megacolon*.

5. A narrowing of the muscle between the stomach and the duodenum is called *pyloric stenosis*.

Terms Related to Oral Cavity Disorders

TERM	WORD ORIGIN	DEFINITION
Aphthous stomatitis AFF thus stoh mah TYE tis	*aphth/o* ulceration *-ous* pertaining to *stomat/o* mouth *-itis* inflammation	Recurring condition characterized by small erosions (ulcers), which appear on the mucous membranes of the mouth. Also called a **canker sore**.
Cheilitis kye LYE tis	*cheil/o* lip *-itis* inflammation	Inflammation of the lips.
Cheilosis kye LOH sis	*cheil/o* lip *-osis* abnormal condition	Abnormal condition of the lips present in riboflavin (a B vitamin) deficiency.
Dental caries KARE ees	*dent/i* teeth *-al* pertaining to	Plaque disease caused by an interaction between food and bacteria in the mouth, leading to tooth decay. Also called **cavities.**
Dental plaque plack		Film of material that coats the teeth and may lead to dental decay if not removed.
Gingivitis jin jih VYE tis	*gingiv/o* gums *-itis* inflammation	Inflammatory disease of the gums characterized by redness, swelling, and bleeding (Fig. 1-8).
Herpetic stomatitis hur PET ick stoh mah TYE tis	*stomat/o* mouth *-itis* inflammation	Inflammation of the mouth caused by the herpes simplex virus (HSV). Also known as a **cold sore** or **fever blister**.
Leukoplakia loo koh PLAY kee ah	*leuk/o* white *-plakia* condition of patches	Condition of white patches that may appear on the lips and buccal mucosa (Fig. 1-9). It is usually associated with tobacco use and may be precancerous.
Malocclusion mal oh KLOO zhun	*mal-* bad, poor *-occlusion* condition of closure	Condition in which the teeth do not touch properly when the mouth is closed (abnormal bite).
Periodontal disease pair ee oh DON tul	*peri-* surrounding *odont/o* tooth *-al* pertaining to	Pathological condition of the tissues surrounding the teeth.
Pyorrhea pye or REE yah	*py/o* pus *-rrhea* flow, discharge	Purulent discharge from the tissue surrounding the teeth; often seen with gingivitis.

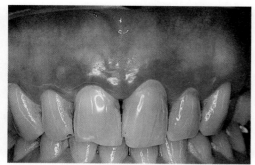

Fig. 1-8 Gingivitis. *(From Eisen D, Lynch DP:* The mouth: diagnosis and treatment, *St Louis, 1998, Mosby.)*

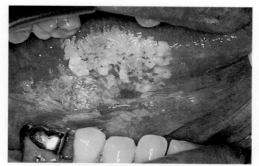

Fig. 1-9 Leukoplakia. *(From Eisen D, Lynch DP:* The mouth: diagnosis and treatment, *St Louis, 1998, Mosby.)*

✧ Exercise 1-8: ORAL CAVITY DISORDERS

Matching.

A 1. dental caries

F 2. gingivitis

E 3. cheilitis

H 4. cheilosis

D 5. aphthous stomatitis

G 6. herpetic stomatitis

I 7. dental plaque

J 8. leukoplakia

C 9. malocclusion

B 10. periodontal disease

A. tooth decay
B. disorder of tissue surrounding teeth
C. abnormal bite
D. canker sore
E. inflammation of the lips
F. inflammation of the gums
G. cold sore
H. abnormal condition of lips
I. material that coats teeth
J. white patches

Terms Related to Disorders of the Esophagus

TERM	WORD ORIGIN	DEFINITION
Achalasia ack uh LAY zsa	*a-* not, without *-chalasia* condition of relaxation	Impairment of esophageal peristalsis along with the lower esophageal sphincter's inability to relax. Also called **cardiospasm, esophageal aperistalsis** (ay per rih STALL sis), and **megaesophagus.**
Dysphagia dis FAY zsa	*dys-* bad, difficult *-phagia* condition of swallowing, eating	Difficulty with swallowing that may be due to an obstruction (e.g., a tumor) or a motor disorder (e.g., a spasm).
Gastroesophageal reflux disease (GERD) gass troh eh sah fah JEE ul	*gastr/o* stomach *esophag/o* esophagus *-eal* pertaining to *re-* back *-flux* flow	Flowing back, or return, of the contents of the stomach to the esophagus caused by an inability of the lower esophageal sphincter (LES) to contract normally; characterized by pyrosis with or without regurgitation of stomach contents to the mouth (Fig. 1-10). **Barrett esophagus** is a condition caused by chronic reflux from the stomach. It is associated with an increased risk of cancer.

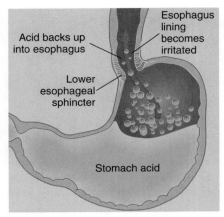

Fig. 1-10 GERD. *(From Black JM, Hawks JH, Keene A: Medical-surgical nursing clinical management for positive outcomes, ed 7, Philadelphia, 2005, Saunders.)*

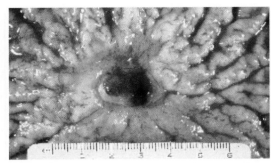

Fig. 1-11 Chronic peptic ulcer. *(From Damjanov I, Linder J: Pathology: a color atlas, St Louis, 2000, Mosby.)*

Terms Related to Disorders of the Stomach

TERM	WORD ORIGIN	DEFINITION
Gastralgia gass TRAL zsa	*gastr/o* stomach -*algia* pain	Gastric pain. Also called **gastrodynia** (gass troh DIH nee ah).
Gastritis gass TRY tis	*gastr/o* stomach -*itis* inflammation	Acute or chronic inflammation of the stomach that may be accompanied by anorexia, nausea and vomiting (N&V), or indigestion.
Peptic ulcer disease (PUD)		An erosion of the protective mucosal lining of the stomach or duodenum (Fig. 1-11). Also called a **gastric** or **duodenal ulcer.**

◆ **Exercise 1-9: ESOPHAGEAL AND STOMACH DISORDERS**

Matching. More than one answer may be correct.

_F_ 1. PUD   _A_ 4. achalasia

_D_ 2. gastralgia   _B_ 5. dysphagia

_C_ 3. gastritis   _G_ 6. GERD

A. cardiospasm
B. difficulty swallowing
C. inflammation of the stomach
D. stomach pain
E. gastrodynia
F. erosion of the gastric mucosa

G. return of the contents of the stomach to the esophagus
H. megaesophagus
I. esophageal aperistalsis

Terms Related to Intestinal Disorders

TERM	WORD ORIGIN	DEFINITION
Acute peritonitis pair ih tuh NYE tis	*periton/o* peritoneum -*itis* inflammation	Inflammation of the peritoneum that most commonly occurs when an inflamed appendix ruptures.
Anal fissure A nul FISH ur	*an/o* anus -*al* pertaining to	Cracklike lesion of the skin around the anus.

Terms Related to Intestinal Disorders—cont'd

TERM	WORD ORIGIN	DEFINITION
Anorectal abscess an oh RECK tul AB ses	*an/o* anus *rect/o* rectum *-al* pertaining to	Circumscribed area of inflammation in the anus or rectum, containing pus.
Appendicitis ah pen dih SYE tis	*appendic/o* appendix *-itis* inflammation	Inflammation of the vermiform appendix (Fig. 1-12).
Colitis koh LYE tis	*col/o* colon *-itis* inflammation	Inflammation of the large intestine.
Crohn disease krohn		Inflammation of the ileum or the colon that is of idiopathic origin. Also called regional **enteritis.**
Diverticulitis dye vur tick yoo LYE tis	*diverticul/o* diverticulum *-itis* inflammation	Inflammation occurring secondary to the occurrence of diverticulosis.
Diverticulosis dye vur tick yoo LOH sis	*diverticul/o* diverticulum *-osis* abnormal condition	Development of diverticula, pouches in the lining of the colon (Fig. 1-13).
Fistula FIST yoo lah		Abnormal channel from an internal organ to the surface of the body.
Hemorrhoid HEM uh royd		Varicose vein in the lower rectum or anus.
Ileus ILL ee us		Obstruction. **Paralytic ileus** is lack of peristaltic movement in the intestinal tract. Also called *adynamic ileus.*
Inflammatory bowel disease (IBD)		Chronic inflammation of the lining of the intestine characterized by bleeding and diarrhea.
Intussusception in tuh suh SEP shun		Inward telescoping of the intestines.
Polyp PAH lip		Benign growth that may occur in the intestines.
Proctitis prock TYE tis	*proct/o* rectum and anus *-itis* inflammation	Inflammation of the rectum and anus. Also called **rectitis**.
Pruritus ani proo RYE tis A nye		Common chronic condition of itching of the skin surrounding the anus.
Ulcerative colitis UL sur uh tiv koh LYE tis	*col/o* colon *-itis* inflammation	Chronic inflammation of the colon and rectum manifesting itself with bouts of profuse watery diarrhea.
Volvulus VOL vyoo lus		Twisting of the intestine.

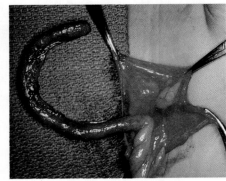

Fig. 1-12 Appendicitis. Note the darker pink color of the appendix, indicating the inflammation. *(From Zitelli BJ, Davis HW: Atlas of pediatric physical diagnosis, ed 4, St Louis, 2002, Mosby.)*

Fig. 1-13 Diverticulosis. *(From Damjanov I, Linder J: Pathology: a color atlas, St Louis, 1996, Mosby.)*

◆ Exercise 1-10: INTESTINAL DISORDERS

Matching.

H	1. polyp	D	8. intussusception
K	2. colitis	G	9. acute peritonitis
O	3. anal fissure	M	10. pruritus ani
C	4. volvulus	E	11. ulcerative colitis
L	5. proctitis	E	12. Crohn disease
R	6. paralytic ileus	N	13. hemorrhoids
P	7. fistula	S	14. IBD
		I	15. diverticulitis
		J	16. diverticulosis
		Q	17. anorectal abscess
		a	18. appendicitis
		b	19. ileus

A. inflammation of the appendix
B. general term for an obstruction
C. a twisting of the intestines
D. inward telescoping of the intestines
E. idiopathic inflammation of ileum or colon
F. profuse watery diarrhea accompanies this condition
G. ruptured appendix puts a patient at risk for this
H. growth on mucous membranes
I. inflammation of pouches in the walls of GI tract
J. abnormal condition of pouches in GI tract
K. inflammation of the large intestine
L. inflammation of the anus and rectum
M. itching of the skin around the anus
N. varicosities around the anus and rectum
O. cracklike lesion in the skin around the anus
P. abnormal channel that forms between the inside and the outside of the body
Q. circumscribed area of purulent material in the distal end of the digestive tract
R. lack of peristaltic movement in intestines
S. erosion of intestinal lining accompanied by bleeding and diarrhea

Terms Related to GI Accessory Organ Disorders

TERM	WORD ORIGIN	DEFINITION
Cholangitis koh lan JYE tis	*cholangi/o* bile vessel *-itis* inflammation	Inflammation of the intrahepatic and extrahepatic bile ducts.
Cholecystitis koh lee sis TYE tis	*cholecyst/o* gallbladder *-itis* inflammation	Inflammation of the gallbladder.
Choledocholithiasis koh lee doh koh lih THY ih sis	*choledoch/o* common bile duct *lith/o* stones *-iasis* condition	Presence of stones in the common bile duct.
Cholelithiasis koh lee lih THY ih sis	*chol/e-* gall, bile *lith/o* stones *-iasis* condition	Presence of stones (**calculi**) in the gallbladder, sometimes characterized by right upper quadrant pain (**biliary colic**) with nausea and vomiting (Fig. 1-14).
Cirrhosis sur OH sis	*cirrh/o* orange-yellow *-osis* abnormal condition	Chronic degenerative disease of the liver, most commonly associated with alcohol abuse (Fig. 1-15).
Hepatitis heh pah TYE tis	*hepat/o* liver *-itis* inflammation	Inflammatory disease of the liver that is caused by an increasing number of viruses, alcohol, and drugs. Currently named by letter, **hepatitis A-G,** the means of viral transmission is not the same for each form.
Hepatitis A	*hepat/o* liver *-itis* inflammation	Virus transmitted through direct contact with fecally contaminated food or water.
Hepatitis B	*hepat/o* liver *-itis* inflammation	Virus transmitted through contaminated blood or sexual contact.
Hepatitis C	*hepat/o* liver *-itis* inflammation	Virus transmitted through blood transfusion, percutaneous inoculation, or sharing infected needles.
Hepatitis D	*hepat/o* liver *-itis* inflammation	Form of hepatitis that manifests itself only in patients who have acquired hepatitis B.

Continued

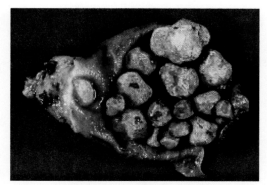

Fig. 1-14   Gallstones in the gallbladder. *(From Damjanov I, Linder J: Pathology: a color atlas, St Louis, 2000, Mosby.)*

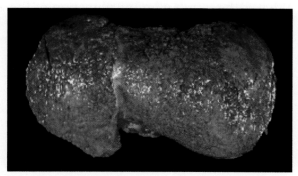

Fig. 1-15   Cirrhosis of the liver. *(From Damjanov I, Linder J: Pathology: a color atlas, St Louis, 2000, Mosby.)*

Terms Related to GI Accessory Organ Disorders—cont'd		
TERM	WORD ORIGIN	DEFINITION
Hepatitis E	*hepat/o* liver *-itis* inflammation	Strain of hepatitis virus that is transmitted through fecally contaminated food or water.
Hepatitis G	*hepat/o* liver *-itis* inflammation	Newer hepatitis virus that can be transmitted by blood.
Jaundice		A yellowing of the skin and sclerae (whites of the eyes) caused by elevated levels of bilirubiin.
Pancreatitis pan kree uh TYE tis	*pancreat/o* pancreas *-itis* inflammation	Inflammation of the pancreas.

◇ **Exercise 1-11: GI ACCESSORY ORGAN DISORDERS**

Fill in the blanks using the following terms.

pancreatitis, hepatitis, cholangitis, choledocholithiasis, cholelithiasis, cirrhosis, cholecystitis

1. What is a chronic degenerative disorder of the liver, usually caused by alcohol abuse?
   _____ cirrhosis

2. What is the term for the presence of stones in the gallbladder? cholelithiasis

3. What is the term for an inflammation of the bile vessels? cholangitis

4. What is the term for the presence of stones in the common bile duct?
   choledocholithiasis

5. What is the term for an inflammation of the pancreas? Pancreatitis

6. What is an inflammatory disease of the liver that is named by letter?
   hepatitis

7. What is the term for an inflammation of the gallbladder? cholecystitis

8. Elevated level of bilirubin resulting in a yellowing of the skin is termed
   jaundice.

Terms Related to Hernias

TERM	WORD ORIGIN	DEFINITION
Femoral hernia FEM uh rul HER nee ah	*femor/o* femur *-al* pertaining to	Protrusion of a loop of intestine through the femoral canal into the groin. Also called a **crural hernia.**
Hiatal hernia hye A tul HER nee ah	*hiat/o* an opening *-al* pertaining to	Protrusion of a portion of the stomach through the diaphragm. Also known as a **diaphragmatic hernia** and **diaphragmatocele** (dye uh frag MAT oh seel) (Fig. 1-16).
Incarcerated hernia in KAR sih ray tid HER nee ah	See **Did You Know?** box	Loop of bowel with ends occluded so that solids cannot pass; herniated bowel can become strangulated. Also called an **irreducible hernia.**
Inguinal hernia IN gwin nul HER nee ah	*inguin/o* groin *-al* pertaining to	Protrusion of a loop of intestine into the inguinal canal.
Strangulation		Constriction of a tubular structure, including intestines, leading to an impedance of circulation.
Umbilical hernia um BILL ih kul HER nee ah	*umbilic/o* umbilicus *-al* pertaining to	Protrusion of the intestine and omentum through a weakness in the abdominal wall (Fig. 1-17). Also known as an **omphalocele.**

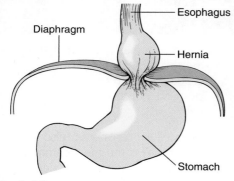

Fig. 1-16   Hiatal hernia. *(From Frazier MS, Drzymkowski JW: Essentials of human diseases and conditions, ed 3, Philadelphia, 2004, Saunders.)*

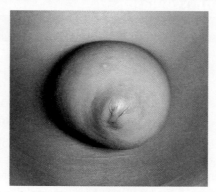

Fig. 1-17   Umbilical hernia. *(From Zitelli BJ, Davis HW: Atlas of pediatric physical diagnosis, ed 4, St Louis, 2002, Mosby.)*

DID YOU KNOW?

Incarcerated hernias acquire their name from the Latin term for *in prison*, meaning that the tissues described are confined, constricted, and *imprisoned.*

Exercise 1-12: HERNIAS

Matching.

A 1. hiatal hernia
B 2. umbilical hernia
F 3. strangulation
C 4. incarcerated hernia
D 5. inguinal hernia
E 6. femoral hernia

A. diaphragmatocele
B. protrusion of part of the intestines and omentum through the abdominal wall
C. irreducible hernia
D. protrusion of intestine in the inguinal canal
E. protrusion of intestine through the femoral canal
F. constriction of a tubular structure

Terms Related to Benign Neoplasms

TERM	WORD ORIGIN	DEFINITION
Cystadenoma	*cyst/o* bladder, cyst *aden/o* gland *-oma* tumor	Glandular tumors that are filled with cysts, these are the most common benign tumors in the pancreas.
Hemangioma	*hem/o* blood *angi/o* vessel *-oma* tumor	The most common type of benign tumor, these are tumors of the blood vessels.
Leiomyoma	*lei/o* smooth *my/o* muscle *-oma* tumor	Smooth muscle tumor that may occur in the digestive tract.
Odontogenic tumor	*odont/o* tooth *-genic* pertaining to produced by	Benign tumors that arise around the teeth and jaw.
Polyps, adenomatous or hyperplastic	*aden/o* gland *-oma* tumor *-ous* pertaining to *hyper-* excessive *plas/o* formation, growth *-tic* pertaining to	Adenomatous (growths that arise from glandular tissue, have potential to become malignant) or hyperplastic (generally, small growths that have no tendency to become malignant) tumors occurring throughout the digestive tract. Polyps may be sessile (flat) or pedunculated (having a stalk).

Terms Related to Malignant Neoplasms

TERM	WORD ORIGIN	DEFINITION	
Adenocarcinoma	*aden/o* gland *-carcinoma* cancerous tumor of epithelial origin	A malignant tumor of epithelial origin that either originates from glandular tissue or has a glandular appearance.	Adenocarcinomas occur throughout the gastrointestinal tract but especially in the esophagus, stomach, pancreas, and colon (Fig. 1-18).
Hepatocellular carcinoma/ hepatoma	*hepat/o* liver *cell/o* little cell *-ular* pertaining to	Malignant tumors of epithelial origin that originate in the liver cells.	Hepatocellular carcinoma (also called hepatoma) is the most common type of liver cancer worldwide.
Squamous cell carcinoma	*squam/o* scaly *-ous* pertaining to	Cancers that have a scalelike appearance.	Squamous cell carcinomas arise from the cells that cover the surfaces of the body. These occur throughout the digestive system.

Please note: Metastatic carcinoma is the most common form of liver cancer, and the liver is the most common site of all metastases. Just remember that this is not a primary tumor but one that has spread from another site.

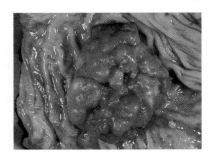

Fig. 1-18   Adenocarcinoma of the esophagus. *(From Damjanov I, Linder J: Andersons' pathology, ed 10, St Louis, 1996, Mosby.)*

Exercise 1-13: NEOPLASMS

Fill in the blank.

1. What type of benign growth is described as either sessile or pedunculated?

   _____ *Polyps* _____

2. What is the most common type of liver cancer? *Hepatocellular carcinoma*

3. Which type of cancer occurs throughout the GI tract but especially in the esophagus, stomach,

   pancreas, and colon? *Adenocarcinoma*

4. What is the term for a benign tumor that arises from around the teeth and jaw?

   _____ *Odontogenic tumor* _____

 Age Matters

Pediatrics

GI congenital disorders are cleft palate, esophageal atresia, Hirschsprung disease, and pyloric stenosis. Although none of these are common, they do require medical intervention that requires surgery. Gastroenteritis and appendicitis—with their possible complications, respectively, of dehydration and peritonitis—are the most common reasons for hospital admissions of children that are related to this body system.

Geriatrics

An aging digestive system is more likely to develop new dysfunctional cell growths (both benign and malignant), so statistics for polyps and colorectal cancer are high for the senior age group. Other diagnoses that appear more often are GERD and dysphagia, hemorrhoids, and Type 2 diabetes mellitus.

 DIAGNOSTIC PROCEDURES

Imaging

Visualizing the internal workings of the digestive system can be achieved with a wide variety of techniques but is usually accomplished through either radiographic imaging or endoscopy, or a combination of the two. Most of the procedures below are a form of radiography, or "taking x-rays." However, because the tissues of the digestive system are soft (as opposed to bone), a radiopaque contrast medium may be necessary to outline the digestive tract. This substance may be introduced into the body through the oral or anal openings, or it may be injected. Fluoroscopy provides instant visual access to deep tissue structures.

DID YOU KNOW?

The term *enema* is derived from the Greek term meaning to send in—as in the intrarectal introduction of fluid for cleansing or medicinal purposes.

Terms Related to Imaging

TERM	WORD ORIGIN	DEFINITION
Barium enema BAIR ee um EN nuh mah	See **Did You Know**? box	Introduction of a barium sulfate suspension through the rectum for imaging of the lower digestive tract to detect obstructions, tumors, and other abnormalities.
Barium swallow		Radiographic imaging done after the oral ingestion of a barium sulfate suspension; used to detect abnormalities of the esophagus and stomach (Fig. 1-19).
Cholangiography koh lan jee AH gruh fee	*cholangi/o* bile vessels *-graphy* recording	Radiographic procedure that captures images of the common bile duct through the injection of a contrast medium into the bile duct, after which a series of digital images is taken (Fig. 1-20).
Cholecystography koh lee sis TAH gruh fee	*cholecyst/o* gallbladder *-graphy* process of recording	Contrast study in which iodine is ingested orally. The gallbladder is then imaged at different time intervals to assess its functioning; this procedure is used to diagnose cholecystitis, cholelithiasis, tumors, and other abnormalities of the gallbladder.
Computed tomography (CT) scan	*tom/o* section, cutting *-graphy* process of recording	Radiographic technique that produces detailed images of "slices" or cross sections of the body; used in the digestive system to diagnose tumors or abnormal accumulations of fluid.
Endoscopy en DAH skuh pee	*endo-* within *-scopy* process of visually examining	General term for any internal visualization of the body using an instrument called an **endoscope**, which has its own fiberoptic light source. The endoscope enters the GI tract through the oral cavity (esophagoscopy, gastroscopy, and esophagogastroduodenoscopy [EGD]), through the anus **(proctoscopy, colonoscopy, sigmoidoscopy),** or through an incision in the abdominal wall **(laparoscopy).**

DID YOU KNOW?

The combining form *man/o* refers to a Greek term meaning scanty. *Man/u* is Latin and refers to the hand. Manometry gets its name from a device that measures a lessening (scanty) amount of air pressure.

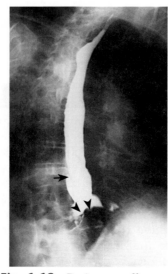

Fig. 1-19   Barium swallow.

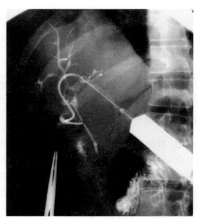

Fig. 1-20   Cholangiography. *(From Ballinger PW, Frank ED: Merrill's atlas of radiographic positions and radiologic procedures, ed 10, St Louis, 2003, Mosby.)*

Terms Related to Imaging—cont'd

TERM	WORD ORIGIN	DEFINITION
Fluoroscopy floo RAH skuh pee	*fluor/o* to flow *-scopy* visually examine	Special kind of x-ray procedure that allows visualization of structures in real time directly on a monitor screen.
Manometry mah NAH met tree	*man/o* scanty *-metry* process of measurement	Test that measures the motor function (muscle pressure) of the esophagus.
Ultrasonography ul trah soh NAH gruh fee	*ultra-* beyond, excessive *son/o* sound *-graphy* process of recording	Use of high-frequency sound waves to image deep structures of the body; used in the digestive system to detect gallstones and tumors.

Terms Related to Laboratory Tests

TERM	WORD ORIGIN	DEFINITION
Biopsy BYE op see	*bi/o* life *-opsy* viewing	Removal and examination of living tissue from the body for diagnostic purposes.
Gamma-glutamyl transferase (GGT) GAM uh GLOO tah mil TRANS fur ace		Blood test to detect increased enzymes that can indicate cirrhosis, hepatitis, acute pancreatitis, acute cholecystitis, or nephrosis, and to test for *Helicobacter pylori* antibodies.
Stool culture		Fecal examination to test for microorganisms in the feces, such as worms, amoebae, bacteria, and protozoa.
Stool guaiac, hemoccult test GWEYE ack HEEM oh kult	*hem/o* blood	Fecal specimen examination to detect hidden blood, which may indicate gastrointestinal bleeding.
Total bilirubin BILL lee roo bin		Blood test to detect possible jaundice (yellowing of the skin), cirrhosis, or hepatitis.

◆ **Exercise 1-14: DIAGNOSTIC PROCEDURES**

Fill in the blanks with the appropriate terms from the following list.

stool culture, hemoccult, total bilirubin, CT scan, barium swallow, cholecystography, guaiac, biopsy, gamma-glutamyl transferase, cholangiography, endoscopy, fluoroscopy, ultrasonography, manometry, barium enema

1. High-frequency sound waves detect a tumor. The imaging technique is called

   ___Ultrasonography___.

2. The patient ingests a contrast medium, after which imaging of the esophagus is done. This is called

   ___Barium swallow___.

3. An iodine compound is swallowed, and a series of images of the gallbladder is taken. This is called _Cholecystography_.

4. A cross-sectional image of the abdomen is taken. This is called a(n) _CT scan_.

5. The common bile duct is imaged radiographically after injection with a contrast medium. This is called _Cholangiography_.

6. A contrast medium was introduced into the patient's rectum, and studies were done of the lower digestive tract. This is called a(n) _Barium enema_.

7. What test measures the motor function of the esophagus? _manometry_

8. A fecal examination that tests for microorganisms is called a(n) _stool culture_.

9. Examination for blood in the stool is done by performing a stool _stool guaiac_ or _hemoccult_ test.

10. Removal of living tissue for diagnostic reasons is called _biopsy_.

11. What type of test is done to test for jaundice, cirrhosis, or hepatitis? _total bilirubin_

12. What is the test for elevated enzymes of _H. pylori_ antibodies? _GGT_

13. What is the general term for a visual examination within the body? _endoscopy_

14. What is the special type of x-ray procedure that images internal structures in real time on a monitor screen? _Fluoroscopy_

Synergy Hospital
781 Magnolia Blvd.
Atlanta, GA 30311

OPERATIVE REPORT

Preoperative diagnosis: Mucous bloody stools
Postoperative diagnosis: Diverticula
Surgical procedure: Colonoscopy

Patient is experiencing change in bowel habits, intermittent rectal bleeding, and some mucus. The procedure was described in detail to the patient, and he seemed to understand the risks, alternative treatments.

The patient was taken to the endoscopy suite, and in the left lateral position, the long colonoscope was inserted without incident. The perirectal area was normal. The rectal ampulla was normal. There were scattered diverticula of the left colon. The left colon, transverse colon, and right colon were otherwise normal. The colonoscope was removed, and the patient returned to the recovery room in satisfactory condition.

Raechel Perez, MD

◇ Exercise 1-15: OPERATIVE REPORT

Using the operative report above, answer the following questions.

1. What was the diagnostic procedure that was performed? _colonoscopy_

2. What was the instrument that was used? _colonoscope_

3. What diagnosis was determined from the procedure? _scattered diverticula of the left colon_

4. What is the "perirectal" area? _rectum_

≋ THERAPEUTIC INTERVENTIONS

When building a therapeutic intervention term that includes the creation of a stoma, the anatomical structures must be named in the order in which they appear in the body system. For example, a **duodenoileostomy** is a new opening between the duodenum and the ileum. The duodenum is listed first because it occurs before the ileum in the digestive system. Other examples are **esophago-gastrostomy** and **jejunocecostomy.** These **"ostomies"** may be either temporary or permanent. If, however, the opening is not between two structures but is to the surface of the body, then the order is (obviously) irrelevant. An example would be a **colostomy**—a new opening of the colon to the surface of the abdomen.

Terms Related to Therapeutic Interventions

TERM	WORD ORIGIN	DEFINITION
Anastomosis ah nas tih MOH sis		New connection created between two (usually hollow) structures that did not previously exist.
Bariatric surgery		A variety of surgical procedures done to control morbid obesity by reducing the size of the stomach and/or by rerouting the small intestine to reduce the absorption of nutrients. These procedures include gastric stapling (gastroplasty), gastric banding, and gastric bypass (Roux en-Y).
Colostomy koh LOSS toh mee	*col/o* colon *-stomy* new opening	Surgical redirection of the bowel to a **stoma** (STOH mah), an artificial opening, on the abdominal wall (Fig. 1-21).
Enema EH nih mah		Method of introducing a solution into the rectum for therapeutic (relief of constipation) or hygienic (preparation for surgery) reasons.
Feeding tubes		**Enteral nutrition**—through a digestive structure (Fig. 1-22). **Parenteral nutrition**—introduced through a structure outside of the digestive system.
Gastrectomy gass TRECK tuh mee	*gastr/o* stomach *-ectomy* removal	Surgical removal of all or part of the stomach.
Gastric gavage gah VAJ		Feeding through a tube in the stomach.
Hemorrhoidectomy heh moh roy DECK tuh mee	*hemorrhoid/o* hemorrhoid *-ectomy* removal	Surgical excision of hemorrhoids.
Herniorrhaphy hur nee OR rah fee	*herni/o* hernia *-rrhaphy* suture	Hernia repair; suture of a hernia.
Laparoscopic surgery lap uh roh SCAH pick	*lapar/o* abdomen *-scopic* pertaining to visually examining	Surgery done through several small incisions in the abdominal wall with the aid of an instrument called a **laparoscope**. A **laparoscopic cholecystectomy** is the removal of the gallbladder (Fig. 1-23).
Laparotomy lap uh RAH tuh mee	*lapar/o* abdomen *-tomy* incision	Any surgical incision in the abdominal wall for the purpose of an operative approach or for exploratory purposes.
Ligation lye GAY shun	*ligat/o* tying *-tion* the process of	Tying off of a blood vessel or duct (e.g., the cystic duct is ligated when the gallbladder is removed during a cholecystectomy).
Lysis of adhesions LYE sis	*lys/o* breakdown *-is* noun ending	Surgical destruction of adhesions (scar tissue that binds two anatomical surfaces), for example, in the peritoneal cavity.
Nasogastric intubation nay soh GASS trick in too BAY shun	*nas/o* nose *gastr/o* stomach *-ic* pertaining to	Placement of a tube from the nose, down the back of the throat, then into the stomach, for the purpose of removing gastric contents. May be termed an *NG tube*.
Paracentesis par ah sen TEE sis	*para-* near, beside *-centesis* surgical puncture	Procedure for withdrawing fluid from a body cavity, most commonly to remove fluid accumulated in the abdominal cavity.
Pylorotomy py lor OT oh me	*pylor/o* pylorus *-tomy* incision	An incision of the pyloric sphincter to correct an obstruction, such as pyloric stenosis.

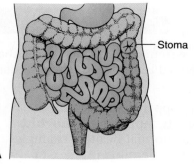
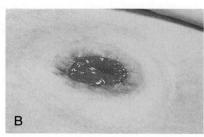

A, Colostomy. **B**, Stoma.

Fig. 1-21 **A,** Colostomy. **B,** Stoma. *(Part A from Beare PG Myers Jr: Adult health nursing, ed 3, St Louis, 1998, Mosby; Part B from Potter PA, Perry AG: Fundamentals of nursing, ed 6, St Louis, 2006, Mosby.)*

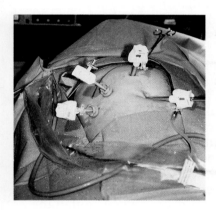

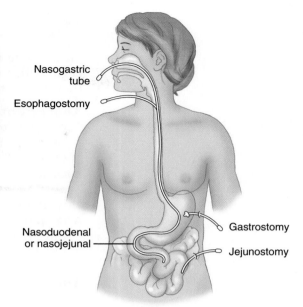

Fig. 1-22 Common placement locations for enteral feeding tubes.

Fig. 1-23 Laparoscopic cholecystectomy. *(From La Brooks M: Exploring medical terminology a student-directed approach, ed 4, St Louis, 2005, Mosby.)*

Exercise 1-16: THERAPEUTIC INTERVENTIONS

Matching.

__B__ 1. removal of fluid from a body cavity

__E__ 2. exploratory surgery of the abdomen

__A__ 3. joining of two hollow tubes or organs

__F__ 4. introduction of a solution in the rectum for cleansing or therapeutic purposes

__H__ 5. tying off a vessel or a duct

__N__ 6. destruction of adhesions

__J__ 7. inserting a tube from the nose to the stomach

__M__ 8. artificial opening

__G__ 9. hernia repair

__L__ 10. name of the instrument used to view the interior of the abdominal cavity

__D__ 11. removal of hemorrhoids

__I__ 12. removal of part of the stomach

__K__ 13. opening of large intestine to the wall of the abdomen

__C__ 14. surgery done through incisions on abdominal wall with aid of laparoscope

A. anastomosis
B. paracentesis
C. laparoscopic surgery
D. hemorrhoidectomy
E. laparotomy

F. enema
G. herniorrhaphy
H. ligation
I. hemigastrectomy
J. nasogastric intubation

K. colostomy
L. laparoscope
M. stoma
N. lysis of adhesions

≋ PHARMACOLOGY

Most of the medications prescribed for the GI system are in drug classes that begin with the prefix *anti-* because they are intended to be *against* the disorders they aim to treat.

Anorexiants (an nor RECK see unts): A class of appetite suppressants designed to aid in weight control, often in an attempt to treat **morbid obesity** (an amount of body fat that threatens normal health). Examples of anorexiants are sibutramine (Meridia) and phentermine (Adipex-P).

Antacids: A group of drugs or dietary substances that buffer (neutralize) or absorb hydrochloric acid in the stomach. Conditions that may be treated with antacids include GERD, pyrosis, and ulcers.

Antidiarrheals: Drugs that provide relief from diarrhea by reducing intestinal motility, inflammation, or loss of fluids and nutrients. Examples include loperamide (Imodium), bismuth subsalicylate (Pepto Bismol), and diphenoxylate with atropine (Lomotil).

Antiemetics: Drugs that prevent or alleviate nausea and vomiting. Examples include scopolamine (Scopace), ondansetron (Zofran), and promethazine (Phenergan).

Antihyperlipidemics: Drugs that reduce total blood cholesterol and, in some cases, also increase HDL cholesterol. Examples include atorvastatin (Lipitor), niacin (NiaSpan), gemfibrozil (Lopid), ezetimibe (Zetia), and cholestyramine (Questran). Natural-based products include Benecol, a plant stanol ester that contains products that can lower total and LDL cholesterol. Soy products contain phytoestrogens that have led to an FDA-approved health claim for reducing risk of heart disease when containing 6.25 g of soy protein per serving.

Cathartics (kuh THAR ticks): Agent that causes evacuation of the bowel by stimulating peristalsis, increasing the fluidity or bulk of intestinal contents, softening the feces, or lubricating the intestine. Cathartics can be classified as either mild (laxatives) or severe (purgatives). Senna (Sennacot) and mineral oil (Fleet Enema) are commonly used purgatives.

Histamine-2 receptor antagonists (H2RAs): Drugs that prevent a portion of the hydrochloric acid production in the stomach for moderate-lasting acid suppression. Examples include famotidine (Pepcid) and ranitidine (Zantac).

Laxatives: Mild medication that causes evacuation of the bowel by increasing the bulk of the feces, softening the stool, or lubricating the intestinal wall. Examples include fiber, docusate (Colace), and bisacodyl (Dulcolax).

Proton pump inhibitors: Drugs that prevent production of hydrochloric acid in the stomach for long-lasting acid suppression. Examples include omeprazole (Prilosec) and pantoprazole (Protonix).

DID YOU KNOW?

Laxative comes from the Latin word *laxare*, meaning to loosen; cathartic comes fro the Greek word *katharsis*, meaning a cleansing.

DID YOU KNOW?

An FDA-approved food supplement, Cholestin, contains lovastatin, so patients must be queried as to their intake of over-the-counter (OTC) supplements to prevent possible overdose and interactions.

◆ **Exercise 1-17: PHARMACOLOGY**

Match each disorder with the type of drug that is used to treat it.

F   1. nausea and vomiting

C   2. chronic GERD

D   3. short-term dyspepsia

E   4. high LDL

G   5. excessive weight gain

A   6. constipation

B   7. intestinal cramping and loose, watery stools

A. laxative
B. antidiarrheal
C. proton pump inhibitor
D. antacid
E. antihyperlipidemic
F. antiemetic
G. anorexiant

Abbreviations

Abbreviation	Definition	Abbreviation	Definition
BaS	Barium swallow	HBV	Hepatitis B virus
BE	Barium enema	IBD	Inflammatory bowel disease
BM	Bowel movement	IBS	Irritable bowel syndrome
CT scan	Computed tomography scan	Lap	Laparoscopy
EGD	Esophagogastroduodenoscopy	LPN	Licensed practical nurse
GB	Gallbladder	N&V	Nausea and vomiting
GERD	Gastroesophageal reflux disease	NPO	Nothing by mouth (L. *nil per os*)
GGT	Gamma-glutamyl transferase	PUD	Peptic ulcer disease
GI	Gastrointestinal	RN	Registered nurse
HAV	Hepatitis A virus		

Exercise 1-18: ABBREVIATIONS

Spell out the abbreviations used in the following examples.

1. The 76-year-old patient complained of no BM in the last week. He had not had a(n) ___bowel movement___.

2. The patient was admitted for suspected GB disease. ___gallbladder disease___

3. The nurse recorded the patient's symptoms as N&V, without a fever. ___Nausea & vomiting___

4. Constant heartburn for Phyllis may have been a result of GERD. ___gastroesophageal reflux disease___

5. Stressful situations were made even more so for Bill when his IBS flared up. ___irritable bowel syndrome___

Careers

Medical-Surgical Nurses

Nursing is a career in high demand. Prospective students can choose between hospital schools that can provide them with either licensed practical nurse (LPN) or registered nurse (RN) credentials or colleges that combine an associate- or bachelor-level degree with the RN credential. A master's or doctoral degree can also be earned in a number of different specialty areas.

Students interested in the nursing field are normally required to have had certain courses with satisfactory grades (usually a C or better) within a given time period specified by each nursing program. These courses normally include high school algebra, biology, and chemistry, or their university equivalents. On completion of a nursing program, students are required to take either a state licensing (for LPN) or registration (for RN) examination before they are permitted to practice.

Most nurses begin their careers as medical-surgical (med-surg) nurses, working in those respective areas for at least 2 years before they branch into a specialty area. Two specialized areas of nursing that require further study include nurse practitioners and certified nurse-midwives.

Continued

Careers — cont'd

Nurse practitioners can conduct physical examinations, provide immunizations, diagnose and treat common illnesses and injuries, and order and interpret x-rays and lab tests. Certified nurse-midwives are responsible for prenatal care of normally healthy women, delivering babies, and conducting follow-up care during the postpartum period.

Further information on nursing programs is available through several avenues. Your local library will have resources to help you locate nursing programs available in your area. Calling your nearby hospitals and universities may also provide information about local programs. If you choose to use the Internet, the following sites may be useful.

The Education and Career Center provides information on private schools, colleges and universities, graduate study, study abroad, summer programs, and distance learning. Their address is http://www.petersons.com/professional/nurslist.html.

The National League for Nursing Accrediting Commission has links to a directory of accredited nursing programs at http://www.accreding-comm-nlnac.org/1999directory-main.htm.

According to the U.S. Bureau of Labor Statistics, opportunities for careers in nursing through 2012 are very good, and employment opportunities are expected to grow faster than the average for all occupations. There is a current nationwide shortage in this largest of all health care occupations.

Careers Related to the Gastrointestinal System

Gastroenterologist

Gastroenterologists are medical doctors who have completed 4 years of an undergraduate degree, 4 years of medical school, a 3-year residency in internal medicine, and a gastroenterology fellowship that takes between 2 and 3 years. These individuals specialize in disorders of the gastrointestinal tract, including the practice of diagnostic endoscopic techniques, such as colonoscopy. The American Board of Colon and Rectal Surgery certifies gastroenterologists for specific procedures. For more information, visit the American Medical Association website for general information on physician careers at http://www.ama-assn.org.

Dentist

Dentists are usually required to complete 4 years of an undergraduate degree and 4 years of dental school. They diagnose and treat dental disorders by removing decay, filling cavities, and extracting and straightening teeth. The work setting is normally a solo practice. Specialties that require additional training include orthodontist, oral and maxillofacial surgeon, pedodontist, periodontist, exodontist, prosthodontist, and endodontist. For more information, visit The American Dental Association at http://www.ada.org.

Dental Hygienist

Dental hygienists examine patients' teeth; take and develop dental x-rays; and remove calculus, stains, and plaque from patients' teeth. They are instrumental in educating patients on good oral health. Although most programs lead to an associate's degree, some dental hygiene programs lead to a certificate, bachelor's degree, or master's degree. Job prospects for dental hygienists through the year 2012 are expected to grow much faster than average for all professions. This profession offers part-time work and flexible scheduling. For more information, contact the Division of Education, American Dental Hygienists' Association at http://www.adha.org.

Dental Assistant

Dental assistants are either trained on the job, or in 1-year programs. They prepare patients for treatment, sterilize and disinfect instruments and equipment, and assist dentists by handing instruments and materials to dentists during procedures. Their job prospects are expected to be excellent through the year 2012. For more information, contact the Commission on Dental Accreditation, American Dental Association at http://www.ada.org and the American Dental Assistants Association at http://www.dentalassistant.org.

Dental Laboratory Technician

These professionals are the technicians who fashion the crowns, bridges, dentures, and other dental prosthetics that are requested by dentists. Using an impression of the patient's mouth, a plaster model is cast. The technicians then build and shape the required teeth to form a close replica of the tooth or teeth that need to be replaced. Training is on the job, in community and junior colleges, in the U.S. Armed Forces, and in vocational-technical institutes. Work settings are usually in medical equipment and supply manufacturing laboratories, which tend to be small and privately owned. For more information, contact the Commission on Dental Accreditation, American Dental Association at http://www.ada.org and the National Board for Certification in Dental Technology at http://www.nadl.org/certifican.shtml.

References

Byrne R: *The 2,548 best things anybody ever said,* New York, 2003, Simon & Schuster.

Franklin B: Letter to Jean-Baptiste Leroy (November 13, 1789). In Bartlett J, Kaplan J, editors: *Bartlett's familiar quotations: a collection of passages, phrases, and proverbs traced to their sources in ancient and modern literature,* ed 16, New York, 1992, Little, Brown.

Rybacki J, Long J: *The essential guide to prescription drugs 2001: everything you need to know for safe drug use,* New York, 2000, Harper Collins.

OBJECTIVES

You will be able to do the following after completing this chapter:

Key Terms
1. Define, appropriately use, and spell all the Key Terms for this chapter.

Structure and Function of the Digestive System
2. Explain the purpose of the digestive system.
3. List the four stages of the digestive process.
4. List the eight distinct areas of the digestive tract through which food passes during digestion.

Digestive Organs
5. Explain the role of the mouth in digestion.
6. Locate three structures in the mouth important to the digestive process.
7. Identify the pharynx and explain its role in digestion.
8. Locate the esophagus and explain its role in digestion.
9. Explain the role of the stomach in digestion.
10. Locate the peritoneum, sphincters, and fundus within the stomach.
11. Explain the role of the small intestine in digestion.
12. Locate the three main parts of the small intestine.
13. Explain the role of the large intestine in the digestive system.
14. Name and locate the four subdivisions of the large intestine.
15. Locate the rectum and explain its role in the digestive system.
16. Locate the anal sphincter and explain its role in the digestive system.

Accessory Organs
17. Name and locate the three accessory organs to the digestive system and describe the role of each in digesting nutrients.

Metabolism
18. Distinguish between anabolism and catabolism.

Diseases and Disorders of the Digestive System
19. List six diseases of the mouth and briefly describe the etiology, signs and symptoms, diagnosis, therapy, and interventions for each.
20. List two disorders of the esophagus and briefly describe the etiology, signs and symptoms, diagnosis, therapy, and interventions for each.

ANATOMY AND PHYSIOLOGY OF THE DIGESTIVE SYSTEM

21. List five disorders of the stomach and briefly describe the etiology, signs and symptoms, diagnosis, therapy, and interventions for each.
22. List three disorders of the small intestine and briefly describe the etiology, signs and symptoms, diagnosis, therapy, and interventions for each.
23. List four disorders of the large intestine and briefly describe the etiology, signs and symptoms, diagnosis, therapy, and interventions for each.
24. List a disorder of the rectum and anal canal and briefly describe its etiology, signs and symptoms, diagnosis, therapy, and interventions.
25. List three diseases of the liver and briefly describe the etiology, signs and symptoms, diagnosis, therapy, and interventions for each.
26. List three disorders of the accessory organs to the digestive system and briefly describe the etiology, signs and symptoms, diagnosis, therapy, and interventions for each.

Colon Tests
27. Explain the purpose of fecal occult testing.
28. Demonstrate the procedure for providing the patient with accurate and complete instructions on the preparation and collection of a stool sample for fecal occult blood testing.
29. Demonstrate the procedure for accurately developing the fecal occult blood slide test.
30. Explain the purpose of sigmoidoscopy.
31. Demonstrate the correct procedure for assisting the physician and patient during sigmoidoscopy.

Patient-Centered Professionalism
32. Analyze a realistic medical office situation and apply your understanding of the digestive system to determine the best course of action.
33. Describe the impact on patient care when medical assistants have a solid understanding of the structure and function of the digestive system.

KEY TERMS

The Key Terms for this chapter have been organized into sections so that you can easily see the terminology associated with each aspect of the digestive system.

digestion Physical and chemical breakdown of food.
elimination Expelling of body wastes.
gastrointestinal (GI) tract Digestive tract.
ingestion Process of taking nutrition into the body.

Structure and Function of the Digestive System

absorption Taking in of nutrients through the stomach and small intestines (villi).
alimentary canal Digestive tract; extends from the mouth to the anus.

Digestive Organs

Mouth
bolus Food broken down by chewing and mixed with saliva ready to be swallowed.
buccal Pertaining to the cheek.

KEY TERMS—cont'd

mandible Lower jawbone.

maxilla Upper jawbone.

mouth Oral cavity; body opening (orifice) through which humans take in food; also used for speech and, at times, breathing.

uvula Small mass of tissue hanging from the soft palate at the back of the mouth.

Tongue

deglutition Act of swallowing.

frenulum Structure that anchors the tongue to the floor of the mouth.

mastication Act of chewing.

taste buds Minute terminal sensory organs of the gustatory nerve located in various areas on the tongue to differentiate sweet, sour, salty, and bitter.

tongue Organ in the mouth used for taste, chewing, swallowing, and speech.

Ducts of Salivary Glands

enzyme Protein produced by living organisms that causes biochemical changes.

parotid gland Salivary gland located at the side of the face in front of and below the external ear.

saliva Watery mixture of secretions from the salivary glands.

sublingual gland Salivary gland located in the front of the mouth, under the tongue.

submandibular gland Salivary gland located below the lower jaw.

Teeth

bicuspids Teeth with two cusps on the grinding surface used for tearing food.

canines Teeth located to the side of the mouth ("eye teeth").

deciduous teeth Teeth that will be lost; commonly called "baby teeth."

incisors Teeth located in the front of the mouth.

molars Back teeth for grinding.

permanent teeth Adult teeth.

Pharynx and Esophagus

epiglottis Flap in the throat at the top of the trachea that prevents chewed food from entering the trachea ("windpipe").

esophagus Muscular tube through which food passes from the pharynx to the stomach.

peristalsis Wavelike motions that propel food through the digestive tract.

Stomach

body Main section of the stomach.

cardiac region Area surrounding the lower esophageal sphincter through which food enters the stomach from the esophagus.

chyme Semiliquid contents of the stomach and small intestines after becoming mixed with stomach acid.

emulsification Process of breaking down fat for digestion.

fundus Top portion of the stomach.

lipase Enzyme that breaks down fat.

lower esophageal sphincter (LES) Sphincter located between the esophagus and the stomach; also called the *cardiac sphincter.*

mesentery Membrane that surrounds the small and large intestines and holds them to the posterior abdominal wall.

omentum Structure that is part of the peritoneum attached to the stomach; folds over and protects the intestines.

pepsin Digestive enzyme found in gastric juice that catalyzes the breakdown of protein.

peritoneum Serous membrane that lines the walls of the abdominal cavity and folds inward to enclose the viscera (internal abdominal organs).

pyloric sphincter Sphincter that allows chyme to exit from the stomach into the small intestine; opening between the stomach and small intestine.

pylorus Area of the stomach closest to the duodenum.

rugae Folds of the stomach that aid in digestion.

sphincters Muscle rings that allow openings to open and close.

stomach Muscular saclike portion of the alimentary canal between the esophagus and small intestines; one of the main digestive organs where food is broken down for digestion.

vagus nerve Nerve that controls secretions of hydrochloric acid, among many other responsibilities.

Small Intestine

bile Fluid secreted by the liver, stored in the gallbladder, and discharged into the duodenum; aids in the breakdown, digestion, and absorption of fats.

duodenum First part of the small intestine.

hepatic portal system Blood vessels carrying blood from intestine to liver; drains intestinal capillaries and feeds hepatic capillaries.

ileum Last part of the small intestine.

jejunum Second part of the small intestine responsible for absorption.

lacteals Absorb nutrients for the lymph system.

small intestine Smaller, upper part of the intestines where digestion is completed and nutrients are absorbed by the blood.

villi Vascular projections of the small intestine that aid in absorption.

Large Intestine

ascending colon Section of the colon located on the right side of the body next to the small intestines.

cecum Large pouch forming the first part of the large intestine.

colon Section of the large intestine extending from the cecum to the rectum.

descending colon Section of the colon located on the left side of the body.

large intestine Portion of the intestine that extends from the small intestine to the anus.

McBurney's point Landmark in the right lower quadrant (RLQ) of the abdomen over the location of the appendix.

sigmoid colon S-shaped section of the colon between the descending section and the rectum.

transverse colon Section of the colon located across the abdomen.

vermiform appendix Wormlike appendage attached to the cecum that is lymphoid tissue.

Rectum

defecation Elimination of feces.

fecal Referring to or consisting of feces.

feces Stool; body waste.

rectum Portion of the digestive tract that extends from the sigmoid colon to the anal canal.

Anal Canal

anal canal Part of the digestive tract between the rectum and the anus.

anal sphincter Muscle ring at the end of the digestive system that allows feces to exit from the body.

anus End of the digestive system.

Accessory Organs and Their Components

common bile duct Duct that enters the duodenum from the gallbladder and liver for release of bile into the intestines.

cystic duct Duct leading from the gallbladder into the common bile duct.

gallbladder Small, muscular sac in which bile secreted by the liver is stored until needed by the body for digestion.

hepatic duct Duct from the liver to the gallbladder.

insulin Hormone that functions to regulate the metabolism of carbohydrates and fats, especially the conversion of glucose to glycogen, which lowers the blood glucose level; necessary for cells to be able to use glucose for energy.

liver Organ that secretes bile; active in formation of certain blood proteins and metabolism of carbohydrates, fats, and proteins.

pancreas Organ that secretes pancreatic juice into the duodenum *(exocrine)* and insulin and other substances into the bloodstream *(endocrine);* has both endocrine and exocrine functions.

pancreatin Medication that is a mixture of the enzymes of pancreatic juice used as a digestive aid.

Metabolism

anabolism Process of converting smaller molecules to larger molecules.

catabolism Process of converting larger molecules into smaller molecules.

metabolism Energy production after the absorption of nutrients; all physical and chemical processes within the body including anabolism and catabolism.

Digestive Diseases and Disorders

Signs and Symptoms

ascites Accumulation of fluid in the peritoneal cavity. May be caused by an obstruction of the portal circulation.

constipation Difficulty in defecation caused by hard, compacted stool.

diarrhea Frequent bowel movements of loose, watery stools.

dyspepsia Difficult digestion; uncomfortable feeling after eating; indigestion.

dysphagia Difficulty swallowing.

emesis Vomiting; forceful expulsion of stomach contents; "throwing up."

flatulence Digestive bowel gas.

hematemesis Vomiting of blood.

idiopathic Disease without an identifiable cause.

jaundice Yellowish discoloration of the skin caused by excessive bilirubin in the blood.

malaise Vague feelings of illness or discomfort.

melena Black, tarry feces caused by free blood in the intestines.

nausea Inclination to vomit.

plaque Food debris and saliva debris that accumulate on the teeth and trap bacteria.

polyps Usually benign growth that can be attached to the mucosal lining of the colon.

regurgitation Reflux into the esophagus of stomach acids and food.

Diseases and Disorders

appendicitis Inflammation of the vermiform appendix.

caries Tooth decay.

celiac sprue Hereditary malabsorption disease coupled with mucosal damage to the small intestine caused by gluten (wheat) intolerance.

cholecystitis Inflammation of the gallbladder.

cholelithiasis Condition in which stones of calcium or cholesterol are in the gallbladder or lodged in the common bile duct; gallstones.

Crohn disease Chronic inflammation of the ileum.

diverticulitis Inflammation of small out-pouches (diverticula) in the colon.

esophagitis Inflammation of the esophagus.

gastric ulcer Lesion of the mucosal lining of the stomach or intestine.

gastritis Inflammation of the stomach.

gastroenteritis Inflammation and irritation of the stomach and intestines.

gastroesophageal reflux disease (GERD) Backup of gastric juices into the esophagus.

gingivitis Inflammation of the gums in the mouth.

glossitis Inflammation of the tongue.

hemorrhoids Dilated veins in the rectum and anus.

hepatitis Inflammation of the liver caused by a viral infection.

hiatal hernia Protrusion of part of the stomach through the diaphragm into the chest cavity.

KEY TERMS—*cont'd*

Hirschprung disease Chronic dilation of the colon; usually congenital.

intussusception Telescoping of one part of the intestine into another; usually occurs in the ileocecal area.

lactose intolerance Deficiency of the enzyme lactase that prevents lactose from being digested properly.

mumps Viral infection of the parotid gland.

pancreatitis Inflammation of the pancreas.

pyloric stenosis Narrowing of the pyloric sphincter between the stomach and the duodenum.

stomatitis Inflammation of the mucous lining of the mouth.

thrush Fungal infection of the mouth.

ulcerative colitis Inflammation of the mucosa of the colon.

Vincent infection Painful ulcerations of the mucous lining of the mouth; commonly called "trench mouth."

volvulus Colon twisting on itself.

Colon Tests

colorectal Pertaining to the colon and rectum.

fecal occult test Test of stool specimen for the presence of minute amounts of blood.

guaiac test Test of hidden (occult) blood in the stool or other body secretions.

sigmoidoscope Instrument used to view the sigmoid region of the colon.

sigmoidoscopy Technique of viewing the sigmoid region of the colon with a sigmoidoscope.

What Would You Do?

Read the following scenario and keep it in mind as you learn about the digestive system in this chapter.

Saril Paratel, age 69, was brought to the physician's office with fever and pain in the right lower quadrant (RLQ) of her abdomen. The pain has lasted for 3 days and has become progressively worse over the last 36 hours. The pain originally started in the umbilical area, but over time it moved to McBurney's point. Last night Saril had nausea and vomiting. She has not had a bowel movement for 4 days. She had dyspepsia for several days before this episode of pain. She has also noticed that fatty foods tend to cause flatulence with some pain in her right upper quadrant (RUQ), radiating into her back at the right shoul-

der. No history of hematemesis is given, but malaise has been present for several weeks. When asked about diarrhea, Saril answers that her stools 5 days ago were soft, formed and frequent; so yes, she had diarrhea. The white blood cell (WBC) count ordered by the physician is reported as WBCs 15,600 with a differential of 76% neutrophils, 6% bands, 25% lymphs, 0% basos, 10% monos, and 1% eos. The physician refers Saril to a surgeon because he wants her to be evaluated for possible appendicitis and to rule out the cause of the RUQ pain.

Would you understand all of the terminology here? Would you be able to explain these findings to Saril if she had questions?

All people need nutrients, water, and electrolytes to live. The digestive system, also known as the *gastrointestinal system,* is responsible for providing these life-sustaining elements to our bodies. Although we can make eating choices, such as whether to eat an apple or a candy bar for a snack, the process of digesting that snack once eaten is handled unconsciously by the components of our digestive system.

The body systems depend on each other to function properly. For example, the digestive system takes food through the pharynx and strives to keep it out of our trachea so that our airway is not blocked and we don't choke. As a medical assistant, you need to comprehend the proper functioning of the digestive system so you can better understand the diseases and disorders that affect it. This understanding will make you a more knowledgeable and effective medical assistant.

STRUCTURE AND FUNCTION OF THE DIGESTIVE SYSTEM

When learning about the body, it is often best to examine the "big picture," or the whole system, before the parts. The function and structure of the whole organ system can shed light on why each part works the way it does.

Function

The process of digestion consists of both the physical breakdown and the chemical breakdown of complex food into simpler substances. This is done so that the food nutrients can be absorbed into the

bloodstream and then used by the body tissues, or those not needed can be eliminated from the body. The digestive organs, accessory organs, and their secretions allow the gastrointestinal (GI) system to move nutrients through four stages: (1) **ingestion,** (2) **digestion,** (3) **absorption,** and (4) **elimination.**

Structure

The **alimentary canal** (digestive tract) is a muscular hollow tube that extends from the mouth to the anus and measures approximately 30 feet. The digestive tract, or **gastrointestinal (GI) tract,** can be divided into several distinct areas and digestive organs through which nutrients pass during digestion. In addition, accessory organs secrete substances that aid in this process (Fig. 2-1).

PATIENT-CENTERED PROFESSIONALISM

- The organs of the digestive system are divided into two categories: those of the GI tract and those of accessory organs of digestion. Why is it important for the medical assistant to understand their general function in digestion and absorption of nutrients?

DIGESTIVE ORGANS

Now that you know the function and structure of the digestive system as a whole, it is time to explore the parts. Nutrients pass through eight distinct areas and digestive organs during digestion: the mouth,

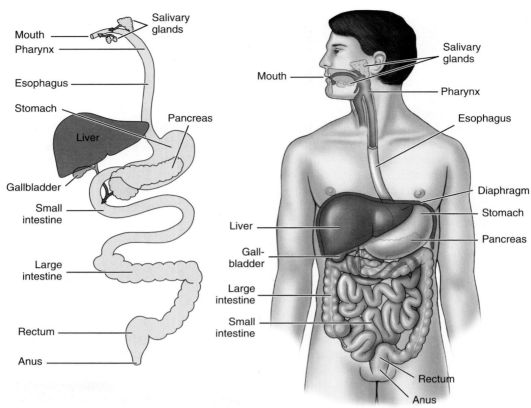

Fig. 2-1 The digestive system. *(From Herlihy B, Maebius NK: The human body in health and illness, ed 2, Philadelphia, 2003, Saunders.)*

pharynx, esophagus, stomach, small intestine, large intestine, rectum, and anal canal.

Mouth

The **mouth** (oral cavity) is where food and nutrients first enter the digestive system. In the mouth food is tasted and physically broken up by the teeth and mixed with saliva, which breaks the food down further with chemicals. When food is chewed and mixed with saliva it becomes a semiliquid form known as a **bolus** (chewed food). Finally, the food is swallowed.

The oral cavity contains the tongue, duct openings of the salivary glands, and the teeth (Fig. 2-2, A). It is an oval-shaped cavity that communicates with the pharynx. A cheek forms the cavity on each side (**buccal** refers to the cheek). The lips protect the front of the mouth. The soft and hard palate form the roof of the mouth, and the tongue forms most of the floor of the mouth. Hanging from the middle of the lower portion of the soft palate is the **uvula,** a finger-like projection that directs food toward the esophagus to aid in swallowing. The **maxilla** forms the upper jaw, and the **mandible** forms the lower jaw to hold the teeth.

Tongue

The **tongue** is the organ for the sense of taste and assists in **mastication** (chewing), **deglutition** (swallowing), digestion, and talking. Located on the tongue are **taste buds** that allow us to taste sweet, sour, salt, and bitter. The tongue is anchored to the floor of the mouth by the **frenulum** and the hyoid bone.

Ducts of the Salivary Glands

The ducts from the salivary glands empty into the mouth (Fig. 2-2, C). These glands secrete approximately 1500 milliliters (ml), or 1½ liters (L), of **saliva** daily. The **parotid gland, submandibular gland,** and **sublingual gland** emit secretions that mix with secretions of the small glands on the floor of the mouth. The parotid gland is the largest of the salivary glands. **Mumps** is a viral infection of the parotid gland that can have complications involving the ovaries and testes. Postadolescent males who contract the disease may become sterile. Saliva lubricates the mouth to enhance the swallowing of food and contains an **enzyme** called *amylase.* Carbohydrate digestion actually begins in the mouth and is assisted by a substance called *ptyalin.*

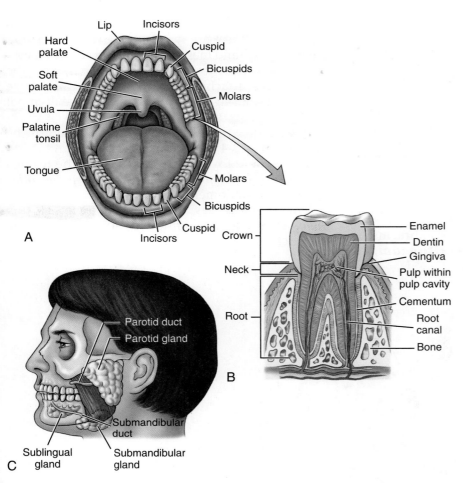

A

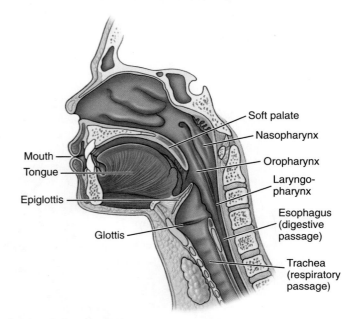

Fig. 2-2 **A,** Structures in the mouth. **B,** Cross-section of a tooth. **C,** Location of the salivary glands. *(From Herlihy B, Maebius NK: The human body in health and illness, ed 2, Philadelphia, 2003, Saunders.)*

Teeth

Two sets of teeth develop during life. The first set is the **deciduous teeth** ("baby teeth"). There are 20 baby teeth, 10 in each jaw: four **incisors,** two **canines,** and four **molars.** These teeth eventually fall out. The second set of teeth is called the **permanent teeth.** Permanent teeth replace the baby teeth. There are 32 permanent teeth, 16 in each jaw: four incisors, two canines, four **bicuspids,** and six molars. Fig. 2-2, *B,* illustrates the longitudinal section of a tooth.

Pharynx

When the bolus is swallowed, it enters the pharynx. As the bolus is being moved through the pharynx, an involuntary reaction occurs that causes the **epiglottis** (flap) to close over the trachea, causing the bolus to enter the esophagus and not the trachea (Fig. 2-3). As food enters the esophagus from the pharynx, a process called **peristalsis** causes wave-like smooth muscle contractions that push food down to the stomach.

Fig. 2-3 The pathway of food from the mouth to the pharynx to the esophagus. *(From Herlihy B, Maebius NK: The human body in health and illness, ed 2, Philadelphia, 2003, Saunders.)*

Esophagus

The **esophagus,** a muscular tube 9 to 10 inches long, connects to the pharynx at its upper end and with the stomach at its lower end. The esophagus carries food mixed with saliva from the mouth to the stomach by way of peristalsis but is collapsed when food is not being transported. The esophagus does not produce digestive enzymes or absorb food. Its sole purpose is to move food along the digestive tract.

Stomach

The esophagus passes through the diaphragm to connect to the **stomach.** The **peritoneum,** a serous membrane, provides protection for the digestive organs. There are two folds of the peritoneum: the omentum and mesentery. The **omentum** hangs in front of the stomach and intestines, and the **mesentery** attaches itself to the small and large intestines, joining them to the posterior abdominal wall for stabilization of the organs.

The esophagus ends in the upper portion of the stomach (Fig. 2-4). The stomach is saclike and serves as a receptacle for food. It is located in the regions of the *epigastric, umbilical,* and *left hypochondriac* areas of the abdomen.

The stomach has the following two **sphincters** guarding the entrance and exit of the stomach:

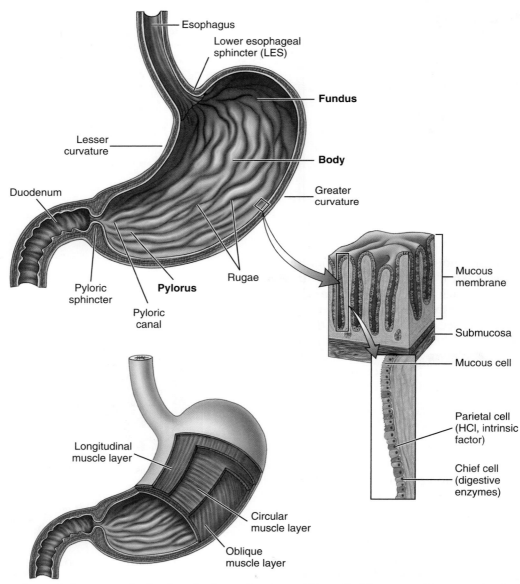

Fig. 2-4 The regions of the stomach: fundus, body, and pylorus. *(From Herlihy B, Maebius NK: The human body in health and illness, ed 2, Philadelphia, 2003, Saunders.)*

- The **lower esophageal sphincter (LES),** or cardiac sphincter, allows food to pass into the stomach. The LES prevents food from re-entering the esophagus as food is converted into **chyme** (a liquid substance) by gastric juices.
- **The pyloric sphincter** allows chyme to exit into the small intestine. The pyloric sphincter keeps food in the stomach until it has been processed and is ready to enter the small intestine as chyme.

The stomach has four different sections, as follows:

1. **Cardiac region:** Area surrounding the LES through which food enters the stomach from the esophagus.
2. **Fundus:** Upper expanded portion of the stomach beside the cardiac region.
3. **Body:** Middle portion of the stomach.
4. **Pylorus:** Bottom portion of the stomach.

The internal lining of the stomach is made up of a mucous membrane that contains folds, referred to as **rugae.** As the stomach fills with food and expands, the folds disappear. The stomach changes food from a semisolid (bolus) to a semifluid substance (chyme). Food remains in the stomach for 1 to 4 hours where it is churned to break it down into usable molecules. The gastric juices contain hydrochloric acid controlled by the **vagus nerve** and enzymes. Hydrochloric acids assist to activate the enzyme **pepsin** for protein breakdown, absorption of iron, and elimination of bacteria. Gastric juices contain the enzyme **lipase** to aid in the breakdown of fats **(emulsification). Gastroenteritis** occurs when extensive inflammation and irritation occur in the lining of the stomach and intestine and is a symptom of many digestive disorders.

Small Intestine

As the chyme exits the stomach through the pyloric sphincter, it enters the **small intestine.** The small intestine is a hollow tube approximately 23 feet long and is located in the abdominal cavity. It is divided into three parts, as follows:

1. The **duodenum** begins at the pyloric sphincter of the stomach; it is only about 10 inches long. **Bile,** which breaks down fats, leaves the gallbladder, and pancreatic juices for sugar breakdown are excreted through ducts into the duodenum. As the duodenum begins to turn downward, it becomes the jejunum.
2. The **jejunum** extends between the duodenum and the ileum; it is about 8 feet in length. Within the jejunum are **villi,** finger-like

projections that contain capillaries allowing nutrients to be absorbed by the blood, and **lacteals** that return nutrients to the lymphatic system (Fig. 2-5). This process is called *absorption.* After nutrients are absorbed, they travel to the liver by way of the **hepatic portal system.**

3. The **ileum** connects to the first part of the large intestine, the **cecum,** by way of the *ileocecal valve.* This valve allows waste material to pass from the ileum into the cecum, but not vice versa. The ileum between the jejunum and cecum is about 12 feet long.

The small intestine produces enzymes that break down sugars, including maltase, sucrase, and lactase. **Lactose intolerance** occurs when there is a deficiency of lactase. Lactase enables digestion of lactose, so if there is a lactase deficiency, lactose is not digested. The enzymes *peptidase* for proteins, *lipase* for fats, and *trypsin* for proteins are also produced in the small intestine. In addition, the small intestine absorbs nutrients, electrolytes, and vitamins.

Large Intestine

The **colon,** or **large intestine,** measures about 5 feet in length. The colon's functions are to (1) absorb water, minerals, and remaining nutrients; (2) synthesize and absorb B-complex vitamins; (3) allow for the formation of vitamin K; and (4) transport solid waste products out of the body.

The **vermiform appendix** is attached to the cecum at the junction of the small intestine. The function of the appendix has been debated, but some believe that it breeds intestinal flora (bacteria) that break down food substances into waste products. Others, however, think it no longer serves a purpose. The colon is subdivided into four parts, as follows (Fig. 2-6):

1. The **ascending colon** travels up (vertical) the right side of the body toward the lower part of the liver.
2. The **transverse colon** moves across the abdomen, below the liver and stomach, and above the small intestine.
3. The **descending colon** travels down the left side of the body and connects to the sigmoid colon.
4. The **sigmoid colon** is the S-shaped structure that joins to the rectum.

Rectum

The **rectum** is continuous with the sigmoid colon and measures about 5 inches in length. It stores all

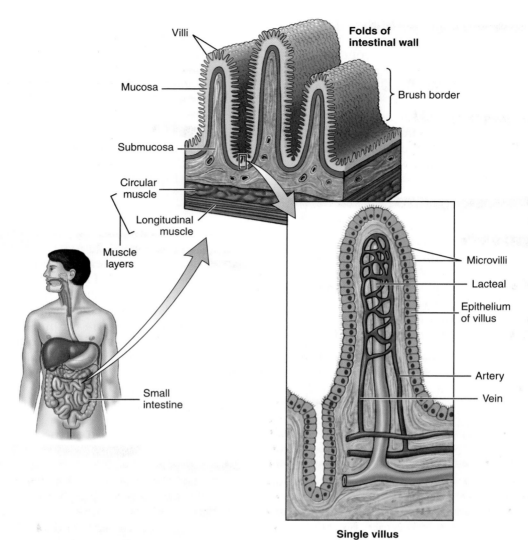

Fig. 2-5   The small intestine. Folds of the intestinal wall showing the villi. *Inset*, A single villus. *(From Herlihy B, Maebius NK: The human body in health and illness, ed 2, Philadelphia, 2003, Saunders.)*

nondigestible wastes until they leave the system as **feces** (adjective form is **fecal**); this process is known as **defecation.**

Anal Canal

The rectum terminates at the **anal canal,** which is about 1½ inches in length. The **anal sphincter** is a ring of muscle at the opening of the **anus.** The sphincter keeps the anus closed until a stool (feces) needs to pass. Stool collects in the rectum and pushes on the walls of the rectum. This pressure causes the anal sphincter to relax, allowing stool to pass out of the body through the anus.

Fig. 2-7 shows the entire digestive process of a carbohydrate, protein, and fat.

PATIENT-CENTERED PROFESSIONALISM

- Food is prepared for use by cells in five basic activities: (1) ingestion, (2) movement, (3) mechanical and chemical digestion, (4) absorption, and (5) defecation. How does each of these basic activities aid in digestion?
- How does it affect patients when medical assistants understand how food is digested?

ACCESSORY ORGANS

The salivary glands (covered in the mouth section), liver, gallbladder, and pancreas are not part of the digestive tract, but they have a role in digestive

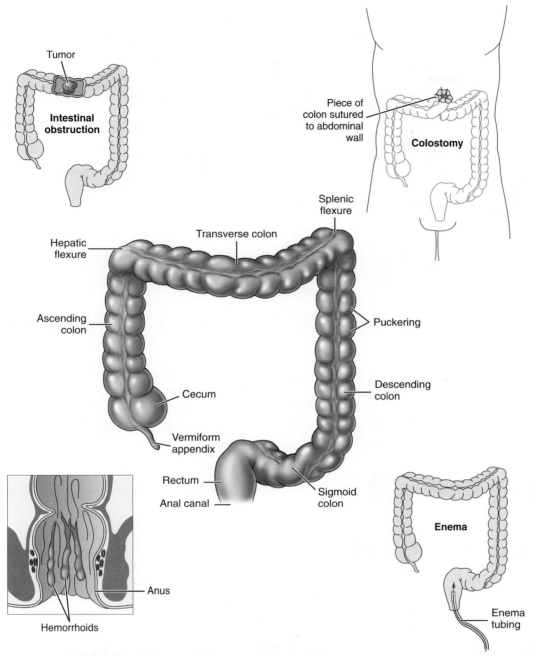

Fig. 2-6 The large intestine, as well as some clinical conditions and procedures affecting the large intestine. *(From Herlihy B, Maebius NK: The human body in health and illness, ed 2, Philadelphia, 2003, Saunders.)*

activities. They all secrete substances that help break down nutrients into a form that is usable by the body. They are considered accessory organs.

The liver, gallbladder, and the pancreas all empty their secretions into the duodenum (Fig. 2-8). It is in the duodenum that the final breakdown of nutrients takes place. The final step depends on the deposit of secretions from the accessory organs. Table 2-1 lists digestive secretions with their role in digestion.

Liver

The **liver** is the largest organ in the digestive system (see Fig. 2-8). It is located in the right hypochondriac and epigastric regions and a small portion of the left hypochondriac area. The liver weighs about 55 ounces. It is connected to the anterior wall of the abdomen by ligaments.

One function of the liver is to produce bile. The chief pigment in bile is called *bilirubin*. The main

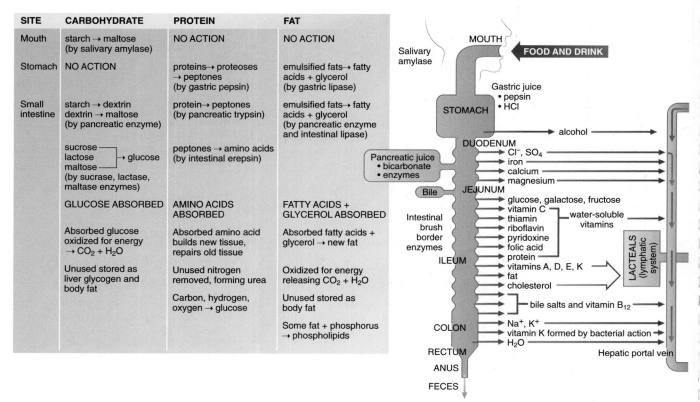

SITE	CARBOHYDRATE	PROTEIN	FAT
Mouth	starch → maltose (by salivary amylase)	NO ACTION	NO ACTION
Stomach	NO ACTION	proteins→ proteoses → peptones (by gastric pepsin)	emulsified fats→ fatty acids + glycerol (by gastric lipase)
Small intestine	starch → dextrin dextrin → maltose (by pancreatic enzyme)	protein→ peptones (by pancreatic trypsin)	emulsified fats→ fatty acids + glycerol (by pancreatic enzyme and intestinal lipase)
	sucrose lactose maltose → glucose (by sucrase, lactase, maltase enzymes)	peptones → amino acids (by intestinal erepsin)	
	GLUCOSE ABSORBED	AMINO ACIDS ABSORBED	FATTY ACIDS + GLYCEROL ABSORBED
	Absorbed glucose oxidized for energy → CO_2 + H_2O	Absorbed amino acid builds new tissue, repairs old tissue	Absorbed fatty acids + glycerol → new fat
	Unused stored as liver glycogen and body fat	Unused nitrogen removed, forming urea	Oxidized for energy releasing CO_2 + H_2O
		Carbon, hydrogen, oxygen → glucose	Unused stored as body fat
			Some fat + phosphorus → phospholipids

Fig. 2-7   The digestive process of carbohydrates, proteins, and fat. *Cl⁻,* Chloride; *CO_2,* carbon dioxide; *HCl,* hydrochloric acid; *H_2O,* water; *K^+,* potassium; *Na^+,* sodium; *SO_4,* sulfur. *(In Peckenpaugh NJ, Poleman CM:* Nutrition essentials and diet therapy, *ed 8, Philadelphia, 1999, Saunders. Modified from Mahan LK, Escott-Stump S:* Krause's food, nutrition, and diet therapy, *ed 9, Philadelphia, 1996, Saunders.)*

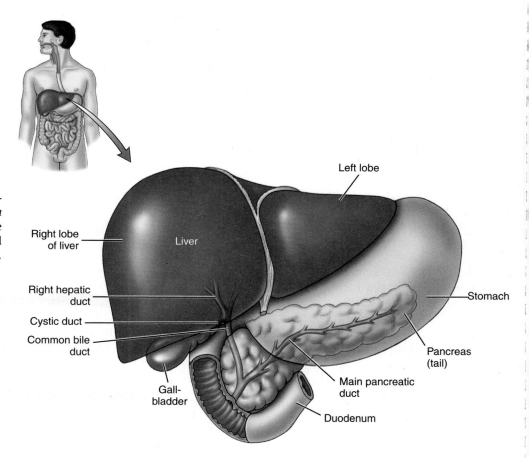

Fig. 2-8   The liver, gallbladder, and pancreas. *(From Herlihy B, Maebius NK:* The human body in health and illness, *ed 2, Philadelphia, 2003, Saunders.)*

TABLE 2-1   Digestive Secretions

Digestive Juice	Source	Substance	Functional Role*
Saliva	Salivary glands	Mucus	*Lubricates bolus of food; facilitates mixing of food*
		Amylase	**Enzyme; begins digestion of starches to disaccharides**
		Sodium bicarbonate	**Increases pH (for optimal amylase function)**
		Water	*Dilutes food and other substances; facilitates mixing*
Gastric juice	Gastric glands	Pepsin	**Enzyme; digest proteins**
		Hydrochloric acid	**Denatures proteins; decreases pH (for optimal pepsin function)**
		Intrinsic factor	**Protects and allows later absorption of vitamin B_{12}**
		Mucus	*Lubricates chyme; protects stomach lining*
		Water	*Dilutes food and other substances; facilitates mixing*
Pancreatic juice	Pancreas (exocrine portion)	Proteases (trypsin, chymotrypsin, collagenase, elastase, etc.)	**Enzymes; digest proteins and polypeptides to peptide and amino acids**
		Lipases (lipase, phospholipase, etc.)	**Enzymes; digest lipids to fatty acids**
		Colipase	**Coenzyme; helps lipase digest fats**
		Nucleases	**Enzymes; digest nucleic acids (RNA and DNA)**
		Amylase	**Enzyme; digests starches**
		Water	*Dilutes food and other substances; facilitates mixing*
		Mucus	*Lubricates*
		Sodium bicarbonate	**Increases pH (for optimal enzyme function)**
Bile	Liver (stored and concentrated in gallbladder)	Lecithin and bile salts	*Emulsify lipids*
		Sodium bicarbonate	**Increases pH (for optimal enzyme function)**
		Cholesterol	Excess cholesterol from body cells, to be excreted with feces
		Products of detoxification	From detoxification of harmful substances by hepatic cells, to be excreted with feces
		Bile pigments (mainly bilirubin)	Products of breakdown of heme groups during hemolysis, to be excreted with feces
		Mucus	*Lubricates*
		Water	*Dilutes food and other substances; facilitates mixing*
Intestinal juice	Mucosa of small and large intestine	Mucus	*Lubricates*
		Sodium bicarbonate	**Increases pH (for optimal enzyme function)**
		Water	*Small amount to carry mucus and sodium bicarbonate*

(From Thibodeau GA, Patton KT: *Anatomy and physiology,* ed 5, St Louis, 2003, Mosby.)
*****Boldface type** indicates a chemical digestive process; *italic type* indicates a mechanical digestive process.

function of bile is the digestion and absorption of fat. Other functions of the liver include the following:

- Metabolizes carbohydrates, fats, and proteins
- Manufactures blood proteins
- Removes toxins, bacteria, and worn-out red blood cells
- Removes waste products from the blood (*detoxification*)
- Manufactures cholesterol
- Stores vitamins A, B$_{12}$, D, E, and K
- Forms antibodies
- Stores simple sugars

Gallbladder

The bile produced by the liver travels to the gall-bladder through the **hepatic duct** for storage. Bile leaves the gallbladder as needed through the **cystic duct.** The hepatic duct and the cystic duct join together and form the **common bile duct.** This duct enters the duodenum just below the pylorus.

The **gallbladder** is a pear-shaped sac about 4 inches long and is lodged under the liver. Its main function is to store bile until needed for digestion. When a meal including fat begins digesting in the stomach, a message is sent to the gallbladder via the nervous system, causing it to contract (squeeze). When this happens, bile enters the duodenum to complete the digestion of fat.

Pancreas

The **pancreas** is divided into three sections: head, body, and tail. It lies behind the stomach and in front of the first and second lumbar vertebrae. The pancreas produces **pancreatin,** which is used in protein breakdown in the duodenum, and **insulin,** which is used in maintaining blood glucose levels.

PATIENT-CENTERED PROFESSIONALISM

- Nutrients are the substances in food that are used as an energy source to fuel the needs of the body. What importance do accessory organs play in the digestive process?
- How might the medical assistant's ability to explain the importance of accessory organs to patients benefit their care and treatment?

METABOLISM

Metabolism is the change, both physical and chemical, that food nutrients undergo after absorp-

tion in the small intestine. The process of metabolism consists of two phases: anabolism and catabolism.

- **Anabolism** (buildup) is considered the "constructive" phase of metabolism because smaller molecules or simple substances are converted to larger molecules or more complex substances (e.g., amino acids converted to proteins).
- **Catabolism** (breakdown) is the opposite of anabolism. Catabolism is the "destructive" phase of metabolism, when larger molecules are converted into smaller molecules (e.g., glycogen converted to pyruvic acid). This process releases energy and is measured in calories. The energy released is used for cell growth and heat production.

Carbohydrates, fats, proteins, and other materials are metabolized to produce the energy needed to keep the body functioning.

PATIENT-CENTERED PROFESSIONALISM

- Metabolism is how the body uses the nutrients absorbed from the food we eat. Why is it important for the medical assistant to understand this process?
- How do anabolism and catabolism differ? What is a situation in which you might need to explain this difference to a patient?

DISEASES AND DISORDERS OF THE DIGESTIVE SYSTEM

Diseases of the digestive tract can be either *acute* (sudden and severe) or *chronic* (of longer duration or recurring). An internist or a gastroenterologist can treat diseases of the digestive tract.

Drugs may be prescribed to treat digestive problems (Table 2-2).

Medical assistants need to be able to recognize the common signs and symptoms of and the diagnostic tests for the different types of digestive system disorders and diseases.

- Study Box 2-1 to familiarize yourself with the common signs and symptoms.
- Study Box 2-2 to learn about common diagnostic tests.
- Study Table 2-3 to understand the diseases and disorders that affect the digestive system.

TABLE 2-2 Digestive Drug Classifications

Drug Classification	Common Generic (Brand) Names
Antacids Buffer or absorb hydrochloric acid (HCl) in the stomach	calcium carbonate (Tums) aluminum and magnesium (Maalox)
Antidiarrheals Provide relief from intestinal cramping and diarrhea	diphenoxylate (Lomotil) loperamide (Imodium)
Antiemetics Prevent or alleviate nausea and vomiting	meclizine (Antivert) prochlorperazine (Compazine)
Cathartics (stimulating laxatives) Cause evacuation of the bowel by stimulating nerves in the intestines resulting in increased peristalsis	senna (Senokot) bisacodyl (Dulcolax)
Laxatives Cause evacuation of the bowel by increasing the bulk of the feces, softening the stool, or lubricating the intestinal wall	methylcellulose (Citrucel) psyllium (Metamucil)
Anti-ulcer agents Prevent or alleviate symptoms of ulcers	esomeprazole (Nexium) lansoprazole (Prevacid)
Antispasmodics Prevent spasms or colic-type actions in the stomach or intestines	dicyclomine (Bentyl) belladonna alkaloids (Donnatal)

BOX 2-1 Common Signs and Symptoms of Digestive Disease

Anorexia	Loss of appetite
Ascites	Accumulation of fluid in the peritoneal cavity; may be caused by an obstruction of the portal (liver) circulation
Colic	Acute abdominal pain
Constipation	Difficulty in defecation caused by hard, compacted stool
Diarrhea	Frequent bowel movements of loose, watery stools
Dyspepsia	Difficult digestion; uncomfortable feeling after eating (e.g., heartburn, bloating, nausea)
Dysphagia	Difficulty swallowing
Emesis	Expulsion of stomach contents; vomiting
Flatulence	Digestive gas
Guarding	Moving away from or flinching when a tender area of the abdomen is touched
Hematemesis	Vomiting of blood
Jaundice	Yellowish discoloration of skin caused by excessive bilirubin in the blood
Melena	Black, tarry feces caused by free blood in the intestines
Nausea	Inclination to vomit
Polyps	Usually benign growths attached to the mucosal lining of the colon
Regurgitation	Reflux of stomach acids and food into the esophagus
Rigidity	Stiff or "boardlike" abdomen
Vomiting	Forceful expulsion of stomach contents; emesis; "throwing up"

BOX 2-2 Diagnostic Tests and Procedures for the Digestive Tract

Abdominal x-ray	Detects and evaluates tumors and other abdominal disorders (flat plate of the abdomen)
Barium enema	Barium sulfate is introduced through the rectum for imaging of the lower bowel (lower GI series)
Barium swallow	Oral ingestion of barium sulfate suspension for imaging of the esophagus (upper GI series)
Cholecystography	Contrast study is done by oral ingestion of an iodine preparation; imaging of the gallbladder occurs at various intervals
Endoscopy	Visualization of the GI tract using an endoscope (Fig. 2-9)
Colonoscopy	Visualization of the large intestine
Laparoscopy	Endoscopic examination of the interior of the peritoneal cavity
Sigmoidoscopy	Endoscopic examination of the sigmoid colon

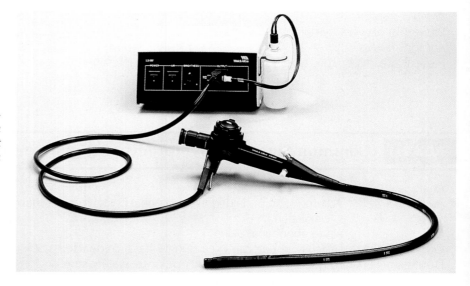

Fig. 2-9 Endoscopy allows the physician to see inside the body. *(From Gerdin J: Health careers today, ed 3, St Louis, 2003, Mosby. Courtesy Welch Allyn, Skaneateles Falls, NY.)*

COLON TESTS

The most common colon procedures done in the medical office are tests for fecal occult blood and sigmoidoscopy. In both these colon procedures, the medical assistant provides the patient with diet and preparatory information and assists the physician during the procedures, making sure equipment and supplies are ready and available when needed.

Fecal Occult Testing

A **fecal occult test,** or **guaiac test** (e.g., Hemoccult), is done to detect the presence of blood in the stool. A fecal occult test cannot identify the *cause* of bleeding; it is performed to screen for **colorectal** bleeding. Positive test results require additional procedures to identify the location of the bleeding.

Bleeding can occur in the stomach, intestines, and other digestive areas.

Colorectal cancer is one possible cause of bleeding. Colorectal cancer is very prevalent in people over 40 years of age, and it is the second most common form of cancer in the United States. Symptoms tend to be general and are often ignored by the patient. Early screening can greatly reduce the risk of colon cancer.

Patient Preparation

During the fecal occult test, a stool specimen is placed on a **test card.** The medical assistant may provide the test card to the physician as part of the rectal examination, or may provide three test cards to the patient to use at home and return to the office for testing. The medical assistant provides the patient with diet instructions before collection of a stool sample. Instructions are also given to the patient on properly collecting the stool sample. Procedure 2-1 explains how to provide a patient with accurate and complete instructions on the preparation and collection of a stool sample for testing. Box 2-3 lists charting information needed to document patient instructions.

Developing Occult Blood Test
The medical assistant is also responsible for accurately developing the occult blood slide test. Regardless of the test card used, a chemical reagent called *guaiac* is impregnated on the testing paper. A developer (hydrogen peroxide) is placed on the guaiac paper directly over the smear. A color change (blue) indicates the presence of blood. Procedure 2-2 explains the process of accurately developing the occult blood slide test. Box 2-4 lists information necessary to chart diagnostic procedures.

Sigmoidoscopy

A **sigmoidoscopy** is a procedure to examine the lower bowel to diagnose and treat conditions that affect this portion of the digestive system. A flexible fiberoptic **sigmoidoscope** is often used to visualize the mucosa of the rectum and sigmoid colon (Fig. 2-10). This instrument magnifies the colon by 10 times and allows the physician to detect lesions, polyps, and other abnormalities. Further testing (e.g., proctoscopy) would be scheduled in a hospital area such as endoscopy, where more extensive equipment is used to evaluate what the sigmoidoscope cannot.

Patient Preparation
Normally, the physician has the patient eat a low-fiber diet the day before the scheduled examination. A mild laxative or an enema may be prescribed the evening before the test, with another enema the morning of the test. The procedure is done early in

Text continued on p. 75

BOX 2-3 **Documentation when Charting for Patient Education**

Before you chart instructions given to a patient, the following information is needed:
1. Date
2. Time
3. Supplies provided (if any)
4. Instructions provided for the procedure
5. Patient's understanding of the instructions
6. Proper signature and credential

BOX 2-4 **Documentation when Charting Diagnostic Testing Procedures**

1. Date
2. Time
3. Name of procedure
4. Results
5. Patient reaction, if any
6. Proper signature and credential

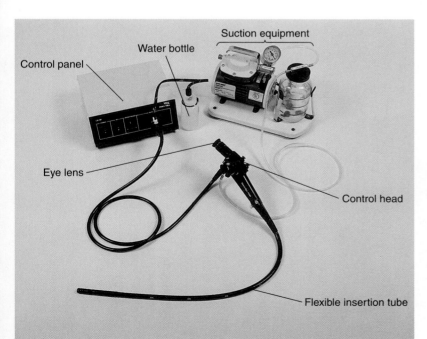

Fig. 2-10 Flexible fiberoptic sigmoidoscope. *(From Bonewit-West K:* Clinical procedures for medical assistants, *ed 6, Philadelphia, 2004, Saunders.)*

TABLE 2-3   Diseases and Disorders of the Digestive System

Disease and Description	Etiology	Signs and Symptoms	Diagnosis	Therapy	Interventions
Mouth					
Gingivitis Infection of gums	Caused by **plaque** around base of teeth	Gums red and inflamed; gums bleed easily	Dentist confirms by oral examination	Removal of plaque and antibiotic therapy	Educate about proper brushing and flossing techniques
Stomatitis Infection of mucous lining of mouth	Viral infection (herpes simplex)	Sudden onset; mouth pain, fever, tenderness of mucosa of mouth	Oral inspection: gums swollen, ulcerations of mouth and throat; viral smear	Symptom relief, including topical anesthetic medications for viral infections	Encourage oral hygiene, including saline or hydrogen
Vincent's infection ("trench mouth") Painful ulcerations of mucous lining of mouth	Secondary infection to gingivitis	Painful ulcerations of gums, excessive salivation, bad breath	Oral examination bleeding gums, ulcerations	Antibiotic and surgery to repair gums	Emphasize good oral hygiene
Thrush Fungal infection of mouth	Caused by the yeast *Candida albicans*	Pale-yellow patches in mouth	Oral examination and laboratory culture	Antifungal medication	Stress good oral hygiene
Caries Tooth decay caused by bacteria and plaque	Bacteria break down sugars in foods; process produces acid, which causes enamel to erode	Toothache	Oral examination with x-ray	Removal of decay	Emphasize good oral hygiene and regular teeth cleaning
Glossitis Inflammation of tongue	Streptococcal infection, vitamin B deficiency, anemia, chronic irritation (e.g., loose dentures, smoking)	Swollen tongue, painful chewing, painful tongue without swelling	Clinical presentation, culture of tongue	Antibiotics, topical anesthetic or analgesics for pain	Stress good oral hygiene and treatment of underlying causes
Esophagus					
Gastroesophageal reflux disease (GERD) Backup of gastric juices into esophagus	Poor cardiac sphincter function resulting in heartburn	Belching, burning sensation in chest and mouth	Patient history and upper gastrointestinal (GI) series to detect erosion and esophageal abnormalities	Head of bed elevated 4 to 6 inches; medication to inhibit gastric juice production	Limit alcohol consumption; lose weight and minimize tobacco use

Disorder	Etiology	Signs and Symptoms	Diagnosis	Treatment	Patient Teaching
Esophagitis Inflammation of esophagus	Reflux of gastric acid causing chemical ingestion	Burning in chest area; pain following eating or drinking	Patient history and upper GI series to detect abnormalities	Bland diet to reduce acid production; medication to promote healing	Diet instruction: consume small meals; avoid spicy foods, caffeine, and alcohol
Stomach **Gastritis** Inflammation of stomach	Causative agent could be *Helicobacter pylori*, bacteria from spoiled food, drugs causing irritation (e.g., aspirin), or stress	Abdominal pain, heartburn	Visualization through gastroscopy Presenting signs and symptoms	Medications (e.g., antacid and those that reduce acid secretions) and antibiotics if causative agent is *H. pylori*	After finding source, if emotional stress, reduce stressful activities
Gastric ulcer Lesion of mucosal lining of stomach or intestine	Breakdown of mucosal lining by stomach acids or *H. pylori*	Epigastric pain	Past history and physical examination upper GI series; endoscopy; gastric analysis	Rest, medications (antibiotics, antacids), surgery	Initiate lifestyle changes to reduce stress, thus reducing acid
Pyloric stenosis Narrowing of pyloric sphincter	Developmental error of sphincter muscle	Projectile vomiting	Clinical evaluation	Surgical intervention	None
Hiatal hernia Protrusion of stomach through diaphragm into chest cavity	Congenital defect in diaphragm	Heartburn when reclining; chest pain and discomfort in chest cavity if overweight	X-ray, upper GI series	Symptoms relieved through medication and lifestyle changes	Lose weight if overweight; smaller meals, sit up straight after eating
Hirschsprung disease (megacolon) Chronic dilation of colon	Unknown	Severe abdominal distention; failure to thrive; explosive, watery diarrhea	Family history; rectal biopsy shows absence of ganglion in wall of colon and rectum	Low-residue diet; surgery to remove impaired section of colon	Provide family with support group information
Small Intestine **Celiac sprue** Malabsorption disease with mucosal damage to small intestine caused by gluten (wheat) intolerance	Immunological reaction to protein	Anorexia, abdominal distention, intestinal bleeding	Biopsy of small intestine to verify villi destruction; symptoms abate on gluten-free diet	Gluten-free diet; corticosteroid treatment in some cases	Encourage adherence to diet

Continued

TABLE 2-3 Diseases and Disorders of the Digestive System—cont'd

Disease and Description	Etiology	Signs and Symptoms	Diagnosis	Therapy	Interventions
Intussusception Telescoping of one part of intestine into another; usually in ileocecal area (Fig. 2-11)	*Adults*: cause may be tumors or polyps *Infants*: cause unknown	*Adults*: obstructive symptoms *Infants*: cry and draw up legs; fever, vomiting	Medical history and x-ray studies of abdomen; laboratory studies show occult blood in stool; barium enema	Surgical intervention, restoration of electrolyte levels	Provide dietary education
Crohn disease Chronic inflammation of ileum	Unknown; theory of autoimmune disease	Chronic diarrhea; cramping abdominal pain	Patient history, barium enema and x-ray studies of abdomen; colonoscopy	Medical management: supplemental support, medications to relieve diarrhea, corticosteroids to reduce inflammation	Stress need for rest; encourage support group
Large Intestine **Appendicitis** Inflammation of vermiform appendix	Blockage of appendix allowing bacteria to multiply	Abdominal pain in right lower quadrant (RLQ), nausea, vomiting, fever, constipation	Symptoms of patient drawing up of knees in response to palpation of RLQ **(McBurney's point)**	Surgical removal	Ensure medical treatment for symptoms No laxatives
Ulcerative colitis Inflammation of mucosa of colon and rectum	Unknown	Bloody diarrhea, abdominal cramping, mucus-containing stools	Clinical symptoms (weight loss, fever, malaise)	Minimize food selections; medications: antidiarrheal and steroidal	Early treatment and diet free of food that is irritating to patient
Diverticulitis Inflammation of small out-pouches (diverticula) in colon	Blockage of diverticulum causing bowel bacteria to multiply	Fever; pain in left lower abdomen that abates after defecation	Sigmoidoscopy, colonoscopy; guaiac testing and elevated erythrocyte sedimentation rate (ESR)	High-residue diet, being careful to avoid seeded fruit and vegetables; rest, medication	Stress need for adherence to diet restrictions
Volvulus Colon twisting on itself (Fig. 2-12)	Abnormal embryonic development	Abdominal pain, nausea, vomiting	Clinical symptoms and GI series (upper and lower)	Surgical intervention	Provide postsurgical diet

Rectum and Anal Canal

Hemorrhoids	Swollen veins caused by blockage or pressure	Inspection and proctoscopy to visualize internal lesions	Prevention of straining and constipation; diet high in fiber, increased water intake; medications as ordered by physician	Encourage adherence to fluid intake and diet high in fiber Stool softener as needed
Dilated veins in rectum and anus (internal or external position)	Rectal pain, itching, protrusion, or bleeding			

Liver

Hepatitis A Inflammation of liver caused by viral infection	Oral contact with feces from infected person (e.g., through prepared food), drinking contaminated water, eating contaminated shellfish	Antibody testing "A" positive; clinical symptoms	Jaundice, fatigue, abdominal pain, loss of weight, diarrhea	Management of symptoms; avoidance of alcohol	Vaccine for prophylaxis, immunoglobulin after prophylaxis; provide prevention education
Hepatitis B Inflammation of liver caused by viral infection	Bloodborne pathogen transmitted through contact with infected person's blood or body fluids*	Antibody testing "B" positive; clinical symptoms	Jaundice, fatigue, abdominal pain, weight loss, diarrhea	Management of symptoms; avoidance of alcohol	Vaccine; use standard precautions in occupation; provide prevention education

Continued

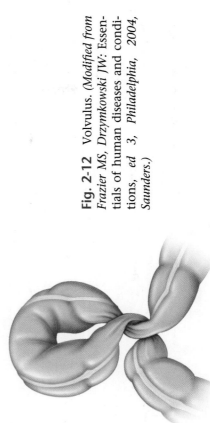

Fig. 2-11 Intussusception. (Modified from Frazier MS, Drzymkowski JW: Essentials of human diseases and conditions, ed 3, Philadelphia, 2004, Saunders.)

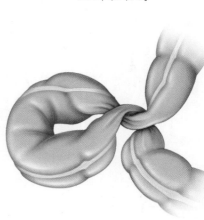

Fig. 2-12 Volvulus. (Modified from Frazier MS, Drzymkowski JW: Essentials of human diseases and conditions, ed 3, Philadelphia, 2004, Saunders.)

TABLE 2-3　Diseases and Disorders of the Digestive System—cont'd

Disease and Description	Etiology	Signs and Symptoms	Diagnosis	Therapy	Interventions
Hepatitis C Inflammation of liver caused by a viral infection	Bloodborne pathogen transmitted through contact with infected person's blood[†]	Jaundice, fatigue, abdominal pain, weight loss, diarrhea	Antibody test for "C"; clinical symptoms	Medication for chronic symptoms; avoidance of alcohol	No vaccine; follow standard precautions (avoid sharing drug and tattooing equipment, toothbrushes, razors); provide prevention education
Pancreas **Pancreatitis** Inflammation of pancreas	Excessive alcohol consumption; bile duct obstructed with gallstones; **idiopathic**	Sudden onset of severe abdominal pain, especially in epigastric area; abdominal distention with vomiting, fever, and tachycardia	Medical history; blood enzymes: amylose level increased	Symptomatic (surgical if obstructed bile duct)	Patient must avoid consuming large amounts of alcohol Diet low in fat
Gallbladder **Cholecystitis** Inflammation of gallbladder	Irritation of gallbladder caused by gallstone becoming lodged in cystic duct	Sudden onset of pain in mid-epigastric area or right upper quadrant (RUQ) that radiates to back in right shoulder area	Ultrasonography and x-rays; elevated series levels of phosphatase	Antibiotic therapy or surgical intervention if antibiotics not adequate	Educate about low-cholesterol diet and weight management to prevent formation of gallstones
Cholelithiasis Gallstones of calcium or cholesterol in gallbladder or lodged in common bile duct	Gallstones leave the gallbladder and cause obstruction in bile duct or fill gallbladder, causing irritation	Jaundice in severe cases; sudden onset of pain in mid-epigastric area or RUQ that radiates to back of right shoulder area	Ultrasonography and x-rays	Surgical intervention; lithotripsy; can be treated medically with medications to dissolve stones	Provide diet management to reduce the risk of forming gallstones

*For example, sharing drug equipment, unprotected sex, and occupational exposure (e.g., needle sticks).
[†]For example, sharing drug equipment, blood transfusions before 1992, and occupational exposure; formerly known as *non-A, non-B hepatitis.*

Procedure 2-1 Instruct the Patient in Obtaining a Fecal Specimen

TASK: Provide the patient with accurate and complete instructions on the preparation and collection of a stool sample for testing.

EQUIPMENT AND SUPPLIES
- Hemoccult slide testing kit:
  Three occult blood slides
  Three applicator sticks
  Diet and collection instruction sheet
- Patient's medical record

SKILLS/RATIONALE

STANDARD PRECAUTIONS ARE TO BE FOLLOWED.

1. **Procedural Step. Sanitize the hands.**
   An alcohol-based hand rub may be used instead of washing hands with soap and water, unless hands are visibly soiled.
   Rationale. Hand sanitization promotes infection control.

2. **Procedural Step. Assemble equipment and supplies.**
   Obtain three fecal occult blood slides. Check the expiration date of each cardboard slide.
   Rationale. It is important to have all supplies and equipment ready and available before starting any procedure to ensure efficiency. Expired slides may render the test results inaccurate.

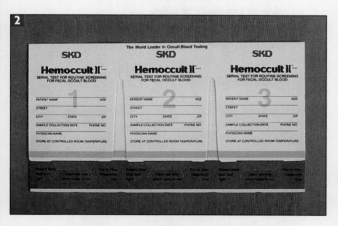

3. **Procedural Step. Obtain the patient's medical record.**

4. **Procedural Step. Escort the patient to the examination room, and greet and identify the patient.**
   Rationale. Identifying the patient ensures that the procedure is performed on the correct patient.

5. **Procedural Step. Explain the procedure to the patient.**
   Inform the patient that the test should not be conducted during a menstrual cycle or in the presence of hemorrhoidal bleeding.

Rationale. Explaining the procedure to the patient promotes cooperation and provides a means of obtaining implied consent. Blood from sources other than fecal matter will provide inaccurate test results.

6. **Procedural Step. Provide the patient with verbal and written instructions.**
   Instructions should outline the correct dietary modifications to begin 48 hours before collection of the first stool sample and should explain that collection continues until all three slide specimens have been collected.
   a. Well-cooked fish and poultry are acceptable, but red or rare meat, processed meat, or liver should be avoided.
   Rationale. Red meat contains animal blood, which could cause a false-positive result.
   b. Vegetables in moderation are acceptable, but broccoli, cauliflower, and radishes should be avoided.
   c. Fruits in moderation are acceptable, but melons should be avoided.
   d. High-fiber foods such as whole-wheat bread, bran cereal, and popcorn are acceptable, but food high in roughage fiber should be avoided.
   e. Medications that contain aspirin, iron, or vitamin C should be avoided.
   Rationale. Following the outlined diet will provide more accurate test results. If the patient does not follow the diet modifications, inaccurate test results will occur.

7. **Procedural Step. Provide the patient with the Hemoccult slide test kit.**
   The kit contains written instructions, three attached cardboard slides, and three wooden applicator sticks (for three separate specimens). Each slide has two squares labeled "A" and "B" containing filter paper impregnated with guaiac.

Continued

Procedure 2-1 Instruct the Patient in Obtaining a Fecal Specimen—cont'd

8. Procedural Step. Instruct the patient to use a ballpoint pen to complete the required information on the front of the card.
This information includes the patient's name, address, phone number, age, and the date of the specimen collection. This information should be completed before collection of specimens.

9. Procedural Step. Inform the patient of the requirements for proper care and storage of the slides.
The slides must be stored at room temperature and protected from heat, sunlight, and strong fluorescent light.
Rationale. Improper storage of the slides may result in deterioration of the guaiac impregnated on the filter paper, leading to inaccurate test results.

10. Procedural Step. Instruct the patient to collect a stool specimen in the toilet from the first bowel movement after the 48-hour preparation period.

11 Procedural Step. Explain the stool collection procedure to the patient.

a. The stool specimen may be collected directly from the stool in the toilet or in a container, on a disposable paper plate, or plastic wrap. Using one of the wooden applicators, obtain a small sample of the stool.
b. Open the front flap of the first cardboard slide (located on the left in the series of three).
c. Spread a very thin smear of the specimen over the filter paper in the square labeled "A."

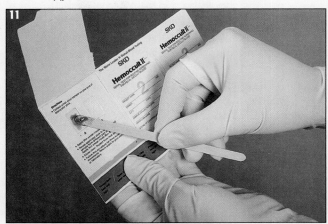

d. Using the opposite end of the same wooden applicator, obtain another small sample from a different area of the stool.

e. Spread a very thin smear of the specimen over the filter paper in the square labeled "B."
f. Close the front flap of the cardboard slide and indicate the date in the space provided.
g. Discard the wooden applicator in a waste container.

Rationale. Occult blood is not always distributed evenly throughout a specimen, so collecting two separate specimens from different areas of the sample provides a greater opportunity to find occult blood. The specimen must be spread thinly to provide adequate penetration through the filter paper.

12. Procedural Step. Instruct the patient to repeat the process on the next two bowel movements, repeating the collection steps.
The specimen from the second bowel movement is placed on the middle slide, and the specimen from the third bowel movement is placed on the slide on the right.

13. Procedural Step. Instruct the patient to allow the slides to air-dry minimally overnight.

14 Procedural Step. Once all three specimens are collected and allowed to air-dry, instruct the patient to place the cardboard slides in the envelope, carefully seal it, and return it as soon as possible to the medical office.

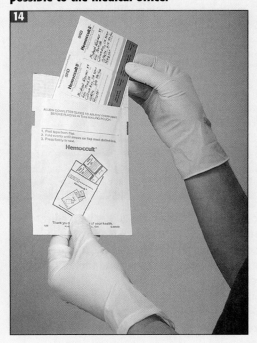

Procedure 2-1 Instruct the Patient in Obtaining a Fecal Specimen—cont'd

15. Procedural Step. Make sure the patient understands the instructions required for patient preparation, collection, and processing of the stool specimens and for storage of the slides.
Allow time for patient questions.
Rationale. Improper patient preparation and technique may lead to inaccurate test results.

16. Procedural Step. Document in the patient's medical record the date that the Hemoccult test and instructions were given to the patient.

17. Procedural Step. Sanitize the hands.
Always sanitize the hands after every procedure or after using gloves.

Charting Example

Date	
1/4/xx	9:30 a.m. Pt. given instructions for diet restrictions and stool collections. Written instructions provided. Pt. verbalizes understanding. — D. Pantalone, CMA (AAMA)

Photos from Bonewit-West K: *Clinical procedures for medical assistants,* ed 6, Philadelphia, 2004, Saunders.

Procedure 2-2 Test for Occult Blood

TASK: Accurately develop the occult blood slide test and document the results.

EQUIPMENT AND SUPPLIES
- Prepared cardboard slides
- Reference card
- Developing solution
- Nonsterile disposable gloves
- Biohazardous waste container
- Patient's medical record

SKILLS/RATIONALE

STANDARD PRECAUTIONS ARE TO BE FOLLOWED.

1. Procedural Step. Sanitize the hands.
An alcohol-based hand rub may be used instead of washing hands with soap and water, unless hands are visibly soiled.
Rationale. Hand sanitization promotes infection control.

2. Procedural Step. Assemble equipment and supplies.
Rationale. It is important to have all supplies and equipment ready and available before starting any procedure to ensure efficiency.

3. Procedural Step. Check the expiration date on the developing solution bottle.
Developing solution bottles must be stored with the cap tightly closed and must be kept from heat and light because the solution contains hydrogen peroxide.
Rationale. Outdated solutions will cause inaccurate test results. The solution must be stored properly because the solution evaporates quickly and is flammable.

4. Procedural Step. Obtain the patient's medical record.

5. Procedural Step. Prepare to develop the slides.
Obtain the specimens from the patient, and identify the specimens as belonging to the patient. The slides may be prepared and developed immediately, or they may be prepared and stored for up to 14 days (at room temperature) before developing.
Rationale. Identifying that the specimens belong to the patient ensures that the procedure is performed on the correct patient.

6. Procedural Step. Apply nonsterile disposable gloves.

7. Procedural Step. Prepare the slides.
Open the back flaps of the cardboard slides (opposite side from where the specimens were applied). Apply two drops of the developing solution to the guaiac-impregnated test paper. The developing solution should not be added directly onto the stool specimen, but should be absorbed through the filter paper into the specimen.

Continued

NOTE: The developing solution may cause irritation to the skin and eyes. If contact occurs, immediately flush the area with water.

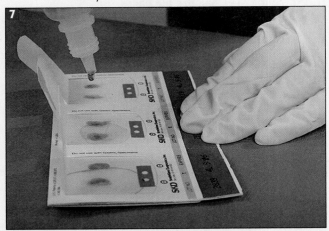

8 Procedural Step. Obtain the test kit reference card.
A reference card is provided with each Hemoccult kit. The reference card provides an illustration of positive and negative results, which can be used as a guide for interpreting results.

9. Procedural Step. Read the test results within 60 seconds.
A positive result is indicated by any trace of blue color on the filter paper on or around the fecal matter. Occult fecal blood in excess of 5 mL per day will result in a positive reaction. If no detectable color change occurs, the result is considered negative.
Rationale. Reading the results in the required time is important because the color reaction will fade after

2 to 4 minutes. The developer containing hydrogen peroxide causes the color reaction because heme, the compound in hemoglobin, oxidizes guaiac.

10. Procedural Step. Perform the quality control procedure, and document the results in the quality control laboratory logbook.
Each Hemoccult kit is supplied with quality control slides.
Rationale. Performing quality control procedures ensures that the test results are accurate and reliable.

11. Procedural Step. Properly dispose of the Hemoccult slides in a biohazardous waste container.
Rationale. Fecal matter is considered a contaminant and should always be disposed of in the appropriate biohazardous waste container.

12. Procedural Step. Remove gloves and sanitize the hands.
Always sanitize the hands after every procedure or after using gloves.

13. Procedural Step. Document the results.
Include the date and time, brand name of the test (Hemoccult), and test results (recorded as positive or negative).

Charting Example

Date	
3/10/xx	Received by mail 3-10-xx. Occult testing done on stool specimens returned. Specimen 1 collected 3/6/xx pos; specimen 2 collected 3/8/xx neg; specimen 3 collected 3/9/xx neg. Dr. notified of results.
	— B. Pizano, CMA (AAMA)

8

INTERPRETING THE HEMOCCULT® TEST

Negative Smears

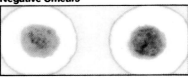

Sample report: negative
No detectable blue on or at the edge of the smears indicates the test is negative for occult blood. (See **LIMITATIONS OF PROCEDURE**.)

Negative and Positive Smears

Positive Smears

Sample report: positive
Any trace of blue on or at the edge of one or more of the smears indicates the test is positive for occult blood.

 **SmithKline Diagnostics, Inc.**
A SMITHKLINE BECKMAN COMPANY
San Jose, CA 95134-1622

Illustrations from Bonewit-West K: *Clinical procedures for medical assistants*, ed 6, Philadelphia, 2004, Saunders.

the morning, when the patient is usually fasting. On arrival, the patient is asked to empty the bladder. The patient is then provided with a gown and placed in the Sims' position.

Assisting with Sigmoidoscopy

During sigmoidoscopy the end of the flexible tube is lubricated and inserted through the anal opening and slowly advanced to the sigmoid colon. Air is blown into the colon through a valve connected to the sigmoidoscope, which allows for better visualization. Suction can be performed to remove feces, mucus, and blood. The intestinal mucosa of the colon is examined while the sigmoidoscope is being inserted and also while it is being withdrawn. Procedure 2-3 explains the process of preparing the patient and assisting the physician and patient during sigmoidoscopy.

PATIENT-CENTERED PROFESSIONALISM

- How would the medical assistant explain the reason for colorectal testing to the patient?
- What role does the medical assistant play before and during colon procedures?

PATIENT-CENTERED PROFESSIONALISM

- The digestive system provides nutrients for the body through many processes. Diseases and disorders of this system can interfere with this process. Why is it important for the medical assistant to understand what signs and symptoms may be present in a patient with a digestive disorder or disease?

Procedure 2-3 Assist with Sigmoidoscopy

TASK: Assist the physician and the patient during sigmoidoscopy.

EQUIPMENT AND SUPPLIES
- Nonsterile disposable gloves
- Sterile specimen container with preservative
- Flexible sigmoidoscope
- 4 × 4-inch gauze squares
- Water-soluble lubricant
- Tissue wipes
- Drape
- Biopsy forceps
- Biohazardous waste container
- Patient's medical record

SKILLS/RATIONALE

STANDARD PRECAUTIONS ARE TO BE FOLLOWED.

1. **Procedural Step. Sanitize the hands.**
An alcohol-based hand rub may be used instead of washing hands with soap and water, unless hands are visibly soiled.
Rationale. Hand sanitization promotes infection control.

2. **Procedural Step. Assemble equipment and supplies.**
Ensure that the light source on the sigmoidoscope is working. Label the specimen container with the patient's name, the date, and the source of the specimen.
Rationale. It is important to have all supplies and equipment ready and available before starting any procedure to ensure efficiency.

3. **Procedural Step. Obtain the patient's medical record.**

4. **Procedural Step. Escort the patient to the examination room, and greet and identify the patient.**

Rationale. Identifying the patient ensures that the procedure is performed on the correct patient.

5. **Procedural Step. Explain the procedure to the patient.**
Rationale. Explaining the procedure to the patient promotes cooperation and provides a means of obtaining implied consent.
Ascertain that the patient's instructions for preparation have been followed.

6. **Procedural Step. Ask the patient if he or she needs to empty his or her bladder before the examination.**
If the physician has ordered that a urine specimen be collected, provide the patient with a specimen container and directions for collection of a urine specimen.
Rationale. An empty bladder allows the patient to tolerate the procedure more comfortably.

7. **Procedural Step. Prepare the patient.**
Provide the patient with a patient gown and drape, and ask the patient to remove all

Continued

Procedure 2-3 Assist with Sigmoidoscopy—cont'd

clothing from the waist down, and put on the gown with the opening positioned in back. Ask the patient to have a seat on the examination table, assisting the patient as needed. Place a drape across the patient's lap.

8. **Procedural Step. Position the patient.**
   Once the physician has examined the patient and is ready to begin the procedure, place the patient into the Sims' or left lateral position.

   NOTE: If the medical office has a sigmoidoscopy table, the patient should first be aligned correctly on the table, then the table should be mechanically adjusted.

9. **Procedural Step. Properly drape the patient so that the drape is placed at an angle and the corner of the drape can be lifted to expose the anus.**
   Some medical offices use fenestrated drapes (drapes with one or more openings), with the circular opening placed over the anus.
   Rationale. Draping the patient reduces exposure and provides warmth.

10. **Procedural Step. Ensure the patient's comfort.**
    Before starting the procedure, reassure the patient that even though the procedure may be uncomfortable, it will last only a short time. Ask the patient to breathe slowly and deeply through the mouth, and encourage the patient to relax the muscles of the anus and rectum.

11. **Procedural Step. Lubricate the physician's gloved index finger.**
    The physician will begin with a digital examination.

12. **Procedural Step. Lubricate the distal end of the sigmoidoscope before the physician inserts the sigmoidoscope into the anus.**
    Rationale. The sigmoidoscope should be well lubricated for ease of insertion.

13. **Procedural Step. Assist the physician with the suction equipment as required.**

14. **Procedural Step. Assist with the collection of a biopsy as needed.**
    Hand the biopsy forceps to the physician, and hold the specimen container to accept the biopsy. Because it is sterile, do not touch the inside of the container.

15. **Procedural Step. On completion of the examination, apply clean gloves and clean the**
    patient's anal area with tissues to remove any excess lubricant.

16. **Procedural Step. Remove gloves and sanitize the hands.**
    Always sanitize the hands after every procedure or after using gloves.

17. **Procedural Step. Assist the patient from the examination table.**
    Assist the patient to a sitting position and allow the patient to rest. Assist the patient off the examination table as needed. Instruct the patient to dress. Provide the patient a restroom to allow the patient to expel air that was used to inflate the colon during the procedure.
    Rationale. The patient should be allowed to rest after the procedure to prevent postural dizziness. Assisting the patient off the examination table as needed prevents falls and injuries.

18. **Procedural Step. Prepare the laboratory requisition form and accompanying specimens.**
    Complete the laboratory requisition form and attach it to the specimen, if a specimen was taken. Transport the requisition form and specimen to the laboratory pathology department in a sealed biohazard transport container.

19. **Procedural Step. Clean the examination room in preparation for the next patient.**
    Discard all contaminated material in a biohazardous waste container. The sigmoidoscope should be sanitized and disinfected according to the manufacturer's recommendations. The sigmoidoscope contains fiberoptics and should be handled with extreme care. Wear nonsterile disposable gloves when cleaning the examination room. Never bring the next patient into an examination room that has items left from the last procedure.

20. **Procedural Step. Document the procedure in the patient's medical record.**

Charting Example

Date	
10/07/xx	9:00 a.m. Sigmoidoscopy c̄ 2 bx transported to Medical Center Laboratory for pathology. Pt. tolerated procedure well. Instructions for follow-up given and questions answered. ——————— M. Parsons, CMA (AAMA)

CONCLUSION

The organs of the digestive system all work together to break food down to a form that can be used by the body cells. The digestive process is responsible for transport of food and wastes, physical and chemical breakdown, absorption of nutrients and water, and elimination of wastes. The digestive system keeps the body in balance by maintaining adequate hydration to include electrolytes and nutrition.

When the digestive system functions properly, it not only performs its tasks but also helps support the other systems of the human body. Medical assistants who are familiar with the structure, function, and pathophysiology of the digestive system are better prepared to deliver high-quality care to the patients with whom they interact in the medical office.

SUMMARY

Reinforce your understanding of the material in this chapter by reviewing the curriculum objectives and key content points below.

1. Define, appropriately use, and spell all the Key Terms for this chapter.
   - Review the Key Terms if necessary.
2. Explain the purpose of the digestive system.
   - The digestive system changes the food and drink we ingest so that our bodies can use the energy from this intake.
   - After absorbing all the nutrients possible, the digestive system eliminates body waste.
3. List the four stages of the digestive process.
   - The digestive and accessory organs allow the gastrointestinal (GI) system to ingest, digest, absorb nutrients, and eliminate waste.
4. List the eight distinct areas of the digestive tract through which food passes during digestion.
   - The GI tract can be divided into eight distinct areas: the mouth, pharynx, esophagus, stomach, small intestine, large intestine, rectum, and anal canal.
5. Explain the role of the mouth in digestion.
   - The mouth is where food enters the digestive system. Food is masticated by the teeth, mixed with saliva and enzymes to help with the digestive process, and transported down the esophagus on its way to the stomach.
   - Food that has been chewed and mixed with saliva is called *a bolus*.
6. Locate three structures in the mouth important to the digestive process.

- The mouth contains the tongue, duct openings of the salivary glands, and the teeth.
- Saliva for digestion is secreted by the salivary glands, which lie outside the mouth but empty into the mouth.
- The teeth are used for mechanical tearing of food.

7. Identify the pharynx and explain its role in digestion.
   - The pharynx (throat) is a long tubelike structure that transports food and liquid to the esophagus for digestion.
   - The bolus enters the pharynx as it is swallowed.
   - The epiglottis closes over the trachea during swallowing, which causes the bolus to enter the esophagus, and not the trachea.
8. Locate the esophagus and explain its role in digestion.
   - The esophagus lies behind the trachea and transports food into the stomach. It is flat except when food is being swallowed.
   - The esophagus carries the bolus to the stomach by the process of peristalsis.
9. Explain the role of the stomach in digestion.
   - The stomach serves as a short-term storage area for food being digested.
   - The stomach is where many chemicals and enzymes are mixed with food. Digestion starts in the stomach, especially the digestion of proteins.
   - The stomach slowly releases a thick near-liquid mass called *chyme* into the small intestine for more digestion and absorption.
10. Locate the peritoneum, sphincters, and fundus within the stomach.
    - The fundus is the top portion of the stomach.
    - Two sphincters guard the entrance and exit of the stomach: the cardiac sphincter at the esophagus and the pyloric sphincter at the small intestine.
    - The peritoneum is a serous membrane that provides protection for the digestive organs.
11. Explain the role of the small intestine in digestion.
    - The small intestine aids in the breakdown of sugars, proteins, and fats.
12. Locate the three main parts of the small intestine.
    - The duodenum begins where the stomach ends.
    - The jejunum contains villi that allow nutrients to be absorbed by the blood.
    - The ileum connects to the cecum (first part of the large intestine).

13. Explain the role of the large intestine in the digestive system.
    - The colon absorbs water, minerals, and remaining nutrients in addition to synthesizing and absorbing B-complex vitamins.
    - The colon allows vitamin K to form.
14. Name and locate the four subdivisions of the large intestine.
    - The colon can be subdivided into the ascending, transverse, descending, and sigmoid colons.
    - The ascending colon travels up the right side of the body toward the lower part of the liver.
    - The transverse colon moves across the abdomen, below the liver and stomach, and above the small intestine.
    - The descending colon travels down the left side of the body and connects to the sigmoid colon.
    - The sigmoid colon joins to the rectum.
15. Locate the rectum and explain its role in the digestive system.
    - The rectum is almost at the end of the digestive system to store waste until it can leave the system as feces.
16. Locate the anal sphincter and explain its role in the digestive system.
    - The anal sphincter regulates defecation by allowing fecal material (waste) to be expelled.
17. Name and locate the three accessory organs to the digestive system and describe the role of each in digesting nutrients.
    - The liver, gallbladder, and pancreas all secrete important substances that aid in digestion.
    - The liver is located in the right hypochondriac and epigastric regions and produces bile that helps digest fats.
    - The gallbladder lies underneath the liver and stores bile until needed to further the digestive process.
    - The pancreas lies behind the stomach and in front of the first and second lumbar vertebrae. It is both an endocrine and exocrine organ and produces pancreatin and insulin.
18. Distinguish between metabolism, anabolism, and catabolism.
    - Metabolism is the physical and chemical change nutrients undergo after absorption that involves both anabolism and catabolism.
    - Anabolism is the buildup of smaller molecules to nutrients the body needs.
    - Catabolism is the breakdown of larger molecules so the byproducts can be used for cell energy.

19. List six diseases of the mouth and briefly describe the etiology, signs and symptoms, diagnosis, therapy, and interventions for each.
    - Diseases of the mouth may affect teeth, tongue, gums, or the mucous lining of the mouth.
    - Review Table 2-3.
20. List two disorders of the esophagus and briefly describe the etiology, signs and symptoms, diagnosis, therapy, and interventions for each.
    - Disorders of the esophagus often involve the backup, or reflux, of gastric juices (acids).
    - Review Table 2-3.
21. List five disorders of the stomach and briefly describe the etiology, signs and symptoms, diagnosis, therapy, and interventions for each.
    - Disorders of the stomach, as with other disorders of the digestive system, may be acute or chronic.
    - Review Table 2-3.
22. List three disorders of the small intestine and briefly describe the etiology, signs and symptoms, diagnosis, therapy, and interventions for each.
    - Review Table 2-3.
23. List four disorders of the large intestine and briefly describe the etiology, signs and symptoms, diagnosis, therapy, and interventions for each.
    - Review Table 2-3.
24. List a disorder of the rectum and anal canal and briefly describe its etiology, signs and symptoms, diagnosis, therapy, and interventions.
    - Review Table 2-3.
25. List three diseases of the liver and briefly describe the etiology, signs and symptoms, diagnosis, therapy, and interventions for each.
    - Hepatitis is recognized in several forms; hepatitis A, B, and C are the most frequently diagnosed types.
    - Review Table 2-3.
26. List three disorders of the accessory organs to the digestive system and briefly describe the etiology, signs and symptoms, diagnosis, therapy, and interventions for each.
    - Disorders of the accessory organs may involve inflammation and problems with gallstones.
    - Review Table 2-3.
27. Explain the purpose of fecal occult testing.
    - Fecal occult testing detects the presence of blood in the stool (screens for colorectal bleeding).

28. Demonstrate the procedure for providing the patient with accurate and complete instructions on the preparation and collection of a stool sample for fecal occult blood testing.
   • Review Procedure 2-1.
29. Demonstrate the procedure for accurately developing the fecal occult blood slide test.
   • Review Procedure 2-2.
30. Explain the purpose of sigmoidoscopy.
   • Sigmoidoscopy examines the lower bowel to diagnose and treat conditions that affect this portion of the digestive system.
31. Demonstrate the correct procedure for assisting the physician and patient during a sigmoidoscopy.
   • Review Procedure 2-3.
32. Analyze a realistic medical office situation and apply your understanding of the digestive system to determine the best course of action.
   • Understanding the normal physiology of the digestive system will help in understanding how the disease process affects this system.
33. Describe the impact on patient care when medical assistants have a solid understanding of the structure and function of the digestive system.

• Medical assistants who understand the physiology of the digestive system will be better prepared to assist with medical procedures, communicate clearly to patients, and perform effective patient teaching.

FOR FURTHER EXPLORATION

1. **Research the stomach and its disorders.** Consider that stress or nervousness can cause an upset stomach. Investigate the physiology of digestion and how gastric secretions are regulated.
   Keywords: Use the following keywords in your search: digestion, gastric secretions, stomach.
2. **Research the liver and its disorders.** The liver has several major functions and can malfunction for many reasons. Investigate the different forms of hepatitis and causes of cirrhosis and treatments.
   Keywords: Use the following keywords in your search: liver, hepatitis, cirrhosis, liver transplant.

WORD PARTS: DIGESTIVE (GI) SYSTEM

Mouth
Combining Forms

cheil/o	lip
dent/i, dent/o	teeth
dips/o	thirst
gingiv/o	gums
gloss/o, lingu/o	tongue
mandibul/o	mandible
maxill/o	maxilla
odont/o	teeth
or/o	mouth
sial/o	saliva
sialaden/o	salivary gland
staphyl/o	uvula; clusters
stomat/o	mouth

Suffix

-ase	enzyme

Pharynx

pharyng/o	throat, pharynx

Esophagus and Stomach
Combining Forms

esophag/o	esophagus
gastr/o	stomach
prote/o	protein
vag/o	vagus nerve

Suffixes

-clysis	washing out
-emesis	vomiting
-pepsia	digestion
-phage	eat or swallow
-phagia	eating or swallowing
-stalsis	contraction

Intestines, Rectum, and Anal Canal
Combining Forms

an/o	anus
append/o, appendic/o	appendix
bil/i	bile
cec/o	cecum
col/o, colon/o	large intestine; colon
diverticul/o	diverticular
duoden/o	duodenum
enter/o	small intestine
fung/i	fungus
glyc/o	sugar

ile/o	ileum
jejun/o	jejunum
lact/o	milk
lip/o	fats
myc/o	fungus
proct/o	anus, rectum
prote/o	protein
py/o	pus
pylor/o	pylorus
rect/o	rectum
sigmoid/o	sigmoid colon
top/o	place or position

Suffixes

-cele	swelling of; hernia, protrusion
-ose	sugar
-pexy	surgical fixation

Accessory Organs
Combining Forms

hepat/o	liver
cholecyst/o	gallbladder
chol/e	bile
choledoch/o	common bile duct
cyst/o	bladder or sac
pancreat/o	pancreas

Abbreviations: Digestive (GI) System

ac	before meals (Latin *ante cibum*)
ALT	alanine transaminase; liver enzyme test
AST	aspartate transaminase; liver enzyme test
BaE, BE	barium enema
GA	gastric analysis
GI	gastrointestinal
IC	irritable colon
IVC	intravenous cholangiogram
NPO, npo	nothing by mouth (Latin *nulle per os*)
SGOT	serum glutamic-oxaloacetic transaminase; AST
SGPT	serum glutamic-pyruvic transaminase; ALT
pc	after meals (Latin *post cibum*)

Chapter Review

Vocabulary Review:

Matching: Match each term with the correct definition.

A. digestion

B. alimentary canal

C. bolus

D. uvula

E. mastication

F. enzyme

G. peristalsis

H. chyme

I. gastroenteritis

J. mesentery

K. peritoneum

L. stomach

M. vagus nerve

N. villi

O. vermiform appendix

P. defecation

Q. liver

R. hepatic duct

___R___ 1. Duct from the liver to the gallbladder

___K___ 2. Serous membrane that lines the walls of the abdominal cavity and folds over and protects the intestines

___A___ 3. Reflux into the esophagus of stomach acids and food

___B___ 4. Digestive tract; extends from the mouth to the anus

___G___ 5. Wavelike motions that propel food through the digestive tract

___L___ 6. Enlarged, saclike portion of the alimentary canal; one of the main organs of digestion

___D___ 7. Small mass of tissue hanging from the soft palate at the back of the mouth

___Q___ 8. Organ that secretes bile; active in the formation of certain blood proteins and the metabolism of carbohydrates, fats, and proteins

___X___ 9. Inflammation of the liver caused by a viral infection

___C___ 10. Food broken down by chewing and mixed with saliva

___F___ 11. Protein produced by living organisms that causes biochemical changes

___N___ 12. Vascular projections of the small intestine for absorption of nutrients

___J___ 13. Membrane that attaches itself to the small and large intestines and holds them in place

___U___ 14. Difficulty in defecation caused by hard, compacted stool; lack of water absorption in the large intestine

___Z___ 15. Colon twisting on itself

S. insulin

T. metabolism

U. constipation

V. flatulence

W. jaundice

X. regurgitation

Y. hepatitis

Z. volvulus

AA. guaiac test

BB. sigmoidoscope

_Q_ 16. Chewing

_A_ 17. Physical and chemical breakdown of food

_O_ 18. Attached to the cecum

_V_ 19. Digestive gas

_I_ 20. Inflammation of the stomach and intestines

_T_ 21. Energy production after the absorption of nutrients

_P_ 22. Elimination of feces

_S_ 23. Hormone functions to regulate the metabolism of carbohydrates and fats, especially the conversion of glucose to glycogen, which lowers the blood glucose level

_H_ 24. Semiliquid contents of the stomach after it has been mixed with stomach acid

_M_ 25. Controls secretions of hydrochloric acid, as well as many other responsibilities

_W_ 26. Yellowish discoloration of the skin due to a breakdown of bilirubin

_BB_ 27. Instrument used to view the sigmoid region of the colon

_AA_ 28. Test for hidden (occult) blood in the stool or other body secretions

Theory Recall

True/False

Indicate whether the sentence or statement is true or false.

_F_ 1. The alimentary canal is a muscular tube that extends from the mouth to the anus and is approximately 30 feet long.

_T_ 2. The liver is the largest organ in the body.

_F_ 3. The trachea carries the bolus to the stomach via the process of peristalsis.

_F_ 4. The duodenum is where the final breakdown of nutrients takes place.

_F_ 5. The LES allows chyme to exit into the small intestine.

_T_ 6. A fecal occult test can identify the cause of rectal bleeding.

Multiple Choice

Identify the letter of the choice that best completes the statement or answers the question.

1. ___A___ is the process of taking nutrition into the body.
   A. Absorption
   B. Elimination
   C. Ingestion
   D. None of the above

2. Which one of the following is not one of the four areas of the taste buds of the tongue?   B
   A. Sweet
   B. Metallic
   C. Salty
   D. Sour

3. The top portion of the stomach is called the A___.
   A. fundus
   B. rugae
   C. body
   D. frenulum

4. The combining form for *mouth* is ___D___.
   A. cheil/o
   B. enter/o
   C. pylor/o
   D. stomat/o

5. A large pouch forming the first part of the large intestine is called the ___B___.
   A. cecum
   B. appendix
   C. colon
   D. jejunum

6. The suffix for *digestion* is ___B___.
   A. -emesis
   B. -pepsia
   C. -stalsis
   D. -phage

7. ___D___ is fluid that is secreted by the liver, stored in the gallbladder, and discharged into the duodenum.
   A. Chyme
   B. Bolus
   C. Feces
   D. Bile

8. The suffix for *hernia* is ___A___.
   A. -cele
   B. -clysis
   C. -pexy
   D. -ose

9. The medical abbreviation that means *before meals* is _C_.
   A. BE
   B. BM
   C. AC
   D. NPO

10. The second part of the small intestine, responsible for absorption, is the _B_.
   A. duodenum
   B. jejunum
   C. vermiform appendix
   D. cecum

11. An organ that has both endocrine and exocrine functions is the _C_.
   A. liver
   B. spleen
   C. pancreas
   D. appendix

12. The medical term for *forceful expulsion of the stomach contents* is _A_.
   A. emesis
   B. dyspepsia
   C. flatulence
   D. ascites

13. The process of converting smaller molecules into larger molecules is called _B_.
   A. cannibalism
   B. metabolism
   C. catabolism
   D. anabolism

14. Frequent bowel movements of loose, watery stools is _D_.
   A. flatulence
   B. ascites
   C. emesis
   D. none of the above

15. Dilated veins in the rectum and anus are called _B_.
   A. caries
   B. hemorrhoids
   C. varicose veins
   D. glossitis

16. The medical term for gallstones is _C_.
   A. cholelithiasis
   B. choledocolithotomy
   C. cholecystitis
   D. diverticulitis

17. _B_ are usually benign growths that can be attached to the mucosal lining of the colon.
   A. Hemorrhoids
   B. Polyps
   C. Caries
   D. None of the above

18. Telescoping of one part of the intestine into another is called __C__.
    A. diverticulitis
    B. gastroenteritis
    C. intussusception
    D. celiac sprue

19. A(n) __C__ is a lesion of the mucosal lining of the stomach or intestine.
    A. pyloric stenosis
    B. volvulus
    C. ulcer
    D. celiac sprue

20. The medical term for *vomiting blood* is __D__.
    A. gastritis
    B. intussusception
    C. ascites
    D. hematemesis

21. __B__ is a viral infection of the parotid glands.
    A. Melena
    B. Mumps
    C. Measles
    D. Ulcers

22. Which one of the following is NOT a stage of digestion? __B__
    A. Ingestion
    B. Respiration
    C. Absorption
    D. Elimination

23. When food is chewed and mixed with saliva, it becomes known as __A__.
    A. bolus
    B. chyme
    C. feces
    D. phlegm

24. The oral ingestion of a suspension for imaging of the esophagus is what type of diagnostic test? __B__
    A. Cholecystography
    B. Barium enema
    C. Barium swallow
    D. Endoscopy

25. When permanent teeth replace baby teeth, there are four __C__.
    A. canines
    B. molars
    C. bicuspids
    D. none of the above

26. A(n) __A__ is a procedure performed to examine and treat a portion of the digestive system.
    A. endoscope
    B. proctology
    C. sigmoidoscopy
    D. none of the above

Sentence Completion

Complete each sentence or statement.

1. The _hepatic duct_ and the cystic duct join together to form the common bile duct.

2. The first set of teeth is called _deciduos teeth (baby teeth)_

3. Gastric juices contain the enzyme _digest protein_.

4. _Lactose intolerance_ is the inability for the body to process dairy products.

5. The _gallbladder_ is the part of the intestinal tract that moves up the right side of the body toward the lower part of the liver.

6. The _rectum_ is continuous with the sigmoid colon and measures about 5 inches in length.

7. The liver, _gallbladder_, and pancreas all empty their secretions into the duodenum.

8. _psyllium_ cause the evacuation of the bowel by increasing bulk of the feces, softening the stool, or lubricating the intestinal wall.

9. Bile leaves the gallbladder through the _hepatic duct_.

10. _NPO_ is the abbreviation for "nothing by mouth."

Short Answers

1. Explain the purpose of the digestive system.

    This is done so that the food nutrients can be absorbed into the bloodstream and used by body tissue or those not needed can be eliminated by the body

2. List the four stages of the digestive process.

    ① ingestion   ④ elimination

    ② digestion

    ③ absorption

3. Explain the role of the mouth in digestion.

    Where food & nutrients are physicaly broken up mixed w/ saliva becomes semiliquid form known as BOLUS.

CHOLELITHIASIS

- Gallstones are hard, pebble like deposits that form inside the gallbladder.
- Symptoms: pain in the right upper/or middle upper abdomen.

  fever

  yellowing of skin (jaundice)

  nausea & vomiting

Often found during routine x-ray / ultrasonography

Treatment: laparoscopic cholecystectomy

In most people gallstones cannot be prevented. In people who are obese, avoid rapid weight loss could prevent gallstones.

PubMed Health / www.ncbi.nlm.nih.gov/pubmedhealth

4. Explain the role of the stomach in digestion.

Stomach is does temporary store the chewed food from esophagus. This food is mixed w/ gastric juices & hydrochloric acid. This mixture is called CHYME

5. Explain the patient preparation for a sigmoidoscopy.

Day before the examination patient must eat low fiber diet, mild enema evening before the test & another enema on the day of examination. procedure done early in the morning w/ fasting. On arrival patient ask to empty bladder then placed in the Sims position on the examination table.

Critical Thinking

1. Using Box 2-1, create a patient history using a minimum of 10 of the terms on the list.

2. Clarence Johansen is 67 years old and has been encouraged by his wife to have a colon check-up. The physician ordered a standard cleansing diet and is going to perform a sigmoidoscopy this afternoon. Explain to Mr. Johansen what a sigmoidoscopy is. Explain why and how the procedure is performed.

Internet Research

Keyword: (Use the name of the condition or disease you select to write about)

Select one condition or disease from Table 2-3. Write a two-paragraph report regarding the condition or disease you selected, listing the etiology, signs and symptoms, diagnosis, therapy, and interventions. Cite your source. (You may not use the information on the tables exclusively for your report.) Be prepared to give a 2-minute oral presentation should your instructor assign you to do so.

What Would You Do?

If you have accomplished the objectives in this chapter, you will be able to make better choices as a medical assistant. Take a look at this situation and decide what you would do.

Saril Paratel, age 69, was brought to the physician's office with fever and pain in the right lower quadrant of her abdomen. The pain has lasted for 3 days and has become progressively worse over the past 36 hours. The pain originally started in the umbilical area, but over time moved to McBurney's point. Last night she had nausea and vomiting. She has not had a bowel movement for 4 days. Saril had dyspepsia for several days before this episode of pain. She has also noticed that fatty foods tend to cause flatulence with some pain in her right upper quadrant, radiating into her back at the right shoulder. No history of hematemesis is given, but malaise has been present for several weeks. When asked about diarrhea, Saril answers that her stools 5 days ago were soft, formed, and frequent, so yes, she had diarrhea. The white blood cell count ordered by the physician is reported as WBC 15,600 with a differential of 76% neutrophils, 25% lymphs, 0% basos, 10% monos, and 1% eos. The physician refers Saril to a surgeon because he wants her to be evaluated for possible appendicitis and to rule out the cause of the right upper quadrant pain.

Use the following information to answer questions.

Type	Range	Function
White blood count (WBC)	5000-11,000	Scavengers during an allergic reaction or an infection
Neutrophil	55%-70%	Phagocytosis
Eosinophil	1%-4%	Allergic reaction
Basophil	0.5%-1%	Allergic reaction
Monocyte	2%-8%	Phagocytosis
Lymphocyte	20%-40%	Immunity

1. What gastrointestinal organs are found in the right lower quadrant?

appendix

2. Where is McBurney's point?

Landmark in the right lower quadrant of abdomen over the location of the appendix

3. What is appendicitis?

Inflammation of vermiform appendix

4. What is hematemesis, and why would this be important in this case study?

Vomitting of blood, to verify the origin of blood expelled

5. What is the difference between emesis and regurgitation?

Emesis - vomitting

Regurgitation - reflux of stomach acids of food into the esophagus

6. Did Saril really have diarrhea? Explain your answer.

No.. she maybe doing frequent bowel movement but her stool was soft & firm, not loose & watery. This could have been because she had not moved for four days already.

7. What did the white blood cell count indicate?

8. How did the white cell differential confirm that Saril might have appendicitis?

9. What organs of digestion are found in the right upper quadrant?

Liver

10. What disease processes might be seen with right upper quadrant pain that radiates into the right back at the shoulder with associated flatulence?

cholecystitis

Application of Skills

Label the diagrams.

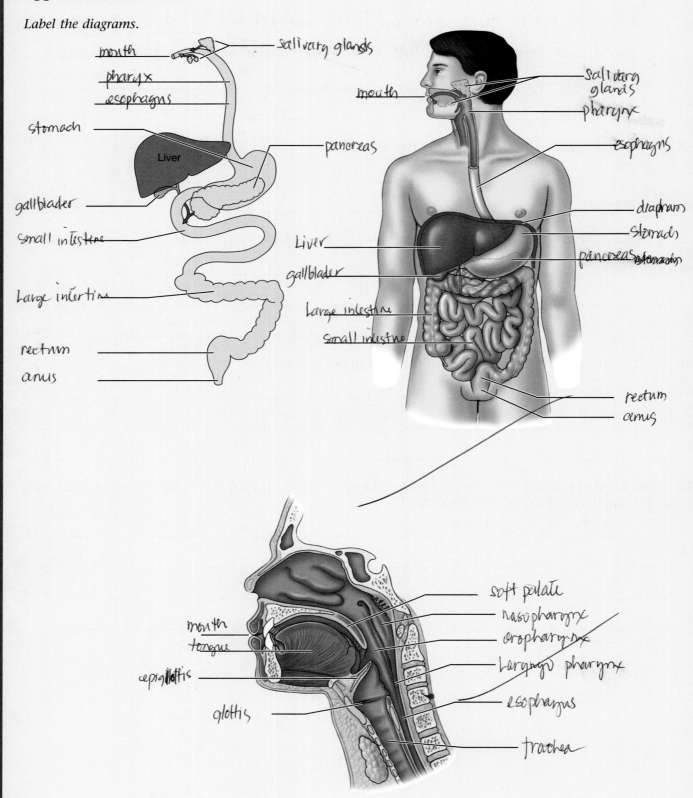

mouth

salivary glands

pharynx

esophagus

stomach

Liver

pancreas

gallbladder

small intestine

Large intestine

rectum

anus

mouth

salivary glands

pharynx

esophagus

diaphram

stomach

pancreas   stomach

Liver

gallbladder

Large intestine

Small intestine

rectum

anus

soft palate

nasopharynx

oropharynx

Laryngo pharynx

esophagus

trachea

mouth

tongue

epiglottis

glottis

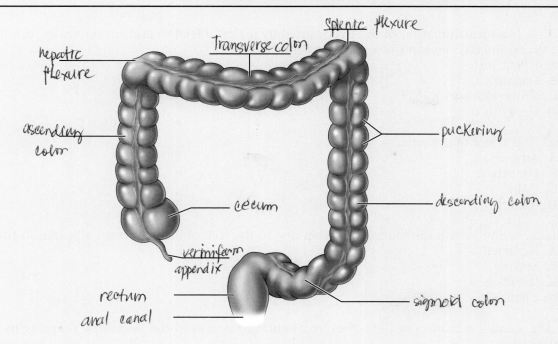

hepatic flexure

Transverse colon

Splenic flexure

ascending colon

puckering

cecum

descending colon

vermiform appendix

rectum

anal canal

sigmoid colon

Trace a hamburger through the alimentary canal.

Chapter Quiz

Multiple Choice

Identify the letter of the choice that best completes the statement or answers the question.

1. A toothache is a symptom of __B__.
   A. glossitis
   B. caries
   C. gingivitis
   D. thrush

2. The therapy for GERD is __A__.
   A. to elevate the head of the bed 4 to 6 inches
   B. the removal of plaque and antibiotic therapy
   C. a bland diet to reduce acid
   D. a gluten-free diet

3. __B__ is the narrowing of the pyloric sphincter.
   A. Intussusception
   B. Pyloric stenosis
   C. Endoscopy
   D. Pyloricectomy

4. __C__ is an inflammation of small out-pouches in the colon.
   A. Gastritis
   B. Colitis
   C. Diverticulitis
   D. Hepatitis

5. _D_ is an inflammation of the liver caused by a viral infection and contracted by coming in contact with an infected person's blood or body fluids.
   A. HIV
   B. Hepatitis C
   C. Crohn disease
   D. Hepatitis B

6. _A_ is a loss of appetite.
   A. Anorexia
   B. Dyspepsia
   C. Colic
   D. Ascites

7. _C_ is a yellowish discoloration of skin due to the lack of breakdown of bilirubin in the blood.
   A. Hematemesis
   B. Melena
   C. Jaundice
   D. Cirrhosis

8. _D_ cause evacuation of the bowel by stimulating nerves in the intestines, resulting in increased peristalsis.
   A. Antacids
   B. Antiemetics
   C. Cathartics
   D. Laxatives

9. _A_ is the physical and chemical change nutrients undergo after absorption.
   A. Metabolism
   B. Anabolism
   C. Catabolism
   D. Hemabolism

10. The _B_ is(are) the largest organ of the digestive system.
    A. heart
    B. liver
    C. lungs
    D. stomach

11. Which one of the following vitamins is NOT stored in the liver?   _C_
    A. A
    B. B$_{12}$
    C. C
    D. E

12. Which one of the following is NOT an accessory organ of the digestive system?   _A_
    A. Appendix
    B. Pancreas
    C. Gallbladder
    D. Liver

13. _D_ occurs when the stomach protrudes through the diaphragm into the chest cavity.
    A. An ulcer
    B. Spastic colon
    C. Appendicitis
    D. A hiatal hernia

14. Which one of the following is the correct spelling for the medical term meaning "inflammation of the gallbladder"?
    A. Koleecystitis
    B. Cholesisitis
    C. Cholecystitis
    D. Coaleesystitis

15. ___B___ are usually benign growths that can be attached to the mucosal lining of the colon.
    A. Hemorrhoids
    B. Polyps
    C. Varices
    D. Ulcers

16. The ___D___ is the portion of the digestive tract that extends from the sigmoid colon to the anal canal.
    A. descending colon
    B. duodenum
    C. ascending colon
    D. rectum

17. The medical term for "difficulty swallowing" is ___B___.
    A. dysphonia
    B. dysphagia
    C. dyspepsia
    D. dysuria

18. The second part of the small intestine responsible for absorption is the ___A___.
    A. jejunum
    B. rectum
    C. duodenum
    D. ileum

19. The ___C___ are the teeth located in the front of the mouth.
    A. molars
    B. canines
    C. incisors
    D. bicuspids

20. Absorption of nutrients takes place in the ___D___.
    A. stomach
    B. pancreas
    C. small intestine
    D. large intestine

21. Patient preparation for a sigmoidoscopy should include ___a___.
    A. an enema
    B. a high-fiber diet
    C. 16 ounces of water
    D. a mild sedative

22. A test card impregnated with guaiac regent is used when testing for occult blood.
    A. True
    B. False

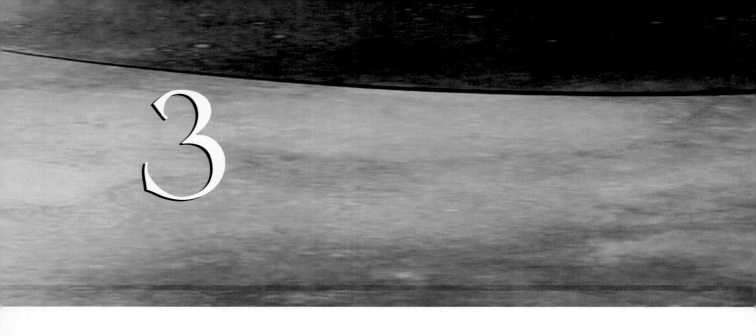

3

OBJECTIVES

You will be able to do the following after completing this chapter:

Key Terms
1. Define, appropriately use, and spell all the Key Terms for this chapter.

Patient Education
2. Explain the importance of patient education.

Dietary Guidelines
3. Explain the purpose of dietary guidelines.
4. List the six food groups included in the food guide pyramid and discuss the recommended daily quantities for a 2000-calorie diet.
5. Explain the purpose of the Nutrition Labeling and Education Act (NLEA), and list the two main panels to consider when looking at a food label.

Principles of Nutrition
6. List and briefly describe five basic principles of good nutrition.
7. Demonstrate how to calculate a patient's body mass index (BMI), and indicate whether a patient is underweight, normal, overweight, or obese according to the chart.
8. List five tips for maintaining nutritional balance in the daily diet.

Nutrients
9. Differentiate between essential and nonessential nutrients.
10. Differentiate fat-soluble vitamins from water-soluble vitamins and list the major sources of each.
11. List nine major minerals and explain the sources of each and the result of deficiency.
12. List seven trace minerals and explain the sources of each and the result of deficiency.
13. Explain why the body needs carbohydrates, fats, and proteins.
14. Explain the importance of water and state the daily recommended amount.

Nutrition Through the Life Span
15. Explain dietary needs during pregnancy and lactation, infancy, toddler age, school age, adolescence, and older adulthood.

Nutrition and Chronic Disease
16. Explain the dietary needs of patients newly diagnosed with human immunodeficiency virus (HIV) and those with acquired immune deficiency syndrome (AIDS).
17. Explain the dietary needs for cancer patients undergoing chemotherapy.

PATIENT EDUCATION AND NUTRITION

Diet Therapy

18. List and briefly describe nine types of therapeutic diets.
19. Explain why fad diets are unhealthy and a poor choice for long-term weight loss.

Patient-Centered Professionalism

20. Analyze a realistic medical office situation and apply your understanding of patient education and nutrition to determine the best course of action.
21. Describe the impact on patient care when medical assistants have a solid understanding of patient education and nutrition.

KEY TERMS

affective Type of learning based on feelings and emotions.

amino acids Building blocks; byproducts of protein breakdown by enzymes.

anorexia Anorexia nervosa is a psychological fear of gaining weight, causing a lack of appetite.

antioxidant Substance that acts against oxidizing agents.

assimilation Taking in of nutrient material.

beriberi Condition caused by a deficiency of thiamine (vitamin B_1).

bile Substance formed by the liver; breaks down vitamins and fats.

bland diet Diet that uses foods that are not irritating to the digestive tract.

body mass index (BMI) Formula that uses a chart to determine a person's predisposition for being overweight.

bulimia nervosa Disorder characterized by compulsive overeating followed by self-induced vomiting or use of laxatives or diuretics.

caloric intake Amount of calories eaten.

calorie Unit of energy.

calorie-controlled diet Diet that minimizes or maximizes the amount of food intake based on caloric intake.

carbohydrates Substances that produce quick energy and are the body's primary source of energy.

cellulose Chief part of the plant cell wall.

cholesterol Type of fat necessary for vitamin D and bile acid production.

cognitive Type of learning based on what the patient already knows and has experienced.

complex carbohydrates Starches.

complex proteins Proteins that contain all the essential amino acids and are found in animal sources.

daily value (DV) Dietary standards that include a range of particular nutrients needed daily to optimize health.

dermatitis Inflammation of the skin caused by irritation or riboflavin deficiency.

diabetic diet Diet for patients who have difficulty with insulin secretion.

display panel Panel on a label that is used for marketing purposes.

enzymes Complex proteins that break down amino acids.

essential nutrients Nutrients that must be supplied to the body from a food source (vitamins, minerals, proteins, carbohydrates, fats, water).

fad diet Diet that is structured to cause the quick loss of weight.

fat-soluble vitamins Vitamins that are stored within the fat tissues of the body (vitamins A, D, E, K).

fatty acids Organic acids produced by the breakdown of fats.

food guide pyramid Tool developed by the U.S. Department of Agriculture (USDA) to provide a visual picture of the six food groups common to the American diet.

glossitis Inflammation of the tongue.

KEY TERMS—*cont'd*

glycemic index Scale that rates carbohydrate foods' effects on blood glucose levels from slowest to fastest.

glycerol Alcohol that is made up of fat.

goiter Enlarged thyroid.

high-fiber diet Diet high in fiber to help with elimination.

hydrogenated Polyunsaturated fats that are made solid.

hypercholesterolemia High level of cholesterol in the blood.

liquid diet Diet consisting of all liquids.

low-cholesterol, low-fat diet Diet low in saturated fats.

low-fiber diet Diet that contains low-residue foods that pass easily through the digestive system.

major minerals Minerals used in significant amounts by the body (calcium, phosphorus, magnesium, sodium, iron, iodine, potassium).

malabsorption Inability of the digestive system to absorb required nutrients.

malnutrition Inadequate nutrition.

minerals Inorganic substances used in the formation of hard and soft body tissues.

monounsaturated fats Fats that are liquid at room temperature and help lower total cholesterol.

night blindness Condition caused by a deficiency in vitamin A.

nonessential nutrients Nutrients provided in the body.

nutrients Chemical substances within food that are released during the digestive process.

nutrition Scientific study of how different food groups affect the body.

Nutrition Labeling and Education Act (NLEA) Federal act of 1990 to assist consumers in identifying nutritional content in food products.

nutritional fact panel Panel on a label that meets the requirements of federal regulatory boards.

obese Grossly overweight.

osteomalacia Abnormal bone softening caused by vitamin D deficiency.

patient education Teaching-learning process that takes place in a medical practice.

pellagra Disease caused by a deficiency of niacin in the body.

pernicious anemia Condition caused by the body's inability to absorb vitamin B_{12}.

polyunsaturated fats Fats that are liquid at room temperature and found in vegetable oil.

portion Actual amount of food consumed at any one time, which may be more or less than a serving.

protein Substance that builds and repairs body tissue and breaks down enzymes so they can be absorbed by the small intestine.

psychomotor Type of learning based on motor skills needed to perform tasks.

psychosocial Pertaining to some form of social action and how it affects an individual.

recommended dietary allowances (RDAs) Established amounts of essential nutrients in a diet that help decrease the risk of chronic disease.

regular diet Diet that contains all foods from the food guide pyramid according to recommended proportions.

rickets Condition in children caused by vitamin D deficiency.

saturated fats Animal fats and tropical oils; solid at room temperature.

scurvy Condition caused by a lack of vitamin C in the diet.

serving Individual quantity of food or drink taken as part of a meal.

simple carbohydrates Sugars that have a high caloric value but no nutritional value.

simple proteins Proteins found in whole grains, beans, nuts, and seeds.

sodium-restricted diet Diet low in sodium-rich foods and seasonings.

soft diet Diet containing foods that are low in residue and easy to digest.

synthesize To make or take in; the body synthesizes substances.

therapeutic diet Diet required for health maintenance, special testing, or disorders.

trace minerals Minerals used by the body in small amounts (copper, cobalt, manganese, fluorine, zinc).

trans-fatty acids Substances formed when polyunsaturated fats are made solid.

triglycerides Dietary fats that have been broken down into fatty acids and glycerol.

unsaturated fats Fats that are liquid at room temperature.

vitamins Organic compounds needed by the body to function.

water-soluble vitamins Vitamins not stored in the body (C, B complex, thiamine, riboflavin, niacin, pantothenic acid, pyridoxine, folic acid, B_{12}).

What Would You Do?

Read the following scenario and keep it in mind as you learn about patient education and nutrition.

Josephine, age 52, has just been diagnosed with type 2 diabetes mellitus related to obesity. Living in the home with Josephine are her mother, Susie, who is 80 years old; Josephine's daughter Jessie, who is 24 and pregnant; and Jessie's two very active children, ages 6 and 2. Susie has been diagnosed with a heart condition and must be on a soft diet that is low in cholesterol and sodium restricted.

Josephine's concern today is how she can maintain a diet acceptable for all the medical conditions in the household while being sure the other family members will eat what is prepared. She thinks the children need sugar, but her mother needs to watch her sugar and salt intake to remain in a stable condition and not gain weight. Susie also needs her meals to be soft and easily chewable because of her decrease in intestinal motility. However, Jessie and her 2-year-old child both need a diet that allows the necessary fiber for adequate bowel activity.

If you were the medical assistant, how might you educate Josephine about nutrition and answer her questions?

One of the most important aspects of the medical assistant's job is patient education.

Patient education is the process of influencing patient behavior and causing the necessary changes in patient knowledge, attitudes, and skills that will maintain or improve the patient's health. Through patient education, medical assistants can help ensure that the prescribed treatment plan will be followed correctly. In addition, patient education is an opportunity to establish and build trusting relationships with patients.

In this chapter, besides learning about patient education, you primarily will learn important concepts of good nutrition. Medical assistants often need to educate patients about good nutrition and provide support and encouragement for patients prescribed a special diet by their physician.

Individuals with inadequate diets and poor nutritional status are more prone to disease. Teaching patients how to make adjustments in their lifestyle (e.g., good nutrition, proper exercise, smoking cessation) is an area in which medical assistants have the opportunity to improve patients' quality of living. To perform effective patient education in the area of nutrition, medical assistants must understand not only patient learning styles and the teaching-learning process but also dietary guidelines, principles of nutrition and nutrients, nutrition through the life span, nutrition for patients with chronic disease, and diet therapy.

PATIENT EDUCATION

The goal of any treatment for a disease or condition is to manage it successfully and eliminate it if pos-sible. Successful management requires that the patient be well informed about the illness, as well as the necessary actions for controlling or correcting it. Changes in patient behavior, including dietary habits, lifestyle, and use of medications, are often important parts of the prescribed treatment plan. Understanding how their illness and is controlled or corrected influences patients' behavior and increases the likelihood that the treatment plan will be followed. Effective **patient education** is the key to helping patients understand the situation and the need for these changes.

A solid understanding of human behavior and effective communication techniques are necessary to perform effective patient education.

In addition to understanding human behavior and communication principles, medical assistants should know about different learning styles, as well as what takes place during the teaching process.

Learning Styles

People learn in different ways. You may have known people who learned best by doing or who learned best by watching someone else. Other people learn best by reading or listening to someone speak about how to do the task. Keeping in mind that people learn in different ways will help you find the best way to educate each individual patient. It is best to discuss expectations and goals with the patient and allow the patient to be part of developing a treatment plan. This also helps the medical assistant determine how the patient learns or processes information.

Three types of learning are cognitive, affective, and psychomotor. Learning experiences that incorporate all three types of learning are most effective because they address the whole patient.

FOR YOUR INFORMATION

Effective Patient Education = Understanding Human Behavior + Good Communication

Applying what you have learned about human behavior interpersonal communication should make the process of patient education easier.

- *Human behavior.* Before a patient will be receptive to changes in behavior, the patient's basic human needs must be met. The patient must feel safe from the embarrassment that can result from lack of knowledge or differing cultural beliefs. For the patient to learn, he or she must be convinced that what is being taught is of value, is an attainable goal, and is something that can be used immediately.
- *Interpersonal communication.* During communication, both verbal and nonverbal messages are sent and received. These messages are influenced by a variety of factors, including environment, personal space, cultural beliefs, perception, developmental stage, language mastery, and a feeling of self-worth. The patient must have the time to listen to the information. For example, if diet information is to be provided to a patient newly diagnosed with diabetes, the patient must have the time available to listen and be able to ask questions.

Cognitive Learning

Cognitive learning is based on what a person already knows or has experienced. Memory or recall can stimulate the thought process, allowing a person to use information to analyze, plan, and evaluate a situation. Patients generally know something about a variety of health issues. When the medical assistant interviews the patient, this information can be used to create a baseline from which to start.

Learning occurs when the patient can understand information presented and when he or she places a significant meaning to its importance. This process may occur when the medical assistant demonstrates adequate knowledge about the subject area.

Affective Learning

A person's **affective** ability is concerned with the person's emotions and feelings. These, along with a person's attitudes, will cause one person to respond to a given situation or illness differently than someone else. In addition, the patient's ability to

learn is affected by his or her emotions, feelings, and attitudes about health care.

The medical assistant's role is to determine how a particular patient's emotions will guide or affect the patient's ability to learn and follow through with established goals. Sincere positive feedback from the medical assistant will build a feeling of confidence in a patient.

Psychomotor Learning

Psychomotor ability relates to movement or muscular activity associated with mental processes. A patient's physical capabilities must be considered when teaching and must be treated with respect at all times throughout the patient education process. The medical assistant must be aware of the patient's ability to perform the required skill.

Teaching Process

The teaching-learning process is a critical part of the medical practice, and again, patient education is an important role of the medical assistant. To perform this role successfully, medical assistants must meet the patient's learning needs. The key to patient teaching is not to focus on how to make the patient do something but to create a situation in which the patient will *want* to do what is needed. The process begins by assessing the patient, moving to form a plan, and implementing the plan and ends by evaluating the process.

Assess

Once the patient's learning needs have been identified, the medical assistant needs to take a quick inventory of the patient's readiness to learn by asking the following questions:

- Is the patient physically and emotionally ready for the health information to be presented? For example, does the patient have any visual or hearing difficulties? Can the patient handle the equipment? Changes associated with aging or disease process may affect the patient's ability to perform a skill.
- Will the patient be able to adapt to any **psychosocial** restrictions (e.g., alcohol)?
- Are the patient's health beliefs, behavior, and expectations in line with the treatment plan?
- What does the patient already know or understand about the illness or procedure? Checking for understanding is a critical element in patient teaching. If the patient lacks knowledge, teaching the basics (vocabulary, pathophysiology of the disease) is a good place to start. Building on prior knowledge provides a

framework with which to modify or elaborate on a subject area.

The medical assistant must be willing to adapt to the patient's needs, educational level, and developmental stage.

Plan

To plan effectively, the patient's learning style must be identified and addressed. What may work for one patient may not work for another. Teaching techniques and methods must allow for the patient's learning style. A variety of tools can be used to improve a person's knowledge about a health care problem.

Provide information in ways that do not involve memorization. Plan to provide a learning experience by connecting events rather than bits and pieces. Local chapters of national organizations develop patient education materials that can serve this purpose (e.g., pamphlets, newsletters, videotapes). When using preprinted material, it is important to consider the reading ability of the patient. Also involve the patient's family and significant others if appropriate during the planning process.

Implement

The medical assistant must know the material being presented to patients well. Pretending to be knowledgeable about a subject area is not acceptable. The environment must be conducive to learning (e.g., comfortable room temperature, good lighting) because learning can take place only when the learner is focused on the material being presented. The patient must understand the language being used and should always be encouraged to ask questions.

When teaching procedures, the medical assistant should try to use the same equipment and supplies that the patient will use at home to demonstrate the required action, as follows:

- The medical assistant must first demonstrate the steps when teaching a skill. *Show* patients what to do; do not tell them. It is better to demonstrate on yourself or a family member because it allows the patient to observe the entire procedure.
- Use multimedia material when possible (e.g., videotapes), and make referrals to appropriate outside resources or agencies for reinforcement of learning.
- If the patient becomes frustrated or distracted, stop the session and reschedule for a time that is more suitable for the patient and caregiver.

Evaluate

When evaluating the patient's ability to learn, use objective data. For example, ask open-ended questions to determine the patient's understanding, or ask the patient to demonstrate the procedure. Always document the date, information provided, and the amount of time spent with the patient. (This is an important step for insurance claims.)

PATIENT-CENTERED PROFESSIONALISM

- How would using the Internet in patient teaching benefit both the medical assistant and the patient?

DIETARY GUIDELINES

Nutrition is the scientific study of how different food groups affect the body. Improper or incomplete nutrition leads to various disorders. Proper and complete nutrition allows people to function effectively, both physically and mentally. It also helps the body resist infection and disease. Food is required for the body to grow, heal, reproduce, and maintain a healthy state. Proper nutrition influences the appearance of a person's hair, eyes, teeth, and complexion. If deprived of proper nutrition, the body is prone to illness and is not able to maintain growth and a healthy state (Table 3-1).

Many American diets have adequate **calories** (units of energy) to get through the day, but they are inadequate in the necessary nutrients to nourish the body's systems. Therefore medical assistants must be prepared to educate patients about healthy eating and explain special diets that may be prescribed by the physician.

To help patients maintain optimal health, medical assistants must understand nutritional standards and must be able to assess the recommended nutritional guidelines in foods that are eaten by the patient daily. In 1941 the National Academy of Sciences and the Food and Nutrition Board published the **recommended dietary allowances (RDAs).** The RDAs reflected the established amounts of essential nutrients in a diet that help to decrease the risk of chronic disease and keep the body in homeostasis. In recent years the RDAs have been replaced on the food label with the term **daily value (DV).** This term better reflects dietary standards that include a range of particular nutrients to optimize an individual's health.

TABLE 3-1	Signs and Symptoms of Poor and Good Nutrition	
Tissues Involved	**Poor Nutrition**	**Good Nutrition**
Hair	Dry and brittle	Shiny
Eyes	Dull and dry	Bright and moist
Skin	Dry and scaling	Smooth, good color, and moist
Mouth		
Lips	Lesions and cracked	Pink color
Tongue	Surface smooth, swollen, and dry	Moist and surface bumpy
Teeth	Dental caries	No caries
Gums	Inflamed and bleeding	Firm and pink

FOR YOUR INFORMATION

Dietary Guideline Updates
The Dietary Guidelines, first published in 1980, must be reviewed every 5 years by law, because the guidelines are used by federal agencies to determine the nutritional content of school lunches.

In May 2005 the U.S. Department of Health and Human Services (DHHS) and Department of Agriculture (USDA) released new guidelines that provided the American public with updated information on food and nutrition. The food guide pyramid and its accompanying dietary guidelines are not solely for public education but influence what products are manufactured and sold and set standards for federal nutrition programs, including school lunches. Dietary guidelines allow an individual to select the types and amounts of foods and adjust them to recognize factors such as age, gender, health status, pregnancy, and other conditions that would affect their daily nutritional needs. The guidelines also identify a relationship between exercise, up to 30 to 60 minutes per day and maintenance of proper weight. Current knowledge about weight, nutrition, and physical activity is used to offer practical advice.

Food Guide Pyramid

The **food guide pyramid** was developed by the USDA to provide a visual picture of the six food groups common to the American diet. The updated pyramid (Fig. 3-1) (www.mypyramid.gov) emphasizes the consumption of fruits and vegetables and indicates that more calories should come from grains rather than meat proteins and dairy products. At least 3 ounces of the recommended 6 ounces of grains should be whole grains because these are complex carbohydrates that supply the muscles and the brain with energy. These foods include bread, pasta, and cereal made from whole grains and brown rice. Limiting fats, oils, and sugars is still advised. The pyramid also emphasizes physical activity by featuring a human figure climbing up the side of the pyramid. A change was made from abstract "servings" to a more concrete measure, such as cups and ounces.

The guidelines represented by the pyramid are not intended to be rigid but rather should be seen as recommendations to encourage people to eat a variety of foods from the six major food groups (Table 3-2). A diet low in fat and containing only moderate use of sugars and salt supports a healthier body. The food pyramid is a tool that provides the information needed to make good choices. Therefore the food pyramid should be used as a guide, not a strict map, for healthier eating. Certain food pyramids have been developed for specific ethnic and cultural groups (Fig. 3-2). Box 3-1 provides information about the relationship between culture and nutrition.

Food Labels

In 1990 the **Nutrition Labeling and Education Act (NLEA)** was passed to assist consumers in identifying nutritional content in food products. Food labels are designed to allow consumers to make informed food choices. Nutritional labeling is required for most foods, except meat and poultry. The information contained on a food label is regulated by the Food and Drug Administration (FDA) and therefore is considered a legal document.

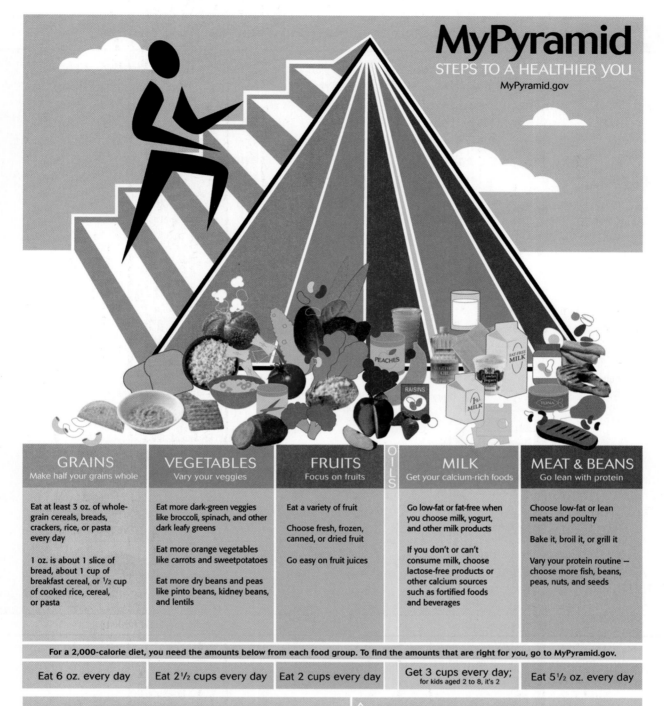

MyPyramid
STEPS TO A HEALTHIER YOU
MyPyramid.gov

GRAINS	VEGETABLES	FRUITS	OILS	MILK	MEAT & BEANS
Make half your grains whole	Vary your veggies	Focus on fruits		Get your calcium-rich foods	Go lean with protein
Eat at least 3 oz. of whole-grain cereals, breads, crackers, rice, or pasta every day	Eat more dark-green veggies like broccoli, spinach, and other dark leafy greens	Eat a variety of fruit		Go low-fat or fat-free when you choose milk, yogurt, and other milk products	Choose low-fat or lean meats and poultry
1 oz. is about 1 slice of bread, about 1 cup of breakfast cereal, or ½ cup of cooked rice, cereal, or pasta	Eat more orange vegetables like carrots and sweetpotatoes Eat more dry beans and peas like pinto beans, kidney beans, and lentils	Choose fresh, frozen, canned, or dried fruit Go easy on fruit juices		If you don't or can't consume milk, choose lactose-free products or other calcium sources such as fortified foods and beverages	Bake it, broil it, or grill it Vary your protein routine — choose more fish, beans, peas, nuts, and seeds

For a 2,000-calorie diet, you need the amounts below from each food group. To find the amounts that are right for you, go to MyPyramid.gov.

Eat 6 oz. every day	Eat 2½ cups every day	Eat 2 cups every day	Get 3 cups every day; for kids aged 2 to 8, it's 2	Eat 5½ oz. every day

Find your balance between food and physical activity
- Be sure to stay within your daily calorie needs.
- Be physically active for at least 30 minutes most days of the week.
- About 60 minutes a day of physical activity may be needed to prevent weight gain.
- For sustaining weight loss, at least 60 to 90 minutes a day of physical activity may be required.
- Children and teenagers should be physically active for 60 minutes every day, or most days.

Know the limits on fats, sugars, and salt (sodium)
- Make most of your fat sources from fish, nuts, and vegetable oils.
- Limit solid fats like butter, stick margarine, shortening, and lard, as well as foods that contain these.
- Check the Nutrition Facts label to keep saturated fats, *trans* fats, and sodium low.
- Choose food and beverages low in added sugars. Added sugars contribute calories with few, if any, nutrients.

MyPyramid.gov
STEPS TO A HEALTHIER YOU

U.S. Department of Agriculture
Center for Nutrition Policy and Promotion
April 2005
CNPP-15

USDA

Fig. 3-1 USDA food guide pyramid. *(U.S. Dept. of Agriculture 2005, CNPP-15)*

TABLE 3-2   Recommended Daily Consumption of the Six Food Groups

Calories	Grains (major source of energy and fiber)	Vegetables (rich sources of fiber, potassium, and magnesium)	Fruits (important sources of fiber, potassium, and magnesium)	Oils (low in saturated fat)	Milk (low-fat/fat-free major source of calcium and protein)	Protein (lean meats, poultry, fish, beans, peas, nuts and seeds)
1000 calories	3 oz	1 cup	1 cup	3 tsp	2 cups	2 oz
2000 calories	6 oz	2½ cups	2 cups	6 tsp	3 cups	5½ oz
3200 calories	10 oz	4 cups	2½ cups	11 tsp	3 cups	7 oz

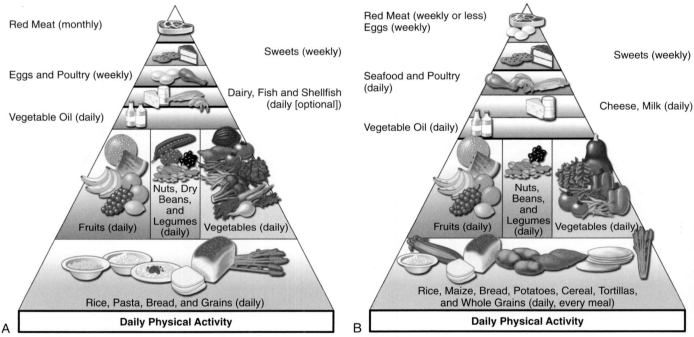

Fig. 3-2 Ethnic Food Guide Pyramid. **A,** An Asian diet indicates that one food group is no better than another. **B,** A Latin American diet includes protein based on plants and grains.

There are two main panels to consider when looking at a food label (Fig. 3-3), as follows:

- The **display panel** is used for marketing purposes.
- The **nutritional fact panel** is designed to meet the requirements of the regulatory boards. This panel is subdivided into two sections. The main (top) section contains product-specific information, and the footnote provides general dietary information. In 2006 the government required labels to list the amount of trans-fatty

acids, fats that have been linked to cardiovascular disease.

Box 3-2 provides the formula for determining fat, carbohydrates, and protein content.

PATIENT-CENTERED PROFESSIONALISM

- Why is it important for the medical assistant to understand the food guide pyramids of different cultures?

BOX 3-1   ## Culture and Nutrition

People eat food not only to meet the nutritional needs of the body but also to feel pleasure and satisfaction, or even comfort in times of stress and sadness. For many, mealtime is a social event, and many joyful occasions are celebrated with food. What is considered a food varies from one culture to another. Most cultures have their own health norms and practices. Knowing a patient's cultural traditions, ethnic background, and religion is important because these factors can influence the person's health and attitudes toward health care.

Attitudes and habits concerning food are the result of culture and society and will influence what foods are eaten most frequently. For example:

- Bread is the main staple in the diet of many countries, especially the Greek diet.
- Persons of German descent often favor pork, noodles, and sauerkraut.

- Italians relish pasta and green leafy vegetables and use large amounts of olive oil when cooking.
- The East-Asian population favors fish and rice as main sources of food.
- Some cultures, such as Indian, use spicy seasonings when cooking.

In recent years, diabetes and gallbladder disease have been increasing among Native Americans. Changes in dietary habits, increased obesity, and genetic factors are thought to have contributed to this increase.

When a person becomes ill, he or she often must adjust food selection depending on their diet restrictions. The medical assistant must understand that a patient's diet is an important part of the patient's lifestyle and ethnicity. Offering suggestions that the patient will find appealing without compromising treatment can be a challenge.

BOX 3-2   ## Calorie Distribution: Fat, Carbohydrate, and Protein Content

Carbohydrates   4 calories per gram
Protein   4 calories per gram
Fat   9 calories per gram

Values from label:
Serving size: 2 tbsp = 12 g total fat, 15 g total carbohydrates, and 8 g protein

8 g protein × 4 calories = 32 calories
15 g carbohydrates × 4 = 60 calories
12 g fat × 9 calories = 108 calories
Total calories: 32 + 60 + 108 = 200 calories per serving
This means that each serving of this product has 200 calories, most of which comes from fat.
By using the values given on the food label, calculate the percentage of calories in food supplied from fat:

$$\text{Grams of fat} \times 9 = \text{Fat calories}$$
$$(\text{Fat calories} \div \text{Total calories}) \times 100 = \% \text{ of calories from fat}$$
$$\textit{Solution: } 12 \text{ g} \times 9 = 108$$
$$(108 \div 200) \times 100 = (10{,}800 \div 20{,}000)$$
$$= 5.9\% \text{ of calories supplied from fat}$$

≋ PRINCIPLES OF NUTRITION

To provide the best patient teaching possible, medical assistants need to understand the basic principles of good nutrition, including the concepts of variety, weight management, balance, and minimizing sugar and sodium.

Variety

The food pyramid encourages eating a variety of foods in moderate amounts to obtain needed nutrients and a **caloric intake** to maintain a healthy body weight. A medical assistant can assist the patient by encouraging him or her to eat something from each food group. The number of servings from

Sample Food Label

The food label can be found on food packages in your supermarket. Reading the label tells more about the food and what you are getting. The nutrition and ingredient information is required by the government.

Nutrition Facts Title
The title "Nutrition Facts" explains the purpose of the label

Serving Size
Similar food products now have similar serving sizes. This makes it easier to compare foods. The FDA set serving sizes for all food groups. They are measurements, not recommendations.

New Label Information
Some label information may be new to you. The new nutrient list covers those most important to your health.

Vitamins and Minerals
Only two vitamins, A and C, and two minerals, calcium and iron, are required on the food label. A food company can voluntarily list other vitamins and minerals in the food.

Label Numbers
Numbers on the nutrition label may be rounded for labeling.

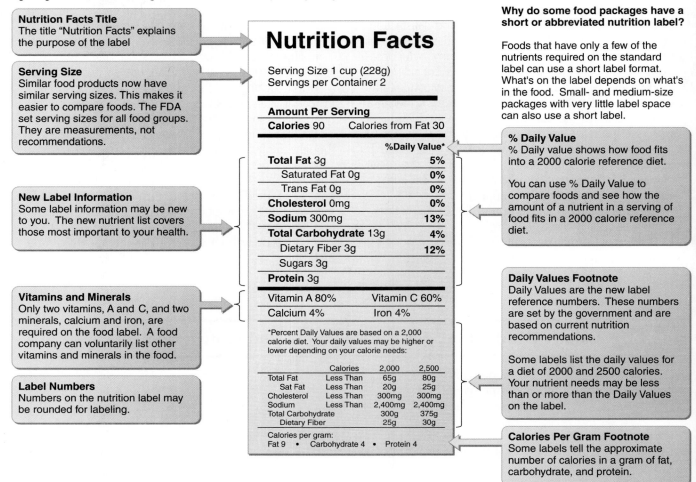

Why do some food packages have a short or abbreviated nutrition label?

Foods that have only a few of the nutrients required on the standard label can use a short label format. What's on the label depends on what's in the food. Small- and medium-size packages with very little label space can also use a short label.

% Daily Value
% Daily value shows how food fits into a 2000 calorie reference diet.

You can use % Daily Value to compare foods and see how the amount of a nutrient in a serving of food fits in a 2000 calorie reference diet.

Daily Values Footnote
Daily Values are the new label reference numbers. These numbers are set by the government and are based on current nutrition recommendations.

Some labels list the daily values for a diet of 2000 and 2500 calories. Your nutrient needs may be less than or more than the Daily Values on the label.

Calories Per Gram Footnote
Some labels tell the approximate number of calories in a gram of fat, carbohydrate, and protein.

Key Points:

- Doubling the serving size also doubles the nutrient value and the calories.

- The calories listed provide a measure of how much energy is received from one serving and those calories derived from fat.

- Consumption of fats, cholesterol, sodium, and sugar in foods should be minimized because research shows they are responsible for chronic illness. It is recommended that these be less than 100% of their Daily Value.

- Nutrients contained in dietary fiber, protein, vitamins, and minerals improve health and assist in reducing disease. It is advised that these nutrients average to 100% daily.

- Foods containing 5% or less of dietary fiber are considered too low in dietary fiber to contribute toward the daily total.

- Foods containing 20% or higher of vitamins and minerals contribute a good amount toward the daily total as needed.

Fig. 3-3 Sample food label.

each food group may have to be modified for some individuals to meet their unique needs, such as those influenced by age, and special conditions, such as pregnancy or diabetes.

Foods that have been highly fortified with vitamins and minerals do not take the place of a well-balanced diet. No single food supplies all the needed nutrients, so a selection of foods from each of the six food groups is necessary daily.

Weight Management

Research shows that being overweight increases a person's risk of developing chronic diseases and conditions such as heart disease, type 2 diabetes, stroke, arthritis, respiratory problems, hypertension, osteoarthritis, and certain cancers. Being overweight causes the heart to work harder, thus increasing the risk for a heart attack.

Restriction of calories and saturated fats may be needed if reduced activity is a concern. The body burns only a certain number of calories per day during normal body functions, and calories not burned turn into fat. Take the lower number of recommended servings, and choose fewer foods

high in caloric count (e.g., fats, sugars, alcoholic beverages).

Problems with weight management can arise when people do not plan ahead for meals. Arriving home tired and hungry often leads to eating fast food (high in fat and sugar) with few or no vegetables. If this cycle continues, it can lead to weight gain. The rationale behind weight management is to pay attention to total caloric intake, not the type of calories, and to adjust exercise regimens according to additional caloric intake.

Body Mass Index

The weight-for-height charts formerly used to determine accepted body weight for an individual have been replaced with the **body mass index (BMI)** chart because the BMI simultaneously takes into account height and weight (Fig. 3-4). BMI is better than the traditional height-weight tables because it is well correlated with total body fat content and applies to both men and women. BMI calculations help determine if a person is overweight, **obese** (more than 20% overweight for gender, height, and body frame), underweight, or at a healthy weight, as determined by the BMI range. For example, a

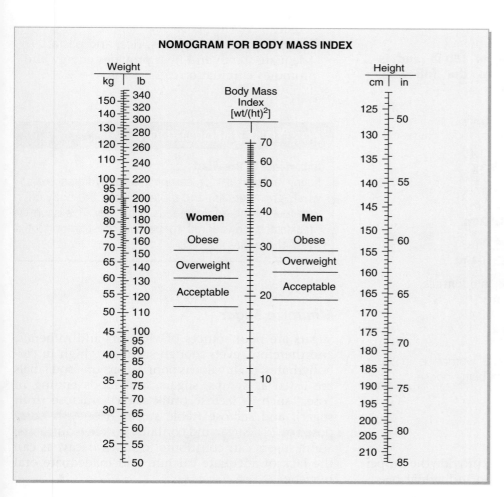

Fig. 3-4 Nomogram for body mass index. *(From Young AP, Kennedy DB:* Kinn's the medical assistant, *ed 9, Philadelphia, 2003, Saunders)*

TABLE 3-3   Body Mass Index (BMI)

Weight Status	BMI
Underweight	Less than 18.5
Normal	18.5 to 24.9
Overweight	25 to 29.9
Obese	Greater than 30

man who weighs 246 lb and is 76 inches tall falls into the obese range.

Children and teens are assessed for being underweight, overweight, and at risk for becoming overweight. BMI for children is gender and age specific. For an adult, BMI uses a person's weight and height to determine a reading and then compares it to an established range (Table 3-3). The Mayo Clinic considers a person overweight if the person has a BMI of 25 to 29.9 and obese if the BMI is 30 or higher.

A mathematical formula is used to calculate BMI. The person's weight in kilograms is divided by the person's height in meters squared.

BMI Calculation
A 46-year-old woman weighs 150 lb and is 60 inches tall. According to the following formula:

$$BMI = Weight\ (kg) \div Height\ (m^2)$$

1.   Convert 150 pounds (lbs) to kilograms
      (2.2 kg is equal to 1 lb)
      $150 \div 2.2 =$ **68 kg**

2.   Convert 60 inches to meters (m)
      (39.37 inches = 1 m)
      $60 \div 39.37 =$ **1.52 m**

3.   Square 1.52 m
      $1.52 \times 1.52 =$ **2.3104 m**

4.   Substitute numbers into formula
      $BMI = kg \div m^2$
      $68 \div 2.3104 = 29.4$
      BMI = 29.4

The BMI chart indicates that the woman is in the overweight range and is close to being obese.

Balance

A balanced diet is encouraged to provide the proper amounts of all nutrients that an individual needs for optimal health. As seen in the food pyramid, each food group has recommendations that contribute to the body's total nutritional needs for a day. Omitting any food group reduces the body's chance of homeostasis. Tips for balancing the daily diet are as follows:

1. Drink eight glasses of water daily (64 ounces). This aids in proper elimination, keeps the body hydrated, and promotes clear skin.
2. Eat low-fat, lean meats (skinless chicken, fish). These supply all the essential amino acids that the body needs to build cells and repair tissue.
   - Three ounces of fish is about the size of a thick checkbook
   - Three ounces of meat or chicken is about the size of a deck of cards
3. Eat a variety of fruits and vegetables daily. These provide nutrient value and roughage (fiber), which helps with elimination.
   - A cup of fruit or vegetables is about the size of a tennis ball
4. Use low-fat or fat-free dairy products. Whole milk can cause unsaturated fatty acids to build in the bloodstream.
   - One ounce of cheese is the size of four dice.
5. Eat plenty of whole grains, rice, and pasta. Adequate starch and fiber provides energy and promotes elimination.

FOR YOUR INFORMATION

Importance of Breakfast
Eating a breakfast of complex carbohydrates (e.g., whole-grain cereals) and proteins starts the body off with fuel for the energy needs of the day. This is why breakfast is considered to be the most important meal of the day.

Minimize Sugar

Sugars are poor sources of vitamins and minerals, and therefore, even though sugars are high in carbohydrates, their value is poor. Sugars on food labels are listed as syrups, sugars, and foods ending in "ose," such as lactose (milk sugar), fructose (fruit sugar), and sucrose (table sugar). Honey is composed of 75% sugar and contains very few nutrients. Some sugars can contribute to tooth decay, as can the lack of adequate calcium and inadequate oral hygiene.

FOR YOUR INFORMATION

The Sweetest Sweetener
Blackstrap molasses contains iron, calcium, potassium, and some B vitamins and is the healthiest of all sweeteners.

Minimize Sodium

Sodium is found naturally in many foods. Therefore the addition of table salt (sodium chloride) when preparing or cooking foods, as well as consumption of large quantities of foods processed with salt, may contribute greatly to cardiovascular disease. In hypertension, for example, sodium in salt causes the body to accumulate fluid, increasing pressure against the blood vessel walls. The recommended intake of sodium per day is 2400 mg. As a comparison, just 1 teaspoon of salt contains approximately 2000 mg of sodium.

PATIENT-CENTERED PROFESSIONALISM

- Why is it important for the medical assistant to be knowledgeable about nutrition and how it applies to weight management?

NUTRIENTS

Nutrients are chemical substances within food that are released and absorbed during the digestive process. Most nutrients provide the body with the energy it needs to maintain body functions, such as maintaining a constant temperature. Nutrients are classified into **nonessential nutrients,** meaning those that are provided in the body, and **essential nutrients,** those that must be taken in from a food source, such as vitamins, minerals, proteins, carbohydrates, fats, and water. Essential nutrients are placed in the five categories of vitamins, minerals, carbohydrates, fats, and proteins.

Vitamins

Vitamins are organic substances that enhance the breakdown of proteins, carbohydrates, and fats. Without vitamins, the breakdown and **assimilation** (the taking in of nutrient material) of foods would not occur. Some vitamins are used in the formation of blood cells and hormones and the production of neurochemical substances. Vitamins are classified into two categories, fat soluble and water soluble.

Fat-Soluble Vitamins

Fat-soluble vitamins are usually absorbed with foods that contain fat and are stored in body fat, the liver, and the kidneys. These vitamins are broken down by **bile,** which is formed by the liver. Fat-soluble vitamins include A, D, E, and K (Table 3-4). Excess intake of these vitamins by taking daily vitamin supplements should be avoided because the body stores these vitamins, and excess can result in serious illness. Beta carotene, found in some fruits and vegetables, is converted by the body to vitamin A.

Water-Soluble Vitamins

Water-soluble vitamins are also important to the body. Vitamin C and B-complex vitamins (thiamine [B_1], riboflavin [B_2], niacin [B_3], pantothenic acid [B_5], pyridoxine [B_6], cyanocobalamin [B_{12}], and folic acid) are not stored in the body and are excreted when in excess. Therefore these vitamins must be consumed daily and are not dangerous when taken as supplements (Table 3-5).

Minerals

Minerals are inorganic substances used in the formation of hard and soft body tissues. Minerals are necessary for muscle contraction, nerve conduction, and blood clotting. Minerals are taken into the body from the foods eaten. The body uses **major minerals,** including calcium, phosphorus, magnesium, sodium, iron, iodine, and potassium, in sufficient amounts (Table 3-6). **Trace minerals,** or trace elements, are used in smaller quantities and include copper, cobalt, manganese, fluorine, and zinc. Trace minerals are found in adequate amounts in most foods (Table 3-7).

Carbohydrates

Carbohydrates produce quick body energy and are the body's primary energy source. Carbohydrates represent the most abundant food source and cost less than foods in the other food groups. **Cellulose** (chief part of the plant cell walls), which is abundant in plant carbohydrates, is important for elimination. During metabolism, carbohydrates produce energy that causes the release of water and carbon dioxide. Unabsorbed glucose increases blood sugar levels and insulin production. The glucose released by the cells is absorbed from the small intestine to be processed in the liver, then converted to glycogen to be stored for use later by the body.

Two types of carbohydrates are starches **(complex carbohydrates)** and unrefined sugars **(simple carbohydrates).** Starches are found mainly in

TABLE 3-4	Fat-Soluble Vitamins		
Vitamin	**Need**	**Source**	**Deficiency**
A	Growth of epithelial tissue; important for vision (especially in dim light) and hormonal production for reproduction and lactation; helps build resistance to infections	Byproducts of animals; milk, eggs, fish oil, liver, green and yellow vegetables and orange and yellow fruits (pumpkin, sweet potatoes, winter squash, carrots, cantaloupe, apricots), dark leafy vegetables (chard, beets, collard, kale, mustard, spinach, turnips), butter, yellow cheese, cream, watercress	**Night blindness**, skin disorders, hair loss, susceptibility to infection
D	Helps body utilize calcium and phosphorus necessary for absorption and metabolism; needed for calcium formation; needed for growth of bones and teeth	Sunlight; butter, eggs, canned fish, herring, salmon, tuna, fish oil, liver, dairy products fortified with vitamin D	**Rickets** (soft bones) in children, **osteomalacia** (soft bones) in adults
E	Use by body remains under study; needed for metabolism of essential fatty acids, absorption of iron, and red blood cell formation; acts as an **antioxidant** (prevents buildup of oxidants) Also used in liquid topical form for scar reduction	Seed oil, wheat germ, nuts, avocados, soybeans, milk products	Breakdown of red blood cells, anemia
K	Needed for blood clotting by forming prothrombin, which is used in producing fibrin for blood clots	Synthesized in intestines by bacteria; assimilated from green leafy vegetables, molasses, apricots, cod liver oil, sunflower oil	Bleeding disorders (e.g., hemorrhages, slow clotting)

TABLE 3-5	Water-Soluble Vitamins		
Vitamin	**Need**	**Source**	**Deficiency**
Vitamin C (ascorbic acid)	Synthesizes and maintains connective tissue; necessary for cholesterol metabolism and cortisol production in adrenal gland; maintains blood vessel strength; used in formation of hemoglobin; aids in utilization of iron in body; vital for healing and acts as an antioxidant	Citrus fruits and juices, broccoli, papayas, mangoes, potatoes, berries, cantaloupe, kiwi, Brussels sprouts, red and green peppers Note: Overcooking destroys most of the vitamin C in foods	**Scurvy** (affects mucous membranes, gums, and skin), slow healing

TABLE 3-5   Water-Soluble Vitamins—cont'd

Vitamin	Need	Source	Deficiency
B-Complex Vitamins			
Thiamine (B_1)	Aids in nervous tissue function; co-enzyme for cellular energy; used in carbohydrate metabolism (turns complex carbohydrates into glucose or fat) helps the functioning of the brain, heart, and nervous system	Brewer's yeast, liver, pork, whole grains, nuts, beans, lentils, oatmeal	Mental confusion, **beriberi** (peripheral nerve disorder), muscle weakness
Riboflavin (B_2)	Used for normal growth; needed for protein, fat, and carbohydrate metabolism; used in formation of liver enzymes; assists adrenal glands to release hormone that stimulates production of stress-relieving hormones; helps red blood cell production	Milk and milk products, greens, whole grains, liver, lean meat, fish, poultry, eggs	**Dermatitis** (inflammation of skin) around mouth, lips, and nose; **glossitis** (inflamed tongue); light sensitivity
Niacin (B_3)	Aids in tissue respiration; used in cellular energy production; synthesizes fat; forms enzymes needed for carbohydrate metabolism *Note:* Formed in body from dietary amino acids	Whole grains, milk, eggs, legumes, lean meats, poultry, fish, and nuts	Dermatitis, diarrhea, mental confusion and irritability, **pellagra**
Pantothenic acid (B_5)	Used in metabolism of fats, carbohydrates, and amino acids; aids in function of adrenal gland; needed to maintain immune system	Brewer's yeast, grains, milk, green vegetables, mushrooms	Reports of burning feet syndrome, cramps, fatigue
Pyridoxine (B_6)	Used in hemoglobin synthesis; formation of red blood cells (RBCs) and neurotransmitters; used in metabolism for amino acid formation; needed for utilization of amino acids; involved in protein, sugar, and fatty acid metabolism	Meats, liver, grains, nuts, bananas, avocados, molasses, mushrooms	Anemia, low level of immunity, peripheral neuropathy, skin disorders
Cyanocobalamin (B_{12})	Needed for nerve synthesis; used in red blood cell development; assists in folic acid metabolism; needed for iron metabolism	Synthesized by gastrointestinal flora; meat, Brewer's yeast, eggs, milk	**Pernicious anemia** (body lacks intrinsic factor to absorb vitamin), sores in mouth, loss of coordination NOTE: **Most seniors lose the ability to make stomach acid, which interferes with the ability to absorb B_{12}**
Folic acid	Needed for hematopoiesis in bone marrow; needed for metabolism of sugar and amino acids; needed for fetal development for neural tube closure; needed for manufacture of antibodies	Liver, green leafy vegetables, beets, cauliflower, broccoli, citrus fruits, Brewer's yeast, eggs, nuts, sweet potatoes	Spina bifida, anencephaly, macrocytic anemia

TABLE 3-6 **Major Minerals**

Vitamin	Need	Source	Deficiency
Calcium (Ca^{++})	Needed for bone and tooth development; regulates nerve stimulation and muscle contraction, especially in heart muscle; forms intracellular cement; assists in blood-clotting process *Note:* Calcium is stored in bones and reabsorbed by blood and tissue	Greens (beets, collards, kale, mustard, spinach, turnips); milk and milk products; canned salmon, sardines; whole-grain cereals, enriched breads; beans, peas, broccoli; cheese, eggs; nuts, seeds, soybeans	Muscle spasms, poorly formed bones and teeth, slow clotting, osteoporosis
Phosphorus (P)	Needed for energy metabolism of cells; combines with calcium in bones and teeth, allowing added strength	Milk and milk products	Fragile bones and stiff joints
Magnesium (Mg)	Needed for metabolism; important for electrical impulse in nerve and muscle cells	Most natural foods	Tremors, foot cramps, irregular heartbeat, convulsions
Sodium (Na$^+$)	Needed in extracellular fluid in cells; aids in normal nerve and muscle function	Most natural foods, especially vegetables and salt	Lack of muscle contractions, dehydration, weakness, cramps *Note:* Excess sodium causes edema and elevated blood pressure
Iron (Fe)	Needed for hemoglobin production and the transport of oxygen in blood; used in cellular respiration and energy production *Note:* Iron is not easily absorbed by the digestive process and can cause gastrointestinal problems such as constipation; foods high in iron need to be eaten along with vitamin C–enriched foods for proper absorption	Whole and enriched grains, dried beans and fruit, egg yolks, shellfish, lean meats and liver, dark-green vegetables, molasses, wine, nuts, soybeans, cocoa, absorbable iron supplements	Impaired behavior, fatigue, iron deficiency anemia *Note:* Women receiving hormone replacement therapy need more iron if they experience uterine bleeding; women taking oral contraceptives may need less iron
Iodine (I)	Needed to synthesize hormone of thyroid gland that regulates metabolism and physical and mental development	Iodized salt, shellfish, garlic, cabbage, turnips, parsley	**Goiter** (enlarged thyroid) *Note:* Low iodine during pregnancy leads to birth defects and possible mental retardation
Potassium (K$^+$)	Maintains normal fluid balance in body; needed for proper functioning of muscle and nervous system	Fresh fruit (apricots, bananas, cantaloupe), citrus juices, dried fruits, raw cauliflower and parsley, whole grains, soybeans, nuts, nonfat milk and tomato juice, potato skins, seafood	Poor nerve conduction, irregular heartbeat and muscle function

TABLE 3-7	Trace Minerals (Elements)		
Vitamin	**Need**	**Source**	**Deficiency**
Copper (Cu)	Found in many enzymes and proteins in brain, blood, and liver; assists in formation of myelin sheath; assists in iron absorption and aids in proper function of vitamin C	Seafood, meat, eggs, whole-grain cereals, nuts	Anemia caused by failure of iron to assist with hemoglobin formation
Cobalt (Co)	Used in magnesium and sugar metabolism; aids in copper absorption; aids in red blood cell production	Brewer's yeast, fruits, vegetables, nuts, whole grains	Pernicious anemia
Manganese (Mn)	Used in energy metabolism; assists in thyroid function	Green vegetables, Brewer's yeast, eggs, fruit, whole grains, tea	Mental confusion
Fluorine (F)	Needed for tooth and bone formation; needed to minimize demineralization of bone	Water with natural or added fluorine	Dental caries, brittle bones
Zinc (Zn)	Forms enzymes; needed for release of vitamin A from liver; aids in protein metabolism and hormone production	Oysters, herring, Brewer's yeast, eggs, beef, peas, dairy, whole-grain foods, nuts, tofu, other shellfish	Impaired growth, poor wound healing, loss of appetite
Chromium (Cr)	Needed for fat and carbohydrate metabolism; aids in production of energy	Fruits, vegetables, Brewer's yeast, wheat germ, meats, molasses	Weight loss, poor glucose removal from blood (type 2 diabetes)
Selenium (Se)	Needed for normal functions of liver and connective tissue; acts as an antioxidant	Protein-rich foods	Osteoarthropathy

grains, legumes, and tubers (e.g., potatoes, yams). Sugars are found in fruits and plants. Complex carbohydrates have the most nutrients. Refined sugars have a high caloric value but are basically empty in nutrient value.

Sources of Carbohydrates and Cellulose

Starches	Sugars	Cellulose
Cereals	Cane and beet sugar	Bran fruits
Breads	Carbonated beverages	Raw vegetables
Pasta	Candy	
Potatoes	Jelly	
Rice	Jams	
Grits		

Fats

Fatty acids and **glycerol** are building blocks of fat that produce oils. Fats are the most concentrated source of energy, but glycogen is the most easily stored form of energy. Glycogen is composed of carbon, hydrogen, and glycerol and is not soluble in water. The body cannot make the essential fatty acids, omega-3 oils, and omega-6 oils.

Dietary fats are broken down into fatty acids and pass into the blood to form **triglycerides** (fatty acids and glycerol), phospholipids, and sterols—namely, cholesterol (lipoprotein). Triglycerides are the most abundant lipids, and they function as the body's most concentrated source of energy.

The American diet takes in more animal fatty acids, cholesterol, and trans-fatty acids that leave the cell membrane in less-than-optimal strength. The cell wall may thus be incapable of holding water, nutrients, and electrolytes. Under current guidelines, the daily allowance of saturated fats is 20 grams. To date, no such limit has been set for trans-fats.

Saturated Fats

Diets high in **saturated fats** have been linked to high cholesterol levels in the blood. Saturated fats are usually solid at room temperature and come from animal fats and tropical oils. Triglycerides are saturated fats that come from butter and lard.

Unsaturated Fats

Unsaturated fats are liquid at room temperature and are referred to as *oils*. Unsaturated fats may be monounsaturated or polyunsaturated, as follows:

- **Monounsaturated fats** are liquid at room temperature and may help lower total blood cholesterol. They are thought to raise high-density lipoprotein (HDL, or "good") cholesterol and lower low-density lipoprotein (LDL, or "bad") cholesterol levels. Monounsaturated fats are found in canola, olive, and peanut oils.

- **Polyunsaturated fats** are also liquid at room temperature. They are thought to lower both HDL ("good") and LDL ("bad") cholesterol levels. Some polyunsaturated fats have a lowering affect on total blood cholesterol. Polyunsaturated fats can be found mainly in vegetable oils. **Trans-fatty acids** are formed when polyunsaturated oils are **hydrogenated,** or made solid. Foods high in hydrogenated oil are margarines, peanut butter, and baked goods.

Research indicates that the cell takes in all fatty acids but that the omega-3 oils (found primarily in whole grains, beans and seeds, and seafood) and the omega-6 oils (found in unsaturated, nonhydrogenated vegetable oils from canola, peanuts, olive, flax, safflower, and sunflower) are the most desirable. The omega oils help maintain smoother skin, promote smoother muscle contractions, allow for better digestion, and support better cardiovascular performance.

Fatty Acid Guidelines

Saturated Fats	Unsaturated Fats
Animal source	Plant source
Raise cholesterol in blood	Lower cholesterol
	Monounsaturated and polyunsaturated

Cholesterol

Cholesterol is necessary for vitamin D and bile acid production. Sources of cholesterol include egg yolks and organ meats, in addition to other animal sources. Although cholesterol is important to the body, too high a level of cholesterol in the blood **(hypercholesterolemia)** is unhealthy and contributes to atherosclerosis and heart disease. As the level of blood cholesterol increases, so does the risk of developing these problems.

Sources of Fats and Cholesterol

Saturated Fats (Animal fats)	Polyunsaturated Fats (Plant fats)	High Cholesterol
Beef	Vegetable oils (liquid)	Organ meats
Pork	Tub margarines made with safflower or corn oil	Shrimp
		Whole milk
Eggs		Lard
Lard		Egg yolks
Solid shortening		Butter, cream
Whole milk		Baked products with butter, eggs, and whole milk

Proteins

Proteins are a group of substances composed of many **amino acids** (building blocks) linked together. Proteins are found in food sources such as whole grains, beans, nuts, and seeds **(simple proteins). Complex proteins** contain all the essential amino acids and are found in animal sources (e.g., eggs, meat, fish, dairy products, poultry). The primary function of proteins is to build and repair body tissue and the formation of **enzymes.** When broken down, amino acids can be absorbed by the small intestine for nutrition. Proteins can also be converted for the body's energy. As the body uses the carbohydrates and fats, it also uses protein from the diet or protein stored in tissue.

There are 22 amino acids in proteins, and of those the body cannot **synthesize** (make) eight of them. A diet containing these eight amino acids is essential for growth and health—thus the name "essential." Foods containing complete proteins contain all the essential amino acids. Both plants and animals provide protein, and it is important to balance the animal protein consumed with the protein from plants.

> ### Eight Essential Amino Acids
> The eight essential amino acids are isoleucine, leucine, lysine, methionine, phenylalanine, threonine, tryptophan, and valine. These essential amino acids can be found in animal sources of protein, milk, and eggs, as well as in peas, beans, lentils, nuts, seeds, and whole grains.

Incomplete proteins should be eaten with other protein sources. When certain amino acids are lacking, the other amino acids will convert to produce the energy needed for tissue growth, causing an excessive excretion of nitrogen from the body. When the body is exposed to increased loss of nitrogen, it responds by being deficient in energy, and **malnutrition** (inadequate nutrition) is evident.

Sources of Protein

Complete Proteins	Incomplete Proteins
Meat	Cereal grains
Poultry	Oatmeal
Cheese	Dried peas and beans
Fish	Peanut butter
Eggs	Nuts
Milk	Soybean products

Water

The body requires large amounts of water each day. This is because water is constantly evaporating as the body produces energy from the foods being eaten. The more protein, salt, caffeine, and alcohol consumed, the more water is needed. Water hydration is also important for removing wastes from the body. The daily recommended amount of water is 2 quarts, or more if you consume salty foods, caffeine, or alcohol.

PATIENT-CENTERED PROFESSIONALISM

- Why must the medical assistant be able to explain the difference between essential and nonessential nutrients when providing patient education?

NUTRITION THROUGH THE LIFE SPAN

For patients of all ages, an important part of the nutritional evaluation is the assessment of the ability to feed oneself, elimination, amount and content of meals, vitamin and other dietary supplements, food preferences and dislikes, food intolerances and allergies, and gastrointestinal (GI) problems. The medical assistant needs to know this information when making assessments of patients' nutritional habits.

Nutritional needs change as people age and go through different life situations.

Pregnancy and Lactation

Meeting nutritional needs during pregnancy and lactation is important to the healthy development of the child.

Nutrition during Pregnancy

Adequate nutrition during pregnancy decreases the chance of some birth defects and assists with embry-onic development. Nutritional needs during pregnancy are best met by consuming the minimal number of recommended servings from the food guide pyramid, as follows:

- Foods high in folic acid are needed to prevent neural tube defects.
- To avoid constipation, diet during pregnancy should be especially high in fiber, and water intake should be increased.
- Increased calcium is essential and can be added by using skim milk, thus avoiding added fats.
- Foods high in vitamin A, such as dark-green leafy vegetables and orange vegetables and fruits, are encouraged.
- Vitamin C intake through citrus is essential.

Pregnant women need encouragement to avoid "empty-calorie" foods (e.g., sweets, junk food). Vitamin supplements are not a replacement for nutrients found in food; iron is considered the only supplement truly needed during pregnancy. Processed foods and nonessential fats and sugars should be avoided, but sodium intake should be maintained through fresh vegetables. Sodium helps increase blood volume and meets fetal requirements.

Nutrition after Childbirth

After birth, the adequacy of breast milk can be measured by the following:

- Adequate weight gain by the infant (1 to 2 pounds per month).
- Number of feedings should be between 8 and 12 in a 24-hour period.
- Diaper changes should consist of at least six wet diapers.

The diet of a lactating mother is the same as the diet during pregnancy to maintain and ensure lactation.

Infants

There are established feeding protocols for an infant's diet. Solid foods are not recommended until age 4 to 6 months for the following reasons:

- Complex carbohydrates (cereal, vegetables, and fruits) are not easily digested, and therefore nutrients are not absorbed.
- The tongue is not able to guide food at such an early age.
- Infants are not able to open and close their mouth to indicate a desire for food.

Adding solid foods as the infant grows older helps replenish depleted iron supplies. Guidelines to add foods are as follows:

- Iron-fortified rice cereal: 4 to 6 months.
- Pureed fruits and vegetables: 6 to 8 months.
  —Add one at a time.
  —Add vegetables first; fruits may be too sweet.
- Pureed meats: 6 to 8 months.
- Diluted juice from a cup: 9 months.
- Finger foods: 9 months.

Egg whites, whole milk, and orange juice are introduced after 1 year of age because these tend to cause allergies in some children.

Toddlers

Toddlers need to be given structured choices for a snack (e.g., offer carrots or sliced apples, or raisins or orange slices). Letting toddlers choose from specific options allows them to demonstrate their independence and autonomy, but it still allows the caregiver to have some control. Toddlers will need smaller servings to avoid feeling overwhelmed because their growth rate slows during this period, reducing the amount of food they need.

Plan meals with the toddler's food preferences in mind (e.g., preferring apples over pears). However, refused foods should be offered again in the future to encourage variety in the diet. In addition, toddlers' feeding skills should be accepted as they are. This means caregivers must understand that hand-mouth coordination has not yet been mastered. Finger foods work well. If a child dislikes a particular food in a food group, the caregiver should be encouraged to find a suitable substitute (e.g., yogurt for milk). Providing nutritious snacks throughout the day can compensate for poor eating at mealtime. The total amount of nutrients consumed during the day is much more important than what is eaten at a single meal.

School-Age Children

School-age children need to have established, regular meal patterns. Breakfast is often earlier than they would like because of school. School-age children may eat lunch at school with other children, and they often trade food. Dietary needs for school-age children include the following:

- Calcium is needed for bone and growth development, so milk is encouraged, as are broccoli and other dark-green vegetables.
- Vitamin A foods assist with vision and healthy skin.
- Vitamin C helps maintain healthy gums and protects against infection.
- Energy is aided by the consumption of breads, pastas, rice, and cereals.

- Snacks should include milk products, fruits, and nuts; sweets and sodas should be avoided.

Adolescents

Major health problems can develop in adolescence because of inadequate nutrition, as well as from overeating or under eating. Peer pressure and food fads may have an influence on the diet of a teenager. Potato chips instead of vegetables and soft drinks instead of milk can lead to obesity, skin problems, and anemia. Teens who obtain sufficient calories from plant protein (e.g., beans, whole grains, soy products) to maintain a healthy weight may avoid protein from meat if they choose. A teenager who is a strict vegetarian may need to take a multivitamin.

The adolescent is entering a time when the body changes and adolescents have a desire to take control. The amount of body fat in girls increases before puberty, and girls also experience long bone growth. Boys develop later but catch up with increased muscle mass and long bone growth.

For many teens, the issues at hand are being accepted by their peers and having a sense of autonomy. These issues are influenced by society's emphasis on being "thin." **Anorexia** (or anorexia nervosa [psychological fear of gaining weight]), **bulimia nervosa** (compulsive overeating followed by self-induced vomiting or laxative or diuretic abuse), and being overweight are conditions that can affect the teenager during this time.

The dietary needs of an adolescent are as follows:

- More calories and nutrients to assist with increases in bone mass, muscle density, and activity of the endocrine system
- Foods high in zinc for energy and growth
- Foods high in calcium, iron, and iodine
- Increased dairy consumption
- Foods high in vitamin B_{12} (animal products)

Aging Individuals

As adults age, their metabolic rates often decrease. Energy levels do not increase as people age, so older adults tend to be less active. When these changes occur and eating habits do not change, older adults tend to put on weight by increasing their fat tissue. Maintaining good bone density during this time is based on physical activity and taking in the needed nutrients so that the weight gain that results is not detrimental to the person's health.

Factors that influence the older adult's dietary consumption and selection of foods include the following:

1. *Income*: Many older adults limit food choices because of cost, thus minimizing protein consumption. Carbohydrates are cheap, easy to fix, store easily, and are consumed more often.
2. *Cultural habits, customs, race, ethnic background, and gender*
3. *Declining health*: Older adults may have trouble chewing and swallowing, which may affect their food choices. The digestive system may not absorb or metabolize needed nutrients from foods as effectively as it once did.
4. *Sense of taste*: The sense of taste alters as people age because of the decreased number of taste buds. Sweets have the greatest taste for many elderly people.

Many older adults use mineral oil as a laxative. This interferes with the body's ability to absorb vital nutrients and should be discouraged.

To assist the elderly patient in nutritional selection, the medical assistant must consider all factors. Knowing the patient's home situation, income, and other demographics will help you guide the patient toward better food selections, as follows:

- The mature adult needs 6 to 8 glasses of water per day to aid in elimination.
- Calcium-rich foods for strong bones and iron-containing foods are needed to help the body use energy.
- Protecting against zinc deficiency helps the wound-healing process.
- Encouraging physical activity is important.

PATIENT-CENTERED PROFESSIONALISM

- Why is it important for the medical assistant to understand the nutritional needs of patients at various stages in the life span?

NUTRITION AND CHRONIC DISEASE

Patients with chronic illness have special nutritional needs. The main goal is to maintain adequate nutrition so that the immune system is at optimal strength. Patients with human immunodeficiency virus (HIV) infection, acquired immunodeficiency syndrome (AIDS), and cancer rely on their defense systems to assist them in maintaining a fight toward better health.

HIV and AIDS

Patients newly diagnosed with HIV infection are encouraged to maintain a diet high in protein, with foods adequate in the essential vitamins, minerals, vitamins A and C, vitamin B_{12}, copper, and zinc. Good nutrition is thought to prevent or delay the onset of AIDS by promoting a healthy immune system.

When HIV progresses to AIDS, the metabolic rate increases as a result of infections, stress, and gastrointestinal (GI) upsets. The medications used to treat AIDS often cause nausea and diarrhea. This causes a loss of appetite and **malabsorption** of nutrients. A diet low in lactose and fat can assist in reducing these GI upsets. The addition of liquid supplements can increase caloric intake and add vitamins and proteins to the diet.

Cancer

It is important for cancer patients undergoing chemotherapy to maintain adequate nutritional intake. A diet high in protein (especially red meats), fats, carbohydrates, vitamins, and fluids is needed to keep up with the increased energy demands. Increased energy is needed because of the high metabolic rate caused by tissue breakdown. Research shows that a diet with adequate nutritional intake prevents weight loss, helps to rebuild body tissue, replaces fluid and electrolyte loss, and provides the patient with a sense of well-being.

As with any patient who has a chronic illness, the patient with cancer suffers from lack of appetite, altered taste, a feeling of fullness, chewing and swallowing difficulties, nausea, and fatigue. The patient should be encouraged to eat small but frequent meals, avoid greasy foods, and limit hot and spicy foods. Serving the patient's favorite foods often assists with taking in nourishment.

PATIENT-CENTERED PROFESSIONALISM

- How can the medical assistant help the patient with a chronic illness understand the importance of nutrition?

DIET THERAPY

A **therapeutic diet** is required in many medical office situations, including preparation for special testing, increasing or decreasing caloric intake, and treating metabolic disorders. It is important for the medical assistant to understand the purpose of various diet therapies, especially in determining which foods are allowed and which should be avoided. To be successful in teaching the patient, the medical assistant must know the patient's current habits and food preferences in addition to the type of therapeutic diet needed.

Regular Diet

A **regular diet** contains all foods from the food guide pyramid and is considered to be adequate and well balanced. It provides generous amounts of all nutrients that an individual needs daily. Modifying this diet to accommodate more fiber, increased nutrients, or increased energy levels leads to a therapeutic diet prescribed to meet the special requirements of the individual patient.

Liquid Diet

A therapeutic **liquid diet** can be in the form of a clear-liquid or a full-liquid diet. Liquid diets should not be used for long periods because of inadequate protein, minerals, vitamins, and calories.

Clear-Liquid Diet
- *Purpose:* Clear liquids are generally the first type of nourishment given to a patient after surgery, in preparation for a colonoscopy, or when fluids have been lost during diarrhea or vomiting. This diet contains minimal residue and consists primarily of dissolved sugar and flavored fluids that provide calories but lack essential nutrients.
- *Recommended foods:* Water, ginger ale, plain gelatin, tea or coffee with sugar, and fat-free broth.
- *Foods to avoid:* Milk and milk products.

Full-Liquid Diet
- *Purpose:* A patient advances to a full-liquid diet after clear liquids. This diet is also prescribed when the patient has difficulty swallowing or an irritated GI tract.
- *Recommended foods:* Continue with clear liquids; custards, ice cream, sherbet, strained soup, puddings, and strained cooked cereals.
- *Foods to avoid:* Any solid food.

Soft Diet

Foods in a **soft diet** are low residue for easy digestion.

- *Purpose:* A soft diet is used to advance past a full-liquid diet, when less strain on the GI system is required, and when there is difficulty chewing.

- *Recommended foods:* Dairy products (to include soft cheese), pureed vegetables, cooked fruit, pastas, ground beef, fish, and chicken.
- *Foods to avoid:* Raw fruits and vegetables, nuts, fried foods, and gas-forming vegetables and meats.

Diabetic Diet

A **diabetic diet** may be prescribed for diabetes or hypoglycemia.

- *Purpose:* Diabetic diets are used with patients who are having difficulty with insulin secretion; this includes both hyperglycemia and hypoglycemia.

The focus is placed on having several small meals of complex-carbohydrate and protein foods. The food intake should match the type of insulin therapy used, exercise performed, and patient's age and weight.

The **glycemic index** rates carbohydrate foods on a scale from the slowest to the fastest with effects on blood glucose levels. It indicates the body's response to a particular food (after eating) compared with a standard amount of glucose. Not all carbohydrates raise the glucose level at the same rate; therefore the index allows an individual to select carbohydrates that take longer to affect blood glucose levels.

Box 3-3 provides food values in the glycemic index. Every carbohydrate is compared with glucose, which has a value of 100. Therefore carbohydrates are given a number relative to glucose in the index. Foods that are thought to be low-glycemic foods seem to have less effect on blood sugars. Foods such as instant rice and white bread have a much higher glycemic value than unprocessed foods such as whole grains and fruits (e.g., grapes, oranges).

- *Recommended foods:* A balance of protein, carbohydrate, and fat.
- *Foods to avoid:* Foods high in sugar (sweets to include baked goods, candy, and syrups).

Calorie-Controlled Diet

A **calorie-controlled diet** may be a low-calorie or a high-calorie diet.

Low-Calorie Diet (1000-1200 Calories)
- *Purpose:* A low-calorie diet reduces calorie intake for overweight and arthritic patients.
- *Recommended foods:* Lean meats, poultry, low-carbohydrate vegetables, fruits, whole grains, and skim milk products.

BOX 3-3   Glycemic Index: Food Values Based on 100 (Glucose)

Beans		Breads		Cereals	
baked	43	bagel	72	cornflakes	83
black	30	pita	57	oatmeal	49
chickpeas	33	rye (whole)	50	Cheerios	74
lentils	30	white	72	All Bran 7	44
Cookies		**Crackers**		**Desserts**	
graham crackers	74	rice cakes	82	angel food cake	67
oatmeal	55	rye	63	blueberry muffin	59
shortbread	64	saltines	72	bran muffin	60
vanilla wafers	77	Wheat Thins	67	pound cake	54
Fruit		**Grains**		**Pasta**	
dates (dried)	103	rice (instant)	91	spaghetti	40
banana	62	sweet corn	55	linguine	50
orange	43	brown rice	59	vermicelli	55
grapes	43	barley	22	mac and cheese	64
Juices		**Milk Products**		**Sweets**	
apple	41	yogurt	38	honey	58
grapefruit	48	milk	34	Lifesavers	70
orange	55	pudding	43	Snickers	41
pineapple	46	ice cream	50	Skittles	70

- *Food to avoid:* Fatty meats, whole milk products, lima beans, corn, peas, beans, snack foods, and desserts.

High-Calorie, High-Protein Diet (>2000 Calories)
- *Purpose:* High-calorie diets are used after surgery, with burn patients, when high fever or infection is present, when weight is below normal (e.g., hyperthyroidism, anorexia), and for patients with fractures.
- *Recommended foods:* All food groups.
- *Foods to avoid:* Fatty foods.

Low-Cholesterol, Low-Fat Diet

Research indicates that when an individual chooses a diet low in fats (**low-cholesterol, low-fat diet**), the person is able to eat a variety of foods needed for nutritional intake. Fats contain twice as many calories as an equal amount of protein or carbohydrates. A diet low in saturated fat and cholesterol helps maintain the blood cholesterol levels below 200 milligrams per deciliter (mg/dL). Total fat intake should be 30% or less of the total calories consumed.

30% Fat Intake
Fat intake should be 30% (or less) of the total calories consumed.

A diet of 1500 calories per day would allow 450 calories to come from fat.

$$1500 \times 0.3 \ (30\%) = 450$$

To determine the number of grams (g) of fat, divide 450 by 9 (9 calories are provided by each gram of fat).

$$450 \div 9 = 50 \text{ g}$$

Therefore, in a diet of 1500 calories per day, 50 or fewer grams of fat should be consumed, or 450 or fewer calories should come from fat.

- *Purpose:* Low-cholesterol and low-fat diets are prescribed for patients with elevated lipids; those with liver, gallbladder, or cardiovascular disease; and patients who are obese.
- *Recommended foods:* Skim milk products, lean fish, poultry, meats, cottage cheese, vegetables,

fruits and their juices, tea and coffee, jelly, and honey.

- *Foods to avoid:* Cheese, whole milk products, fatty meats (pork, bacon, ham, sausage, duck, goose, fatty fish), chocolate, and fried foods.

Sodium-Restricted Diet

Another type of therapeutic diet is the **sodium-restricted diet.**

- *Purpose:* Sodium-restricted diets are prescribed for patients with kidney disease, high blood pressure, or cardiovascular disease and those who have edema.
- *Recommended foods:* Natural foods without additives.
- *Foods to avoid:* Processed foods, added table salt, condiments, pickles, and olives.

Renal Failure Diet

The **renal failure diet** is ordered when a patient's kidneys are not able to get rid of all the wastes in the blood.

- *Purpose:* This diet controls the amount of protein and phosphorus the patient consumes. The diet may also restrict the amount of sodium and potassium the patient consumes.
- *Recommended foods:* Per day—1 ounce of protein, 1/2 cup of nondairy product, 1 slice of bread (Italian, light rye), 1/2 cup of vegetables—alfalfa sprouts, green or wax beans, cabbage, lettuce (1 cup), fruit—canned pears, applesauce, blueberries (1/2 cup).
- *Foods to avoid:* Processed foods, more than 1 ounce of meat, chicken, fish, eggs, dairy products, beans, peas, nuts, colas, beer, and cocoa.

Bland Diet

A **bland diet** may also be prescribed as a therapeutic diet.

- *Purpose:* Bland diets help prevent irritation of the GI tract (e.g., colitis, ulcers).
- *Recommended foods:* Foods low in fiber, mild seasonings, dairy, eggs, well-cooked vegetables, boiled and broiled meats, fish, poultry, and pastas.
- *Foods to avoid:* Fried foods or highly seasoned foods, alcohol or carbonated beverages, condiments, pickled products, and raw vegetables.

Low-Fiber Diet

The **low-fiber diet** is another therapeutic option.

- *Purpose:* A low-fiber diet decreases the work of the intestines (e.g., in patients with colitis, ileitis, or diverticulitis).
- *Recommended foods:* Broiled, boiled, or baked meats; fish and poultry; pastas; dairy products; well-cooked vegetables; fruit and vegetable juices; and canned fruit.
- *Foods to avoid:* Fresh fruits and vegetables, fried foods, nuts, and pickled products.

High-Fiber Diet

A **high-fiber diet** may also be needed as a therapeutic option.

- *Purpose:* A high-fiber diet helps with elimination.
- *Recommended foods:* All vegetables, raw and cooked fruits, and whole-grain foods, (including breads, grains, and cereals).
- *Foods to avoid:* Fatty foods.

FOR YOUR INFORMATION

What Is Organic?
Poultry, eggs, and meats that come from animals that have not been fed hormones or antibiotics are considered organic. Organic crops are grown without pesticides, including synthetic fertilizers or sewer sludge. Legally, foods with the USDA's green and white sticker must be grown or raised according to certain federal standards.

Fad Diets

A **fad diet** is one that offers quick weight loss but has no long-term advantages. Research has shown that although weight loss is quick, if steps are not taken to revise eating habits, dieters regain much of the weight, if not more, by the end of the first year.

- The *Atkins diet* stresses low carbohydrates, high protein, and fats.
- The *cabbage soup diet* is a 7-day diet plan that requires a special soup to be eaten each day, with certain foods introduced each day as well.
- The *negative-calorie diet* allows only certain foods to be eaten that the body tends to burn faster.
- The *South Beach diet* is based on reducing carbohydrates initially and changing the eating habits overall for a lifetime to exclude many white flour and sugar food items.

Fad diets can result in electrolyte loss, dehydration, kidney disease, gout, and calcium depletion, which in turn can result in hospitalization. There is no substitute for eating a healthy diet, making good nutrition a habit, and ensuring adequate exercise.

PATIENT-CENTERED PROFESSIONALISM

- How does the medical assistant use information relevant to different diet therapies?
- How should the medical assistant answer a question about a fad diet that a patient is considering?

CONCLUSION

The medical assistant who understands basic nutritional concepts and the reasons for a particular diet therapy can assist the patient in following the prescribed dietary regimen. Unless the body receives the nutrients it requires, fat and muscle are used to supply the body's daily energy needs. The basic life process needed to circulate the blood throughout the body, move muscles in order to breathe, and maintain the body temperature requires a certain amount of energy. Therefore adequate nutrition is required daily.

Nutrition is the key to the healing process, but other factors affect the body's ability to absorb or take in the required nutrients. These factors include the state of a person's digestive system, an individual's mental issues with regard to physical appearance (e.g., "perfect" body), and economic inability to purchase nutritious foods. Dealing with the nutrition issues of patients is not only about the type of food they eat; as a medical assistant, you must also address the person as a whole. During patient teaching, consider what disease processes are affecting a patient's ability to eat, whether the patient is on a limited income, and whether the patient is depressed or has low self-esteem.

Educating patients about following through with treatment plans, improving their nutrition, and improving their overall health is one of the most important responsibilities of the medical assistant.

SUMMARY

Reinforce your understanding of the material in this chapter by reviewing the curriculum objectives and key content points below.

1. Define, appropriately use, and spell all the Key Terms for this chapter.
   - Review the Key Terms if necessary.

2. Explain the importance of patient education.
   - The purpose of patient education is to influence a patient's behavior toward a certain goal.
   - Understanding effective communication techniques and human behavior is necessary to provide optimal patient education.
3. Explain the purpose of dietary guidelines.
   - Dietary guidelines provide the public with information about the amounts of essential nutrients in a diet that assist in decreasing the risk of chronic disease.
4. List the six food groups included in the food guide pyramid and discuss the recommended daily quantities for a 2000-calorie diet.
   - Review Table 3-2
   - Grains (half should be whole-grain) 6 oz
   - Vegetables (variety) 2½ cups
   - Fruits (2 cups)
   - Milk (3 cups)
   - Vegetables (3-5 servings)
   - Fruits (2-4 servings)
   - Meat and beans 5½ oz
   - Consumption of fats, sodium, and sugar in foods; fat sources from fish, nuts, and vegetable oils
5. Explain the purpose of the Nutrition Labeling and Education Act (NLEA), and list the two main panels to consider when looking at a food label.
   - The NLEA was enacted to assist consumers in identifying nutritional content in food products.
   - Food labels allow consumers to make better choices.
   - The display panel is used for marketing purposes, and the nutritional fact panel meets the requirements of federal regulatory boards.
   - The calories listed show how much energy is received from one serving and how many calories are derived from fat.
6. List and briefly describe five basic principles of good nutrition.
   - Five principles of good nutrition are variety (eating different foods in moderation), weight management (restricting calories to maintain weight), balance (eating proper amounts of foods), minimizing sugar (restricting poor-value calories), and reducing sodium (found naturally in many foods).
   - Doubling the serving size also doubles the nutrient value and the calories.
7. Demonstrate how to calculate a patient's body mass index (BMI), and indicate whether a patient is underweight, normal, overweight, or obese according to the chart.

- BMI = Weight (kg) ÷ Height (m^2).
- Review Table 3-3.

8. List five tips for maintaining nutritional balance in the daily diet.
   - Drinking water; eating low-fat lean meats; eating a variety of fruits and vegetables; using low-fat or fat-free dairy products; and eating plenty of whole grains, rice, and pasta are tips for maintaining balance in the daily diet.

9. Differentiate between essential and nonessential nutrients.
   - Essential nutrients must be taken from a food source (vitamins, minerals, proteins, carbohydrates, fats, water).
   - Nonessential nutrients are provided within the body.
   - Nutrients contained in dietary fiber, protein, vitamins, and minerals improve health and assist in reducing disease. It is advised that these nutrients average to 100% daily.
   - Foods containing 5% or more of dietary fiber are considered to be contributing toward the daily total.
   - Foods containing 20% or higher of vitamins and minerals contribute a good amount toward the daily total.

10. Differentiate fat-soluble vitamins from water-soluble vitamins and list the major sources of each.
    - Review Tables 3-4 and 3-5.

11. List nine major minerals and explain the sources of each and the result of deficiency.
    - Review Table 3-6.

12. List seven trace minerals and explain the sources of each and the result of deficiency.
    - Review Table 3-7.

13. Explain why the body needs carbohydrates, fats, and proteins.
    - Carbohydrates are the body's primary energy source.
    - Fats are the body's stored energy.
    - Proteins build and repair body tissue and break down enzymes into amino acids.

14. Explain the importance of water and state the daily recommended amount.
    - Water keeps the body hydrated and is important for eliminating waste.
    - The daily recommended amount of water is 2 quarts.

15. Explain dietary needs during pregnancy and lactation, infancy, toddler age, school age, adolescence, and older adulthood.
    - The amounts and types of nutrients vary depending on age and physical state, which determine how well the body can absorb and use the nutrients.

16. Explain the dietary needs of patients newly diagnosed with HIV and those with AIDS.
    - Newly diagnosed HIV patients need a diet high in protein and adequate in essential vitamins, minerals, vitamins A and C, vitamin B$_{12}$, copper, and zinc that will prevent or delay the onset of AIDS by promoting a healthy immune system.
    - Patients with AIDS may have gastrointestinal upset, stress, and infections, so a diet low in lactose and fat should help reduce nausea and diarrhea; increased caloric intake, vitamins, and proteins are also important.

17. Explain the dietary needs for cancer patients undergoing chemotherapy.
    - Patients undergoing chemotherapy need to maintain adequate nutritional intake to prevent weight loss, rebuild body tissue, replace fluid and electrolyte loss, and promote a sense of well-being. A diet high in protein, fats, carbohydrates, vitamins, and fluids is needed to maintain energy.

18. List and briefly describe nine types of therapeutic diets.
    - Therapeutic diets include liquid (clear or full liquid), soft (low residue, easy to digest), diabetic (small meals with complex carbohydrates), calorie controlled (low calorie or high calorie depending on whether the goal is to lose or gain weight), low cholesterol, low fat (restricted animal fat intake), sodium restricted (natural foods without additives), bland (nonirritating to gastrointestinal tract), low fiber (decreases work of intestines), and high fiber (increases work of intestines to help with elimination).

19. Explain why fad diets are unhealthy and a poor choice for long-term weight loss.
    - Fad diets can result in electrolyte loss, dehydration, kidney disease, gout, and calcium depletion.
    - Fad diets do not change a person's eating behavior for the long term and may actually increase weight gain.

20. Analyze a realistic medical office situation and apply your understanding of patient education and nutrition to determine the best course of action.
    - Medical assistants must understand both patient education techniques and nutrition to provide optimal education for their patients.

21. Describe the impact on patient care when medical assistants have a solid understanding of nutrition and how it relates to the patient's treatment plan.

- Nutrition knowledge is a valuable tool for the promotion of health care because it helps promote actions that benefit the patient.

- Nutritional information in the medical practice is an ongoing topic, because the effects are seen throughout the patient's life span and assist during treatment of an illness.

FOR FURTHER EXPLORATION

1. **Research food guide pyramids for a certain age group.** Children need nutrients that promote growth, for example, but getting a child to eat is sometimes a difficult task. Elderly persons may need fewer calories because they tend to be less active. Both groups have certain nutritional needs that must be met to promote tissue growth and maintain body function.
Keywords: Use the following keywords in your search: food guide pyramid, elderly nutrition, toddler food guide, adolescent nutritional needs.

2. **Research the policies that the American Medical Association (AMA) adopted in 2007 to promote healthier food options to fight obesity in Americans.** Combating obesity by promoting healthier food options is a concern of the AMA. The AMA focused on replacing trans-fats with healthier fats and oils, nutritional labeling at fast-food and chain restaurants and tailoring items in food assistance programs to better address the health care needs of Americans.
Keywords: Use the following keywords in your search: AMA obesity, AMA healthier food, AMA trans fat.

3. **Research metabolic syndrome.** Metabolic syndrome is a combination of medical disorders that increase the risk of developing cardiovascular disease and diabetes.
Keywords: Metabolic syndrome, syndrome X, insulin resistance, Reaven syndrome, or CHAOS.

Chapter Review

Vocabulary Review

Matching

Match each term with the correct definition.

A. affective

B. anorexia nervosa, anorexia

C. antioxidant

D. beriberi

E. bulimia nervosa

F. cellulose

G. cognitive

H. dermatitis

I. display panel

J. fad diet

K. glossitis

L. goiter

M. hydrogenated

N. major minerals

O. malabsorption

P. monounsaturated fats

Q. night blindness

R. osteomalacia

___T___ 1. Minerals used by the body in small amounts

___F___ 2. Chief part of a cell wall

___N___ 3. Minerals used in significant amounts by the body

___I___ 4. Type of learning based on motor skills to perform tasks

___a___ 5. Type of learning based on feelings and emotions

___M___ 6. Polyunsaturated fats that are made solid

___2___ 7. Vitamins not stored in the body

___I___ 8. Panel on a label used for marketing purposes

___S___ 9. Disease caused by a deficiency of niacin in the body

___V___ 10. Condition caused by a lack of vitamin C in the diet

___D___ 11. Condition caused by a deficiency of thiamine

___Q___ 12. Condition caused by a deficiency of vitamin A

___Y___ 13. Dietary fats that have been broken down into fatty acids and glycerol

___J___ 14. Diet that is structured to cause quick loss of weight

S. pellagra

T. psychomotor

U. rickets

V. scurvy

W. synthesize

X. trace minerals

Y. triglycerides

Z. water-soluble vitamins

___O___ 15. Inability of the digestive system to absorb required nutrients

___R___ 16. Condition in children caused by vitamin D deficiency

___B___ 17. Psychological fear of gaining weight, lack of appetite

___K___ 18. Inflammation of the tongue

___H___ 19. Inflammation of the skin caused by irritation or riboflavin deficiency

___N___ 20. To make or take in

___E___ 21. Disorder characterized by compulsive overeating followed by self-induced vomiting or use of laxatives or diuretics

___U___ 22. Abnormal bone softening caused by vitamin D deficiency

___G___ 23. Type of learning based on what the patient already knows and has experienced

___L___ 24. Enlarged thyroid

___C___ 25. Substance that acts against oxidizing agents

___P___ 26. Fats that are liquid at room temperature and help lower total cholesterol

Theory Recall

True/False

Indicate whether the sentence or statement is true or false.

___T___ 1. The information on the food label is considered a legal document.

___F___ 2. Foods that have been fortified with vitamins and minerals take the place of a well-balanced diet.

___T___ 3. Sodium is found naturally in many foods.

___T___ 4. Effective patient education is the key to helping patients understand the situation and the need for change.

___F___ 5. It is okay for the medical assistant to tell the patient that he or she is not knowledgeable about the material being presented but that they will learn it together.

Multiple Choice

Identify the letter of the choice that best completes the statement or answers the question.

1. The food guide pyramid was developed by the _D_.
   A. DHHS
   B. FDA
   C. RDA
   D. USDA

2. Honey is composed of _D_ % sugar.
   A. 10
   B. 25
   C. 50
   D. 75

3. _D_ are organic substances that enhance the breakdown of proteins, carbohydrates, and fat.
   A. Carbohydrates
   B. Minerals
   C. Nutrients
   D. Vitamins

4. Complex carbohydrates supply the _B_ with energy.
   A. heart and lungs
   B. muscles and brain
   C. brain and heart
   D. lungs and muscles

5. _D_ is a type of learning.
   A. Affective
   B. Cognitive
   C. Psychomotor
   D. All of the above

6. RDAs are the nutritional guidelines that are published as the recommended dietary allowances, the name of which has been changed to read _A_.
   A. recommended daily allowances
   B. daily allowances
   C. daily values
   D. has not been changed and still reads the same

7. _C_ is an example of a fat-soluble vitamin.
   A. Vitamin B
   B. Vitamin C
   C. Vitamin K
   D. All of the above

8. _D_ mg is the recommended intake of sodium per day.
   A. 1200
   B. 1500
   C. 2000
   D. 2400

9. _B_ are liquid at room temperature and may help lower blood cholesterol.
   A. Saturated fats
   B. Monounsaturated fats
   C. Polyunsaturated fats
   D. Fatty acids

10. There are _C_ amino acids in protein.
    A. 10
    B. 15
    C. 22
    D. 24

11. The recommended amount of water to ingest is _C_ daily.
    A. 16 ounces
    B. 1 quart
    C. 2 quarts
    D. 3 quarts

12. _A_ is (are) a group of substances composed of many amino acids linked together.
    A. Proteins
    B. Carbohydrates
    C. Cholesterol
    D. Minerals

13. High-protein diets are often used _C_.
    A. before surgery
    B. when an infection is present
    C. with hypothermia
    D. all of the above

14. The daily allowance of saturated fats is _B_ grams.
    A. 10
    B. 20
    C. 25
    D. 30

15. A diet low in saturated fats and cholesterol helps maintain the blood cholesterol at levels below _____.
    A. 100
    B. 200
    C. 250
    D. 300

16. Fad diets can result in _C_.
    A. revised eating habits
    B. slowed weight loss
    C. rapid weight loss
    D. long-term weight loss

17. Dietary fats break down into fatty acids and are passed into the blood to form _D_.
    A. phospholipids
    B. enzymes
    C. hormones
    D. all of the above

18. The Mayo Clinic considers a person overweight when his or her body mass index is __C__.
    A. 10 to 19.9
    B. 20 to 25.9
    C. 25 to 29.9
    D. 30 to 35.9

19. Which one of the following is not affected by proper nutrition? _D_
    A. hair
    B. teeth
    C. reproduction
    D. all of the above are affected

20. __A__ produce(s) quick energy.
    A. Carbohydrates
    B. Protein
    C. Fatty acids
    D. Unsaturated fats

Sentence Completion

Complete each sentence or statement.

1. _Cognitive_ learning is based on what a person already knows or has experienced.

2. _Nutrition_ is the scientific study of how different food groups affect the body.

3. _C & B_ vitamins are not stored in the body.

4. _Carbohydrates_ are inorganic substances used in the formation of hard and soft body tissue.

5. _Saturated fat_ are usually solid at room temperature.

6. The primary function of _____ is to build and repair tissue and the formation of enzymes.

7. _____ is necessary for vitamin D and bile acid production.

8. _unsaturated fat_ are liquid at room temperature and are thought to lower both HDL and LDL cholesterol levels.

9. _Fiber_ is important for elimination.

10. A person's _affective learning_ ability is concerned with the person's emotions and feelings.

7 days meal plan

	Monday
fast	whole-wheat toast w/ cheese, tomato
k	fruit
h	salad w/ chicken
k	Fat-free potato chips
er	pork stir-fry
k	fruit
	TUESDAY
akfast	cooked wheat cereal w/ raisins
ack	fruits
unch	egg salad sandwich
nack	mini-yogurt
Dinner	chicken burger
nack	2-gram crackers
	WEDNESDAY
akfast	Toast w/ peanut butter & jelly, juice
nack	fruit
unch	pasta, salad
nack	1 slice of deli turkey, carrot sticks
inner	pizza, salad
nack	fruits
	THURSDAY
ackfast	cereal w/ seeds & raisins
ack	fruit
Lunch	soup, crackers, fruit
snack	mini-yogurt
inner	cheese & mushroom omelet
nack	fruit

FRIDAY

Breakfast	Scramble egg w/ tomato on toast
Snack	fruit
Lunch	tuna salad w/ whole-wheat crackers
Snack	fat-free potato chips
Dinner	chicken w/ BBQ sause, veggies, graham crackers (dessert)
Snack	mini-yogurt

SATURDAY

Breakfast	cereal
Snack	mini-yogurt
Lunch	turkey breast salad
Snack	fruit
Dinner	homemade burger
Snack	graham crackers

SUNDAY

Breakfast	cooked wheat cereal
Snack	fruit
Lunch	chicken salad
Snack	fat-free potato chips
Dinner	veggie stir-fry w/ rice
Snack	mini-yogurt

Short Answers

1. List the two main panels of a food label and explain each.

   New Level information   - nutrients list covers most important to your health

   Daily value - see how the amount of a nutrient in a serving of food fits in
   a 2000 calorie reference diet.

2. List and explain the five tips for a balanced diet.

   Drinking water; eating low-fat lean meats; eating a variety of fruits & vegetables,
   using low-fat / or fat-free dairy products, & eating plenty of whole grains,
   rice & pasta are tips for maintaining balance in the daily diet.

3. Explain three conditions for which a medical assistant should be looking when doing an inventory of the patient's readiness to follow a new health plan.

   Assess the patients physical & emotional readiness. Then you can plan patients
   needs & gradually implement until they get used to their new diet routine.

Critical Thinking

Select one of the four following diets and make a plan for three meals a day with a morning and afternoon snack diet for 7 days. Each diet should include a calorie count, fat count, carbohydrate count, and salt intake, regardless of which diet is selected.

1. A 1200-calorie diet

2. Low-fat diet

3. Low-carbohydrate diet

4. Low-sodium diet

Monday	Tuesday	Wednesday	Thursday	Friday	Saturday	Sunday
BF whole Wheat toast w/ cheese tomato						

Internet Research

Keywords: South Beach diet, Atkins' diet, Weight Watchers' diet, low-fat diet

Choose one topic to research: South Beach diet, Atkins' diet, Weight Watchers' diet, or low-fat diet, or pick a diet you are interested in learning more about. Write a one-page paper describing the advantages and disadvantages of the diet you selected to research. Cite your source. Be prepared to give a 2-minute oral presentation should your instructor assign you to do so.

What Would You Do?

If you have accomplished the objectives in this chapter, you will be able to make better choices as a medical assistant. Take a look at this situation and decide what you would do.

Josephine, age 52, has just been diagnosed with type 2 diabetes mellitus related to obesity. Living in the home with Josephine are her mother, Susie, who is 80 years old; Josephine's daughter Jessie, who is 24 and pregnant; and Jessie's two very active children, ages 6 and 2. Susie has been diagnosed with a heart condition and must be on a soft diet that is low in cholesterol and sodium restricted.

Josephine's concern today is how she can maintain a diet acceptable for all the medical conditions in the household while being sure the other family members will eat what is prepared. She thinks the children need sugar, but her mother needs to watch her sugar and salt intake to remain in a stable condition and not gain weight. Susie also needs her meals to be soft and easily chewable because of her decreased intestinal motility. However, Jessie and her 2-year-old child both need a diet that allows the necessary fiber for adequate bowel activity.

If you were the medical assistant, how might you educate Josephine about nutrition and answer her questions?

1. Why are learning styles important for the medical assistant to understand when teaching medical knowledge to the patient?

    To validate the facts regarding giving advices to patients.

2. Why is it now so important for Josephine to read food labels? What information is found on these?

    Ability to balance each family members diet.

    Basically all the information on nutrition facts per serving size.

3. Why is diet so important for Josephine to follow in the treatment of type 2 diabetes mellitus? Why does she need to know the glycemic index of foods?

Diabetic people had to follow carefully their diet. Glycemic index should be know to maintain their glucose level.

4. What special requirements will be needed for Susie so that she maintains a low-cholesterol diet?

Should maintain diet low in saturated fat & cholesterol.

5. Jessie's children want to eat pizza and French fries as their friends do. How will this affect the dietary changes of Josephine, Susie, and Jessie?

This will definetly affect their dietary routeen, as much as possible they should be avoiding fast foods.

6. Because Jessie has elevated blood pressure and early signs of edema in the legs and feet, what type of diet would you expect her to maintain for the remainder of her pregnancy?

Sodium - Restricted Diet and High Fiber diet

7. What is found in a diabetic diet? A low-sodium diet?

    Dieta- Balance of protein, carbohydrate & fat.

    Low - Low - sodium diet - natural foods w/o additives.

8. What effect would low income have on this family?

    I dont see any effect being low income, all of them can maintain
    a high fiber diet by just eating all natural food such as vegetable,
    fruits & dairy.

9. What effect would culture have in planning this diet if the family were of Greek or Italian ethnicity?

    They can use other alternative or if not less sodium & more on
    fiber.

10. Why is body mass index (BMI) a better guide for obesity than height-weight charts?

11. Why is it important that Josephine include a variety of foods in the diet for all members of the family?

    She should introduce other alternative for all the family members
    for them to maintain a well balanced diet according to their
    Illnesses.

Chapter Quiz

Multiple Choice

Identify the letter of the choice that best completes the statement or answers the question.

1. __A__ are building blocks; byproducts of protein breakdown by enzymes.
   A. Amino acids
   B. Carbohydrates
   C. Major minerals
   D. Trans-fatty acids

2. __B__ is learning based on what a person already knows or has experienced.
   A. Affective learning
   B. Cognitive learning
   C. Individual learning
   D. Psychomotor learning

3. Honey is __D__ % sugar.
   A. 20
   B. 40
   C. 60
   D. 75

4. __B__ are chemical substances within food that are released and absorbed during the digestive process.
   A. Minerals
   B. Nutrients
   C. Vitamins
   D. Carbohydrates

5. __A__ are in liquid form at room temperature and may help lower total blood cholesterol.
   A. Monounsaturated fats
   B. Polyunsaturated fats
   C. Trans-fatty acids
   D. None of the above

6. A medical assistant pretending to be knowledgeable about a subject is not acceptable.
   A. True
   B. False

7. The acceptable level of saturated fats daily is __C__ grams.
   A. 10
   B. 15
   C. 20
   D. 25

8. An adult should consume a minimum of __D__ of water a day.
   A. 16 ounces
   B. 32 ounces
   C. 1 quart
   D. 2 quarts

9. Sodium is found naturally in foods.
   A. True
   B. False

10. Cholesterol is necessary for vitamin _C_ and bile production.
    A. A
    B. C
    C. D
    D. E

11. A patient undergoing chemotherapy for cancer must have a diet high in _D_.
    A. carbohydrates
    B. fats
    C. vitamins
    D. all of the above

12. A body mass index of higher than _B_ is considered to be obese.
    A. 20
    B. 30
    C. 40
    D. 50

13. _D_ is a condition caused by the body's inability to absorb vitamin B_{12}.
    A. Beriberi
    B. Night blindness
    C. Pellagra
    D. Pernicious anemia

14. The key to patient teaching is not to focus on how to make a patient do something but to create a situation in which the patient will want to do what is needed.
    A. True
    B. False

15. Vitamin _D_ is a fat-soluble vitamin.
    A. B_6
    B. B_{12}
    C. C
    D. K

16. _B_ are inorganic substances used in the formation of soft and hard tissues.
    A. Amino acids
    B. Carbohydrates
    C. Minerals
    D. Vitamins

17. _C_ are the building blocks of fat that produce oil.
    A. Fatty acids
    B. Saturated fats
    C. Unsaturated fats
    D. None of the above

18. An infant should be fed between __B__ times in a 24-hour period.
    A. 6 and 8
    B. 8 and 12
    C. 10 and 14
    D. 12 and 15

19. A food label is a legal document.
    A. True
    B. False

20. With a diagnosis of cancer, the patient should eat a __B__ diet.
    A. full-liquid
    B. high-protein
    C. regular
    D. soft

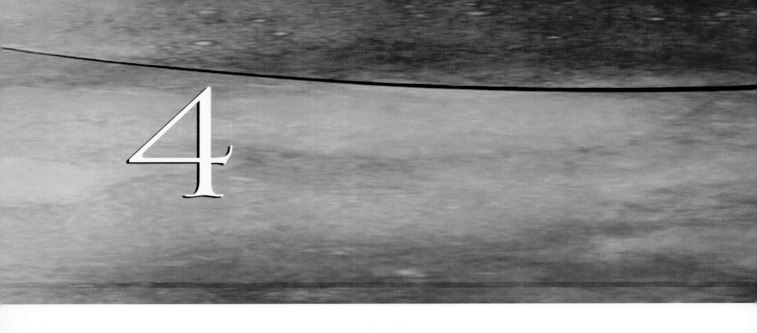

4

OBJECTIVES

You will be able to do the following after completing this chapter:

Key Terms
1. Define, appropriately use, and spell all the Key Terms for this chapter.

Situations Requiring First Aid
2. Explain what a medical assistant should do first in an emergency situation.
3. Define first aid, and list two guidelines that protect health care workers and victims from disease transmission.
4. List one situation requiring first-aid attention for each of the seven body systems.

Incident Reporting
5. Explain the purpose of an incident report.
6. List the information needed to accurately complete an incident report.

Office Emergencies
7. Explain what causes fainting.
8. List seven guidelines for the emergency care of a patient who has fainted.
9. Describe the symptoms of a heart attack, and explain the purpose of cardiopulmonary resuscitation (CPR).
10. List 10 guidelines for the emergency care of a patient who has heart attack symptoms.
11. Explain how a stroke differs from a heart attack, and identify the signs of obstructed airway and cardiac arrest.
12. List six guidelines for the emergency care of a patient who has had a stroke.
13. List seven types of shock and explain what causes each.
14. List eight guidelines for the emergency care of a patient who has symptoms of shock.
15. Explain what a seizure is and what may cause one.
16. List eight guidelines for the emergency care of a patient who has had a seizure.
17. List and describe the two methods for controlling bleeding.
18. Explain the emergency care for patients with thermal, chemical, or electrical burns.
19. Differentiate between heat exhaustion and heat stroke.
20. Explain considerations for the emergency care of a patient with hypothermia and frostbite.
21. List the main goal for the emergency care of a fracture.
22. List four guidelines for assessing the degree of a dislocation.
23. List five guidelines for emergency care of a patient who has ingested poison.
24. List four guidelines for the emergency care of a patient who has inhaled poison.
25. Identify the symptoms of bites and stings.
26. Explain the difference between insulin shock and diabetic ketoacidosis (diabetic coma).
27. Demonstrate the correct procedure for performing the Heimlich maneuver.

BASIC FIRST AID AND MEDICAL OFFICE EMERGENCIES

Bandaging
28. List three common uses for bandages.
29. Differentiate between an elastic bandage and a Kling-type bandage.
30. List and briefly describe five basic bandage turns.
31. Demonstrate the procedure for properly applying a tubular gauze bandage to a affected area.

Basic Life Support
32. Explain the "CAB" guidelines for performing CPR.
33. Demonstrate the correct procedure for opening a victim's airway.
34. Demonstrate the correct procedure for performing rescue breathing.
35. Demonstrate the correct procedure for performing one-person adult CPR.
36. Demonstrate the correct procedure for performing two-person adult CPR.
37. Explain what an AED is, and describe how it is used.
38. Explain how to perform pediatric CPR.
39. Demonstrate the correct procedure for performing one-person infant CPR.

Disaster Preparedness
40. Discuss the difference between natural and man-made disasters.
41. Discuss the advantage of registering with a disaster preparedness team.

Patient-Centered Professionalism
42. Analyze a realistic medical office situation and apply your understanding of handling office emergencies to determine the best course of action.
43. Describe the impact on patient care when medical assistants have a solid understanding of the knowledge and skills necessary to assist patients in office emergencies.

KEY TERMS

anaphylactic shock Severe allergic reaction caused by hypersensitivity to a substance (e.g., foreign protein).

automated external defibrillator (AED) Machine that analyzes a patient's cardiac rhythm and delivers an electric shock if indicated.

bandage turn Method of arranging a bandage on a body part.

bleeding Loss of blood from a ruptured, punctured, or cut blood vessel.

burn Injury or destruction of tissue caused by excessive physical heat, chemicals, electricity, or radiation.

cardiac arrest Cessation of heart activity.

cardiogenic shock Condition that occurs when the cardiac muscles can no longer pump blood throughout the body.

cardiopulmonary resuscitation (CPR) Action performed to restore breathing and cardiac activity.

cerebrovascular accident (CVA) Lack of oxygen to the brain caused by narrowed or ruptured cerebral vessels.

choking Inability to breathe caused by a blockage in the trachea.

circular turn Bandage application in which each turn overlaps the previous turn.

conscious Awake; aware of one's surroundings.

KEY TERMS—*cont'd*

defibrillation Electrical shock to the heart to maintain heart rhythm.

diabetic ketoacidosis State that occurs when there is too much glucose and not enough insulin in a patient's blood, and ketones are produced; acute insulin deficiency (also called *diabetic coma*).

disaster Event that creates destruction and or an adverse consequence.

direct pressure Pressure applied directly over a wound.

dislocation Injury that occurs when one end of a bone is separated from its original position in a joint.

elastic bandage Bandage containing elastic that stretches and molds to the body part to which it is applied.

epilepsy Chronic brain disorder in which an individual has seizures.

epistaxis Nosebleed.

first aid Temporary care given to an injured or ill person until the victim can be provided complete treatment.

first-degree burn Burn that involves only the epidermis.

figure-eight turn Bandage turn that is applied on a slant and progresses upward and then downward to support a dressing or joint.

fracture Break or crack in a bone caused by trauma or disease.

frostbite Form of hypothermia that occurs when body tissues freeze.

full-thickness burn Burn that destroys the epidermis and dermis to include the nerve endings; third-degree burn.

heat exhaustion Form of hyperthermia marked by pale, cool, and clammy skin, shallow respirations, and weak pulse.

heat stroke Form of hyperthermia caused by dehydration causing a loss of consciousness.

Heimlich maneuver Abdominal thrust used in an emergency to dislodge the cause of a blockage.

hemorrhagic shock Shock caused by inadequate blood supply to tissues as a result of trauma, burns, or internal bleeding.

hyperglycemia High blood sugar level; can cause diabetic coma.

hyperthermia Increased body temperature.

hypoglycemia Low blood sugar level; can cause insulin shock.

hypothermia Decreased body temperature.

immobilization Prevention of movement; inability to move.

incident Any unusual event that is not consistent with the routine activity within a health care facility.

incident report Document that describes any unusual occurrence that happens while a person is on the property of a health care facility.

indirect pressure Pressure applied over an arterial pressure point.

insulin shock State that occurs when the body has too much insulin and not enough glucose (food) to use the insulin; severe hypoglycemia.

Kling-type bandage Gauze bandaging material that stretches and molds to irregular-shaped areas.

Kussmaul breathing Breathing pattern that begins with very deep, gasping respirations that become rapid and are associated with severe diabetic acidosis and coma.

metabolic shock Type of shock caused by excessive loss of body fluids and metabolites (body chemicals).

neurogenic shock Loss of nerve control over the circulatory system causing decreased blood supply to an area.

partial-thickness burn Burn depth that damages the epidermis or the epidermis and dermis; second-degree burn.

poison Substance that causes injury, illness, and even death; toxin.

psychogenic shock Psychological stress on the body.

respiratory arrest Cessation of breathing.

"rule of nines" Method of evaluating a surface area of a burn; the surface is divided into regions with percentages assigned.

second-degree burn Burn that damages both the epidermis and dermis; partial-thickness burn.

seizure Sudden involuntary muscle activity leading to a change in level of consciousness and behavior.

septic shock Severe infection with toxins that prevent blood vessels from constricting, causing blood to pool away from vital organs.

shock Progressive circulatory collapse brought on by insufficient blood flow to all parts of the body.

spiral reverse turn Bandage turn that progresses upward and reverses on itself at intervals to assist in making the bandage fit.

spiral turn Bandage turn in which the bandage progresses upward and each spiral overlaps the previous turn.

splint Firm material used to immobilize above and below a fracture to prevent further damage.

sprain Full or partial tear of a ligament caused by trauma of a joint.

strain Stretching or tearing of a muscle or tendon caused by trauma.

stroke Cerebrovascular accident (CVA); condition caused by narrowed cerebral vessels, hemorrhage into the brain, and formation of an embolus or thrombus, resulting in a lack of blood supply to a portion of the brain.

syncope Fainting.

synergy Bringing together; bonding.

third-degree burn Burn that destroys the epidermis and dermis to include the nerve endings; full-thickness burn.

tubular gauze Gauze bandage made in a tubular shape that can be used to cover rounded body parts.

unconscious Not responding to stimuli.

within normal limits (WNL) Values found within established guidelines.

What Would You Do?

Read the following scenario and keep it in mind as you learn about first aid and office emergencies.

Mariah has type 1 diabetes mellitus and takes insulin on a regular basis. Dr. Naguchi is aware that Mariah does not follow her diet as she should and that her exercise habits are not consistent, so her diabetes is often not stable.

Mariah lives in the southern United States, where it is currently 100° F outside and very humid. Earlier today, Mariah was in the garden gathering vegetables. Later she started canning the vegetables. Her house has minimal air-conditioning. In her haste to complete what needed to be done in the garden, Mariah did not eat her lunch as she should have, although she took her entire dose of insulin.

During the afternoon Mariah began to feel weak, experiencing dizziness and sweating, and her skin felt cool and clammy. Don, her husband, drove her the three blocks to Dr. Naguchi's office because she started complaining of chest pain and difficulty breathing. As soon as she arrives, Mariah appears to faint and falls, injuring her left ankle. As the medical assistant, Janis is the first health care professional to see what is happening to Mariah. After seeing Mariah, Dr. Naguchi orders an x-ray of her ankle to see whether she has a sprain, strain, or fracture.

If you were in Janis's place, would you know what to do in this situation?

Occasionally, medical emergencies occur in the medical office. Medical assistants are expected to respond according to the nature of the emergency. If the physician is present, the medical assistant alerts the physician and assists with the needs of the patient as directed. If the physician is not available, the medical assistant must assess the situation, call 911, and provide first aid as needed until help arrives.

Emergency situations can also occur outside the medical office; as a trained health care worker, you would be expected to manage the situation according to your scope of training until complete medical care can be obtained. The skills for handling medical office emergencies can be applied in "street" emergencies. Medical assistants need to understand the situations that require first aid, types of emergencies and what should be done for each, and how to perform basic life support procedures to be able to handle these situations.

SITUATIONS REQUIRING FIRST AID

Emergency situations require medical assistants to prioritize both the urgency of the situation and the status of the patient. Circulatory and respiratory symptoms are of primary concern and have first priority. Once the medical assistant begins providing emergency care, he or she must call 911 if appropriate, or have someone else place the call. Box 4-1 lists the information that will be requested when making a 911 call. Once emergency care is started, the medical assistant must stay with the victim until help arrives.

BOX 4-1   911 Information

Be prepared to provide the following information when calling 911:
1. Name of caller and verification of address, to include floor level and room or suite number.
   - If using a cell phone, exact location including complete address, floor level, and room or suite number
2. Name and condition of the victim.
   - Patient's chief complaint and any known conditions
   - Observable signs and symptoms
   - Vital signs, if known
3. Care already given.

Example of Prioritizing Urgency and Patient Status

A car crashes outside the medical facility. The medical assistant reaches the car and sees the driver holding her chest, having difficulty breathing, and she is bleeding from a laceration on her forehead. The medical assistant must determine which illness or injury to attend to first. The circulatory and respiratory symptoms (holding chest, having difficulty breathing) take priority. The laceration is not life threatening and can be attended to when the patient is stable.

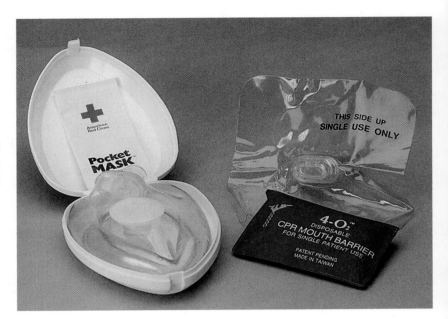

Fig. 4-1 Cardiopulmonary resuscitation (CPR) mouth barriers. *(From Young AP, Kennedy DB: Kinn's the medical assistant, ed 9, Philadelphia, 2003, Saunders.)*

First aid is the temporary care given to an injured or ill person until the victim can be provided complete emergency treatment. In the medical office, a medical assistant may be required to perform lifesaving first-aid measures (e.g., cardiopulmonary resuscitation [CPR]), as well as basic first aid (e.g., applying a simple dressing to a skin break). Providing first aid should be done in ways that protect the health care worker and the victim from disease transmission. Therefore **Standard Precautions** should be followed when providing first aid, as follows:

- Wear protective gloves to avoid contact with blood and body fluids if possible.
- Do not touch areas that are soiled with blood, mucus, or other biohazardous materials without a barrier between you and the victim (Fig. 4-1).

Table 4-1 lists situations that may require first-aid attention, and Box 4-2 provides general guidelines for providing emergency care.

PATIENT-CENTERED PROFESSIONALISM

- Why must the medical assistant be able to recognize and quickly assess any situation that requires first aid or CPR?

INCIDENT REPORTING

An **incident** is any unusual event that is not consistent with the routine activity within a health care facility. This includes a patient, visitor, or an

TABLE 4-1	Situations Requiring First Aid
Body System Affected	**Situation**
Circulatory	Fainting
	Chest pain or heart attack
	Stroke
	Shock
	Bleeding
Respiratory	Obstructed airway (choking)
	Allergic reactions (anaphylaxis)
Digestive	Poisoning
Integumentary	Burns
	Wounds
	Heat or cold emergencies
Musculoskeletal	Sprains and strains
	Fractures and dislocations
Nervous	Seizures
Endocrine	Diabetic ketoacidosis
	Insulin shock

employee of the health care facility. Examples of an incident include falls, accidental needle-stick injury, medication error, or carelessness in performance of a procedure whether it leads to an injury of a patient or not. When an incident occurs, the health care professional involved or the person, often the medical assistant, who witnesses the incident, completes an **incident report**. The incident report is a document that describes any unusual occurrence that happens while a person is on the premises of

BOX 4-2 Guidelines for Providing Emergency Care

Important: Assess the emergency for your own safety first to avoid creating another emergency.

1. Know your limits. Only do what is in your scope of training.
2. Stay calm and speak in a normal tone of voice. This assists in keeping the patient (if conscious), and other people around, calm. Explain what has happened and the extent of your training.
3. Practice Standard Precautions and follow the OSHA Bloodborne Pathogen Standards.
4. Assess the situation quickly and check for possibilities of life-threatening injuries. Use the "ABC" method to assess the patient:
   Airway
   Breathing
   Circulation
   This can be accomplished by (A) looking at the rise and fall of the patient's chest, (B) listening for air entering and leaving the patient, and (C) feeling for the patient's pulse.
5. Know how to acquire emergency medical response (e.g., call 911).
6. Do not move the patient unless he or she is in harm's way. Keep the person lying down.
7. Keep the patient warm (e.g., blanket, coats).
8. Look for a medical alert tag on the patient's wrist or neck.
9. Move bystanders away from the person. Do ask if anyone knows what happened.
10. Never leave the patient until emergency medical personnel have arrived and taken over. Provide information that you have observed.

---

a health care facility. Think of an incident report as part of the medical facility's quality improvement plan or assessment tool for risk management.

Completing the Incident Report

It must be understood that completing an incident report is not an admission of negligence or placing blame on any one person but a way to gather factual information of a problem that exists. A written report of the incident must be completed within 24 hours of the occurrence. The report must include the following observed, objective, and chronological information:

- Person's name
- Location and time of occurrence
- Factual description of what occurred and what was done:

- Sequence of events leading up to the event (include victim's own words)
- Assessed extent of injury incurred (objective findings of health care professional reviewing)
- Observation of factors that may have contributed to the incident (e.g., wet floor observed in bathroom where Amanda Packo fell)

The medical assistant must remember that the incident report is not a permanent part of the medical record and should not be referred to in the medical record. This action legally protects the health care facility and personnel involved.

Trend Analysis

A *trend analysis* is the ongoing review of data to detect significant patterns. Incident reports should indicate that an occurrence happens infrequently. If, after a review of incident reports, a different pattern begins to emerge, such as an unusual number of falls in a particular examination room, it can be the result of a dangerous condition. This adverse trend analysis identifies occurrences that need immediate attention.

PATIENT-CENTERED PROFESSIONALISM

- Why is it necessary to complete an incident report even if there is no apparent injury?

OFFICE EMERGENCIES

Despite efforts to prevent emergencies in the medical office with effective facilities management, Occupational Safety and Health Administration (OSHA) requirements, and Standard Precautions, office emergencies still occur. Medical assistants must be alert to unusual noises (screams, loud noises, breaking glass), unusual sights (overturned chair, fire), unusual odors (smell of smoke, unrecognizable odors), and the unusual appearance or behavior of a patient (slurred speech, difficulty breathing, erratic behavior, or pale, moist skin). If the patient involved in an office emergency is **conscious**, the medical assistant can assess the patient's condition by asking questions. Also, stabilizing care can begin until help arrives. If the patient is **unconscious**, a 911 call should be made and care provided until help arrives.

Sudden illnesses that occur in the medical office often have similar symptoms. The medical assistant may not know the exact cause of the illness but can react to visual and auditory clues. For example, unusual breathing patterns may alert another individual that there is a problem. Chest pain should be treated as a heart attack because it is better to err on the side of caution.

Some form of emergency equipment should be present in a medical office. Fig. 4-2 shows a standard emergency cart, and Table 4-2 lists equipment, supplies, and medications often stored on an emergency cart. Medical assistants cannot prescribe medications, but they can administer prescribed medications, be responsible for checking the cart to make certain that medications are not outdated, and ensure that all supplies are present. The emergency cart should be inventoried on a regular basis, and it should be documented that the supplies have been checked. Fig. 4-3 illustrates various items included on the cart that are used for airway management for a patient in respiratory distress.

Fainting

Fainting, or **syncope**, is a temporary loss of consciousness caused by an inadequate blood supply to the brain. Patients often describe the sensation before fainting as "everything is going dark." Following this sensation, they lose consciousness.

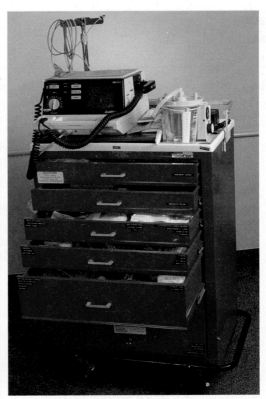

Fig. 4-2 Standard emergency cart with defibrillator for use in emergencies.

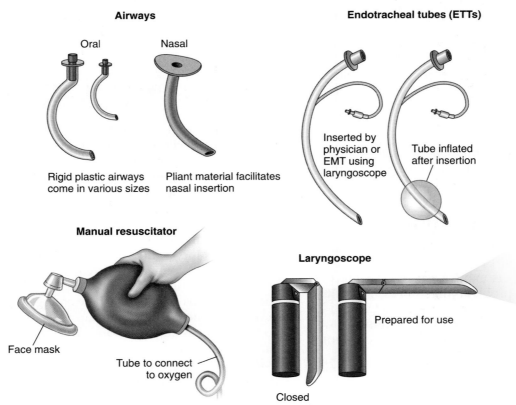

Fig. 4-3 Equipment for emergency airway management. *EMT,* Emergency medical technician. *(From Hunt SA:* Saunders fundamentals of medical assisting, *Philadelphia, 2002, Saunders.)*

TABLE 4-2   Basic Medical Office Emergency Cart

Type of Equipment	Supplies Needed	Generic (Trade) Medications	Treatment
Equipment and Supplies			
Defibrillator with pads	ECG machine with cable/pads	adenosine (Adenocard)	Ventricular tachycardia
Oxygen tank and airway management	Flow meter, tubing, mask, nasal cannula	aminophylline	Acute bronchospasm (e.g., emphysema, bronchitis)
	Suction machine with tubing and catheters		
	Airways, both oral and nasal in assorted sizes	atropine	Bradycardia caused by hypotension
	Laryngoscope (handle and blades), assorted sizes	albuterol (Proventil)	Acute bronchospasm
		diazepam (Valium)	Seizures and acute anxiety attacks
	Endotracheal tubes	digoxin (Lanoxin)	Atrial tachycardia
	Ambu bag	diphenhydramine (Benadryl)	Hypersensitivity reactions
Intravenous (IV) supplies	Tourniquet		
	Alcohol wipes	dopamine (Intropin)	Hypotension from cardiogenic shock
	Betadine swabs	epinephrine (Adrenalin)	Restoring cardiac rhythm in cardiac arrest and acute allergic reactions
	Surgical tape		
	Angiocaths and butterfly needles (assorted sizes)	furosemide (Lasix)	Congestive heart failure and pulmonary edema
	IV tubing	isoproterenol (Isuprel)	Bradycardia that does not respond to atropine
	Arm board		
	IV fluids:	lidocaine (Xylocaine)	Ventricular arrhythmias after MI
	Dextrose 5% (D_5W)	naloxone (Narcan)	Narcotic overdose
	Normal saline (NS)	nitroglycerin (Nitrostat)	Chest pain associated with angina and MI
	Lactated Ringer's solution	nitroprusside (Nitropress)	Elevated blood pressure in hypertensive crisis
	IV cutdown tray	norepinephrine (Levophed)	Hypotensive emergencies
General Supplies			
	Gloves (sterile and nonsterile)	methylprednisolone (Solu-Medrol)	Acute allergic reactions when epinephrine is not effective
	Scissors (bandage, operative)		
	Hemostat	phenobarbital	Seizures, especially febrile seizures
	Syringes and needles (assorted sizes)	phenytoin (Dilantin)	Seizures, especially tonic-clonic
	Biohazard containers	procainamide (Pronestyl)	Ventricular arrhythmias when lidocaine is not effective
	Sterile gauze squares (2 × 2, 4 × 4)		
	Water-soluble lubricant	sodium bicarbonate	Acidosis after MI
	Penlight	verapamil (Calan)	Ventricular tachycardia that does not respond to adenosine
	Pen and paper		
	Pocket mask	activated charcoal	Ingested poisons
	Kling dressings	ammonia ampules	Fainting
	Blood pressure cuffs (all sizes)	glucagons or glucose	Hypoglycemia
	Stethoscope		

ECG, Electrocardiogram; *MI*, myocardial infarction.

Patients may complain of dizziness and nausea. They may appear pale, have cool skin, and be sweating. The body usually falls in a supine position, allowing the blood to flow back to the brain. Although fainting is not dangerous, the fall can cause injury. When patients regain consciousness, they sometimes experience confusion and anxiety.

If a patient indicates that he or she feels faint or lightheaded, it is best to have the patient sit down and lower the head to knee level (Fig. 4-4, A). Alternately, have the patient lie down in a supine position on the floor or examination table with the feet slightly elevated (Fig. 4-4, B). These positions increase the blood flow to the brain. Ask the patient if he or she has ever experienced this before, and if so, under what circumstances. Because fainting is a symptom of low blood sugar (hypoglycemia), heart attack (myocardial infarction), dehydration, and other diseases, this quick assessment assists you in determining what to do next. Patients have been known to become lightheaded when they see needles, such as during a blood drawing procedure, so be prepared.

Guidelines for care of a patient who has fainted are as follows:

1. Quickly assess any life-threatening situation that may have caused the fainting.
2. Check for any medical alert tags or alert cards, because these provide information about certain medical conditions (e.g., diabetes; Fig. 4-5).
3. Move all furniture out of the way and keep the patient in a supine position. Slightly elevate the legs above the level of the heart (10-12 inches). If the patient vomits, turn the head to the side to prevent choking.

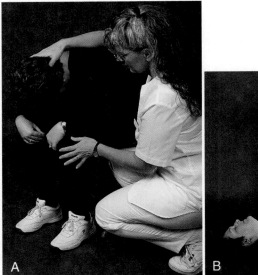
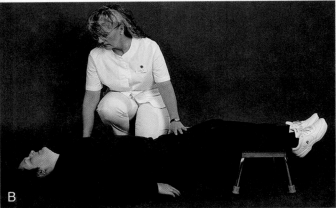

Fig. 4-4 **A,** Prevention of fainting. **B,** Prevention and treatment of fainting. *(From Bonewit-West K: Clinical procedures for medical assistants, ed 6, Philadelphia, 2004, Saunders.)*

Fig. 4-5 Diabetic medical identification. **A,** Diabetic medical alert bracelet. **B,** Diabetic wallet alert card. *(From Bonewit-West K: Clinical procedures for medical assistants, ed 6, Philadelphia, 2004, Saunders.)*

4. Check and clear the airway, and determine if any injuries were sustained during the fall. Loosen any tight clothing.
5. Apply a damp, cool cloth to the patient's face.
6. Calm the patient as he or she awakens.
7. Ask if the patient has any known medical conditions. Do not allow the patient to sit upright immediately.

Chest Pain (Heart Attack)

Chest pain can be a sign of a heart attack and should be treated as an emergency until a medical diagnosis can be made. Symptoms include dusky skin color; diaphoresis; a bluish discoloration to the lips and nail beds; shortness of breath (SOB); and a rapid, weak pulse. Chest pain is described as "heavy" or "crushing" in the sternum area and may radiate down the left arm, jaw, and up into the shoulder area.

Guidelines for the care of a patient who has symptoms of a heart attack are as follows:

1. Call for emergency assistance (911) and alert the physician.
2. Place the patient in a comfortable position, usually semireclining.
3. Assess the airway.
4. Loosen any tight clothing.
5. Ask if the patient is conscious; if he or she is, ask if he or she is taking any "heart" medication.
6. Administer any medications the patient may be taking (e.g., nitroglycerin, aspirin).
7. Administer oxygen with the physician's order.
8. Take the patient's vital signs.
9. Keep the patient warm.
10. Comfort and reassure the patient.

Stroke

A **stroke**, or **cerebrovascular accident (CVA)**, occurs when the brain does not receive oxygen. This may result from a burst or blocked blood vessel leading to the brain or from pressure on the cerebral artery caused by a brain tumor. Stroke symptoms vary according to the severity and location of the blockage. A patient may complain of a severe headache with no known cause, sudden confusion, or vision changes that make it difficult to focus. A stroke is often painless and is usually the result of narrowed cerebral vessels caused by high blood pressure, heart disease, smoking, diabetes, and elevated cholesterol. It may also be caused by a hemorrhage or bleeding into the brain or an embolus or thrombus in the brain. Keep in mind that if a stroke occurs on the left side of the brain, the damage will be noticeable to the right side of the body, and vice versa.

FOR YOUR INFORMATION

Recognizing Stroke Warning Signs

The warning signs of stroke can be easily learned using the acronym **FAST:**

Facial weakness or numbness
Arm weakness or numbness
Speech difficulty
Time to call 911

Guidelines for the care of a patient who has a stroke are as follows:

1. Call for emergency assistance (911) and alert the physician.
2. Assess the patient's airway. Turn the patient's head to the side to prevent the patient from choking on vomitus. A head tilt keeps the tongue from blocking the airway.
3. Elevate the head and shoulders slightly by placing a jacket or folded towel underneath. This relieves intracranial pressure.
4. Keep the patient quiet and warm. Maintain a confident attitude. Even though a patient may not be able to communicate, the person can hear what is being said. Anxiety can worsen the stroke.
5. If the patient develops difficulty with breathing, turn the patient on the side (paralyzed side down).
6. Take the patient's vital signs.

Shock

Shock is the progressive circulatory collapse of the body brought on by insufficient blood flow to all parts of the body. If left untreated, death can occur. Typical causes of shock include allergic reactions, exposure to extremes in heat or cold, heart attack, trauma, loss of blood, severe burns, and electrical shock. Symptoms include pale, cool skin; rapid pulse and breathing; disorientation; restlessness; and cyanosis around the lips and nail beds. Table 4-3 describes different types of shock and possible causes.

Guidelines for the care of a patient who has symptoms of shock are as follows:

1. Seek emergency assistance.
2. Maintain the patient's airway.
3. Place the patient in a supine position with the feet elevated above the heart (10-12 inches).
4. If bleeding is external, provide control by applying direct pressure.
5. Keep the patient warm and calm.

TABLE 4-3 Types of Shock

Type of Shock	Description
Anaphylactic	Severe allergic reaction brought about by insect sting, drugs, foods, or any inhaled or ingested substance
Cardiogenic	Cardiac muscles can no longer pump blood throughout the body; therefore the blood flow lessens, blood pressure drops, and the heart has difficulty pumping blood
Hemorrhagic	Multiple trauma, severe burns, and internal bleeding all result in inadequate blood supply to tissues
Neurogenic	Spinal or head injuries cause loss of nerve control over the circulatory system, causing decreased blood supply to an area
Metabolic	Diabetic coma, insulin shock, vomiting, and diarrhea result in loss of body fluids and metabolites, causing an imbalance in the body
Psychogenic	Psychological stress on the body causes shock (e.g., death in family, fear, high anxiety)
Septic	Severe infection produces toxins that prevent the blood vessels from constricting; blood pools away from vital organs

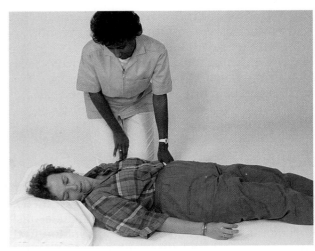

Fig. 4-6 Protect the person's head during a seizure. *(From Sorrentino SA: Assisting with patient care, St Louis, 1999, Mosby.)*

1. Quickly remove any objects from the area that could cause injury.
2. Maintain an open airway. ***Do not place anything between the patient's teeth.*** This could become an airway obstruction and cause vomiting.
3. Protect the patient's head by placing a folded towel, pillow, or clothing underneath the head (Fig. 4-6).
4. Loosen any tight clothing that would interfere with breathing, and remove eyeglasses.
5. Do not restrain the patient. Avoid overstimulation; this may cause further seizures.
6. After seizure activity ceases, turn the victim to the side with the head extended and face slightly downward to help secretions drain and to allow the tongue to remain free of the airway.
7. Assess the patient's vital signs.
8. Allow the patient to rest after the seizure subsides. Reassure the patient and make him or her as comfortable as possible. If a seizure occurs in the waiting room, move the patient to the examination room when fully conscious. Document the incident and the care provided.

6. Do not give anything by mouth.
7. Never leave the patient alone.
8. Take the patient's vital signs.

Seizures

A **seizure** is a sudden involuntary muscle activity leading to a change in level of consciousness and behavior. Seizures are normally brief and are brought about by a change in electrical activity in the brain. **Epilepsy**, a chronic brain disorder, accounts for many cases of seizure activity, but seizures can also be brought on by head trauma, high fever, and even low blood sugar.

Guidelines for the care of a patient who has a seizure are as follows:

Bleeding

Bleeding is the loss of blood from a ruptured, punctured, or cut blood vessel. The severity of bleeding depends on whether the bleeding is from an artery, vein, or capillary. The more blood vessel damage present, the more life threatening the incident becomes. The average adult has a blood volume of 8 to 10 pints. A loss of 25% to 40% of the total volume can be fatal. Fig. 4-7 shows the effects of

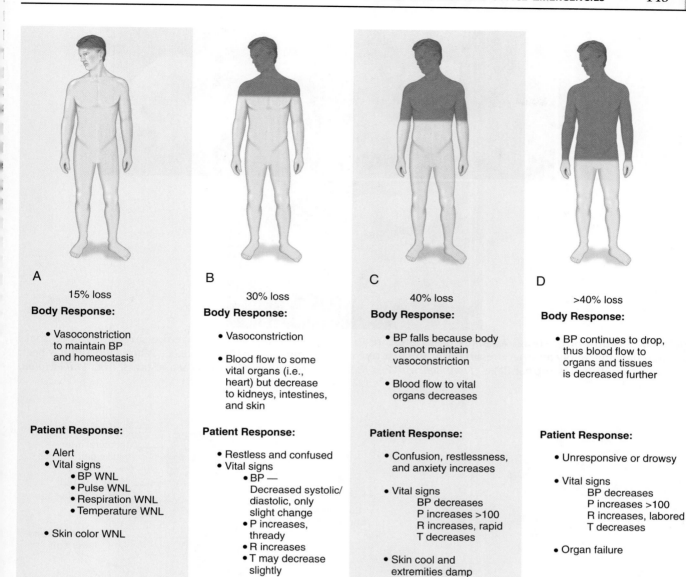

A

15% loss

Body Response:

- Vasoconstriction to maintain BP and homeostasis

Patient Response:

- Alert
- Vital signs
  - BP WNL
  - Pulse WNL
  - Respiration WNL
  - Temperature WNL
- Skin color WNL

B

30% loss

Body Response:

- Vasoconstriction
- Blood flow to some vital organs (i.e., heart) but decrease to kidneys, intestines, and skin

Patient Response:

- Restless and confused
- Vital signs
  - BP — Decreased systolic/diastolic, only slight change
  - P increases, thready
  - R increases
  - T may decrease slightly
- Skin color pale, cool, and dry

C

40% loss

Body Response:

- BP falls because body cannot maintain vasoconstriction
- Blood flow to vital organs decreases

Patient Response:

- Confusion, restlessness, and anxiety increases
- Vital signs
  BP decreases
  P increases >100
  R increases, rapid
  T decreases
- Skin cool and extremities damp

D

>40% loss

Body Response:

- BP continues to drop, thus blood flow to organs and tissues is decreased further

Patient Response:

- Unresponsive or drowsy
- Vital signs
  BP decreases
  P increases >100
  R increases, labored
  T decreases
- Organ failure

Fig. 4-7 The body's response to blood loss. *BP*, Blood pressure; *P*, pulse; *R*, respiration; *T*, temperature; *WNL*, within normal limits.

blood loss from a patient and indicates how the body of the patient reacts to the blood loss.

- *Artery damage.* External arterial bleeding is easy to identify because the wound spurts bright-red blood. The blood is coming directly from the heart and is rich in oxygen (the reason for the bright-red appearance). If an artery is severed, the blood loss is rapid and severe. This type of injury requires direct pressure over the wound, as well as indirect pressure over the artery closest to the wound.
- *Vein damage.* When a vein is damaged, the blood flow is steady from the wound and is dark red. Since venous blood has less oxygen and contains more waste products than arterial

blood, its color is darker. Injury to a vein is easier to control with direct pressure than injury to an artery.
- *Capillary damage.* A capillary injury does not flow freely, but drips slowly or oozes. It forms a clot by itself or with the aid of a pressure dressing over the wound and seals off quickly.

Bleeding can be controlled by the use of direct or indirect pressure. **Direct pressure** is applied directly over the wound (Fig. 4-8), whereas **indirect pressure** is applied over an arterial pressure point (Fig. 4-9). When an extremity is injured, applying pressure and elevating the bleeding limb above heart level slow the flow of blood and allow the wound to clot faster.

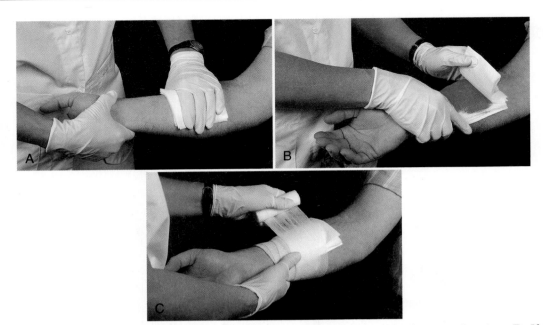

Fig. 4-8 Control of bleeding. **A**, Apply direct pressure to wound with large, thick gauze dressing. **B**, If blood soaks through dressing, apply another dressing over the first one and continue to apply pressure. **C**, When bleeding has been controlled, apply a pressure bandage. *(From Bonewit-West K:* Clinical procedures for medical assistants, *ed 6, Philadelphia, 2004, Saunders.)*

Fig. 4-9 Pressure points to decrease arterial bleeding. *(From Hunt SA:* Saunders fundamentals of medical assisting, *Philadelphia, 2002, Saunders.)*

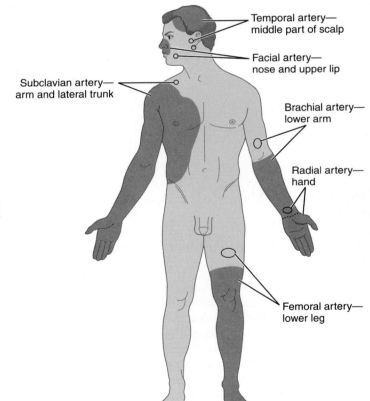

Temporal artery— middle part of scalp

Facial artery— nose and upper lip

Subclavian artery— arm and lateral trunk

Brachial artery— lower arm

Radial artery— hand

Femoral artery— lower leg

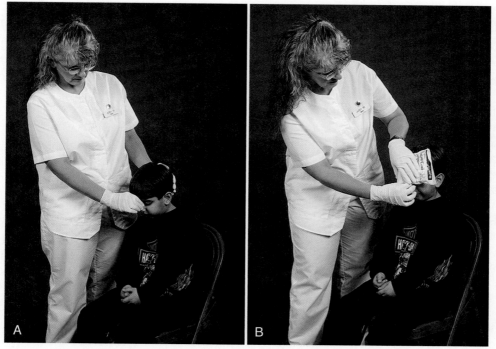

Fig. 4-10   Care of a nosebleed. **A,** With the patient sitting and tilting the head slightly forward, apply direct pressure by pinching the nostrils together. **B,** An ice pack can be applied to the bridge of the nose to help control bleeding. *(From Bonewit-West K:* Clinical procedures for medical assistants, *ed 6, Philadelphia, Saunders, 2004.)*

Epistaxis (nosebleed) can be caused by trauma, hypertension, high altitude, or an upper respiratory infection. The patient should be in a sitting position with the head tilted slightly forward (Fig. 4-10, *A*). This prevents blood from going down the back of the throat and causing nausea. The nostrils should be pinched together to assist in clotting. An ice pack can be placed at the back of the neck or at the top of the nose area (Fig. 4-10, *B*). The ice pack causes vasoconstriction of the blood vessels and is usually applied for 15 minutes. After the bleeding has stopped, the patient should be cautioned not to blow the nose because this would loosen the blood clot. Inability to stop the bleeding requires further emergency treatment, so the patient should be taken to a hospital.

Simple wound care for an abrasion or laceration is accomplished by cleaning the area with mild soap and water, rinsing, and blotting dry with a clean dressing. The purpose of wound care is to prevent infection, so cleaning and protecting the wound are important. After cleaning the site, a dressing is applied to protect the wound from further contamination and absorb any fluids. Tape is used to secure the dressing.

Burns

A **burn** is an injury to or destruction of body tissue caused by excessive physical heat (e.g., scalding water, hot iron), chemicals, electricity, or radiation. Box 4-3 reviews the depth and classification of burns, as well as the use of the "rule of nines" to evaluate surface area.

Proper treatment is started after both the depth and the total surface area of the burn have been determined. It is important to know what caused the burn (e.g., heat, chemical), the length of time the person was exposed (e.g., to the heat, chemical), and if the person has any medical conditions.

Call 911 in the following burn situations:

- Patient has breathing difficulties.
- Patient has burns to the head, neck, hands, feet, or genital area.
- Patient has chemical or electrical burns.
- Patient is very young or elderly.

Heat or Thermal Burns

Heat or thermal burns are best handled by taking the following actions:

1. Remove the person from the source of the burn (if this can be done without danger to yourself).
2. Cool the burned area by flushing with cool water or applying wet cloths.
3. Cover the burn with a dry sterile dressing or clean cloth.
4. In extreme cases, assess for respiratory and circulatory complications.
5. If necessary, start CPR and alert 911.

BOX 4-3   Depth and Classification of Burns

The depth of the burn and the extent of body surface area covered will determine its severity. Depth of burns is classified as either **partial-thickness burns** or **full-thickness burns.**

- Partial-thickness burns are divided into first-degree and second-degree burns.
  - **First-degree burns** are dry, red, painful, and slightly swollen and involve only the epidermis (e.g., sunburn).
  - **Second-degree burns** damage both the epidermis and the dermis. Symptoms include redness, swelling, and pain (because of nerve involvement), and the area is moist and blistered.
- Full-thickness burns are **third-degree burns.** The epidermis and dermis are destroyed, and the underlying tissues are damaged. Patients with third-degree burns have little or no pain because the nerve endings are damaged. The damaged tissue appears white, tan, brown, black, or cherry red.

The surface area is evaluated according to the **"rule of nines."** The total body surface is divided into regions with assigned percentages related to the number 9 (e.g., arm to include shoulder to fingertip [front and back] 9%).

Chemical Burns

Chemical burns are best treated by removing the irritant from the skin as quickly as possible.

- Dry chemicals must be brushed off of the skin *before* flushing the area with water. Adding water to the chemical may activate it and cause greater damage.
- Liquid chemicals need to be flushed immediately with large amounts of water.
- Both dry and liquid chemical burns need to be covered with a dry sterile dressing after flushing.

Always remove clothing and jewelry that may trap chemicals against the skin or on which chemicals may have spilled.

Electrical Burns

Electrical burns occur when an electric current passes through the body (e.g., lightning, electricity). A victim who has apparently been affected by some form of electrical power must be approached carefully. Assess the situation, and if a power line is down, wait for the power company to turn it off.

BOX 4-4   Signs and Symptoms of Heat Emergencies

- Altered mental status (e.g., confusion, unresponsive to questions)
- Complaints of dizziness or fainting
- Weakness or feelings of exhaustion
- Muscle cramps
- Rapid, pounding heart rate

Be certain the electrical source is off before administering first aid. At the scene, safety is a priority because you cannot provide assistance if you are injured by the electric current. Check the breathing and pulse of the victim and provide CPR if needed. Check for an entrance point and an exit point, and treat accordingly.

Exposure

Exposure to excessive heat or cold causes localized tissue damage.

Hyperthermia

Hyperthermia (increased body temperature) can manifest itself as either heat stroke or heat exhaustion. Typical signs and symptoms of heat exposure emergencies are listed in Box 4-4. Treatments include removing the patient from the hot environment, gradually cooling the body by fanning, and comforting the patient until help arrives.

Heat exhaustion occurs when the body is subjected to excessive heat (e.g., furnace room at steel plant, lack of ventilation in room with excessive heat). Symptoms include excessive sweating and skin that appears pale and feels cool and clammy. The patient may appear confused or disoriented and may complain of headache, weakness, nausea, and being tired. People suffering heat exhaustion normally have increased shallow respirations; temperature of 101° to 102° F; and a weak, rapid pulse. They should be moved to a cooler environment, have restrictive clothing loosened, be provided large amounts of fluids, and have a cold compress applied to the forehead. If the patient feels faint, the treatment includes placing the patient in a supine position with the feet slightly elevated.

Heat stroke, or sunstroke, occurs when the body is subjected to high temperatures and humidity for long periods. The body becomes dehydrated, which causes a decrease in circulating blood. The patient's skin feels hot and is red and dry (not sweating). The patient acts confused, has a high body temperature (106° F or higher), and has increased pulse and respirations. The patient's pupils are equal but dilated, and the patient may complain of feeling weak and being dizzy. Treatment requires that the person be placed in a cool area. Clothes that retain body heat should be removed. Apply cool water to the patient's skin and ice packs to areas where heat is released in the body (e.g., armpits, back of neck, groin). Slightly elevate the patient's head and shoulders. Take vital signs when equipment is available, and transport the patient for further medical attention as soon as possible.

FOR YOUR INFORMATION

Elderly persons are more prone to heat-related emergencies because their circulatory systems are less able to compensate for the stresses brought on by the heat.

Hypothermia

Hypothermia (decreased body temperature) can occur slowly when a person is exposed to extremely low temperatures for long periods, or it can occur rapidly, as when someone falls through ice or into extremely cold water. The body loses its ability to generate heat when experiencing hypothermia. Signs and symptoms of hypothermia are listed in Box 4-5. Treatment includes removal of wet clothing and application of warm clothing. Provide a hot liquid to drink and place a hot water bottle on the neck, groin, and under each arm until help arrives.

Frostbite is the freezing of body tissue. Frostbite occurs when the tissues are subjected to extreme cold over time. The patient complains of numbness, which progresses to loss of feeling in the affected area. At first the skin appears red and has a sensation of burning and itching. The skin feels cold, is hard to the touch, and may appear white in the fingertips or toes. Pressure should not be applied,

---

BOX 4-5   Signs and Symptoms of Hypothermia

- Decreased mental status (confusion, unresponsive to voice or touch)
- Abnormal skin temperature
- Decreased motor function (poor coordination, difficulty with speech)
- Slow pulse and respiration
- Shivering (and in late stages, lack of shivering)

---

and the patient should not walk on frostbitten feet. The tissue should be protected, and immediate medical attention must be sought.

Treatment for frostbite requires the body part to be gradually rewarmed in water, which should not exceed 105° F. The area should not be rubbed, but it can be placed against another body part to rewarm. The person can be offered hot drinks, which will dilate the blood vessels, and should not smoke because this causes vasoconstriction.

Musculoskeletal Injuries

Medical assistants must also be prepared to give first aid for musculoskeletal injuries that may be brought to or occur in the medical office.

Fracture

A **fracture** is any break or crack in the bone caused by trauma or disease. The appearance of a deformity is a sign that a fracture has occurred. Swelling and pain often occur in the affected area. An *open* fracture pierces through the skin, a *closed* fracture does not pierce the skin, and a *greenstick* fracture bends but does not break the bone.

The main goal for the emergency care of a fracture is to immobilize the part above and below the fracture to prevent further damage. A **splint** immobilizes the affected body part and can be made from any firm material available (e.g., cardboard, rolled newspapers). A covering of soft material is placed over the splint and held in position with rolled bandage gauze. A sling can be made to elevate the extremity and help reduce swelling (Fig. 4-11). Many devices are available to repair (reduce) a fracture, and the choice depends on the angle and severity of the break (Fig. 4-12).

Dislocation

A **dislocation** occurs when one end of a bone is separated from its original position in a joint, usually by trauma. The patient experiences pain over the joint and loses motion. To assess the degree of dislocation, do the following:

1. Check the distal pulse to make certain the extremity below the dislocation is receiving a blood supply. For example, with a shoulder injury, check the radial pulse.
2. Splint above and below the dislocated joint.
3. Keep the patient warm and observe for shock.
4. Apply an ice pack to the area.

Sprain

A **sprain** is a full or partial tear of a ligament. Care should be taken to keep the injured area immobile. In accordance with the acronym RICE, begin

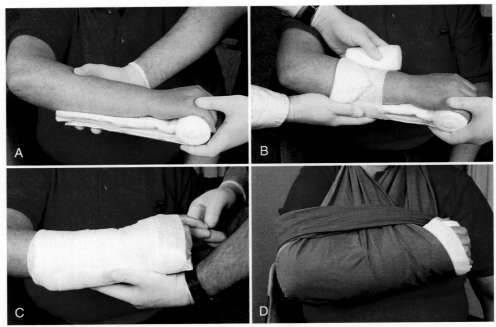

Fig. 4-11 Emergency care of a fracture. **A**, A splint should immobilize the area above and below injury. **B**, A splint is held in place with a gauze roll bandage. **C**, After a splint is supplied, pulse below the splint should be checked to make sure the splint has not been applied too tightly. **D**, A sling can be used to elevate the extremity to reduce swelling. *(From Henry M, Stapleton E: EMT prehospital care, ed 2, Philadelphia, 1997, Saunders.)*

Fig. 4-12 Devices used to reduce a fracture. *(Modified from Beare PG, Myers JL: Principles and practice of adult health nursing, ed 3, St Louis, 1998, Mosby.)*

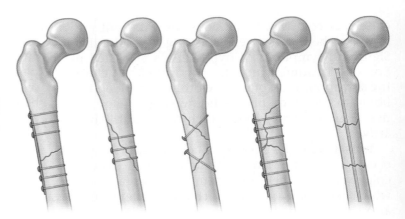

treatment within 10 to 20 minutes of the injury, as follows:

- **R**est the injured area by splinting the area.
- **I**ce the area because cold reduces bleeding, swelling, and muscle spasms in injured muscles.
- **C**ompress the area by wrapping with an elastic bandage to minimize swelling.
- **E**levate the injured area to heart level if possible. This reduces circulation to the affected area.

Strain
A **strain** is a stretching or tearing of a muscle or tendon. As with a fracture, immobilize the area.

Have the person assume a comfortable position to take pressure off the injured muscle. Apply heat to the area, and provide support if available.

Poisons

A **poison** is any substance that causes injury, illness, and even death in an individual. Signs and symptoms of having ingested a poison are listed in Box 4-6.

Ingested Poison
Ingested poisons are taken in by mouth and travel through the digestive system. When poison has been ingested, always call the nearest poison control

BOX 4-6   Signs and Symptoms of Poison Ingestion

- Altered mental status (confusion)
- Chemical burns around the mouth
- Breath odor of chemical
- Difficulty breathing
- Nausea
- Vomiting
- Abdominal pain
- Diarrhea

center for advice; inform the center of the type of poison ingested and, if a medication is involved, the name of the medication, dosage, and the number of pills taken or missing from the bottle. If the person does not know how many pills were taken, the number remaining in the bottle can be subtracted from the number dispensed.

Emergency care for a person who has ingested poison is as follows:

1. Call 911.
2. Maintain the airway.
3. Position the patient to keep the airway clear.
4. Induce vomiting if the manufacturer or the poison control center provides this recommendation. Vomiting prevents absorption of the remainder of certain poisons if done within 1 to 2 hours of ingestion. Activated charcoal is the substance of choice for neutralizing poisons that have been swallowed. It should be administered only if the airway is clear and the patient's mental status is not impaired. *Do not induce vomiting* unless instructed to do so by the poison control center. If the patient has ingested corrosive or caustic (burning) materials or petroleum products (e.g., bleach, cleaners), rinse the mouth with cool water, without swallowing. The American Academy of Pediatrics no longer recommends the use of ipecac syrup.
5. Position the patient leaning forward to prevent aspiration of stomach contents.

Be prepared for poisoning; always have the poison control center's phone number posted at the receptionist's desk. Patients will often call the office first.

Inhaled Poison

Inhaled poison vapors and fumes usually result from a fire or chemical spill (e.g., carbon monoxide, cleaning solvents). Emergency care is as follows:

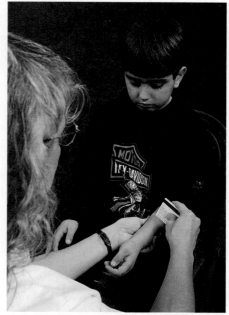

Fig. 4-13 Removing a honeybee stinger and venom sac using the edge of a credit card. *(From Bonewit-West K: Clinical procedures for medical assistants, ed 6, Philadelphia, 2004, Saunders.)*

1. Call 911.
2. Protect yourself, and remove the patient from the source.
3. Loosen clothing that may affect breathing.
4. Assess breathing and perform rescue breathing or CPR if necessary.

Injected Poison

Injected poisons can be drugs or venom from spider, snake, and other insect bites. For insect stings, the area should be washed with soap and water after the stinger has been removed (Fig. 4-13). Observe the patient for signs of an allergic reaction, such as redness, swelling, and difficulty breathing. Symptoms and treatments for bites and stings are listed in Table 4-4.

Diabetic Emergencies

Two types of emergencies can affect the diabetic patient: insulin shock **(hypoglycemia)** and diabetic ketoacidosis **(hyperglycemia).**

Insulin Shock

Insulin shock (low blood sugar level) occurs when the patient has taken too much insulin; has not eaten enough to use up the insulin taken; or has exercised heavily, using up available glucose in the body. The patient appears pale, and the skin feels cool and clammy. Patients usually complain of being lightheaded or hungry. They may appear

TABLE 4-4 Treatment Guidelines for Bites and Bee Stings

Bite or Sting	Symptoms or Signs	Treatment Guidelines
Snake bite, spider bite, scorpion bite	Pain Swelling Redness Bleeding	1. Ask victim to lie still with bitten area lower than the heart 2. Tie strip of cloth, shoestring, watchband, or belt about 3 inches above bite, making sure one finger can fit between strip and skin 3. Wash bitten area thoroughly with soap and water 4. Do not cut bite unless you have special training 5. Observe for signs of shock 6. *Snake or spider:* Try to identify markings on snake or type of spider; if dead, bring to emergency department (ED) 7. Transport victim to ED as soon as possible
Human and animal bites	Pain Swelling Redness Bleeding Human bites worst	1. Wash bite thoroughly with soap and water 2. Control bleeding by applying direct pressure; ice may be applied 3. Raise injured limb above level of the heart (helps control bleeding) 4. When bleeding stops, apply clean bandage (not too tight) 5. *Wild animal:* Try to capture or kill animal (without being bitten yourself) 6. *Domestic animal:* Obtain name and address of owner to report to health department 7. Seek medical attention for victim
Tick bites	Pain Tick may be attached	1. Remove tick if attached by cutting off its oxygen supply; cover tick with petroleum jelly or any oil, or gasoline; remove tick when it backs out of skin 2. Wash area thoroughly with soap and water 3. Seek medical attention if bite becomes infected or victim becomes sick, has joint pain, or develops rash on palms of hands (Lyme disease or Rocky Mountain spotted fever)
Bee stings	Pain Swelling Raised lump Stinger may be attached	1. If honeybee stinger attached, remove it carefully with tweezers, or scrape it with edge of knife or credit card (see Fig. 4-13) 2. Avoid squeezing venom sac on tip of stinger 3. Wash area thoroughly with soap and water 4. Elevate stung area above the heart and apply ice to control swelling 5. Antihistamines may help localized swelling 6. Seek medical attention if site becomes infected or victim shows signs of severe allergic reaction (hives, itching, wheezing)

restless or appear agitated. Vital signs are **within normal limits (WNL).**

To assess the situation, ask the patient if food was eaten after taking insulin. If the patient did not eat or had time for only minimal food, provide the patient with sugary nourishment (e.g., orange juice, white sugar dissolved in water, glucose gel or tablets) followed by proteins and fats, such as peanut butter, which will maintain the glucose level. The blood glucose level should be assessed with a glucose meter. If the condition does not improve, seek emergency assistance.

Diabetic Ketoacidosis

Diabetic ketoacidosis occurs when glucose builds up in the patient's blood without sufficient insulin, and ketones (acid waste byproducts) are produced. This situation requires a 911 call. A change in the patient's medical condition (e.g., infection, common cold) or glucose overload when eating without adequate insulin can lead to ketoacidosis. The patient tends to be confused and has diminished responsiveness. The skin feels hot and dry and is reddened. The patient's vital signs are severely affected. Respirations become very deep and gasping, then become rapid **(Kussmaul breathing),** and the pulse is thready and weak. A sweet or fruity odor caused by acetone buildup is detected. The physician will order a glucose level to assess the need for insulin to be given immediately (stat).

Choking

Choking is caused by a blockage in the trachea or from a swelling of the larynx caused by an injury. Box 4-7 lists possible food and household choking hazards, especially for children.

- A partial airway obstruction begins with a coughing episode and progresses to the patient not being able to breathe.

BOX 4-7	Possible Food and Household Choking Hazards

Pieces of meat and uncooked vegetables
Nuts
Hard candy
Marshmallows
Chunks of peanut butter
Balloons
Coins
Pen caps

- With a complete airway obstruction, the patient cannot speak or breathe. The face will redden and will rapidly change to purple if the obstruction is not removed.

Patients who are conscious can usually indicate they are choking by clutching at their throat (Fig. 4-14). This nonverbal communication is referred to as the "universal sign for choking." If the cough is forceful, allow the person to continue coughing because this type of action indicates air is getting into the lungs. If the coughing fails to dislodge the obstruction, emergency action is needed to remove the cause of the obstruction. The type of action depends on whether the patient is conscious or unconscious.

Conscious Individuals

The **Heimlich maneuver,** or *abdominal thrust,* is an emergency procedure used to dislodge the cause of a blockage. Abdominal thrusts are recommended only for conscious patients with an airway obstruction.

The Heimlich maneuver is performed as follows (Procedure 4-1):

1. The rescuer wraps his or her arms around the patient from behind.
2. The rescuer's fist, with thumb facing the abdomen of the victim, is placed just below the sternum and xiphoid process and above the umbilicus. The other hand is placed over the fist.

Fig. 4-14 A choking person will usually clutch the throat. This is considered to be the universal distress signal. *(From Sorrentino SA:* Assisting with patient care, *ed 2, St Louis, 2004, Mosby.)*

Procedure 4-1 Perform the Heimlich Maneuver

TASK: Remove airway obstruction and restore breathing to an adult.

EQUIPMENT AND SUPPLIES
- Nonsterile disposable gloves (when available)
- Pocket ventilation mask (for unresponsive patient, when available)
- Adult-sized CPR mannequin (approved for FBAO practice)

SKILLS/RATIONALE

STANDARD PRECAUTIONS ARE TO BE FOLLOWED.

1. **Procedural Step. Assess the victim.**
   Ask the victim, "Are you choking?" If the victim responds in the affirmative, ask, "Can you speak?" If the victim is unable to speak, assure the victim that you are going to help. The universal signal for choking is to place the hands crossed at the throat.
   Rationale. If the victim can speak or can cough forcefully, the victim should be encouraged to continue coughing; this indicates air exchange even if an obstruction is present. If the victim cannot speak and has a weak cough or is wheezing, this indicates a partial airway obstruction, which must be removed immediately before respiratory arrest occurs.

2. **Procedural Step. Position yourself behind the victim.**
   With feet slightly apart, stand behind the victim and wrap your arms around the victim's waist

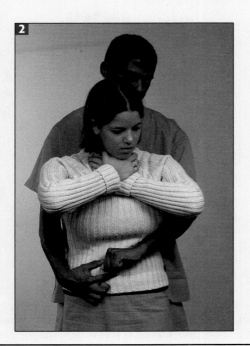

with the fist and thumb against the abdomen, above the umbilicus, and below the sternum and xiphoid process.
   Rationale. Standing directly behind the victim with an open stance provides a secure position for support should the victim become unconscious.

3. **Procedural Step. Grasp your fist with your other hand, and place the thumb of that fist toward the victim.**

4. **Procedural Step. Press your fist into the victim's abdomen with a quick inward and upward thrust.**
   Each thrust must be separate and distinct. The force behind the first thrust must be the greatest.
   Rationale. After the first thrust, the victim will reflexively guard, making it more difficult to generate enough force to push out the obstruction.

5. **Procedural Step. Repeat thrusts until the obstruction is removed or until the victim becomes unconscious.**

6. **Procedural Step. If the victim becomes unconscious or unresponsive, immediately activate the emergency response system.**
   Rationale. If not relieved of the obstruction, the victim will go into respiratory arrest, which will ultimately lead to cardiac arrest. The quicker the victim can be transported to an emergency facility or receive advanced care (tracheotomy), the greater is the chance of survival.

7. **Procedural Step. Apply gloves if available, and open the victim's mouth to perform a finger sweep.**
   If the object is in the mouth, remove it.

8. **Procedural Step. Attempt ventilation.**
   Open the victim's airway using the head-tilt, chin-lift or jaw thrust maneuver. Using a protective barrier, if available, provide the victim with two slow breaths in an attempt at ventilation. If ventilation is unsuccessful, reposition the head and try again.
   You should see the chest rise and fall if ventilation occurs.

Procedure 4-1 Perform the Heimlich Maneuver—cont'd

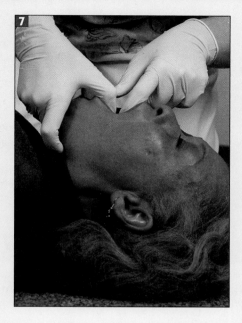

9. **Procedural Step. Position yourself for chest thrusts (compressions).**
   If ventilation is unsuccessful, kneel at the victim's side. Locate the sternum and place your hand below the nipple line and the other hand on top of the first hand.

10. **Procedural Step. Administer 30 chest compressions, then 2 breaths.**
    Use only the heels of your hands to administer compressions.

11. **Procedural Step. Return to the victim's head, reposition the head, and look in the airway.**
    If the object is visible and loose, remove it.

12. **Procedural Step. If the obstruction has not released, repeat Steps 9 to 11 until EMS arrives or the obstruction is expelled.**

13. **Procedural Step. If the obstruction is expelled, monitor the victim's breathing and circulation.**
    If the victim has a pulse but is not breathing, perform rescue breathing. If the victim is not breathing and has no pulse, initiate CPR.

14. **Procedural Step. Remain with the victim until he or she has stabilized or EMS assumes responsibility for the victim.**

CPR, Cardiopulmonary resuscitation; *FBAO,* foreign body airway obstruction; *EMS,* emergency medical services.

3. An upward thrust is done in an attempt to dislodge the foreign body in the trachea (Fig. 4-15). This pushes the diaphragm up, forcing air from the lungs and the obstruction from the trachea.

Unconscious Individuals

For individuals who are unconscious, a combination of chest compressions and looking into the airway is used instead of the Heimlich maneuver. If the patient is unconscious and slightly blue and no air movement is evident, do the following:

1. Check the airway by looking in and if the object is visible and loose, remove it, then reposition the head and neck and attempt to breathe.
2. Reposition the patient if necessary, and kneel beside the patient.

3. Give five abdominal thrusts with the heel of the hand. Always look into the airway after each abdominal thrust, and repeat as needed.

An infant with a complete airway obstruction, manifested by the inability to cry or breathe, should have alternating blows to the back and chest thrusts to dislodge the foreign body forcibly from the airway.

PATIENT-CENTERED PROFESSIONALISM

- What are some general guidelines to help the medical assistant best handle an office emergency?
- Why is knowledge of how to handle each specific type of office emergency critical to the safety of the patients who visit the office?

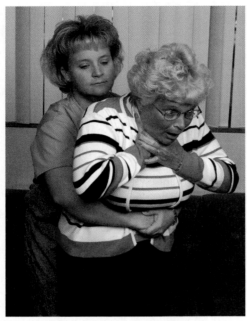

Fig. 4-15 Abdominal thrusts with the person standing. *(From Sorrentino SA: Assisting with patient care, ed 2, St Louis, 2004, Mosby.)*

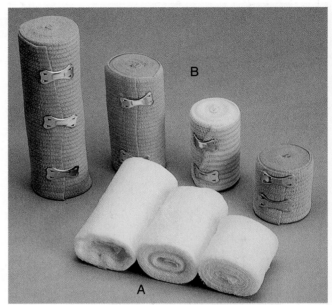

Fig. 4-16 **A,** Cloth bandages. **B,** Elastic bandages. *(From Young AP, Kennedy DB: Kinn's the medical assistant, ed 9, Philadelphia, 2003, Saunders.)*

BANDAGING

Bandages have many uses, including the following:

- Support or **immobilization** of an injured body part.
- Securing a dressing (e.g., gauze) in place.
- Application of pressure to control bleeding.

Medical assistants need to be familiar with the types of bandages available and the basic bandage turns.

Types of Bandages

The two types of bandages most often used by the medical assistant are elastic cloth bandages and wrinkled gauze–type roller bandages such as Kling bandages. Tubular gauze is also used in some medical offices.

- **Elastic bandages** can be stretched and molded around a body part. They can be removed and reused on the same patient as long as they are not soiled (Fig. 4-16, *A*).
- **Kling-type bandages** stretch but are not elastic. They mold around irregular areas and are most often used to hold dressings in place on the head or extremities (Fig. 4-16, *B*).
- **Tubular gauze** bandages consist of loose, elastic cotton fibers in a tubular roll and use a

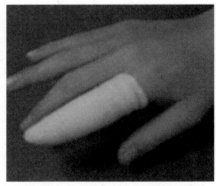

Fig 4-17 Tubular gauze bandage application. *(From Zakus SM: Mosby's clinical skills for medical assistants, ed 4, St Louis, 2001, Mosby.)*

metal tube for application. Essentially, tubular gauze is used to cover rounded body parts such as fingers and toes (Fig. 4-17). Tubular gauze can also be applied over a sterile dressing to keep the dressing in place. Procedure 4-2 explains the process of applying a tubular gauze bandage.

It is important to inspect the patient's skin for any break or swelling when applying a bandage. In addition, be sure not to impair circulation when applying the bandage.

Bandage Turns

There are basically five **bandage turns** that are used either to support or to secure: the circular,

Procedure 4-2 Apply a Tubular Gauze Bandage

TASK: Properly apply a gauze bandage to the affected area.

EQUIPMENT AND SUPPLIES
- Tube gauze applicator
- Roll of tubular gauze
- Adhesive tape
- Patient's medical record

SKILLS/RATIONALE

STANDARD PRECAUTIONS ARE TO BE FOLLOWED.

1. **Procedural Step. Sanitize the hands.**
   An alcohol-based hand rub may be used instead of washing hands with soap and water, unless hands are visibly soiled.
   Rationale. Hand sanitization promotes infection control.

2. **Procedural Step. Assemble equipment and supplies.**
   Tube gauze applicators come in a variety of sizes. Select a size that is slightly larger than the appendage to be bandaged. Select a tube gauze width that is wide enough to fit over the appendage but narrow enough to ensure a snug fit.
   Rationale. It is important to have all supplies and equipment ready and available before starting any procedure to ensure efficiency. The applicator should be larger than the body part to allow the gauze to slide easily over it.

3. **Procedural Step. Obtain the patient's medical record.**

4. **Procedural Step. Escort the patient to the examination room, greet and identify the patient, and ask the patient to have a seat on the end of the examination table.**
   Rationale. Identifying the patient ensures the procedure is performed on the correct patient.

5. **Procedural Step. Explain the procedure to the patient.**
   Rationale. Explaining the procedure to the patient promotes cooperation and provides a means of obtaining implied consent.

6. **Procedural Step. Prepare the bandage.**
   Pull a sufficient length of gauze from the boxed roll, approximately 6 to 10 times the length of the appendage, depending on the desired thickness of the completed bandage. Cut the length of gauze from the roll. Spread one end of the tube gauze apart by inserting your fingers into the opening. Slide the now-open end of the tube gauze onto the applicator. Continue to push the tube gauze onto the applicator until the entire length of gauze has been loaded onto the applicator.

7. **Procedural Step. Gently slide the applicator over the proximal end of the appendage.**

8. **Procedural Step. Anchor the bandage at the proximal end of the appendage with the fingers of your nondominant hand, and pull the applicator away from the proximal end toward the distal end.**
   Rationale. The tube gauze must be held in place to prevent it from sliding. If the bandage is not secured, the appendage will not be completely covered.

9. **Procedural Step. Pull the applicator approximately 1 inch past the distal end of the patient's appendage.**
   Continue to hold the bandage in place with your fingers at the proximal end.
   Rationale. The bandage must extend beyond the length of the patient's appendage in order to secure it at the distal end.

10. **Procedural Step. Rotate the applicator one full turn to anchor the bandage.**
    Rationale. Anchoring the bandage holds it securely in place.

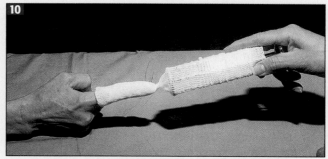

11. **Procedural Step. Fit the applicator back over the distal end of the appendage, and gently push forward toward the proximal end of the patient's appendage.**
    Rationale. Moving the applicator forward applies a second layer of bandaging material to the patient's appendage.

Continued

Procedure 4-2 Apply a Tubular Gauze Bandage—cont'd

12. **Procedural Step. Repeat Steps 9 to 11 to accomplish the number of layers needed.**
13. **Procedural Step. Finish the last layer at the proximal end, remove the applicator, and trim the excess gauze as needed.**

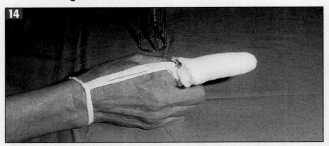

14 **Procedural Step. Apply adhesive tape at the base of the appendage to secure the bandage.**
An alternative to adhesive tape is to secure the length of tube gauze remaining on the applicator around the patient's wrist or ankle.

This is done by cutting the length of tube gauze down two sides, bringing it over the back of the hand or foot, and tying the two now-loose ends around the patient's wrist or ankle.

NOTE: The tube gauze should never cross the patient's palm or sole.

15. **Procedural Step. Sanitize the hands.**
Always sanitize the hands after every procedure or after using gloves.
16. **Procedural Step. Document the procedure.**
Include the date, time, and location of the bandage application.

Charting Example

Date	
3/10/xx	10:30 a.m. Tubular gauze bandage applied to the index finger of the ® hand. ———— E. Simons, CMA (AAMA)

Photos from Young AP, Kennedy DB: *Kinn's the medical assistant,* ed 9, Philadelphia, 2003, Saunders.

---

spiral, spiral reverse, figure-eight, and recurrent turns. It is important to remember that all bandaging begins at the distal end and proceeds proximally.

1. The **circular turn** is used on areas that are uniform in width, such as the fingers, toes, head, and wrist (Fig. 4-18). Each turn overlaps the previous turn. A circular turn can also be used to anchor a bandage.
2. A **spiral turn** is used where body parts are uniform in circumference, such as the arms and legs (Fig. 4-19). The bandage progresses upward, and each spiral turn overlaps the previous turn by ½ inch.
3. The **spiral reverse turn** is used when the area to be bandaged is of various widths, such as the forearm and lower legs (calf area) (Fig. 4-20). By reversing the turn, a smoother fit is accomplished, with less bulkiness. Each turn repositions the bandage downward and folds on itself as in the spiral turn.
4. The **figure-eight turn** is most often used to hold a dressing in place or to support a jointed area, such as the ankle and wrist. The bandage is applied on a slant and progresses upward, then downward, around the body part being wrapped (Fig. 4-21).

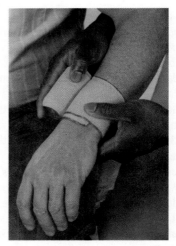

Fig. 4-18 A circular bandage turn anchors a bandage.

5. The **recurrent turn** is most frequently used for a stump area or for the head (Fig. 4-22). The bandage is first anchored by using a circular turn and then moves back and forth over the end of the part to be bandaged. Each turn overlaps the next turn.

It is important to remember that once the bandage has been applied to the body part, the area

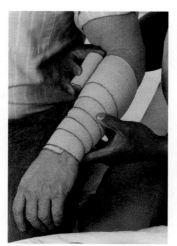

Fig. 4-19 A spiral bandage turn is used to wrap the arm or leg. Always wrap from distal to proximal.

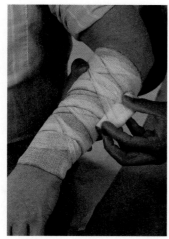

Fig. 4-20 In a spiral reverse bandage turn, the direction of the spiral changes each time the bandage is brought around the limb.

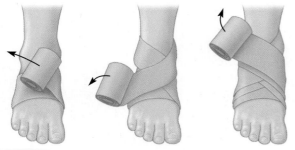

Fig. 4-21 Use of figure-eight bandage turns for the ankle. *(Modified from Bonewit-West K: Clinical procedures for medical assistants, ed 6, Philadelphia, 2004, Saunders.)*

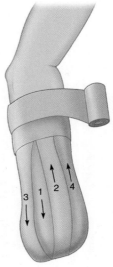

Fig. 4-22 A recurrent bandage turn is used for a below-the-knee amputee. *(Modified from Bonewit-West K: Clinical procedures for medical assistants, ed 6, Philadelphia, 2004, Saunders.)*

below the bandage must be checked. Checking below the site for *capillary refill* (blood to fingers or toes) ensures that the application of the bandage is not too tight. Typical signs that circulation may be impaired include swelling, a pale or bluish color to the skin, coolness to the touch, and a complaint of pain, numbness, or tingling to the area.

Fig. 4-23 illustrates various bandage-wrapping techniques for various body parts.

PATIENT-CENTERED PROFESSIONALISM

- Why must the medical assistant understand how the different types of bandages are to be used?
- What could happen if the medical assistant applied the wrong type of bandage turn?

BASIC LIFE SUPPORT

Cardiac arrest is the sudden cessation of heart activity. It can occur at any time without warning. Unless the patient's heart activity is restored quickly, permanent brain damage or death will occur. If a patient stops breathing **(respiratory arrest)** because of an airway obstruction, the heart can still pump for several minutes. Current American Heart Association Guidelines recommend beginning any adult rescue as if the heart has stopped (Procedure 4-5). After giving 30 chest compressions, the airway

Foot and ankle

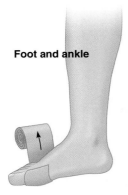

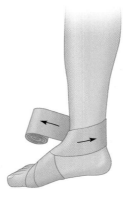

Use 3-inch width. Hold foot at right angle to leg. Start bandage on right of foot just back of the toes.

Pass bandage around foot from inside to outside. After two or three complete turns around foot, ascending toward the ankle on each turn, make a figure eight turn by bringing bandage up and over the arch -

to the inside of the ankle - around the ankle - down over the arch - and under the foot.

Repeat the figure-eight wrapping two to three times. Fasten end by pressing the last 4 to 6 inches of unstretched bandage to the preceding layer.

Lower leg

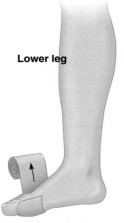

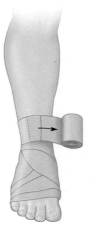

Use 3- to 4-inch width depending on the size of the leg. A leg wrap requires two rolls of bandage. Hold foot at right angle to leg. Start bandage on ridge of foot just back of the toes.

Pass bandage around foot from inside to outside. After two complete turns around foot, make a figure-eight turn by bringing bandage up over the arch - to the inside of the ankle - around the ankle -

down over the arch - and under the foot. Start circular bandaging, making the first turn around the ankle. To begin the second roll of bandage, simply overlap the unstretched ends by 4 to 6 inches, press firmly, and continue wrapping.

Wrap bandage in spiral turns to just below the kneecap. Fasten end by pressing the last 4 to 6 inches of unstretched bandage to the preceding layer.

Knee

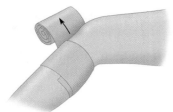

Use 4-inch width. Bend knee slightly. Start with one complete circular turn around the leg just below the knee.

Start circular bandaging, applying only comfortable tension. Cover kneecap completely.

Continue wrapping to thigh just above the knee. Fasten end by pressing the last 4 to 6 inches of unstretched bandage to the preceding layer.

Fig. 4-23 Bandage-wrapping techniques illustrating the circular, spiral, and figure-eight turns.

Wrist

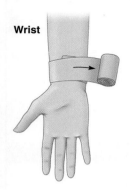 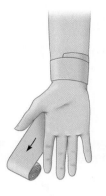 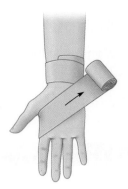 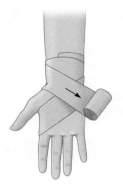 

Use 2- or 3-inch width. Anchor bandage loosely at the wrist with one complete circular turn.

Carry the bandage across the back of the hand, through the web space between the thumb and index finger

and across palm to the wrist

Make a circular turn around the wrist and once more carry the bandage through the web space and back to the wrist.

Start circular bandaging, ascending the wrist. Fasten end by pressing last 4 to 6 inches of unstretched bandage to the preceding layer.

Elbow

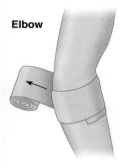  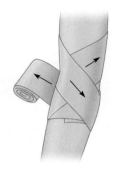 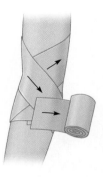 

Use 3- or 4-inch width, depending on the size of the arm. Two rolls of bandage are required to complete the wrap. Start with a complete circular turn just below the elbow.

Wrap bandage in loose figure eights

to form a protective bridge across the front of the elbow joint.

Fasten end by pressing 4 to 6 inches of unstretched bandage to the preceding layer. Start second bandage with a circular turn below the elbow

over the first wrap. Continue spiral bandaging over the elbow, ascending to the lower portion of the arm. Fasten end with a circular turn.

Shoulder

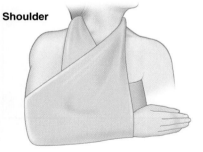  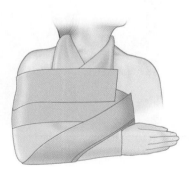

A shoulder wrap is used to provide additional support for an arm in a sling. Use 4- or 6-inch width. One or two rolls of bandage may be used. Start under the free arm.

Carry the bandage across the back, over the arm in the sling, across the chest and back under the free arm in complete circular, overlapping turns. Fasten the end by pressing 4 to 6 inches of unstretched bandage to underlying bandage.

Additional support can be obtained with a second bandage. Start at the back just behind the flexed elbow in the sling. Carry the bandage under the elbow, up over the forearm, around the chest and back, and repeat. Fasten end.

Fig. 4-23, cont'd

Procedure 4-3 Open an Airway

TASK: Open the airway of an unresponsive victim using the head-tilt, chin-lift or jaw thrust maneuver.

EQUIPMENT AND SUPPLIES
- Nonsterile disposable gloves (if available)
- Adult-sized CPR mannequin

SKILLS/RATIONALE

STANDARD PRECAUTIONS ARE TO BE FOLLOWED.

Head-Tilt, Chin-Lift Maneuver

1 **Procedural Step. Tilt the head.**
Apply gloves if available. Place one hand on the forehead and the fingers of the other hand under the chin.
Rationale. This lifts the tongue base away from the throat.

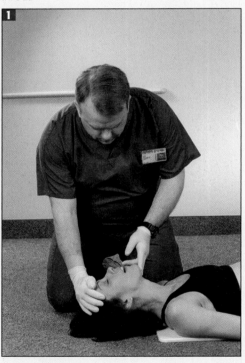

2. **Procedural Step. Apply gentle pressure to the forehead while lifting the chin upward until the teeth are touching but the mouth is not completely closed.**
The thumb may be used to move the lower lip away from the upper lip, if necessary.
3. **Procedural Step. Look, listen, and feel for air movement.**
If there is no air movement, proceed with rescue breathing.

Jaw Thrust Maneuver
1. **Procedural Step. Position yourself above the victim's head.**
2. **Procedural Step. Place both thumbs on the victim's cheekbones, and place the index and middle fingers on both sides of the lower jaw where it angles toward the ear.**
3. **Procedural Step. While using the cheekbones to stabilize the head, lift the jaw upward, *without tilting the head or flexing the cervical spine.***
4. **Procedural Step. Look, listen, and feel for air movement.**
If there is no air movement, proceed with rescue breathing.

is opened and rescue breathing is begun. Procedure 4-3 describes how to open an airway, and Procedure 4-4 outlines the technique for rescue breathing. Remember, always assess the situation before taking action. If the victim is not responsive or is unconscious, follow the basic "CAB" guidelines:

- *Compressions* should be started immediately at a rate of 100/minute.
- *Airway* must be open.
- *Breathing* must be assessed.

Be especially aware of any head or neck trauma that could be associated with a spinal injury.

Cardiopulmonary Resuscitation

Cardiopulmonary resuscitation (CPR) is performed to restore breathing and cardiac activity to the heart. CPR must be started as quickly as possible, because this activity provides oxygen to the vital organs until more advanced care can be provided.

Procedure 4-4 Perform Rescue Breathing

TASK: Restore breathing.

EQUIPMENT AND SUPPLIES
- Nonsterile disposable gloves (if available)
- Pocket ventilation mask (if available)
- Adult-size CPR mannequin

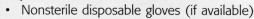

SKILLS

STANDARD PRECAUTIONS ARE TO BE FOLLOWED.

1. **Procedural Step. Establish unresponsiveness.**
   Tap the victim on the shoulder and shout, "Are you OK?" Wait for a response. If no response, proceed with rescue breathing.
2. **Procedural Step. Open the airway with the head-tilt, chin-lift or jaw thrust maneuver.**
   Apply gloves, if available. Look, listen, and feel for breathing. Assess for 5 seconds. Once the need for rescue breathing has been established, alert EMS, then seal your mouth or mask completely around the victim's mouth while pinching the nose and maintaining an airway.
3. **Procedural Step. Deliver two smooth breaths while observing for chest rise out of the corner of your eye.**

Each breath should take 1½ to 2 seconds to deliver. Take your mouth away from the victim's mouth or mask after each breath so that you can take another breath. Avoid breathing the exhaled air from the victim.

4. **Procedural Step. Assess for circulation.**
   If the pulse is present, administer one breath every 5 seconds for an adult and one breath every 3 seconds for an infant or child until the victim begins to breathe adequately.
5. **Procedural Step. If breathing does not resume, continue with Steps 3 and 4 until EMS arrives and assumes responsibility.**

---

1. Before beginning CPR, 911 (EMS) should be called and an AED (automated external defibrillator) should be obtained if available.
2. Place the person in a supine position on a hard surface.
3. If there is no AED, begin compressions using the heels of both hands. An individual without CPR training should continue compressions until help or an AED arrives.
4. After 30 compressions, an individual who has been trained in CPR should put on gloves (if available) and open the airway. The *head tilt–chin lift method* is often used.
5. Begin rescue breathing, using a pocket mask if available. Give two breaths and 30 chest compressions using the heels of both hands.

See Procedure 4-5 for one-person adult CPR. If two rescuers are available, the second rescuer should call 911 and go to get an AED if it is available while the first rescuer begins compressions.   Then the second rescuer can join with the first to perform two-person CPR (Procedure 4-6).

Automated External Defibrillator

The **automated external defibrillator (AED)** is a machine that analyzes the patient's cardiac

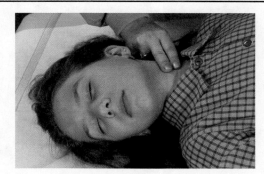

Fig. 4-24   A child older than 1 year can have the carotid artery palpated.

rhythm and can deliver an electrical shock (**defibrillation**) to the heart to stop an erratic rhythm or restart the cardiac cycle. The chance of surviving sudden cardiac arrest decreases by 10% with every minute that passes without action. Technological advances allow these machines to be operated by almost everyone with minimal training.

There are two types of external defibrillators: fully automatic and semi-automatic. An AED should not be attached to a patient who is responsive. Also, transdermal patches should be removed because they often have an aluminum backing, or the patch's paste medium is reactive to defibrillation. Be sure that the patient is not touching metal, and be

Procedure 4-5 Perform One-Person Adult CPR

TASK: Restore breathing and circulation to an adult.

EQUIPMENT AND SUPPLIES
- Nonsterile disposable gloves (if available)
- Pocket ventilation mask (if available)
- Adult-size CPR mannequin

SKILLS/RATIONALE

STANDARD PRECAUTIONS ARE TO BE FOLLOWED.

1. **Procedural Step. Establish unresponsiveness.**
   Tap the victim on the shoulder and shout, "Are you OK?" Wait for a response. If there is no response, call 911 and go to get an AED if one is available.

2. Locate the xiphoid process. Place your index and middle fingers of the hand closest to the victim's feet along the margin of the ribs, then slide up to the bottom of the breastbone (two fingers). Place the heel of the hand closest to the victim's head next to the fingers, and place the heel of the other hand directly over the hand on the sternum; interlock the fingers to avoid pressure in the area of the ribs.

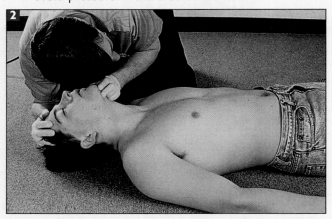

3. **Procedural Step. Begin chest compressions at a rate of 100 compressions per minute.**
   During compressions, it is important to count out loud "1 and 2 and 3 and 4" and so on.
   Rationale. Counting out loud forces the rescuer to breathe. It is natural to hold the breath in times of emergency and excitement.

4. **Procedural Step. Maintain correct body position.**
   While performing chest compressions, your shoulders, elbows, and the heels of your hands should be in alignment directly over the victim's sternum.

Rationale. This position gives you the most control, inflicts the least amount of damage to the victim's ribs, and provides the most effective compressions."

5. **Procedural Step. Perform 30 compressions.**

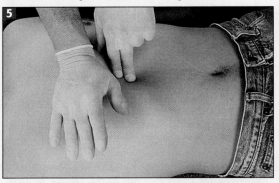

6. **Procedural Step. Open the airway with the head-tilt, chin-lift, or jaw thrust method.**
   Apply gloves, if available. Look, listen, and feel for breathing. Assess for 5-10 seconds. Seal your mouth or mask completely around the victim's mouth while pinching the nose and maintaining an airway. (Use your CPR mask if available.)

7. **Procedural Step. Deliver two smooth breaths while observing for chest rise out of the corner of your eye.**
   Each breath should take 1½ to 2 seconds to deliver. Take your mouth away from the victim's mouth or mask after each breath so that you can take another breath. Avoid breathing the exhaled air from the victim. Continue compressions and breaths at a ratio of 30 : 2.

8. **Procedural Step. After 5 cycles (about 2 minutes) use the AED (if available) according to the directions on the device to administer 1 shock. Use pediatric pads if available on a child (ages 1-8).**
   Continue CPR for two minutes, then administer a second shock. If an AED is not available, continue CPR until help arrives.

9. **Procedural Step. Continue with CPR until the victim stabilizes or EMS arrives and assumes responsibility.**

Photos from Young AP, Kennedy DB: *Kinn's the medical assistant,* ed 9, Philadelphia, 2003, Saunders.

Procedure 4-6 Perform Two-Person Adult CPR

TASK: Restore breathing and circulation to an adult using two people.

EQUIPMENT AND SUPPLIES
- Nonsterile disposable gloves (if available)
- Pocket ventilation mask (if available)
- Adult-size CPR mannequin

SKILLS/RATIONALE

STANDARD PRECAUTIONS ARE TO BE FOLLOWED.

1. **Procedural Step. Establish unresponsiveness.**
Tap the victim on the shoulder and shout, "Are you OK?" Wait for a response. If there is no response, one person calls 911 and goes to get an AED if one is available.

2. One rescuer should locate the xiphoid process and place the index and middle fingers of the hand closest to the victim's feet along the margin of the ribs, then slide up to the bottom of the breastbone (two fingers). Place the heel of the hand closest to the victim's head next to the fingers, and place the heel of the other hand directly over the hand on the sternum; interlock the fingers to avoid pressure in the area of the ribs.

3. **Procedural Step. Begin chest compressions at a rate of 100 compressions per minute.**
During compressions, it is important to count out loud "1 and 2 and 3 and 4" and so on.
Rationale. Counting out loud forces the rescuer to breathe. It is natural to hold the breath in times of emergency and excitement.

4. **Procedural Step. Maintain correct body position.**
While performing chest compressions, your shoulders, elbows, and the heels of your hands should be in alignment directly over the victim's sternum.
Rationale. This position gives you the most control, inflicts the least amount of damage to the victim's ribs, and provides the most effective compressions.

5. **Procedural Step. Perform 30 compressions.**

6. **Procedural Step. This step would be performed by the first rescuer or the second rescuer if he or she has finished calling 911 and obtaining an AED.**
Open the airway with the head-tilt, chin-lift, or jaw thrust method. Apply gloves, if available. Look, listen, and feel for breathing. Assess for 5-10 seconds. Seal your mouth or mask completely around the victim's mouth while pinching the nose and maintaining an airway. (Use your CPR mask if available.)

7. **Procedural Step. Deliver two smooth breaths while observing for chest rise out of the corner of your eye.**
Each breath should take 1½ to 2 seconds to deliver. Take your mouth away from the victim's mouth or mask after each breath so that you can take another breath. Avoid breathing the exhaled air from the victim.

8. One rescuer continues with chest compressions while the other rescuer gives breaths at a ratio of 30 : 2. Compressions should stop while breaths are given. Rescuers can change places.

9. **Procedural Step. After 5 cycles (about 2 minutes) use the AED (if available) according to the directions on the device to administer 1 shock.**
Use pediatric pads if available on a child (ages 1-8). Continue CPR for two minutes, then administer a second shock. If an AED is not available, continue CPR until help arrives.

sure that there isn't a large amount of water on the chest.

Fully Automatic Defibrillator
The fully automatic external defibrillator requires the rescuer to place two defibrillator patches on the patient's chest, connect the lead wires, and turn on the AED. The machine will analyze and shock the victim with no action by the rescuer. After three shocks, check the pulse. The machine will state "clear the patient" before delivering the shocks, or "no shock indicated" if the AED does not detect a shockable rhythm. Once it is determined the patient has no pulse, CPR should begin. Even after successful resuscitation, the AED should not be disconnected because ventricular fibrillation could occur.

Semi-Automatic Defibrillator
The semi-automatic defibrillator requires the rescuer to attach the patches and leads to the patient's chest, turn on the AED, and press a button. The computer analyzes the rhythm, and the computer-synthesized voice advises the rescuer what steps to take.

Pediatric CPR

Children (age 1 to 8) in cardiac arrest usually have experienced trauma or a respiratory emergency rather than a cardiovascular problem. After the rescuer determines that the child is unresponsive, a quick assessment is performed. The nature of any spinal, bone, or neck injuries may be obvious from the child's location and position. If the child is moved, the head and neck must be supported firmly to avoid twisting or tilting the neck.

- As with an adult victim, follow the CAB guidelines, but a single rescuer should begin with two minutes (5 cycles) of CPR before calling 911. If alone, begin by giving 30 chest compressions. The child must be in a supine position and on a hard surface. Locate the xiphoid process on the chest. Place the heel of the hand over the lower half of the sternum between the nipple line and the xiphoid process (Fig. 4-25). The compressions-to-ventilation ratio is 30 to 2. After the first 30 compressions, the child's airway must be opened. If a neck injury is suspected, the head-tilt, chin-lift method should be avoided and the jaw thrust used instead.
- After the airway is opened, it is important to listen and look for breathing for no more than 10 seconds. If the victim is not breathing, rescue breathing should begin, giving two slow breaths. The volume and pressure used to deliver each breath must be sufficient to make the chest rise. Breaths given too fast could cause gastric distention in the child. After about two minutes a single rescuer should call 911 and use an AED if it is available. If a second person is present, that person should call 911 and locate an AED while the first rescuer begins chest compressions.

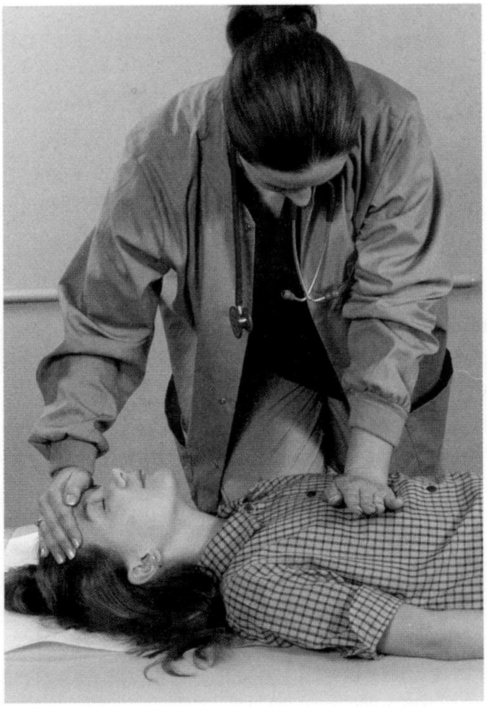

Fig. 4-25 With a pediatric patient, the heel of the rescuer's hand is placed over half the sternum.

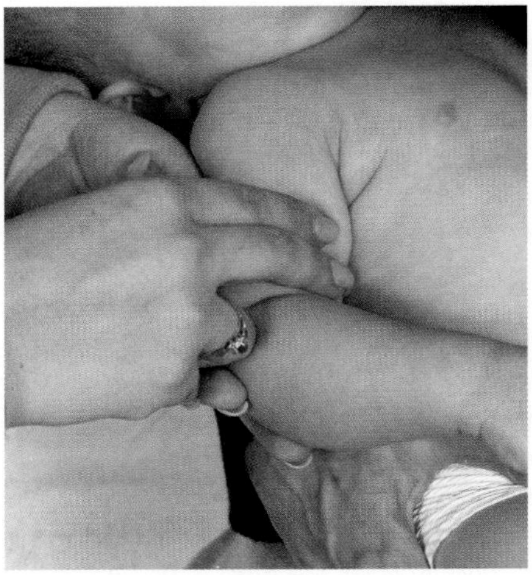

Fig. 4-26 Assess circulation in the infant by palpating the brachial artery.

Infant CPR

An infant found in cardiac arrest is assessed in the same manner as a child or an adult. Check the infant for movement or responsiveness. If the infant is unresponsive, begin CPR. One rescuer should perform CPR for about two minutes (5 cycles) and then stop to call 911. If another person is present, he or she should call 911 while the first rescuer performs CPR. An AED should not be used on an infant younger than one year old.

Be sure the infant is on a flat surface. Chest compressions should begin on the lower half of the sternum by placing the index and middle finger on the sternum (Fig. 4-27). Compress the infant's chest about 1½ inches. Give 30 gentle compressions, at a rate of 100 per minute. Tip the infant's head back by lifting the jaw and pressing down on the forehead. Look and listen for a few seconds. If the infant is not breathing, cover the infant's nose and mouth and give two slow breaths. Watch for the chest to rise. If it does not, reposition the head and try again. If necessary, sweep the infant's mouth and/or perform first aid for a choking baby. If the breath goes in, give a second breath and continue the cycle of 30 compressions. Procedure 4-7 provides instructions for infant CPR.

Procedure 4-7 Perform One-Person Infant CPR

TASK: Restore breathing and circulation to an infant.

EQUIPMENT AND SUPPLIES
- Nonsterile disposable gloves (if available)
- Pocket ventilation mask (if available)
- Infant-size CPR mannequin

SKILLS

STANDARD PRECAUTIONS ARE TO BE FOLLOWED.

1. **Procedural Step. Establish unresponsiveness.**
   Gently shake or click the sole of the foot, then position the infant on its back on a hard surface.
2. **Procedural Step. Perform 30 compressions.**
   Place the middle and ring fingers in the midline and one finger below the nipple line. Depress the lower sternum 1½ inches at a rate of 100 compressions per minute.
3. **Procedural Step. Maintain correct body position while performing chest compressions.**
4. **Procedural Step. Check for an open airway using the head-tilt, chin-lift maneuver.**
5. **Procedural Step. Look, listen, and feel for breathing for 5-10 seconds.**
6. **Procedural Step. If the infant is not breathing, maintain head position, make a seal over the infant's mouth and nose, and give two breaths.** Observe the chest rise and fall.
7. **Procedural Step. Give 2 gentle puffs of air after every 30 compressions.**
8. **Procedural Step. Perform CPR for 5 cycles (about 2 minutes).**
9. **Procedural Step. If alone, call 911 at this point, then continue CPR.**
10. **Procedural Step. Continue with CPR until the victim stabilizes or EMS arrives and assumes responsibility.**
11. **Procedural Step. Continue with CPR until the victim stabilizes or EMS arrives and assumes responsibility.**

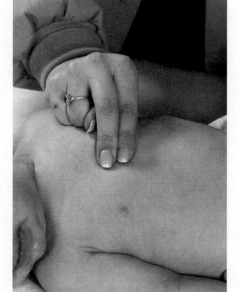

Fig. 4-27 Proper position for chest compressions for CPR for an infant.

PATIENT-CENTERED PROFESSIONALISM

- Why is it important for the medical assistant to be knowledgeable and skilled in cardiopulmonary resuscitation?

DISASTER PREPAREDNESS

What were your first thoughts when you saw the word **disaster** (an event that creates destruction and or adverse consequences)? Terrorist attack! Since September 11, 2001 this has become an automatic response and because of that event has produced an even greater awareness of biological and chemical agents. What about Katrina? This hurricane devastated New Orleans, not only because of its heavy rain and strong winds but also because of the flooding when the levees broke. Disaster preparedness is nothing more than making plans to prevent, if possible, an event that causes destruction and, if unable to prevent it, to respond and recover as quickly as possible.

Disasters can be divided into two major categories: natural and man-made. Box 4-8 provides a list

BOX 4-8   Types of Disaster

Natural Disasters	Man-Made Disasters
Hurricanes	Terrorism
Tornadoes	Bioterrorism
Earthquakes	Chemical spills
Floods	Nuclear accidents
Wildfires	Transportation accidents
Blizzard	Train, airplane, bridge collapse
Heat waves	Volcanic eruptions
Tsunamis	Infectious disease
(tidal waves)	SARS
Landslides	West Nile virus
	Civil unrest

of catastrophic events that require an immediate response from the community and various agencies (e.g., American Red Cross, the Salvation Army, and Public Health Department), health care professionals (e.g., licensed health care professionals [physicians, registered nurses], and, soon to be added, allied health professionals [e.g., medical assistants, licensed practical nurses]). Effective emergency preparedness requires cooperation, communication, and coordination between all these groups. Collaboration (cooperation) strengthens coordination efforts, reduces overlap of assignments, and adds **synergy** to the disaster team. Working together optimizes resource use and coordinates efforts to promote the health and safety of the community affected by the disaster.

Prepare

How can a community prepare for so many types of disasters? The answer to that question is that it cannot. What can be done, however, is to understand that each type of disaster is unique but the planning and preparation are similar. Preparedness is the key to a successful disaster response. Preparing includes identifying resources that will be needed in the event of a disaster (e.g., communication equipment, supplies, and vehicles) and how these resources should be used.

Plan

The advantage of having a disaster preparedness plan is it provides a way to maximize the efforts of the team by providing a well-documented process that assists in the timely response and recovery of the area. Disaster planning requires the use of a management system approach. The plan will identify a designated "Chief" who is responsible for all

functions of the plan unless they have been delegated. Typical duties include identification of priorities, coordination with outside agencies, and the approval of the team's action plan. The team can consist of, but is not limited to, the following:

Safety officer—monitors safety of those affected and response team's adherence to personal protective equipment (PPE) protocols.
Logistics officer—is responsible for supplies, equipment, food, and communication support.
Operations officer—directs activities and maintains discipline.

Some states, to support the need of health care providers to increase their emergency (disaster) preparedness, have enacted statutes that require disaster training as a requirement to renew their professional license. The Commission on Accreditation of Allied Health Education Programs (CAAHEP) proposes the inclusion of allied heath care professions to the disaster team. The rational is that allied health professionals routinely provide health care services needed in a disaster situation and therefore can reduce the shortage of providers in an emergency situation.

Practice

Drills or practice sessions provide all team members with a clear understanding of their responsibilities during a disaster. Drills help in evaluating the effectiveness and efficiency of the plan and in the coordination and use of the resources. Practice in advance of an emergency allows everyone concerned to be better able to handle any situation.

Medical Assistant's Role

The role medical assistants can play in times of emergency is to supplement existing emergency and public health resources by contributing their vast knowledge and abilities during a crisis. This can be done by registering with an emergency preparedness unit before a disaster occurs. Registering has many advantages:

- Skills and competencies can be verified beforehand.
- The medical assistant knows details of the unit's action plan.
- The medical assistant knows expectations.
- The medical assistant receives advanced training.
- The medical assistant is provided with liability protection.

Not registering in advance presents problems:

- There is often not enough time to verify credentials and competencies

- Food and shelter accommodations are inadequate to provide for last-minute personnel.
- The medical assistant may get in the way because he or she does not know the plan.

Several agencies have formed to assist in organizing an emergency health care workforce that could help during a disaster to meet the increased patient/victim care and increased needs of the community. The *Emergency System for Advanced Registration of Volunteer Health Professionals (ESAR-VHP)* was initiated to provide a method for the supplemental health care workforce to be mobilized to respond immediately to a mass casualty event. An issue that arose in the aftermath of the World Trade Center destruction was the use of health care professional volunteers in an emergency or mass casualty event. Hospital administrators reported that they were unable to use medical volunteers because they were unable to verify the volunteer's basic identity, licensing, credentials (training, skills, and competencies), and employment.

The *Emergency Management Assistance Compact (EMAC)* is a congressionally ratified organization that provides aid from its list of health care volunteers in cases of an emergency. The *Medical Reserve Corps (MRC)* establishes teams of volunteer medical and public health professionals to contribute their skills in times of community need. A group that is composed of nonmedical volunteers is the *Community Emergency Response Team (CERT)*.

By becoming active members of a disaster preparedness team, medical assistants avoid getting in the way in the aftermath of a disaster because their role will be defined in advance of the emergency and within their scope of training. The use of medical assistants on a disaster preparedness team draws on their experience working with patients.

CONCLUSION

The purpose of performing first-aid measures is to provide emergency care within the scope of practice. When providing emergency care, the medical assistant must take care that the victim experiences no further injury. Detecting and responding to the situation in a competent manner is paramount. To do this, always assess the situation before beginning first aid. If a patient is conscious, permission to treat must be obtained. If the patient refuses, do not start any emergency care.

The Good Samaritan law was enacted to encourage people to assist others during an emergency situation. This law provides legal protection to those people who provide emergency care to ill or injured persons and minimizes the fear of legal consequences. The care provided can never exceed the scope of a person's training.

Medical assistants who are prepared to give first aid in office emergencies can make a difference in the lives of their patients. Because accidents can happen at any time, knowing what to do to assist the patient in each situation is essential.

SUMMARY

Reinforce your understanding of the material in this chapter by reviewing the curriculum objectives and key content points below.

1. Define, appropriately use, and spell all the Key Terms for this chapter.
   - Review the Key Terms if necessary.
2. Explain the purpose of an incident report.
   - The incident report documents the exact details of the occurrence while the facts are fresh in the minds of those who witnessed the event.
3. List the information needed to accurately complete an incident report.
   - Observed, objective, and chronological information is required. This includes the person's name, location and time of the incident, and any factual description of what occurred and what was done as a result of the incident.
4. Explain what a medical assistant should do first in an emergency situation.
   - Emergency situations require the medical assistant to prioritize both the urgency of the situation and the status of the patient.
5. Define first aid, and list two guidelines that protect health care workers and victims from disease transmission.
   - First aid is the temporary care given to an injured or ill person until he or she can be provided with complete treatment.
   - Health care workers should wear protective gloves to avoid contact with blood and body fluids.
   - Areas that are soiled with blood, mucus, or other body fluids should not be touched without a barrier (e.g., CPR mouth barriers).
6. List one situation requiring first-aid attention for each of the seven body systems.
   - Review Table 4-1.
7. Explain what causes fainting.
   - Fainting is caused by an inadequate blood supply to the brain.
8. List seven guidelines for the emergency care of a patient who has fainted.
   - Assess for life-threatening cause; check for medical alerts; keep the patient supine and

elevate the legs; check the airway and loosen clothing; apply a damp cloth to the face; calm the patient; and ask about medications.

9. Describe the symptoms of a heart attack, and explain the purpose of cardiopulmonary resuscitation (CPR).
   - Dusky skin color; diaphoresis; bluish lips and nail beds; shortness of breath; and rapid, weak pulse are all symptoms of a heart attack.
   - Chest pain can be a sign of heart attack.
   - The purpose of CPR is to keep oxygen moving to the lungs and blood circulating throughout the body.

10. List 10 guidelines for the emergency care of a patient who has heart attack symptoms.
    - Always call for emergency assistance in a possible heart attack situation.
    - If a patient is exhibiting signs of a heart attack, follow these guidelines: call 911; position the patient comfortably; assess the airway; loosen clothing; determine if the patient is conscious and taking medication; administer the medication; administer oxygen; take vital signs; keep the patient warm; and comfort the patient.

11. Explain how a stroke differs from a heart attack, and identify the signs of obstructed airway and cardiac arrest.
    - A stroke occurs when the brain does not receive oxygen because of a burst or blocked blood vessel or pressure on the cerebral artery; a heart attack occurs because heart tissue is deprived of blood supply.
    - Stroke symptoms vary according to severity but can include facial and arm weakness or numbness, severe headache, sudden confusion, visual changes, and speech difficulty.
    - Heart attack victims may complain of chest pain, be diaphoretic, have shortness of breath, be cyanotic, and have altered vital signs.
    - A person with an obstructed airway will not be able to breathe or speak, whereas a heart attack victim may be able to breathe or have breath restored, and the heart muscle is affected.

12. List six guidelines for the emergency care of a patient who has had a stroke.
    - Keep in mind that if stroke occurs on the left side of the brain, damage will be to the right side of the body, and vice versa.
    - If a patient has had a stroke, follow these guidelines: call 911; assess the airway; elevate the head; keep the patient warm; turn the

patient on the side if there is difficulty breathing; take vital signs.

13. List seven types of shock and explain what causes each.
    - Review Table 4-3.

14. List eight guidelines for the emergency care of a patient who has symptoms of shock.
    - Seek medical assistance; maintain the airway; place the patient supine with the feet elevated; apply direct pressure to external bleeding; keep the patient warm; do not give the patient anything orally; do not leave the patient alone; take vital signs.

15. Explain what a seizure is and what may cause one.
    - A seizure is a sudden involuntary muscle activity with a change in behavior and level of consciousness.
    - Seizures are brought on by a change in the electrical activity of the brain.

16. List eight guidelines for the emergency care of a patient who has had a seizure.
    - Remove objects from the area; maintain the airway; protect the head; loosen clothing; do not restrain the patient and avoid overstimulation; turn the patient to the side after a seizure; assess vital signs; allow the patient to rest.

17. List and describe the two methods for controlling bleeding.
    - Bleeding can be controlled by direct and indirect pressure.
    - Direct pressure is applied directly to the wound itself.
    - Indirect pressure is applied to the artery that supplies blood to the injured area.

18. Explain the emergency care for patients with thermal, chemical, or electrical burns.
    - The surface area of the burn is evaluated according to the "rule of nines."
    - Proper treatment is started after both depth and total surface area have been determined.
    - It is important to know the cause of the burn, length of exposure, and any medical condition.

19. Differentiate between heat exhaustion and heat stroke.
    - Heat exhaustion occurs when the body is subjected to excessive heat; symptoms include excessive sweating and pale, cool, clammy skin.
    - Heat stroke (sunstroke) occurs when the body is exposed to extreme heat and high humidity for long periods; symptoms include dry, hot, reddened skin and body temperature of 106° F or higher.

20. Explain considerations for the emergency care of a patient with frostbite.
    - Pressure should not be applied to frostbitten areas, and the patient should not walk on frostbitten feet.
    - The area should not be rubbed, and the body part needs to be gradually rewarmed.
21. List the main goal for the emergency care of a fracture.
    - Immobilization of the fractured area is the main goal of emergency care.
22. List four guidelines for assessing the degree of a dislocation.
    - Check the distal pulse; splint above and below the dislocated joint; keep the patient warm and observe for shock; apply an ice pack to the injured area.
23. List five guidelines for emergency care of a patient who has ingested poison.
    - Call the poison control center for advice when a patient has ingested poison.
    - Call 911; maintain the airway; position the patient to keep the airway clear; induce vomiting if recommended; position the patient leaning forward.
24. List four guidelines for the emergency care of a patient who has inhaled poison.
    - Call 911; protect yourself and remove the patient from the source of vapors and fumes; loosen clothing; assess breathing and perform rescue breathing or CPR if necessary.
25. Identify the symptoms of bites and stings.
    - Review Table 4-4.
26. Explain the difference between insulin shock and diabetic ketoacidosis (diabetic coma).
    - Insulin shock occurs when the body has too much insulin and not enough glucose.
    - Diabetic ketoacidosis occurs when there is too much glucose and not enough insulin in the blood, and ketones are produced.
27. Demonstrate the correct procedure for performing the Heimlich maneuver.
    - Review Procedure 4-1.
28. List three common uses for bandages.
    - Bandages can be used for support or immobilization, to hold dressings in place, and to apply pressure to control bleeding.
29. Differentiate between an elastic bandage and a Kling-type bandage.
    - An elastic bandage (Ace bandage) is made of cloth and contains elastic; it can be reused on the patient if not soiled.
    - A Kling-type bandage is made of stretchy loose fibers but contains no elastic.
30. List and briefly describe five basic bandage turns.
    - Circular bandage turn overlaps the previous turn.
    - Spiral bandage turn progresses upward, and each spiral overlaps the previous turn.
    - Spiral reverse bandage turn progresses downward and overlaps.
    - Figure-eight bandage turn is applied on a slant and progresses upward and then downward to support a dressing or joint.
    - Recurrent bandage turn is used for a stump or the head and begins with a circular turn and progresses back and forth, overlapping each turn.
31. Demonstrate the procedure for properly applying a tubular gauze bandage to an affected area.
    - Review Procedure 4-2.
32. Explain the "ABCs" to follow before starting any type of resuscitation.
    - Airway must be open, breathing assessed, and circulation checked by feeling for a pulse.
33. Demonstrate the correct procedure for opening a victim's airway.
    - Review Procedure 4-2.
34. Demonstrate the correct procedure for performing rescue breathing.
    - Review Procedure 4-3.
35. Demonstrate the correct procedure for performing one-person adult CPR.
    - Review Procedure 4-4.
36. Demonstrate the correct procedure for performing two-person adult CPR.
    - Review Procedure 4-5.
37. Explain how to perform pediatric CPR.
    - Assess the child for obvious spinal, bone, or neck injuries once it is determined that the child is unresponsive.
    - Open the airway, begin rescue breathing, and check the pulse. If there is no pulse, begin chest compressions.
38. Demonstrate the correct procedure for performing one-person infant CPR.
    - Review Procedure 4-7.
39. Explain what an AED is, and explain how it is used.
    - An automated external defibrillator (AED) analyzes cardiac rhythm and delivers electric shock (defibrillation) to the heart to stop an erratic rhythm or restart the cardiac cycle.
40. Discuss the difference between natural and man-made disasters.
    - Natural disasters are the result of the forces of nature, and man-made disasters result from man's intervention causing an event of destruction.

41. Discuss the advantages of registering with a disaster preparedness team.
    * Skills and competencies can be verified.
    * The medical assistant knows details of the unit's action plan.
    * The medical assistant knows expectations.
    * The medical assistant receives advanced training.
    * The medical assistant is provided with liability protection.

42. Analyze a realistic medical office situation and apply your understanding of handling office emergencies to determine the best course of action.
    * Medical assistants must be prepared to act in emergency situations in the medical office; they must be aware of what is going on around them and must be prepared to act on the knowledge they have.

43. Describe the impact on patient care when medical assistants have a solid understanding of the knowledge and skills necessary to assist patients in office emergencies.
    * When the medical assistant is knowledgeable and skillful when emergencies arise in the medical office, the patient benefits.
    * Quick assessment by the medical assistant can prevent a delay in appropriate treatment.
    * When the medical assistant is prepared for medical emergencies, patient confidence is established in the medical practice.

FOR FURTHER EXPLORATION

Research risk factors of a stroke. Certain medical and hereditary conditions increase the risk of a stroke (e.g., diabetes, African-American race, family history of stroke).

Keywords: Use the following keywords in your search: National Heart, Lung, and Blood Institute; National Stroke Association; American Heart Association; hypertension.

Chapter Review

Vocabulary Review

Matching

Match each term with the correct definition.

A. anaphylactic shock

B. automated external defibrillator

C. burn

D. cardiac arrest

E. cerebrovascular accident

F. defibrillation

G. direct pressure

H. epistaxis

I. fracture

J. full-thickness burn

K. Heimlich maneuver

L. hemorrhagic shock

___A___ 1. Severe infection with toxins that prevent blood vessels from constriction, causing blood to pool away from vital organs

___D___ 2. Sudden cessation of breathing and heart activity

___W___ 3. Not responding to stimuli

___I___ 4. Break or crack in a bone caused by trauma or disease

___O___ 5. Breathing pattern that begins with very deep, gasping respirations that become rapid and are associated with severe diabetic acidosis

___U___ 6. Cerebrovascular accident; condition caused by narrowing cerebral vessels; hemorrhage into the brain; and formation of an embolus or thrombus resulting in a lack of blood supply to the brain

___Y___ 7. Form of hyperthermia caused by dehydration causing a loss of consciousness

___Z___ 8. Chronic brain disorder in which an individual has seizures

___A___ 9. Severe allergic reaction caused by hypersensitivity to a substance

___K___ 10. Methods of evaluating a surface area of a burn; the surface is divided into regions with percentage assigned

___V___ 11. Fainting

___I___ 12. Firm material used to immobilize above and below a fracture to prevent further damage

___F___ 13. Electrical shock to the heart to maintain heart rhythm

M. hypothermia

N. insulin shock

O. Kussmaul breathing

P. metabolic shock

Q. neurogenic shock

R. "rules of nines"

S. seizure

T. splint

U. stroke

V. syncope

W. unconscious

X. septic shock

Y. heat stroke

Z. epilepsy

AA. bandage turns

BB. elastic bandage

___L___ 14. Shock caused by inadequate blood supply to tissues as a result of trauma, burns, or internal bleeding

___B___ 15. Machine that analyzes a patient's cardiac rhythm and delivers an electric shock if indicated

___Q___ 16. Loss of nerve control over the circulatory system causing decreased blood supply to an area

___J___ 17. Burn that destroys the epidermis and dermis to include the nerve endings; third-degree burn

___M___ 18. Decreased body temperature

___C___ 19. Injury or destruction of tissue caused by excessive physical heat, chemicals, electricity, or radiation

___S___ 20. Sudden involuntary muscle activity leading to a change in level of consciousness and behavior

___E___ 21. Lack of oxygen to the brain caused by narrowing or ruptured cerebral vessels

___K___ 22. Abdominal thrust used in an emergency to dislodge the cause of a blockage

___H___ 23. Nosebleed

___P___ 24. Type of shock caused by excessive loss of body fluids and metabolites

___G___ 25. Pressure applied directly over a wound

___N___ 26. State that occurs when the body has too much insulin and not enough glucose to use the insulin; severe hypoglycemia

___BB___ 27. Bandage containing elastic that stretches and molds to the body part to which it is applied

___EE___ 28. Bandage turn used for a stump or the head that begins with a circular turn and progresses back and forth, overlapping each turn until the area is covered

___AA___ 29. Gauze bandage made in a tubular shape that can be used to cover rounded body parts

CC. figure-eight turn

DD. recurrent turn

EE. tubular gauze

FF. Kling-type bandage

GG. Incident report

___*CC*___ 30. Bandage turn that is applied on a slant and progresses upward and then downward to support a dressing or joint

___*DD*___ 31. Method of arranging a bandage on a body part

___*FF*___ 32. Gauze bandaging material that stretches and molds to irregular-shaped areas

___*GG*___ 33. Document that describes any unusual occurrence.

Theory Recall

True/False

Indicate whether the sentence or statement is true or false.

___F___ 1. When a patient is having an epileptic seizure, it is important to place something between the patient's teeth.

___F___ 2. Indirect pressure is applied over the wound.

___T___ 3. Insulin shock occurs when a patient has taken too much insulin in relation to the amount of food eaten, causing the available glucose to be depleted.

___T___ 4. Abdominal thrust is an emergency procedure used to dislodge the cause of a blockage.

___F___ 5. All chemical burns should be washed with water immediately.

Multiple Choice

Identify the letter of the choice that best completes the statement or answers the question.

1. ___D___ occurs when the brain does not receive enough oxygen.
   A. Cerebrovascular accident
   B. Heart attack
   C. Shock
   D. Fainting

2. Epilepsy seizures can be brought on by ___C___.
   A. low blood sugar
   B. high fever
   C. head trauma
   D. all of the above

3. Arterial blood is a ___a___ color.
   A. bright red
   B. dark red
   C. pale red
   D. none of the above

4. __b__ occurs when the body is subjected to excessive heat.
   A. Heat exhaustion
   B. Heat stroke
   C. Sunstroke
   D. Hypothermia

5. __b__ is a fracture of a bone that does not break but bends the bone.
   A. Compound
   B. Greenstick
   C. Simple
   D. Open

6. __b__ can lead to ketoacidosis.
   A. Infection
   B. Glucose overload
   C. Common cold
   D. All of the above

7. With infant CPR, the medical assistant needs to give __a__ compressions, at a rate of 100 per minute, to _____ ventilation.
   A. 3:1
   B. 5:1
   C. 8:1
   D. 10:1

8. When a patient feels lightheaded, the medical assistant needs to __a__.
   A. stand the patient up
   B. have the patient lower head to knee level
   C. help patient to lithotomy position
   D. place a warm compress on forehead

9. __a__ occurs when one end of a bone is separated from its original position in a joint.
   A. Dislocation
   B. Fracture
   C. Sprain
   D. Strain

10. A patient who is having a CVA will complain of __c__.
    A. lightheadedness
    B. warm tingly sensation
    C. sudden confusion
    D. difficulty concentrating

11. Epistaxis can be caused by __B__.
    A. low altitude
    B. upper respiratory infection
    C. hypotension
    D. exercise

12. __a__ is when the cardiac muscle can no longer pump blood throughout the body.
    A. Cardiogenic shock
    B. Hemorrhagic shock
    C. Insulin shock
    D. Septic shock

13. The body temperature of a person with heat exhaustion is _B_.
    A. 100° to 102°
    B. 101° to 102°
    C. 102° to 103°
    D. 103° to 104°

14. With a sprain, the RICE treatment must begin within _a_.
    A. 10 to 20 minutes
    B. 30 minutes
    C. 45 minutes
    D. 1 hour

15. Treatment for hypothermia requires the body part to be gradually warmed in water, which should not exceed _a_ degrees.
    A. 99
    B. 100
    C. 105
    D. 108

16. There are _a_ basic bandage turns used either for support or to secure a dressing.
    A. two
    B. four
    C. five
    D. eight

17. A _a_ bandage is used on areas that are uniform in width, such as fingers and wrists.
    A. circular
    B. figure eight
    C. recurrent
    D. spiral turn

18. A _c_ turn bandage is used when the area to be bandaged is of varying widths, such as the forearm and the lower calf of the leg.
    A. figure eight
    B. recurrent
    C. spiral
    D. spiral reverse turn

Sentence Completion

Complete each sentence or statement.

1. __First aide__ is the temporary care given to an injured or ill person until the victim can be provided complete emergency treatment.

2. __Syncope__ is a temporary loss of consciousness caused by an inadequate blood supply to the brain.

3. __Shock__ is a progressive circulatory collapse of the body brought on by insufficient blood flow to all parts of the body.

4. __Bleeding__ is the loss of blood from a ruptured, punctured, or cut blood vessel.

5. __Heat stroke__ occurs when the body is subjected to high temperatures and humidity for a long period of time.

6. A(n) _splint_ immobilizes an affected body part and can be made from any available firm material.

7. Respirations that become very deep and gasping and then become rapid is known as

_____ breathing.

8. _Burn_ is an injury to or destruction of body tissue caused by excessive physical heat.

9. _recurrent turn_ bandage is most frequently used for a stump area or for the head.

10. A(n) _Figure of eight_ bandage application is when each turn overlaps the previous turn.

11. After a bandage has been applied, it is very important that the medical assistant check for

body part below the bandaged area.

12. A(n) _Figure eight_ turn bandage is most often used to hold a dressing in place or support a joint area.

Short Answers

1. Explain the symptoms of a heart attack.

Chest pain in the sternum area & may radiate down the left arm, Jaw & up onto the shoulder area.

2. List the four steps in wound care.

1. Direct preassure over the wound

2. apply another dressing, continue preassure

3.

4 apply preassure bandage.

3. Explain what the acronym RICE stands for.

R - rest the injured area by splinting the area

I - ice the area

C - compress the area

E - elevate the injured area

4. List three uses for bandages.

-support the immobilization of an injured body part

- securing a dressing in place.

- application of pressure to control bleeding

5. List and explain the three types of bandages most commonly used in a medical office.

Elastic bandages — can be stretched or molded around the body part -

Kling-type — stretch but not elastic

Tabular gauze — consist of loose elastic cotton fibers

Critical Thinking

1. You and a friend are out on a lunch-time jog when she starts complaining of shortness of breath. You both write it off as being out of shape and continue. Once back at the office, you notice your friend's lips are bluish in color and her skin tone is gray. You ask her if she is feels okay. She states that she is sweaty and her chest feels a little heavy. What would you do next? Explain what the friend's statement tells you.

2. Use the following information to complete an incident report:

Date: 9/21/20XX
1:30 p.m.: You were in examination room #2 when you heard someone calling for help. Upon investigating, you found Mrs. Jessie Cash, a patient of Doctor Morales, on the floor of the patient bathroom. She says that she felt a bit dizzy when she went to get up from the toilet and eased herself to the floor. Dr. Morales examines Mrs. Cash and does not observe any broken bones. Her blood pressure is 130/90, pulse is 90, and respirations are 20. Doctor Morales requests that her blood glucose level be checked, and it is 100. She is helped to her feet and escorted to an examination room for further observation. After 30 minutes, her vital signs remain stable, and she states she is fine. She had come into the office today for a blood pressure check and a renewal of her allergy medication.

Jessie Cash, Mrs.
10290 Eagles Glen Ave.
Anywhere, USA 56790
555-765-3467
DOB: 7/30/46

XYZ MEDICAL CENTER

Date of Incident: 9/21/20XX   **Time:** 1:30 pm   a.m./p.m.

Location of Incident: Patients bathroom

Name of injured person: Jessie Cush

Address: 10290 Eagle Glen Ave, Anywhere USA 54790

Phone Number: 555-765-3467

Date of birth: 7/30/46   Male ____   Female ✓

Who was injured person? (circle one) (Patient)   Visitor   Employer

Description of incident: Was in the ER#2 when I heard someone asking for help. And found Mrs. Cash on the bathroom floor.

What was the nature of the injury to the person: Patient got dizzy

Action taken: vital signs taken & glucose level checked.

Injury requires hospital visit?   **Yes:** ____   **No:** ✓

Name of hospital: _____

Address: _____

Signature of injured party:

_____ **Date** ____

***No medical attention was desired and/or required.**

Signature of injured party:

_____ **Date** ____

Person reporting incident: Ney P   **Date** ____

Signature: nb

3. You have been selected to be part of the crisis management team at your school. Your assignment is the following:

   - List the expectations of the crisis management team in a disaster setting.
   - Develop competencies for the medical assistant related to the organization and management of disaster preparedness, response, and recovery.
   - Create a list of community resources needed for an emergency situation, including names, telephone numbers, and contact persons.
   - Participate in a tabletop exercise as provided by your instructor.

4. Discuss what must be included in an emergency plan for a physician's office

Internet Research

Keyword: CERT

Research the emergency preparedness in your own area. Cite your source. Be prepared to give a 2-minute oral presentation should your instructor assign you to do so.

What Would You Do?

If you have accomplished the objectives in this chapter, you will be able to make better choices as a medical assistant. Take a look at this situation and decide what you would do.

Mariah has type 1 diabetes mellitus and takes insulin on a regular basis. Dr. Naguchi is aware that Mariah does not follow her diet as she should and that her exercise habits are not consistent, so her diabetes is often not stable.

Mariah lives in the southern United States, where it is currently 100° F outside and very humid. Earlier today, Mariah was in the garden gathering vegetables. Later she started canning the vegetables. Her house has minimal air-conditioning. In her haste to complete what needed to be done in the garden, Mariah did not eat her lunch as she should have, although she took her entire dose of insulin.

During the afternoon Mariah began to feel weak, experiencing dizziness and sweating, and her skin felt cool and clammy. Don, her husband, drove her the three blocks to Dr. Naguchi's office because she started complaining of chest pain and difficulty breathing. As soon as she arrives, Mariah appears to faint and falls, injuring her left ankle. As the medical assistant, Janis is the first health care professional to see what is happening to Mariah. After seeing Mariah, Dr. Naguchi orders an x-ray of her ankle to see whether she has a sprain, strain, or fracture.

If you were in Janis's place, would you know what to do in this situation?

1. What are the external factors that could have caused the symptoms that Mariah showed?

   She took her insulin w/o eating lunch. Too much insulin w/o enough
   to use up the insulin & exaustion too much from gardining.

2. How should Janis handle this problem when several persons are in the waiting room with Don and Mariah?

That is when triage will be followed.

3. What questions should Janis immediately ask Don?

Is she taking any medication, if yes what for.
And how it was administered

4. What recent activities could have contributed to Mariah's problems?

Climate
administration of insulin w/o food taken w/ith

5. If Mariah fainted and you were the medical assistant, what would you do for her immediately while someone was notifying the physician?

Lay her in a supine position slightly elevate the legs above the level
of the heart. Check is clear airway

6. Knowing that Mariah has diabetes, what might you think happened, and what would you expect Dr. Naguchi to order for her?

Insulin shock

7. Why would you be suspicious of hyperthermia? What should Janis do for these symptoms?

Because of the present climate of 100° humid, and the activities she had done.

8. What symptoms does Mariah have that might indicate a heart attack?

chest pain ā difficulty of breathing.

9. How do a sprain, strain, and fracture differ, and how is each treated? What treatment is common to all three conditions?

Sprain :

applying splint to immobilize the area -

Strain -

Fracture -

Chapter Quiz

Multiple Choice:

Identify the letter of the choice that best completes the statement or answers the question.

1. _____ can lead to ketoacidosis.
   A. Infection
   B. Common cold
   C. Glucose overload
   D. All of the above

2. With vein damage, the color of the external bleeding will be _C_.
   A. bright red
   B. light red
   C. dark red
   D. pale red

3. _____ shock is when there is a loss of nerve control over the circulatory system, causing decreased blood supply to an area.
   A. Insulin
   B. Metabolic
   C. Neurogenic
   D. Psychogenic

4. Patients who are being seen for heat exhaustion will have a core temperature of _____ degrees.
   A. 99 to 101
   B. 101 to 102
   C. 102 to 103
   D. 103 to 104

5. When performing adult CPR, the first thing that must happen is _____.
   A. to start compressions
   B. to call 911
   C. to perform rescue breathing
   D. to call for help

6. A sprain is a full or partial tear of a ligament.
   A. True
   B. False

7. _____ is a form of hyperthermia marked with pale, cool, and clammy skin.
   A. Shock
   B. Heat exhaustion
   C. Heat stroke
   D. None of the above

8. _A_ burn is a burn that destroys the epidermis and dermis, including the nerve endings.
   A. Full-thickness
   B. First-degree
   C. Second-degree
   D. Minor

9. Heimlich maneuver should be done only on conscious patients with an airway obstruction.
   A. True
   B. False

10. A child must be older than __*a*__ years to feel for the carotid pulse as a part of CPR.
    A. 1
    B. 3
    C. 5
    D. 7

11. When one end of bone is separated from its original position in a joint, it is called __*B*__.
    A. dislocation
    B. fracture
    C. strain
    D. sprain

12. When an area is being warmed because of frostbite, the warming solutions should be no warmer than __*b*__ degrees.
    A. 105
    B. 120
    C. 125
    D. 130

13. A(n) _____ fracture pierces through the skin.
    A. closed
    B. open
    C. greenstick
    D. compound

14. Treatment for a sprain should begin within __*a*__ minutes.
    A. 10 to 20
    B. 15 to 30
    C. 20 to 40
    D. 30 to 45

15. When a patient has an epileptic seizure, it is important to remember not to place anything between the patient's teeth because it could become an airway obstruction.
    A. True
    B. False

16. The __*a*__ bandage application is most commonly used to hold dressings in place or support a joint area.
    A. circular turn
    B. figure-eight turn
    C. spiral reverse
    D. recurrent turn

17. _____ bandages are used to mold around irregular areas and are most often used to support dressings.
    A. Elastic
    B. Fabric
    C. Kling
    D. Tubular

18. The _____ bandage is most often used for a stump area.
    A. figure-eight
    B. recurrent
    C. spiral
    D. spiral reverse

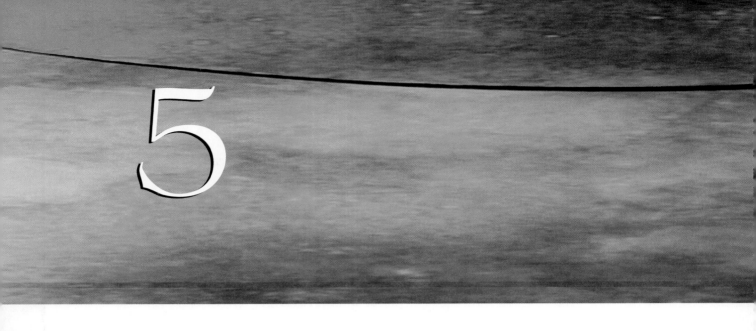

OBJECTIVES

You will be able to do the following after completing this chapter:

Key Terms
1. Define, appropriately use, and spell all the Key Terms for this chapter.

Accounting Principles
2. State the accounting equation.
3. Explain the differences among assets, liabilities, and owner's equity.
4. Explain the difference between a debit and a credit.
5. List three types of assets in a medical office.
6. Demonstrate the correct procedure for establishing a petty cash fund, maintaining an accurate record of expenditures, and replenishing the fund as necessary.
7. Explain what an accounts receivable "aging" report shows.
8. Differentiate among the following financial statements: income statement, statement of owner's equity, and balance sheet.

Bookkeeping Procedures
9. List three types of forms used on a pegboard system to record the daily transactions.
10. List two advantages of using a pegboard bookkeeping system.
11. Demonstrate the correct procedure for posting service charges and payments using the pegboard system.
12. List four advantages of using a computerized bookkeeping system.

Banking Procedures
13. List the five requirements of banks for checks being deposited, and explain the importance of confirming these five items when accepting checks from patients.
14. Define "third-party" check, "postdated" check, and check "paid in full."
15. List seven security tips for check writing.
16. Differentiate between restrictive endorsement and blank endorsement.
17. Demonstrate the correct procedure for preparing a bank deposit.
18. List four methods of making deposits and briefly explain each.
19. Demonstrate the correct procedure for reconciling a bank statement.

Billing and Collections
20. List four ways in which a patient statement can be prepared.
21. Demonstrate the correct procedure for explaining professional fees before providing services.

FINANCIAL MANAGEMENT

22. Explain how an adjustment affects the balance of a patient's account, and list four reasons that an adjustment might be made.
23. Describe the collection process, including the role of third-party payers.
24. Demonstrate the correct procedure for establishing payment arrangements on a patient's account.
25. List four guidelines for making telephone calls to collect debts.
26. Demonstrate the correct procedure for explaining a statement of account to a patient.
27. Demonstrate the correct procedure for collecting delinquent accounts.

Payroll Processing
28. List six laws that affect earnings and withholdings and briefly explain each.
29. Differentiate between gross wages and net pay.
30. List the three principal deductions from the employee's gross pay that are required by federal law.
31. List the four types of information in the employee earnings record.

Patient-Centered Professionalism
32. Analyze a realistic medical office situation and apply your understanding of medical office financial management to determine the best course of action.
33. Describe the impact on patient care when medical assistants have a solid understanding of the financial aspects of a medical office.

KEY TERMS

ABA number Number on all checks that identifies a payer's bank and location; assigned by American Bankers Association (ABA).

accounting Numerical language of business that describes its activities.

accounting equation Equation that expresses the relationship among assets, liabilities, and owner's equity.

accounts receivable (AR) Record of patient transactions showing an amount due.

adjustment Addition or deduction of a designated amount to a balance owed.

aging report Report that shows how long a debt has gone unpaid.

asset Anything of value owned by a business that can be used to acquire other items.

balance sheet Report on the financial condition of a business on a certain date.

bank statement Document that lists all the banking activities for a set period.

blank endorsement Type of endorsement in which only a signature is listed on the back of a check.

bookkeeping Systematic recording of business transactions, such as money owed and money paid.

co-insurance Fixed percentage of a medical cost that is paid by the patient.

co-payment Fixed fee that is paid by the patient at each office visit.

credit Amount representing a payment; recorded on the right side of an accounting sheet.

daysheet Journal for recording the day's activities.

debit Amount representing a charge or debt owed; recorded on the left side of an accounting sheet.

debtor Person owing a debt.

KEY TERMS—*cont'd*

dependent Person for whom another person is financially responsible.

deposit Money placed in an account of a financial institution.

deposit slip Listing of all cash and checks to be deposited to a certain account of a business's financial institution.

employee earnings record Document that shows individual employee earnings and deductions.

Employee's Withholding Allowance Certificate (Form W-4) Form that each new employee fills out to declare exemption from tax withholding for earnings.

encounter form Source document for billing purposes that contains patient account information and insurance codes for the date of service; also known as a *superbill.*

endorse To sign or place (e.g., stamp) a signature on the back of a check that transfers the rights of ownership of funds to a financial institution.

exemption Amount of money earned that is not taxable.

Fair Labor Standards Act Legislation providing the standards for payment of hourly and salaried employees.

Federal Employees' Compensation Act Legislation that covers federal government workers for work-related injuries.

Federal Insurance Contributions Act (FICA) Legislation that provides funds to support retirement benefits, dependents of retired workers, and disability benefits.

Federal Truth in Lending Act Legislation requiring a disclosure statement that informs a patient of a procedure's total cost, including finance charges; required when the patient will make more than four payments.

Federal Unemployment Tax Act (FUTA) Legislation that requires employers to pay tax based on employee's earnings to cover benefits if the employee becomes unemployed.

fee schedule Listing of a physician's charges for services.

financial statements Reports that indicate the financial condition of a business.

gross wages Total amount of money earned before deductions are taken.

income statement Report showing the results of income and expenses over time.

ledger cards Records of debit and credit activity of a patient in the practice.

liability Amount owed; debt.

Medicare tax Tax collected to support the federal health insurance program for people age 65 and older.

net income Resulting figure when income is greater than expenditures.

net loss Resulting figure when expenditures exceed income.

net pay Total amount of money paid for work, minus deductions.

nonsufficient funds (NSF) Indication that the payer did not have sufficient funds in the bank to cover the amount of a check written.

one-write system Pegboard system.

out-of-town check Check drawn on a bank account that is not local.

owner's equity Amount remaining after liabilities are subtracted from assets.

paid in full Endorsement qualifying that the balance of an account is zero after acceptance of a check.

payable Representing liability; accounts payable are money and funds owed to someone else (e.g., vendor).

payee Person receiving payment of a debt.

payer Person paying a debt.

payroll Employees' salaries, wages, bonuses, net pay, and deductions.

payroll register Document that shows information about earnings and deductions for each employee.

pegboard Device used to write the same information on several forms at one time.

pegboard system Recording system using a pegboard designed to increase the efficiency of recording daily transactions; called also *one-write system.*

petty cash Amount of cash kept on hand to be used for making payments for incidental supplies.

postdated Using a written future date, as in postdated check.

professional discounts Discount given to other professionals working in the same field as a provider.

qualified endorsement Type of endorsement that qualifies the acceptance of a check received; done when one person accepts payment for another.

receipt-charge slip Charge form with two parts: right side lists previous balance, treatments, and patient's name; left side lists charge for treatments, payments received, and current balance; also called *statement-receipt.*

reconciled State of a checkbook and a bank statement being in balance.

restrictive endorsement Type of endorsement in which the payee indicates a sole purpose for funds; ex: endorsement "for deposit only" on the back of a check for deposit with signature indicates that check is to be used for that purpose only (deposited to that particular account) and therefore cannot be exchanged for cash.

salary Predetermined amount of pay for a designated period.

special endorsement Type of endorsement in which a payee signs a check made out to the payee over to another payee.

statement Document indicating the activity in an account.

statement of owner's equity Report that shows changes in the owner's financial interest over time.

statement-receipt Receipt-charge slip.

State Unemployment Tax Act (SUTA) Legislation mandating that the state collect tax money for benefits to be used by workers who become unemployed.

superbill Encounter form.

T-account Tool used to analyze the effect of a transaction on an account.

Tax Payment Act Legislation requiring employers to withhold tax based on a scale, and to pay it to the Internal Revenue Service.

KEY TERMS—cont'd

third-party check Check signed over to another party, who is not the original payee.

transaction Financial activity of a business.

voucher Paper showing the date, amount of transaction, what was purchased, and who purchased the item.

wages Money paid for work done by an employee and calculated by multiplying the hourly wage rate times the number of hours worked.

workers' compensation System that provides insurance to the employer for a worker injured on the job.

write-off Amount of money not able to be collected.

What Would You Do?

Read the following scenario and keep it in mind as you learn about the financial aspects of a medical practice in this chapter.

Meredith is the office manager for a private physician. She is responsible for the financial management of the office. She is the person who tracks the assets and liabilities for the accountant and interprets "owner equity" so that the physician will know the net value of the practice. As part of her job description Meredith also disburses petty cash. She makes sure that the vouchers, with receipts attached, and the cash on hand balance at the end of each workday. As each patient leaves the office,

the payments for office visits are collected. The goal is to collect whatever is necessary from patients (co-payment, co-insurance) on the day of service. If patient receivables are current, outstanding insurance claims become the main focus for accounts receivable. Another one of Meredith's duties is to approve or disapprove of professional discounts and write-offs as fee adjustments. Finally, she generates collection letters and telephone calls for overdue and delinquent accounts.

Would you be able to perform these responsibilities in the medical office?

The front-office duties and responsibilities of a medical assistant vary according to the type of medical practice. The person at the front desk typically is responsible for clerical and basic bookkeeping duties. This requires accurate recording of the physician's charges and receipts for payment of services. The office manager usually prepares the payroll and handles accounts payable and accounts receivable. In most practices, the daily journals, disbursement records, and payroll records are forwarded to an accountant who completes the quarterly income and disbursement summaries for income tax purposes.

Even though others handle many financial aspects of the medical practice, it is important for you to understand basic bookkeeping and accounting principles and procedures. An understanding of the "big picture" will help you manage whatever parts of the system for which you may be responsible. Also, because fees, billing, and collection directly relate to patients, efficient handling of these aspects will improve patients' overall experience.

ACCOUNTING PRINCIPLES

Accounting is considered the "language" of business because it describes the activities of a business.

Effective accounting records provide the medical practice with accurate and timely information regarding the financial activities and condition of the practice. The accounting process analyzes, classifies, records, summarizes, and interprets the **transactions** (financial activities) or activities of the business in financial terms. Accounting and bookkeeping are not the same activity. Accounting involves the design and management of the financial operating system; it specifies how bookkeeping should be done. **Bookkeeping** is the basic process of recording the financial activities of the business.

Medical assistants need to understand the accounting equation, assets and liabilities, and the various types of financial statements used for medical office accounting.

Assets, Liabilities, and Equity

Assets, liabilities, and equity are three important accounting principles.

- *Assets.* A medical practice has many items of value. It acquires items such as cash, equipment, and supplies that will be used to conduct the daily activities of the practice. Anything of value that is owned by the medical practice is an **asset.** Assets have value because they can be used to acquire other items of value or to operate the medical practice.

- *Liabilities.* An amount owed by the medical practice is called a **liability.** Liabilities are debts and include what the business owes its creditors (e.g., business loans, charge accounts, vendors).
- *Owner's equity.* The amount remaining after the liabilities are subtracted from the assets is called **owner's equity.** Owner's equity is the investment the physician or physicians have made in the medical practice. When a medical practice is being started, the owner puts an initial investment of cash into the practice. This infusion of cash increases the cash asset and owner's equity and funds the operation of the business.

Assets, liabilities, and equity are all a part of the accounting equation. A T-account is used to represent the accounting equation.

Accounting Equation

An equation that expresses the relationship among assets, liabilities, and owner's equity is called the **accounting equation.** The accounting equation is stated as follows:

$$Assets = Liabilities + Owner's\ equity$$

The total of the amounts on the left side of the equation (assets) will always be equal to the total of the amounts on the right side (liabilities + owner's equity).

For example, if the office pays $50 cash for medical supplies, the cash account decreases, but the medical inventory supply account increases by the same amount. This keeps the equation in balance because the total assets have remained the same and the liabilities and owner's equity remain unchanged.

Cash + Medical supplies = Liabilities + Owner's equity

Opening balance:

$$1000 + 500 = 600 + 900$$

After transaction:

$$(1000 - 50) + (500 + 50) = 600 + 900$$
$$950 + 550 = 600 + 900$$

Therefore each side of the equation is equal.

If the office had charged the $50 in medical supplies, how would the equation change, and would it be in balance?

After transaction:

$$1000 + (500 + 50) = (600 + 50) + 900$$
$$1000 + 550 = 650 + 900$$

Instead of $50 being subtracted from cash, $50 was added to liabilities, and the accounting equation is still in balance.

NOTE: Total assets and total liabilities have each increased by the same amount. Owner's equity cannot increase by increasing liabilities; it can increase only through the owner contributing more equity to the business or the business earning a profit.

T-Accounts

The accounting equation can be represented as a T, as shown in Fig. 5-1. As seen with the previous example of the purchase of medical supplies, a transaction changes the balance of two different accounts in the accounting equation. When using the T-account, an amount recorded on the left side of the T is called a **debit,** and an amount recorded on the right side is called a **credit.** The **T-account** is the basic tool used to analyze the effect of a transaction on accounts. A debit entry will *increase* the value of an asset account but will *decrease* a liability and owner's equity account.

Using the above example, T-accounts would appear as follows:

After transaction:

1000	+	500		=		600	+		900
		+50				+50			
1000	+	550		=		650	+		900
D	C	D	C		D	C		D	C
1000		500			600				900
		50			50				

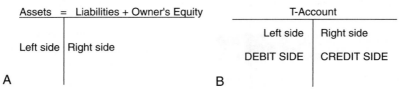

Fig. 5-1   **A,** Accounting equation in T-account form. **B,** T-account showing the debit side *(left)* and credit side *(right).*

Asset accounts (e.g., cash, equipment owned) have normal debit balances (D, left side), and liability and owner's equity accounts have normal credit balances (C, right side). Because asset accounts have normal debit balances, they increase on the debit side and decrease on the credit side. Liability and owner's equity accounts increase on the credit side and decrease on the debit side.

It is important to remember that each transaction will change the balance of at least two specific accounts, one on each side of the T-account. For example, disbursing cash will decrease cash (a credit). The other half of the transaction must be a debit that offsets the credit to the cash account. That debit can be an increase in an asset (e.g., increase in inventory) or a decrease in a liability (debit) that was paid through the original disbursement of cash (credit).

Types of Assets

Although the specific assets of a medical practice will vary, some types of assets are common to many medical practices: cash, accounts receivable, and miscellaneous assets such as property and equipment.

Cash

A medical practice receives cash for services rendered. This may be in the form of a payment from a patient (either full payment or a co-payment) or by the insurance company. Petty cash is another cash asset of the medical office.

Petty Cash

Petty cash is an amount of cash kept on hand used for making small payments for incidental supplies. Ideally, "cash control" (having a record of what money is spent and how) is best maintained when payments are made by check. Some expenses are small, however, and writing a check is not time- or cost-effective. In these situations a separate cash fund for making small cash payments is maintained

(the petty cash fund). Each office will decide on the actual dollar amount kept in the fund, but essentially the fund should provide for small cash purchases for a month. The petty cash account is an asset and has a debit, or positive, balance.

Each time a payment is made from the petty cash fund, a numbered form, or **voucher,** is prepared (Fig. 5-2). The voucher shows the date and purpose of the withdrawal, to whom the money was paid, and the amount of the payment. Petty cash vouchers are kept in the petty cash box until the fund is replenished.

Every time petty cash is paid out, the transaction should also be recorded in the petty cash record (Fig. 5-3). Employees requesting reimbursement from the petty cash fund should submit proof of their expenditures, such as a receipt, and it should be attached to the voucher. The amount in the petty cash box decreases with each payment. Eventually, the fund needs to be replenished. When reconciling a petty cash fund, the person responsible for the fund totals the vouchers, distributes the total into proper categories, and reimburses the fund for the amount of the vouchers to bring the cash balance back up to the original amount. Procedure 5-1 explains the process of accounting for petty cash.

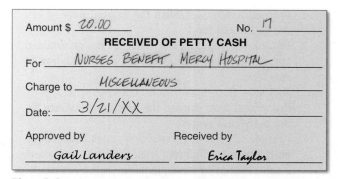

Fig. 5-2 Petty cash voucher. *(From Kinn ME: Woods MA: The medical assistant, ed 8, Philadelphia, 1999, Saunders.)*

No.	Date	Description	Amount	Office Exp.	Auto.	Misc.	Balance
	04/01	FUND ESTABLISHED					50.00
1	04/02	POSTAGE DUE	.55	.55			49.45
2	04/08	PARKING FEE	6.00		6.00		43.45
3	04/10	DELIVERY CHARGE	2.32			2.32	41.13
4	04/25	STATIONARY SUPPLIES	3.38	3.38			37.75
		TOTAL	12.25				
		BALANCE	37.75	3.93	6.00	2.32	
	CH# 374		12.25				50.00

Fig. 5-3   Petty cash record. *(From Kinn ME: Woods MA: The medical assistant, ed 8, Philadelphia, 1999, Saunders.)*

For example, if the amount initially put in the petty cash fund is $50.00, and at the end of the month the vouchers total $49.10 and $0.90 remains, there is no shortage or surplus of money in the petty cash fund. In this case a check is written for $49.10 and then cashed to bring the account back to $50.00.

However, if at the end of the month the voucher total is $48.00, but only $1.00 remains, this means there is a shortage of $1 in the fund. A shortage slip is made out to account for the missing money ($1.00), and a check is written for $49.00. The voucher total plus the shortage slip will account for the $49.00 check. (See Procedure 5-3.)

Accounts Receivable

Accounts receivable (AR) are used to record patient transactions when an amount is still due (owed) to the office (e.g., when an insurance payment has not yet arrived). A charge to a patient's AR account will increase the account balance, and a payment or adjustment will decrease the balance. The information provided by the AR account assists in managing the cash flow of the practice. This account represents credit extended to the customer (e.g., how much money is owed to the practice by patients). Think of AR as an account that is for "collection of past services."

Procedure 5-1 Manage an Account for Petty Cash

TASK: Establish a petty cash fund, maintain an accurate record of expenditures, and replenish the fund as necessary.

EQUIPMENT AND SUPPLIES
- Petty cash box or envelope
- Petty cash expense record
- Petty cash vouchers with receipts or list of petty cash expenditures
- Two blank checks
- Calculator
- Pen or pencil

SKILLS/RATIONALE

1. **Procedural Step. Establish the amount needed in the petty cash fund.**
2. **Procedural Step. Write a check for the determined amount, and put the cash in the petty cash box or envelope.**
   Rationale. This establishes a petty cash fund.
3. **Procedural Step. Record the beginning balance to the petty cash record.**
4. **Procedural Step. Prepare a petty cash voucher for each amount withdrawn from the fund, and attach a sales receipt or an explanation of the payment.**
   Rationale. The vouchers, sales receipts, and explanations of payment will be used for audit purposes.
5. **Procedural Step. Enter each expense in the petty cash expense record, allocating them to the correct disbursement categories. Calculate the new balance.**
   Rationale. Bringing forward the new balance after each entry keeps the balance current and helps determine when it is time to restore the fund to its original balance.
6. **Procedural Step. At the end of the month or when the fund balance has reached the established minimum, count the remaining currency in the petty cash box.**
7. **Procedural Step. Total all vouchers in the petty cash box.**

8. **Procedural Step. Add the voucher total to the amount in the petty cash fund. This should equal the original amount.**
   Rationale. The total of the remaining cash and the total of the expense vouchers should equal the amount originally in the petty cash fund.
9. **Procedural Step. Prepare a check for "cash" for the amount that was used for expenses (total of the vouchers). Enter the check number on the petty cash expense record.**
   This check should be categorized in the disbursement journal by the categories on the petty cash receipt.
10. **Procedural Step. After the replacement check is cashed, add the money back to the cash box.**
11. **Procedural Step. Record the amount added to the fund on the expense record.**
12. **Procedural Step. Bring the balance forward.**

NOTE: Petty cash is usually kept in a locked drawer or locked box; it is generally not kept at the front desk. Usually only one person on staff is responsible for petty cash. Change for patients should not be made from the petty cash fund; there should be separate funds for that purpose. Staff should never be permitted to borrow from petty cash.

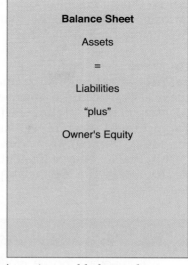

Income Statement	Statement of Owner's Equity	Balance Sheet
Revenue (income)	Owner's Equity (beginning)	Assets
"minus"	"plus"	=
Expenses	Additional Investments	Liabilities
=	"plus"	"plus"
Net Income/Loss	Net Income	Owner's Equity
	"minus"	
	Withdrawals	
	=	
	Ending Owner's Equity	

Fig. 5-4 Financial statements: income statement, statement of owner's equity, and balance sheet.

Aging of Accounts

An AR report that is beneficial to the financial success of the medical practice is the **aging report,** which shows the "age" of the debt, or how long the debt has gone unpaid. The following categories are used to identify accounts that are overdue:

- *Current:* These accounts include services that were provided within the month, and the accounts have not yet been sent an end-of-month statement.
- *0-30:* These accounts include services within the month and have been sent an end-of-month statement.
- *31-60:* These accounts reflect 2 months of billing services and need attention.
- *61-90:* These accounts have received 3 months of billing invoices, are long overdue, and may be sent to a collection agency.
- *Over 90:* These accounts are seriously overdue and should be in collection.

The longer an account "ages," the less likely the practice is to recover the amount due in full.

Miscellaneous Assets

Assets such as cash and accounts receivable in a medical office are easy to identify. However, a medical practice may own the property and the building where the medical office is located. The medical supplies, equipment, and furniture in the facility are all things of value owned by the business and are considered assets.

Types of Liabilities

Liabilities are debts owed by the medical practice. Liabilities are written as **payable** (e.g., notes

payable, accounts payable, wages payable). Think of a note payable as a "loan," accounts payable as "credit charges," and wages payable as "money due to employees."

Financial Statements

Financial statements are reports that tell the owner (physician) the fiscal (financial) condition of the practice. The owner uses these statements to consider expansion of the practice, budget for additional staff and equipment, and make salary adjustments (Fig. 5-4).

Income Statement

An **income statement** shows the results of income (revenues) and expenses over time, usually a month or year. The income statement shows money earned by the medical office and the expense of doing business. Another name for the income statement is a *profit and loss statement* or a *statement of income and expenses.* The income statement condenses the results of the activities into one figure, either **net income** or **net loss.** The income statement is prepared first so that the result (net income or loss) can be recorded in the statement of owner's equity, which is prepared next.

Statement of Owner's Equity

The **statement of owner's equity** reports the changes in the owner's financial interest during a reporting period and why the investment has changed. The net income or net loss amount is needed before the statement of owner's equity can be prepared. An investment or cash inflow to the medical practice will increase owner's equity, and withdrawals will decrease it. The ending balance (capital) on the statement of owner's equity is used on the balance sheet, so this statement must be prepared before the balance sheet.

Balance Sheet

The **balance sheet** reports the financial condition of a medical practice on a given date, usually the end of each month. It shows what the medical practice owns and owes, as well as the amount of owner's equity (capital). By reviewing the balance sheet with the income statement, the physician is able to assess the financial position of the practice.

Fig. 5-5 Medical assistant using pegboard system to record the day's activities.

PATIENT-CENTERED PROFESSIONALISM

- Why is it important for the medical assistant to understand basic accounting principles?
- If a medical assistant asked for a salary raise, which financial statements would provide information to the medical practice to make such a decision?

BOOKKEEPING PROCEDURES

Bookkeeping involves the systematic recording of financial business transactions. The person performing this function must understand the entire accounting system. A medical assistant performs bookkeeping tasks when recording all financial transactions on the daysheet or entering the information into a computerized management system. The recorded data are organized and reported on a timely basis so that appropriate financial statements can be prepared.

Many offices use a computerized patient accounting system for their daily bookkeeping tasks. Computerized bookkeeping is becoming increasingly common. Bookkeeping can also be done with the pegboard system.

Pegboard System

The **pegboard system,** or **one-write system,** is a type of recording system designed to increase the efficiency of recording daily transactions (Fig. 5-5). It is used most often for three types of documents or forms: payroll, general ledgers, and accounts receivable. The **pegboard** is a special device used to write the same information on several forms at one time (Fig. 5-6).

The name *pegboard* comes from the pegs along one side of the board. The forms used with this device have holes punched along one side. Each of the forms is placed on the pegs. Thus the lines on

Fig. 5-6 Use of a daysheet provides a record of patients seen, charges, and payments for a given day. *(Courtesy Bibbero Systems, Inc., Petaluma, Calif; phone [800] 242-2376; fax [800] 242-9330; www. bibbero.com.)*

each form are aligned, one beneath the other, and information written will be correctly positioned on each form. When an entry is made on the form on the top page of the pegboard, the data are reproduced on all the other forms beneath it at the same time. This happens because the forms are printed on NCR (no carbon required) paper, which is chemically treated to allow the transfer of entries from one sheet to another. Carbonized strips are on the form in specific places that must be recorded more than once. Remember that anything you write on the top sheet will show on the NCR sheets, so do not place miscellaneous papers or forms (e.g., phone messages) on top of the pegboard and write on them.

The pegboard has two major purposes: (1) It provides a solid writing base for writing on the forms by hand, and (2) information is recorded on several forms at once, thus saving time and reducing the chance of error.

When a patient arrives for the scheduled office visit, the medical assistant attaches either the receipt-charge slip or the encounter form (superbill) to the pegboard to register the patient, and then to the front of the patient's medical record. The physician completes the information on the form and returns the chart, with the form, to the front desk, where the medical assistant enters the dollar amount on the form from the **fee schedule** for all treatments. Daysheets, various charge forms, and ledger cards are used on the pegboard system, and the medical assistant needs to understand how to post service charges and payments using this system.

Daysheet

The **daysheet** acts as a journal for recording the day's activities. It provides a record of the patients seen, charges, and payments received on a daily basis (Fig. 5-7). Each day, all columns of the daysheet are totaled and checked for accuracy. The daysheet lets the physician know the amount of money collected for the day and the amount still owed.

Charge Forms

Several types of charge forms are used in the medical office. Two common charge forms are the encounter form and the receipt-charge slip.

ENCOUNTER FORM

The **encounter form,** or **superbill,** is a charge form that lists the ICD-9 and CPT codes most frequently used in the medical practice. Fig. 5-8 shows a completed encounter form. Note the blank spaces for adding codes and a space for the physician to indicate when the patient should return for follow-up. Also included is a financial box to list financial data, such as outstanding balance.

RECEIPT-CHARGE SLIP

The **receipt-charge slip,** or **statement-receipt,** is a charge form with two parts. The right side is the *charge slip,* listing the previous balance, treatments, and the patient's name (statement). The left side lists financial data, such as the charges for certain treatments, payments received (receipt), and the current balance (Fig. 5-9). The left portion of this form is returned to the patient as a *receipt* for any payment given to the physician that day.

Ledger Cards

When arriving for a scheduled appointment, a new patient is asked to complete a patient information (registration) sheet. This completed data sheet provides the demographic and insurance information needed to prepare a patient ledger card (Fig. 5-10).

Ledger cards contain demographics (name, address, phone number) about the patient as well as important billing information. When the patient is provided treatment, the ledger card is inserted between the charge slip (the encounter form or statement-receipt) and the daysheet. The type of service and the charges are recorded (charges for each service should be listed on the physician's fee schedule). Payment is recorded, and the current balance is listed. The ledger card is a permanent record for each patient and contains the up-to-date status of the patient's account. Many offices photocopy the ledger cards and mail them to patients as account statements.

Posting Payments

When a patient visits the medical office and makes a payment, it is recorded immediately. Payments may be in the form of check, cash, or credit card. Payments are also received electronically or in the mail from the insurance company, as well as from the patient at a later date.

Procedure 5-2 explains the process of posting service charges and payments using a pegboard.

Procedure 5-3 explains how to record charges and credits using a pegboard.

IMMEDIATE PAYMENT BY CREDIT CARD

A patient may offer to pay for services with a credit card. The medical practice must have an agreement with the credit card company. The agreement indicates a service charge will be applied to each transaction made by the medical office. Often a flat fee or a small percentage of the total payment goes to the credit card company as per the agreement. When the payment is processed, the patient receives a hard copy of the transaction as a receipt. The transaction is posted on the ledger card, recording all information (credit card company, total amount, and date).

PAYMENT BY MAIL

Payments from patients are sometimes received in the mail after the appointment. In this situation the ledger card is pulled and positioned on the appropriate line on the daysheet. The payments are posted on the ledger card and daysheet.

PAYMENT FROM THIRD-PARTY PAYERS

Payments from insurance companies (third-party payers) usually do not cover the total amount, so

Text continued on p. 202

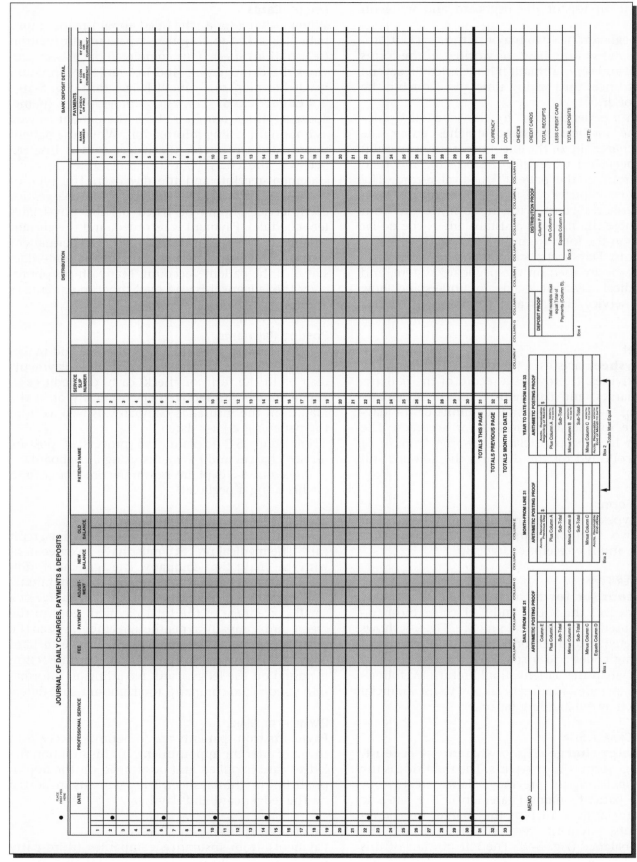

Fig. 5-7 Sample daysheet used with a pegboard system. (*Courtesy Bibbero Systems, Inc., Petaluma, Calif; phone [800] 242-2376; fax [800] 242-9330; www.bibbero.com.*)

Blackburn Primary Care Associates, PC
1990 Turquoise Drive
Blackburn, WI 54937
(608) 555-8857

Howard M. Lawler, MD   11
Joanne R. Hughes, MD   21
Ralph Garcia Lopez, MD   31
TAX ID NO. 00-00000000

GUARANTOR NAME AND ADDRESS	PATIENT NO.	PATIENT NAME	DOCTOR NO.	DATE
Darla Sissle 468 Maple Street Blackburn, WI 54937		Darla Sissle	21	6/5/XX

	DATE OF BIRTH	TELEPHONE NO.	INSURANCE		
			CODE	DESCRIPTION	CERTIFICATE NO.
	2/17/32	555-2075		CPC	21 - 58624

OFFICE - NEW				OFFICE - ESTABLISHED				OFFICE - CONSULT				PREVENTIVE CARE - ADULT			
X	CPT	SERVICE	FEE	X	CPT	SERVICE	FEE	X	CPT	SERVICE	FEE	X	CPT	SERVICE	FEE
	99201	Prob Foc/Straight			99211	Nurse/Minimal			99241	Prob/Foc/Straight			99385	18-39 Initial	
	99202	Exp Prob/Straight			99212	Prob Foc/Straight			99242	Exp Prob/Straight			99386	40-64 Initial	
	99203	Detailed/Low			99213	Exp Prob/Low	(55)		99243	Detailed/Low			99387	65+ Initial	
	99204	Compre/Moderate			99214	Detailed/Moderate			99244	Compre/Moderate			99395	18-39 Periodic	
	99205	Compre/High			99215	Compre/High			99245	Compre/High			99396	40-64 Periodic	
												99397	65+ Periodic	

GASTROENTEROLOGY				CARDIOLOGY & HEARING				INJECTIONS & IMMUNIZATION				REPAIR & DERMATOLOGY			
X	CPT	SERVICE	FEE	X	CPT	SERVICE	FEE	X	CPT	SERVICE	FEE	X	CPT	SERVICE	FEE
	45300	Sigmoidoscopy Rig			93000	ECG (Global)	(55)		86585	TB Skin Test			17110	Warts: #	
	45305	Sigmoid Rig w/bx			93015	Stress Test (Global)			90716	Varicella Vaccine				Tags: #	
	45330	Sigmoidoscopy Flex			93224	Holter (Global)			90724	Flu Vaccine				Lesion Excis	
	45331	Sigmoid Flex w/bx			93225	Holter Hook Up			90732	Pneumovax				Lesion Destruct	
	45378	Colonoscopy Diag			93227	Holter Interpretation			90718	TD Immunization			SIZE CM:	SITE:	
	45380	Colonoscopy w/bx			94010	Pulm Function Test							MALIG:	PREMAL/BEN:	
	46600	Anoscopy			92551	Audiometry Screen			90782	Injection IM*				(Check One Above)	
									90788	Injection IM Antibiot*				Simple Closure	

OTHER				SUPPLIES/DRUGS*											
				DRUG NAME:					Injection joint*				Intermed Closure		
				UNIT/MEASURE:			SM	MED	MAJOR			SIZE CM:	SITE:		
				QUANTITY			(circle one)								
							FOR ALL INJECTIONS, SUPPLY DRUG				10060	I&D Abscess			
							INFORMATION				10080	I&D Cyst			

DIAGNOSTIC CODES: ICD-9-CM

- ☐ 789.0 Abdominal Pain
- ☐ 795.0 Abnormal Pap Smear
- ☐ 706.1 Acne Vulgaris
- ☐ 477.0 Allergic Rhinitis
- ☐ 285.9 Anemia, NOS
- ☐ 281.0 Pernicious
- ☐ 411.1 Angina, Unstable
- ☐ 427.9 Arrhythmia, NOS
- ☐ 440.9 Arteriosclerosis
- ☐ 714.0 Arthritis, Rheumatoid
- ☐ 414.0 ASHD
- ☐ 493.90 Asthma, Bronchial W/O Status Ast.
- ☐ 493.91 Asthma, Bronchial W/ Status Ast.
- ☐ 466.1 Bronchiolitis, Acute
- ☐ 466.0 Bronchitis, Acute
- ☐ 727.3 Bursitis
- ☑ 786.50 Chest Pain
- ☐ 574.20 Cholelithiasis
- ☐ 372.30 Conjunctivitis, Unspecified
- ☐ 564.0 Constipation
- ☐ 496 COPD
- ☐ 692.9 Dermatitis, Allergic
- ☐ 250.01 Diabetes Mellitus, ID
- ☐ 250.00 Diabetes Mellitus, NID
- ☐ 558.9 Diarrhea
- ☐ 562.11 Diverticulitis
- ☐ 562.10 Diverticulosis

- ☐ 782.3 Edema
- ☐ 492.8 Emphysema
- ☐ V16.0 Family History of Diabetes
- ☐ 780.6 Fever of Undetermined Origin
- ☐ 578.9 G.I. Bleeding, Unspecified
- ☐ 727.41 Ganglion of Joint
- ☐ 535.0 Gastritis, Acute
- ☐ V72.3 Arrhythmia, NOS
- ☐ 748.0 Headache
- ☐ 550.90 Hernia, Inguinal, NOS
- ☐ 054.9 Herpes Simplex
- ☐ 053.9 Herpes Zoster
- ☐ 708.9 Hives/Urticaria
- ☐ 401.1 Hypertension, Benign
- ☐ 401.0 Hypertension, Malignant
- ☐ 402.90 Hypertension, W/O CHF
- ☐ 244.9 Hypothyroidism, Primary
- ☐ 380.4 Impacted Cerumen
- ☐ 487.1 Influenza
- ☐ 564.1 Irritable Bowel Syndrome
- ☐ 464.0 Laryngitis, Acute
- ☐ 454.9 Leg Varicose Veins
- ☐ 424.0 Mitral Valve Prolapse
- ☐ 412 Myocardial Infarction, Old
- ☐ 715.90 Osteoarthritis, Unspec. Site
- ☐ 620.2 Ovarian Cyst

- ☐ 614.9 Pelvic Inflammatory Disease
- ☐ 685.1 Pilonidal Cyst
- ☐ 462 Pharyngitis, Acute
- ☐ 627.1 Postmenopausal Bleeding
- ☐ 625.4 Premenstrual Tension
- ☐ 782.1 Rash
- ☐ 569.3 Rectal Bleeding
- ☐ 398.90 Rheumatic Heart Disease, NOS
- ☐ 431.9 Sinusitis, Acute, NOS
- ☐ 782.1 Skin Eruption, Rash
- ☐ 845.00 Sprain, Ankle
- ☐ 848.9 Sprain, Muscle, Unspec. Site
- ☐ 785.6 Swollen Glands
- ☐ 246.9 Thyroid Disease, Unspecified
- ☐ 463 Tonsillitis, Acute

- ☐ 474.0 Tonsillitis, Chronic
- ☐ 465.9 Upper Respiratory Infection, Acute
- ☐ 599.0 Urinary Tract Infection
- ☐ V03.9 Vaccination/Bacterial Dis.
- ☐ V06.8 Vaccination/Combination
- ☐ V04.8 Vaccination, Influenza
- ☐ 616.10 Vaginitis, Vulvitis, NOS
- ☐ 780.4 Vertigo
- ☐ 787.0 Vomiting, Nausea
- ☐ ___ _____
- ☐ ___ _____
- ☐ ___ _____
- ☐ ___ _____

RETURN APPOINTMENT		BALANCE DUE			
__7__ Days _____ Weeks _____ Months		DATE OF SERVICE	CPT CODE	DIAGNOSIS CODE(S)	CHARGE
Authorization Number: ▶ _____					

Place of Service:
(✓) Office
( ) Emergency Room
( ) Inpatient Hospital
( ) Outpatient Hospital
( ) Nursing Home

TOTAL CHARGE	$ 110
AMOUNT PAID	$ 100
PREVIOUS BAL	$ 100
BALANCE DUE	$ 110

Check #: _____

(Circle Method of Payment)
CASH   (CHECK)   MC   VISA

Physician's Signature

▶ *Joanne R. Hughes, MD*

Fig. 5-8 Encounter form (superbill). *(From Hunt SA:* Saunders fundamentals of medical assisting, *Philadelphia, 2002, Saunders.)*

6/5/xx	Intermediate Exam, EKG	110	100		110	100	Darla Sissle
DATE / Family member	DESCRIPTION	TOTAL FEE	PAYMENT	ADJ.	BALANCE	PREVIOUS BALANCE	PATIENT'S NAME
			CREDITS				

This is your RECEIPT for this amount

This is a STATEMENT of your account to date

Please present this slip to receptionist befor leaving office

BLACKBURN PRIMARY CARE ASSOCIATES, PC
1990 Turquiose Drive
Blackburn, WI 54937
608-555-8857

B–Biopsy
C–Consultation
CPX–Complete Physical
ECG–Electrocardiogram
E.R.–Emergency Room
H.A.–Hospital Admit
H.V.–Hospital Visit
IOV–Initial Ofc. Visit
INJ–Injection
LAB–Laboratory
N.C.–No Charge
O.V.–Office Visit
L–Limited
C–Comprehensive
ROA–Rec'd on Acct.
S–Surgery
X–X-Ray

OFFICE VISIT	55	—
CONSULTATION		
ECG	55	—
INJECTION		
LABORATORY		
X-RAY		
SURGERY		
TOTAL	110	—

Thank You

YOUR NEXT APPOINTMENT WILL BE

PATIENT NAME	DATE	DAY	TIME
Darla Sissle	6	10	3:00

1000

1000 ___DAYS___WKS___MO.

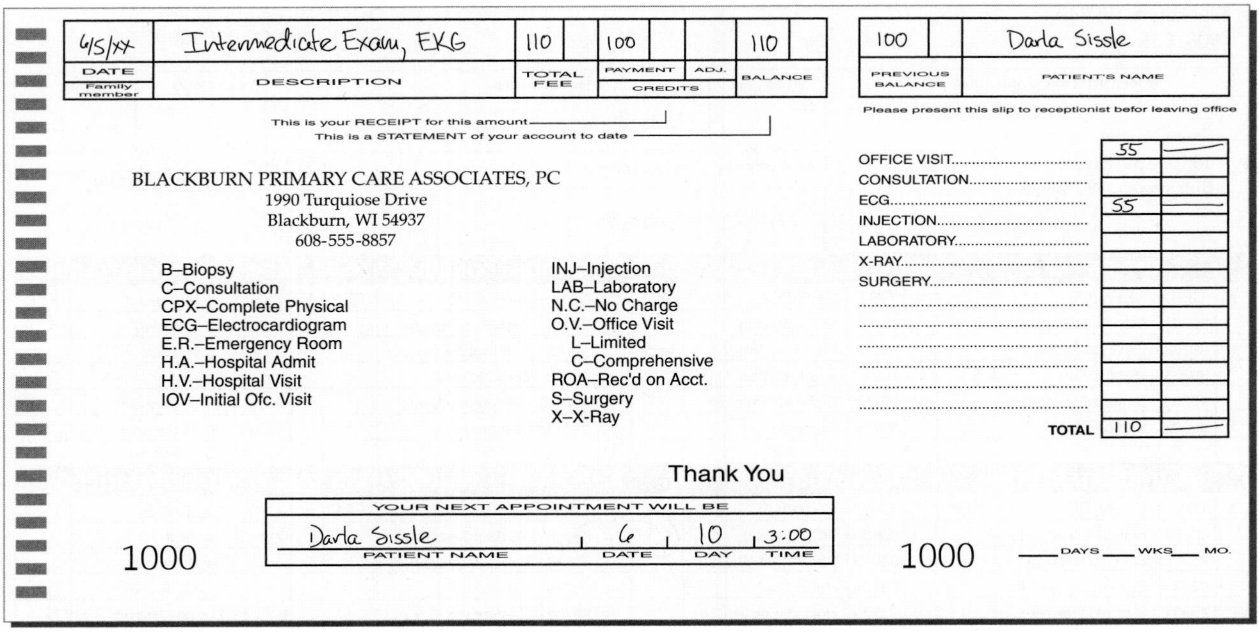

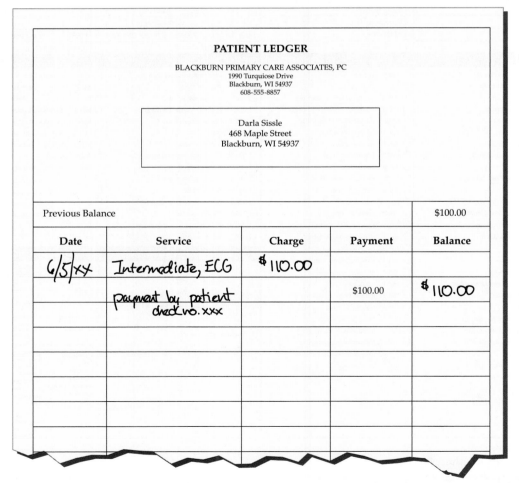

Fig. 5-9 Receipt-charge slip for the pegboard system. *(From Hunt SA:* Saunders fundamentals of medical assisting, *Philadelphia, 2002, Saunders.)*

PATIENT LEDGER

BLACKBURN PRIMARY CARE ASSOCIATES, PC
1990 Turquiose Drive
Blackburn, WI 54937
608-555-8857

Darla Sissle
468 Maple Street
Blackburn, WI 54937

Previous Balance				$100.00
Date	**Service**	**Charge**	**Payment**	**Balance**
6/5/xx	Intermediate, ECG	$110.00		
	payment by patient check no. xxx		$100.00	$110.00

Fig. 5-10 Patient account ledger. *(From Hunt SA:* Saunders fundamentals of medical assisting, *Philadelphia, 2002, Saunders.)*

Procedure 5-2 Post Service Charges and Payments to the Patient's Account

TASK: Post service charges and payments using a pegboard.

EQUIPMENT AND SUPPLIES
- Pegboard
- Calculator
- Pen, pencil
- Daysheet (daily journal)
- Receipt-charge slips
- Ledger cards
- Previous day's balance
- List of patients and services
- Fee schedule

SKILLS/RATIONALE

1. **Procedural Step. Prepare the pegboard:**
   a. Place a new daysheet on the board.
   b. Place a series of receipt-charge slips over the pegs aligning the top receipt with the first open writing line on the daysheet.
   Rationale. This should be done every morning before scheduled appointments arrive so that the office is prepared to receive patients.

2. **Procedural Step. Using a pen, date the daysheet with the current date, then carry forward the balances from the previous day's financial activity.** To "carry forward" means to record the totals from the previous daysheet on the new sheet you have just prepared.
   Rationale. It is important that a ballpoint pen be used to ensure that the information is transferred through all layers of the pegboard system. Carrying forward balances ensures that all totals are current.

3. **Procedural Step. Pull ledger cards for patients scheduled for appointments that day.**

4. **Procedural Step. Align the ledger card.** When a patient arrives, insert the ledger card under the first receipt, aligning the first available writing line of the card with the carbonized strip on the receipt.
   Rationale. It is important to align the ledger card accurately with the receipt to ensure correct posting of information to the receipt, ledger card, and daysheet.

5. **Procedural Step. On the receipt-charge slip, enter the date and the patient's name.** Also enter on the daysheet any existing balance from the patient's ledger card in the Previous Balance column and the number of this receipt in the Receipt Number column.

6. **Procedural Step. Detach the charge slip from the receipt and clip it to the patient's chart.**
   Rationale. The physician then can mark the slip to indicate the service(s) performed for the patient during the appointment.

7. **Procedural Step. Remove the ledger card from the pegboard.**
   Rationale. Removing the ledger card from the pegboard prepares you to be ready to make entries for other patients.

8. **Procedural Step. Complete the ledger card.** When the completed charge slip is returned at the end of the visit, enter on it the appropriate fee(s) for the service(s) provided, using the office's fee schedule.

9. **Procedural Step. Locate on the pegboard the receipt with the number that matches the number on the patient's charge slip.**
   Rationale. This is done to make certain that it is the correct receipt.

10. **Reinsert the patient's ledger card over the daysheet and under the correct receipt.**

11. **Procedural Step. Complete the receipt.**
    a. Enter the professional service code and services provided.
    b. Write the fee for the patient's visit on the receipt.
    Rationale. This will serve as the patient's receipt of services.

12. **Procedural Step. Ask the patient for payment; record the payment amount and the new balance for the patient's account.**
    Rationale. This brings the patient's account up to date and provides current information for the patient.

13. **Procedural Step. Remove the completed receipt from the pegboard and give the patient the receipt.**

14. **Procedural Step. Refile the ledger card according to office procedure.**

15. **Procedural Step. Repeat Steps 4 through 14 for each patient or receipt of payment for the day.** If this sheet is filled during the day, prepare a new sheet and continue the day's activities. Then, at the end of the day, fill in the Total Sheet Numbers at the top of the form.

Continued

Procedure 5-2 Post Service Charges and Payments to the Patient's Account—cont'd

16 Procedural Step. At the end of the day, total all columns of the daysheet using a pencil until totals have been verified as accurate. This consists of two parts.

a. Add up the amounts shown in columns A, B1, B2, C, and D, plus the total of the cash column, the total of the checks columns, and the total to deposit.

Rationale. This determines the figures that need to be entered in the "Totals This Page" row.

b. Add the figure in column A in the "Totals This Page" row and the figure in column A in the "Totals Previous Page" row. Do the same for columns B1, B2, C, and D.

Rationale. This determines the figure that needs to be entered in the "Totals Month to Date" row.

17. Procedural Step. Write in ink the proof totals on the bottom of the daysheet and add the total number of pages in the Sheet Number space at the top of the daysheet page(s).

16

DAILY LOG OF CHARGES AND RECEIPTS

DATE 1/4/xx   SHEET NUMBER _____

DATE	FAMILY MEMBER	PROFESSIONAL SERVICES		CHARGE	CREDITS PYMTS.	CREDITS ADJ.	NEW BALANCE	PREVIOUS BALANCE	NAME	RECEIPT NUMBER		CASH	CHECKS		PRACTICE SUMMARY Dr. A. Dr. B.	
1/4	Pat	OC, I, L, XR	CK	80 00	55 00		80 00	55 00	Gerald Morris	1197	1		55 00	80.00	
1/4	Ruth	OC, PAP, L		55 00	- 0 -		55 00	- 0 -	Ruth Jensen	1198	2				55.00
1/4	Debra	OC, EKG	CA	53 00	25 00		95 00	67 00	John Walters	1199	3	25 00			53.00
1/4	Peter	OS		175 00	- 0 -		175 00	- 0 -	Peter Brown	1200	4			175.00	
1/4	Sue	OB	CK	350 00	100 00	20 00	250 00	20 00	George Lawson	1201	5		100 00		350.00
1/4	Trudy	OC	CK	25 00	40 00		- 0 -	15 00	David Chalmers	1202	6		40 00		25.00
1/4	Martha	OC, I	CA	40 00	40 00		- 0 -	- 0 -	Ralph Franklin	1203	7	40 00			40.00
1/4	Billy	OC, XR	CK	85 00	50 00		63 00	28 00	Doris Thomas	1204	8		50 00	85.00	
1/4	Andy, Jr.	OC, I		45 00	- 0 -		45 00	- 0 -	Andrew Carson	1205	9				45.00
1/4	Pam	OS, M		95 00	- 0 -		95 00	- 0 -	Pamela Unger	1206	10			95.00	
1/4	Alice	OC, L	CA	35 00	35 00		81 00	81 00	Henry Young	1207	11	35 00		35.00	
1/4	Tina	OC, PAP	CK	35 00	35 00		- 0 -	- 0 -	Leonard Adams	1208	12		35 00		35.00
1/4	Catherine	OC, L		40 00	- 0 -		86 00	46 00	Catherine Mills	1209	13			40.00	
1/4	Frank	PE		45 00	- 0 -		45 00	- 0 -	Frank George	1210	14			45.00	
1/4	Dwight	HC Medicaid	CK	40 00	40 00	12 00	50 00	62 00	Dwight Nelson, Sr.	1211	15		40 00		40.00
										16				
										17				
										18				
										19				
										20				
										21				
										22				
										23				
1/4		BCBS	CK		275 00		35 00	310 00	Jason Phillips		24		275 00		
1/4		Medicaid	CK		51 00	16 00	- 0 -	67 00	Barbara Worth		25		51 00		
1/4		ROA	CA		30 00		- 0 -	30 00	R. Olson		26	30 00			
1/4		PRV	CK		268 00		13 00	281 00	Howard Rogers		27		268 00		
1/4		ROA	CK		52 00		- 0 -	52 00	Jane Klein		28		52 00		
										29				
										30				
										31				
										32	130 00	966 00	555.00	643.00

TOTALS		Col. "A"	Col. B-1	Col. "B-2	Col. C	Col. D		
	THIS PAGE	1198 00	1096 00	48 00	1168 00	1114 00		
	PREVIOUS PAGE	2981 00	3152 00	59 00	1916 00	2146 00		
	MONTH-TO-DATE	4179 00	4248 00	107 00	3084 00	3260 00		

TOTAL DEPOSIT 1,096 00

PROOF OF POSTING			ACCOUNTS RECEIVABLE CONTROL		ACCOUNTS RECEIVABLE PROOF	
COL. D TOTAL	$ 1114.00	PREVIOUS DAY'S TOTAL	$ 10,302.00	ACCTS. REC. 1ST OF MONTH	$ 10,532.00
PLUS COL. A TOTAL	$ 1198.00	PLUS COL. A	$ 1,198.00	PLUS COL. A-MO. TO DATE	$ 9,179.00
SUB TOTAL	$ 2312.00	SUB TOTAL	$ 11,500.00	SUB TOTAL	$ 14,711.00
LESS COLS. B-1 & B-2	$ 1144.00	LESS COLS. B-1 & B-2	$ 1,144.00	LESS B-1 & B-2 MO. TO DATE	$ 4,355.00
MUST EQUAL COL. C	$ 1168.00	TOTAL ACCTS. REC.	$ 10,356.00	TOTAL ACCTS. REC.	$ 10,356.00

CASH PAID OUT	
	$
	$
	$
	$

CASH CONTROL	
BEGINNING CASH ON HAND	$ 100.00
RECEIPTS TODAY (COL. B-1)	1,096.00
TOTAL	1,196.00
LESS PAID-OUTS	- 0 -
LESS BANK DEPOSIT	1,096.00
CLOSING CASH ON HAND	$ 100.00

Figure courtesy Colwell, a division of Patterson Companies, Inc., St. Paul, Minn, (800) 637-1140.

Procedure 5-3 Record Adjustments and Credits to the Patient's Account

TASK: Record adjustments such as insurance payments, write-offs, professional discounts, and nonsufficient funds (NSF) using a pegboard.

EQUIPMENT AND SUPPLIES
- Pegboard
- Calculator
- Pen, pencil
- Daysheet (daily journal)

- Ledger cards
- Previous day's balance
- List of patients and services
- Fee schedule

SKILLS/RATIONALE

Refer to the figure for Step 16 in Procedure 5-2 as you complete this procedure.

Recording Adjustments

When an adjustment is necessary (e.g., insurance payment is less than charge based on contractual agreement; overpayment to account is made), the amount of the adjustment is entered in column B2.

To determine a new balance for the patient, add together the patient's previous balance and any current charges, then subtract from this sum any credits that appear in column B1, as well as the adjustment that shows in column B2. This produces the patient's new balance.

1. **Procedural Step. Pull the patient's ledger card and align it with the first available empty row on the daysheet.**
   Rationale. It is important to align the ledger card accurately to ensure correct posting of information to the ledger card and daysheet.
2. **Procedural Step. Fill out the ledger card, entering the date and the following information:**
   a. Notation of the payment.
   b. "Received on Account" (ROA) in the "Professional Services" area.
   c. Amount of the payment in the "Payment" column.
   d. Amount of the adjustment in the "Adjustment" column.
   e. New balance (calculated as stated above).
3. **Procedural Step. Refile the ledger card according to office procedure.**
4. **Procedural Step. Provide a refund if the patient's account has a credit balance (e.g., patient makes payment at time of service, then patient's insurance company is billed and makes subsequent payment).**

a. To eliminate a credit balance, you must debit the account.
b. Place the amount of the refund in the adjustment column in brackets, indicating it is a **_debit,_** not a credit adjustment.
c. Write "Refund to Patient" in the description column.
d. Write and mail a check to the patient in the amount of the refund.

Recording Nonsufficient Funds

NSF situations are considered a "charge" and are accounted for on the daysheet in column A. Entering an NSF on the daysheet is similar to entering a charge for a professional service. If a notice of nonsufficient funds is received in the mail, enter this information in column A by writing "NSF" in the "Professional Services" column. In column A, enter the sum of the returned check itself, plus any service charge your office makes for an NSF.

1. **Procedural Step. Pull the patient's ledger card and align it with the first available empty row on the daysheet.**
   Rationale. It is important to align the ledger card accurately to ensure correct posting of information to the ledger card and daysheet.
2. **Procedural Step. Fill out the ledger card, entering the date and the following:**
   a. Notation of "NSF" (including check number) in the "Professional Services" area.
   b. Amount of the NSF (check amount + service charge) in the "Fee" column.
   c. New balance.
3. **Procedural Step. Refile the ledger card according to office procedure.**
   NOTE: A receipt-charge slip is typically not used when entering an NSF on the daysheet.

the account must be adjusted after an insurance payment is received. Adjustments are made according to the agreement between the insurance company and the physician about how much can be charged for a service. For example, Medicare has specified "allowable" charges for services. When a physician agrees to accept Medicare patients, he or she must not charge more than the Medicare "allowable" amount. The difference between the physician's charge and the correct Medicare payment must be "adjusted" on (deducted from) the patient's account; the patient is not charged for this difference. (This process is explained further in the Billing and Collections section.)

Computerized Account Management

There are many computerized account management systems for medical offices. The procedures used are similar to those of the pegboard system. The current date is verified each morning because this is the date recorded when posting the business transaction of the medical office. An encounter form is attached to the patient's chart. When returned to the front desk, the patient's account is "pulled up" on the computer, the current charges are entered (posted), and payments and adjustments are made. A receipt can be printed for the patient. At the end of the workday, a daysheet (daily journal) can be printed and all entries verified. Computerized systems will automatically post the daily transactions to each patient's account and total all activities for the day.

Advantages of using various types of computerized systems include the following:

1. Claims to insurance companies can be submitted electronically.
2. Reports of financial and billing information can be more detailed and printed easily.
3. Less room is needed for storage of paper records.
4. Entering data into one screen can automatically update other electronic forms.

PATIENT-CENTERED PROFESSIONALISM

- How is the pegboard system enhanced by the requirements used in bookkeeping?

BANKING PROCEDURES

The medical assistant responsible for administrative duties will receive payments for physician services in the form of cash, check, or credit card. When accepting a check for payment, the medical assistant must be aware of the basic check requirements necessary to make the payment valid. Sometimes the medical assistant may be asked to complete a check when purchasing office supplies or to complete a bank deposit at the end of the day. Understanding how to perform these duties correctly will make your job easier, whether these are your responsibilities or those of another medical assistant.

Checks

Although you may be familiar with writing checks, you should take a few precautionary steps when accepting and writing checks in the medical office. Understanding these precautions protects both the patient and the practice.

Accepting Checks

Checks received for medical services will be from a patient (personal check), an insurance company, or both. For example, a patient may make a co-payment with a check, and the portion of the service fee for which the insurance company is responsible can also be paid to the office in the form of a check. Medical assistants need to understand what information should be verified and follow office procedure on different types of checks.

CHECK REQUIREMENTS
When accepting a check for payment, you must verify the following information:

1. *Correct provider name* (the **payee**). Check the spelling, as well as any credentials or titles (e.g., Rosa Parks Clinic; Pete Pierson, MD).
2. *Current date.* Check to verify that the date and year are correct and that the check is not **postdated** (a postdated check has a future date written on it).
3. *Correct amount.* Make sure the written amount on the check is the same as the number amount.
4. *Current address and phone number.* Verify that the demographic data (name, address) on the check matches the patient's information on file.
5. *Affixed signature.* Verify that the person who signed the check (the **payer**) is listed on the check.

By confirming this information, you can prevent potential problems later with the bank or the patient.

DIFFERENT TYPES OF CHECKS
The medical office should have a written policy that states how the front desk is to handle "out-of-town"

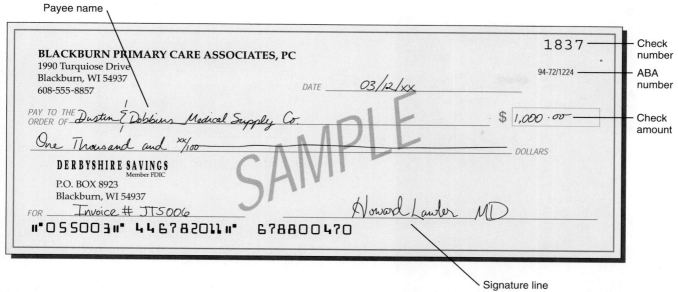

Payee name

Check number

ABA number

Check amount

BLACKBURN PRIMARY CARE ASSOCIATES, PC
1990 Turquiose Drive
Blackburn, WI 54937
608-555-8857

1837

94-72/1224

DATE _03/12/xx_

PAY TO THE ORDER OF _Dustin & Dobbins Medical Supply Co._ $ _1,000.00_

One Thousand and xx/100 DOLLARS

DERBYSHIRE SAVINGS
Member FDIC
P.O. BOX 8923
Blackburn, WI 54937

FOR _Invoice # JTS006_ _Howard Lawler MD_

⑈055003⑈ 44678 2011⑈ 678800470

Signature line

Fig. 5-11 Completed check. *(Modified from Hunt SA:* Saunders fundamentals of medical assisting, *Philadelphia, 2002, Saunders.)*

checks, third-party checks, and checks that are marked "paid in full."

- **Out-of-town checks** are written on an account in a bank that is not local. Some offices do not accept out-of-town checks.
- **Third-party checks** are "made out" to someone else but "signed over" to the medical practice. Third-party checks usually are not accepted because the medical office does not know the payer. An exception is an insurance check made out to the patient and endorsed by the patient to the medical practice.
- Checks marked **paid in full** should not be accepted unless the amount does cover the entire current balance. If the amount on a check that is marked "paid in full" does not cover the full amount, a notation above the endorsement should indicate that the payment is received toward an account balance.

Writing Checks

Payment by check provides the medical office with an excellent record of spending. By looking back at the check register (record of checks written, to whom, and for what amount), the physician or office manager can see where the money of the practice is going. Trends can be seen and budgets prepared more easily. The cancelled check, when received from the bank with the bank statement, serves as a receipt and a permanent record. Most banks do not return cancelled checks each month but will return them on request. The bank does provide the check numbers on the bank statement, so they may be reconciled with the checkbook.

Different styles of checks include end stub, wallet style, and book style. The type chosen for the medical practice depends on the needs and preferences of the person responsible for handling funds. Many physicians choose the end-stub style checks because they provide a place for recording important information about the payee or the reason the check was written.

The medical assistant may be required to fill out the necessary information on a check and then present it for an authorized signature (Fig. 5-11). If you are asked to write checks, follow these security tips for check writing:

1. Only authorized office personnel may sign the check. Each authorized person must have a signature card on file at the bank.
2. The record portion of the end-stub style should be filled in before the check is completed.
3. All lines should be filled in closest to the left end of the line to prevent additions to the line. When the item written is completed, a long line should be added to fill out the line.
4. Check amounts are written with numbers and words. This eliminates misinterpreting the amount intended on the check.
5. Write the number amount in the box directly next to the dollar sign to reduce the chance of an additional number being added. Some medical offices use a check-writing machine that makes small perforations across the amount to prevent alterations.
6. Enter the cents as number of cents over the number one hundred (e.g., $\frac{10}{100}$ for 10 cents).

Fig. 5-12 Accurate records reflect the competence of the staff. The medical assistant should use a calculator when adding numbers and should be careful not to transpose numbers when performing financial activities such as preparing deposit slips.

7. Write the amount in words on the blank line that ends in "Dollars" *under* the line that starts with "Pay to the order of."

Deposits

A **deposit** is when money (cash or checks) is prepared and sent to a financial institution to be placed in an account. Deposits are usually made at the end of each business day (Fig. 5-12). The medical assistant may be responsible for preparing or making deposits, so it is important to understand the concept of endorsement, how to use a deposit slip, and various deposit methods.

Endorsement

The physician or designated person must **endorse** the checks before they can be deposited. (Endorsing transfers all rights to another party, in this case the financial institution where the checks will be deposited.) This can be accomplished by having the physician sign each check in ink in the designated area on the back (Fig. 5-13), or most often, the endorsement is obtained by stamping the back of each check with a specially designed stamp. Most medical offices prefer using a stamp because the check can be endorsed immediately on receiving the check for

Fig. 5-13 Physician's endorsement on the back of a check in the designated area.

payment. The stamp can include the physician's signature with special instructions (e.g., "Alan Dean, M.D. For deposit to account of within named payee only").

- "For Deposit Only" is a form of **restrictive endorsement** because it limits what can be done with the check.
- A **blank endorsement** is when the payee (person to whom the check is written) signs only his or her name on the back of the check.
- A **special endorsement** includes words that specify to whom the endorser makes the check payable, such as when a patient signs the back of an insurance check over to the medical practice for payment on their account (e.g., "Charlie Baker (patient) Pay to the order of Alan Dean, M.D.").
- Occasionally, a **qualified endorsement** is used to prevent future liability of the endorser. An attorney uses a qualified endorsement to accept a check on behalf of a client (e.g., "Paid in Full").

Deposit Slip

After the checks have been endorsed, a **deposit slip** is prepared. A deposit slip is completed each business day and is presented to the bank with the monies (cash, checks) so the deposit will be properly credited to the correct bank account. Most deposit slips are preprinted with the depositor's name, address, and the account number into which the money is being deposited. Most medical practices use deposit slips that are in duplicate form so a receipt can be kept for the deposit. Deposit slips are located at the end of the checkbook, or may be separate documents in a book. They have a place for recording the date and columns in which to record the amount of cash (currency and coin) and individual checks (Fig. 5-14).

When recording checks, the payer's name (name of the person who wrote the check) can be listed. Sometimes the **ABA number** (number assigned by the American Bankers Association to identify the

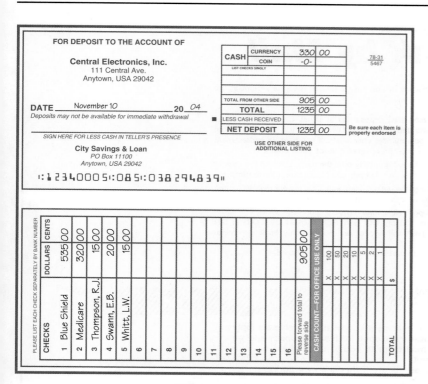

Fig. 5-14 Front and back of a completed deposit slip. *(From Young AP, Kennedy DB: Kinn's the medical assistant, ed 9, Philadelphia, 2003, Saunders.)*

payer's bank and location) is used. The ABA number is located on the upper right corner of each check as a whole number followed by a hyphen and ending with a "fraction" (e.g., 94-72/1224).

Procedure 5-4 outlines the correct process for preparing a bank deposit.

Deposit Methods

Deposits can be made in several ways, including the following:

- *In person.* The deposit is handed to the teller, who in turn verifies the information contained on the deposit slip and provides a deposit receipt. Automated (or automatic) teller machines (ATMs) allow the deposit of monies into an account without a teller.
- *By mail.* This type of deposit is best used when the deposit consists only of checks. Special deposit forms are provided to the user by the bank, and a receipt can be made and later verified by the bank (Fig. 5-15).
- *Electronic.* Electronic banking allows for all deposits to be made directly to a person's bank account. This is usually done by insurance companies, which have made prior arrangements with the medical practice. The receipt of funds can be verified by viewing computerized banking records or through a statement sent to the medical office.
- *Night deposit.* The bank provides the business with a key to the night depository and a special bank bag. The customer opens the locked

drawer and places the bag into the drawer. The following morning, the bank verifies the deposit slip, credits the proper account, and forwards a deposit receipt to the customer.

No matter what deposit system is used, it is important to remember that the deposit receipt is a financial document and must be retained to verify a transaction.

Statement Reconciliation

Each month the bank will mail a **bank statement** (statement of all banking activities for a set period) to the medical practice along with all canceled checks (Fig. 5-16). Bank statements also list each deposit made, any service charges, interest received, and any other fees (e.g., ordering of checks, NSF checks). These statements must be **reconciled** monthly (put into agreement with the checkbook).

Reconciling a bank statement compares the checks written on the medical practice's account to those received by the bank. Any checks written or deposits deposited after the closing date of the bank statement are subtracted from or added to the balance. The bank reconciliation may be done on the back of the statement or on separate sheets of paper (Fig. 5-17). Any errors found on the statement must be reported immediately to the bank. Procedure 5-5 shows how to reconcile a bank statement.

Bank by Mail

Make your deposits in one easy step and get your receipt at the same time! Here's how:

1 Complete your personalized deposit slip as usual. Endorse the reverse side of all checks with the words "FOR DEPOSIT ONLY," sign your name and place your account number underneath. If you have an endorsement stamp, you may stamp the reverse side of each check.

2 In the detachable panel below, neatly print the name to which the deposit is to be credited, and write all applicable transaction information.

3 Peel back and remove the detachable panel. *This is your deposit receipt.* Please retain it as no other receipt will be mailed.

4 Be sure to place deposit slips, loan payment coupons, checks, etc. inside the envelope before mailing. DO NOT SEND CASH OR COIN in this envelope. Your deposit will appear on your monthly bank statement.

Please keep the detachable receipt for your records.

022000

☐ Please indicate if you wish to receive a supply of these envelopes for future deposits and we will mail them to you at the address on your receipt.
☐ Please indicate if this is a new address.

PLEASE DETACH AND RETAIN FOR YOUR RECORDS.

ACCOUNT NO.	AMOUNT	TRANSACTION ENCLOSED
_____	$ _____	☐ Deposit for Checking Account
_____	$ _____	☐ Deposit for Savings Account
_____	$ _____	☐ Payment on Loan
_____	$ _____	☐ Other_____

LIFT HERE ▲ Bank of America

TODAY'S DATE _____   TELEPHONE NO. _____   022000

THIS COPY IS FOR YOUR RECORDS. PLEASE REMOVE AND RETAIN.

NAME _____

ADDRESS _____   CITY/STATE/ZIP _____

Fig. 5-15 Example of bank-by-mail deposit envelope. *(Courtesy Valley Bank of Nevada, Las Vegas. In Young AP, Kennedy DB:* Kinn's the medical assistant, *ed 9, Philadelphia, 2003, Saunders.)*

PATIENT-CENTERED PROFESSIONALISM

- If you were responsible for receiving payments from the patient made by check, what information would you verify?
- Why is it important for the medical assistant to be aware of how to do a bank deposit and reconcile a bank statement, even when this is not a typical duty?

≋ BILLING AND COLLECTIONS

A patient is billed (sent a statement for the balance on the account) when all fees are not collected at the time of service, or not paid by his or her insurance company after a claim has been filed. Patients with outstanding balances are billed monthly, even when an insurance claim is pending. Collection is the process of obtaining payment for services. "Aging" accounts that are "delinquent" with unpaid balances are sent to collection agencies for further attempts at payment for services already rendered.

Billing

A patient's **statement**, or bill of what is owed, can be prepared in the following ways:

- *Photocopy of ledger card.* This is the easiest method because the ledger card contains current account information. A window envelope is used to accommodate the folded statement. The statement is folded in such a way that the patient's name and address show

Procedure 5-4 Prepare a Bank Deposit

TASK: Correctly prepare a bank deposit for the day's receipts and complete appropriate office records related to the deposit.

EQUIPMENT AND SUPPLIES
- Currency (cash and coin amounts)
- Checks for deposit (amounts for deposit)
- Deposit slip
- Endorsement stamp (optional)
- Deposit envelope

SKILLS/RATIONALE

Refer to Fig. 5-14 throughout this procedure.

1. **Procedural Step. Organize currency, including coins.**
   Place bills in order with the largest denomination on top, and arrange so that all bills are faceup and in the same direction.
   Rationale. Organizing the currency facilitates processing of the deposit at the bank.

2. **Procedural Step. Accurately count and total the currency, then record the total on the bank deposit slip.**
   Record the individual pieces on the back of the deposit slip. (Write down the number of $20 bills, $10 bills, and so on.)

3. **Procedural Step. Prepare the checks that will be included in the deposit.**
   Endorse each check, using a restrictive endorsement.
   Rationale. To transfer the title and to protect the checks from loss or theft, a restrictive endorsement needs to be placed on the back side of each check.

4. **Procedural Step. Fill out the deposit slip.**
   a. List each check separately on the back of the deposit slip.
   b. Total the amount of the checks.
   c. Record the total on both the back and the front of the deposit slip.

   NOTE: Record the checks starting with the largest amount and ending with the smallest amount. Some practices prefer that checks be added to the deposit slip in the order in which they were received. Checks may be recorded using the payer's name, or, if the bank prefers, the ABA number can be used instead (upper right corner of each check; see Fig. 5-11).

5. **Procedural Step. Total the amount of currency and checks, and enter the total on the front of the deposit slip.**
   This figure will be entered as the net deposit if no cash is being withdrawn.

6. **Procedural Step. Record the total amount of the deposit in the office checkbook.**
   Rationale. This keeps the account accurate and allows for reconciliation of the balance.

7. **Procedural Step. Write the date of the deposit (that day's date) on the front of the deposit slip.**

8. **Procedural Step. Make a photocopy of the front and back of the deposit slip for the office record if a duplicate deposit slip was not made.**
   Rationale. This is important for purposes of verification of the deposit, should this become necessary.

9. **Procedural Step. Place the currency, checks, and completed deposit slip in an envelope or bank bag for transporting to the bank.**

through the window, so there is no need to address the envelope, which saves time.
- *Prepared statement.* A statement is prepared from the information included on the ledger card. This method is time-consuming because it requires not only typing the information on a separate sheet of paper but also addressing the envelope.

- *Outside billing services.* This method requires that all patient-related financial records be given to an independent service to perform the billing process. Practices may find that this type of service, although expensive, allows for better cash flow. Many practices prefer this type of service to hiring full-time in-house billing employees, who would require benefits.

0821-402054

#821

Ililmuldldlulumlululdldluulllludlmululululudull

N
2

CALL (888) 555-2932
24 HOURS/DAY, 7 DAYS/WEEK
FOR ASSISTANCE WITH
YOUR ACCOUNT.

PAGE 1 OF 2   THIS STATEMENT COVERS: 6/22/XX THROUGH 7/22/XX

INTEREST CHECKING
0821-402054

SUMMARY

PREVIOUS BALANCE	252.10		MINIMUM BALANCE	142.55
DEPOSITS	68.74 +		AVERAGE BALANCE	220.00
INTEREST EARNED	.18 +		ANNUAL PERCENTAGE	
WITHDRAWALS	109.55 −		YIELD EARNED	.96 %
CUSTOMER SERVICE CALLS	.00 −			
INTERLINK/PURCHASE FEE	.00 −		INTEREST EARNED 20xx	2.23
MONTHLY CHECKING FEE AND OTHER CHARGES	.00 −			
▶ NEW BALANCE	**211.47**			

CHECKS AND WITHDRAWALS	CHECK 202	DATE PAID 7/05	AMOUNT 15.05	CHECK 203	DATE PAID 7/15	AMOUNT 94.50
DEPOSITS					DATE POSTED	AMOUNT
	CUSTOMER DEPOSIT				7/22	68.74
	INTEREST PAYMENT THIS PERIOD				7/22	.18
BALANCE INFORMATION	DATE 6/22	BALANCE 252.10	DATE 7/05	BALANCE 237.05	DATE 7/15 7/22	BALANCE 142.55 211.47

24 HOUR CUSTOMER SERVICE

EACH ACCOUNT COMES WITH 3 COMPLIMENTARY CALLS PER STATEMENT PERIOD.

CALLS TO 24 HOUR CUSTOMER SERVICE THIS STATEMENT PERIOD: 0

INTEREST INFORMATION

FROM	THROUGH	INTEREST RATE	ANNUAL PERCENTAGE YIELD (APY)
6/22	7/22	1.00%	1.01%

INTEREST RATE/APY AS OF 7/22/XX IF YOUR BALANCE IS

$ 0 - 4,999 . . . . .1.00%		1.01%
$ 5,000 - 9,999 . . . . .1.00%		1.01%
$ 10,000 AND OVER. 1.00%		1.01%

CALL 1-888-555-2932 IN CALIFORNIA ANYTIME FOR CURRENT RATES.

MEMBER FDIC

STATEMENT

Fig. 5-16 Example of bank statement. *(From Young AP, Kennedy DB:* Kinn's the medical assistant, *ed 9, Philadelphia, 2003, Saunders.)*

THIS WORKSHEET IS PROVIDED TO HELP YOU BALANCE YOUR ACCOUNT

1. Go through your register and mark each check, withdrawal, Express ATM transaction, payment, deposit or other credit listed on this statement. Be sure that your register shows any interest paid into your account, and any service charges, automatic payments, or Express Transfers withdrawn from your account during this statement period.

2. Using the chart below, list any outstanding checks, Express ATM withdrawals, payments or any other withdrawals (including any from previous months) that are listed in your register but are not shown on this statement.

3. Balance your account by filling in the spaces below.

ITEMS OUTSTANDING		
NUMBER	**AMOUNT**	
TOTAL	$	

ENTER

The NEW BALANCE shown on this statement _ _ _ _ _ _ _ _ _ _ _ _ _ $_____

ADD

Any deposits listed in your register $_____
or transfers into your account $_____
which are not shown on this $_____
statement.   +$_____

                         TOTAL _ _ _ _ _ _ _ +$_____

CALCULATE THE SUBTOTAL _ _ _ _ _ _ _ $_____

SUBTRACT

The total outstanding checks and withdrawals from the chart at left _ _ _ _ _ _ _ −$_____

CALCULATE THE ENDING BALANCE

This amount should be the same as the current balance shown in your check register _ _ _ _ _ _ _ _ _ _ _ _ _ $_____

IF YOU SUSPECT ERRORS OR HAVE QUESTIONS ABOUT ELECTRONIC TRANSFERS

If you believe there is an error on your statement or Express ATM receipt, or if you need more information about a transaction listed on this statement or an Express ATM receipt, please contact us immediately. We are available 24 hours a day, seven days a week to assist you. Please call the telephone number printed on the front of this statement. Or, you may write to us at United Trust Company, P.O. Box 327, Anytown, USA.

1) Tell us your name and account number or Express card number.

2) As clearly as you can, describe the error or the transfer you are unsure about, and explain why you believe there is an error or why you need more information.

3) Tell us the dollar amount of the suspected error.

You must report the suspected error to us no later than 60 days after we sent you the first statement on which the problem appeared. We will investigate your question and will correct any error promptly. If our investigation takes longer than 10 business days (or 20 days in the case of electronic purchases), we will temporarily credit your account for the amount you believe is in error, so that you may have use of the money until the investigation is completed.

Fig. 5-17 Reverse side of bank statement to be used for reconciling a checking account. *(From Young AP, Kennedy DB: Kinn's the medical assistant, ed 9, Philadelphia, 2003, Saunders.)*

Procedure 5-5 Reconcile a Bank Statement

TASK: Correctly reconcile a bank statement with the checking account.

EQUIPMENT AND SUPPLIES
- Ending balance of previous statement
- Current bank statement
- Canceled checks for current month
- Checkbook stubs
- Calculator
- Pencil

SKILLS/RATIONALE

Refer to the figure below throughout this procedure.
1. **Procedural Step. Compare the closing balance of the previous statement with the beginning balance of the current statement.**
   a. Look on the previous statement where it states "New Balance."
   b. Look on the current statement where it states "Previous Balance."
   Rationale. These balances must be in agreement to continue with the reconciliation process.
2. **Procedural Step. Compare the checks written with the items on the statement.**
   Rationale. This verifies that the statement reflects the correct amounts.

NOTE: Because most banks no longer send canceled checks back to their clients, the check register must be used for this comparison of check numbers to the statement.
3. **Procedural Step. Place a checkmark (✔) in the reference area of the check register to reflect that these checks have cleared the bank.**
   Rationale. This will help later when you need to identify the outstanding checks.
4. **Procedural Step. List and total the outstanding checks from this statement, as well as any outstanding checks from previous bank reconciliations.**

Alan T. Slatkin, M.D.
BANK RECONCILIATION
JUNE 20XX

BALANCE PER BANK STATEMENT		**$525.00**
+ Deposit in Transit		
June 28	$291.47	
June 29	$94.21	$385.68
		$910.68
- Oustanding Checks		
#137 June 19	$200.00	
#145 June 27	$150.00	$350.00
		$560.68
BALANCE PER BANK STATEMENT		**$575.68**
Services Charge		$10.00
NSF Check		$5.00
ADJUSTED CHECKBOOK BALANCE		**$560.68**

PREPARED BY:

DATE:

Figure modified from Chester GA: *Modern medical assisting*, Philadelphia, 1998, Saunders.

Procedure 5-5 Reconcile a Bank Statement—cont'd

5. **Procedural Step. Complete the bank statement reconciliation worksheet on the back of the bank statement, or apply the bank statement reconciliation formula.**
   a. Enter the new balance from the current bank statement ("Bank statement balance"). *(This is the starting point for the formula.)*
   b. Enter total amount of outstanding checks from the compiled list.
      NOTE: Do not include any certified checks as outstanding because their amount has already been deducted from the account.

6. **Procedural Step. Reconcile deposits.**
   Compare the check register and deposit slips to the bank statement to make sure that all deposits were made in the correct amount and to identify any deposits made that are shown in the check register but not on the statement.
   Rationale. This verifies that the statement reflects the correct amounts.

7. **Procedural Step. Add interest.**
   If the office's checking account is an "interest-bearing" account:
   a. Add amount of the interest earned to the account deposit at this time.
   b. Add interest deposit to the check register.

8. **Procedural Step. Update the bank statement reconciliation formula with any deposits that are in** the check register but are not shown on the statement.

9. **Procedural Step. Enter the corrected bank statement balance.**

10. **Procedural Step. Total any bank charges that appear on the bank statement and subtract them from the checkbook balance.**
    Such charges may include service charges, automatic withdrawals, ATM, payments, and NSF checks.
    Rationale. This provides a corrected checkbook balance.

11. **Procedural Step. If the checkbook balance and the statement balance do not agree, check the following items, then repeat the process as required:**
    a. Check your arithmetic.
    b. Remember to include *all* the outstanding checks.
    c. Remember to record *all* deposits or interest earned; make sure you did not record anything twice.
    d. Make sure no figures are transposed. (If the amount of the error is divisible by 9, you may have done this.)
    e. Make sure you remembered to correct your checkbook balance at the time of the previous statement.

- *Computerized billing.* Medical offices that are computerized have the advantage of being able to generate all statements from information in the patient accounts. Billing cycles can be run on demand, and more detailed financial reports can be generated for accounts receivable management.

The statement should always contain a notice clearly stating the office's payment policy (e.g., payment due on receipt).

Fee Policy

A patient should always be informed of the fee policy of the office. Most offices have a sign in the reception area that states "payment is due at the time of service." If the patient is a "self-pay" (e.g., bill is paid by the patient, not by insurance), an estimate of the total costs should be discussed before the appointment. If the patient has insurance, it is acceptable to ask for the patient's portion of the total cost, whether the deductible, the **co-insurance** (percentage of total charge not paid by insurance), or the **co-payment** (usually $10 to $20 per visit), at the time of service. Procedure 5-6 outlines the process of explaining professional fees before providing services.

The collection process begins with the patient's first visit and continues with each subsequent visit. New patients should be made aware of billing policies at the time of appointment to be ready to make payment and avoid embarrassment. Problems can arise later if the patient fails to make a payment on the day of service. Some practices will attach a finance charge if accounts are not kept up to date. The explanation for this charge should be included in the brochure on office policy. Patients may have questions about their statements, and the medical assistant must be prepared to help explain billing.

Billing Cycles

Each medical office chooses a billing cycle that meets the needs of the medical practice. Two forms are generated by the billing department: the

Procedure 5-6 Explain Professional Fees Before Services Are Provided

TASK: Explain the physician's fees so that the patient understands his or her obligations before receiving services.

EQUIPMENT AND SUPPLIES
- Physician's fee schedule
- Surgical cost estimate
- Estimate of medical expenses form
- Private area for discussion

SKILLS/RATIONALE

1. **Procedural Step. Take the patient to a private area for discussion of fees.**
2. **Procedural Step. Display a professional attitude toward the patient during the discussion.**
   Demonstrate a willingness to provide answers and look for solutions to payment arrangements, ensuring the patient has a thorough understanding of what will be expected.
   Rationale. Discussing long-term medical fees is often stressful for the ill patient and requires the medical assistant to be professional, understanding, and caring while remaining firm.
3. **Procedural Step. Provide the patient with an estimate of anticipated fees before services are provided.**
   Emphasize that what is being discussed is an estimate and that the actual cost may be

different depending on what types of services are ultimately provided.
   Rationale. In cases involving surgery or long-term treatment (e.g., chemotherapy), patients are given an estimate of medical expenses. This informs the patient of what insurance benefits will or will not cover and if alternative payment arrangements need to be made.
4. **Procedural Step. Determine whether the patient has specific concerns that may hinder payment.**
   Rationale. This provides an opportunity for making special arrangements, if needed.
5. **Procedural Step. Make appropriate arrangements for a discussion between the physician and patient if further explanation is necessary.**

CMS-1500 claim form to the insurance company and the bill (statement) to the patient. Most funds come from insurance payments, so practices try to file claims within 1 or 2 days of the date of service. Now, especially with electronic claim filing, the turnaround time is much faster for claim settlement, which improves the practice's cash flow. Types of cycle billing include the following:

- *Daily.* This method is used if the practice is large and patient accounts are divided into small sections. Claims are generally sent out every day.
- *Weekly.* Claims to insurance companies may be sent in batches on a weekly basis (e.g., all the Blue Cross claims are run at the same time). Statements to patients can be spaced according to the alphabet and divided into four sections for the month. For example, statements A-F could be sent out the first week, G-M the next week, N-S the next, and T-Z the last week of

the month. This type of billing spreads the return payments over the month for ease of posting and better cash flow.
- *Biweekly (or semimonthly).* Patient statements are sent every 2 weeks, or twice a month on the 15th and the 30th, with half sent on each date.
- *Monthly.* All the patient statements are sent together at the same time of the month, usually at the beginning of the month or last week of the month.

Fee Adjustments

The daysheet has a column for making adjustments. An **adjustment** is an amount that is added or subtracted from the physician's fee, changing the patient's account balance. To make an adjustment to a fee, only the ledger card and the daysheet are needed. Adjustments change the amount owed in patient accounts for various reasons, including discounts (credit), write-offs (credit), returned checks (debit), and overpayments (credit). Occasionally, an adjustment is needed for an incorrect charge because the service was not coded or documented correctly (usually the incorrect charge is voided [adjusted], and the correct charge or code is rebilled).

Professional Discount

Professional discounts are sometimes given to other health care professionals and their families. If a professional discount is to be given, a note in the service column should indicate the reason for the discount (e.g., "courtesy" or "professional discount"). This includes accepting only what the insurance has paid, not asking the patient for the difference (co-insurance) if allowed, and not accepting co-payments. The amount is subtracted from the account balance. Many physicians no longer do this because insurance companies are not responsible for the entire fee if a discount has been applied. Their contention is that the discount is not applied for all their subscribers, only those who are health care professionals or family, and therefore is not equitable.

Write-off

A **write-off** is done when a portion or the entire amount of the charges cannot be collected. If a patient has declared bankruptcy, the entire amount must be written off. Portions of fees may need to be written off if the physician's fee is above the "allowable" amount in an agreement with a third-party payer (insurance companies, Medicare, Medicaid). Insurance payments are based on contracted amounts and usually cover only a portion of the service fee charged. Because of the contract, the balance remaining cannot be charged back to the patient. This may also be done for other reasons (e.g., bankruptcy) or when the person cannot pay the bill because of personal circumstances and the physician or representative subtracts an amount from the bill owed.

The amount written off is subtracted from the account balance. Money received from a collection agency (company that collects debts that are overdue and then keeps a "finder's fee," or percentage, of the amount collected) provides only for the office's percentage share; the agency's portion of the recovered balance is another example of a write-off.

Returned Checks

When a patient does not have enough funds in his or her bank account, a check may be returned for **nonsufficient funds (NSF).** If the check cannot be resubmitted to the bank, the amount of the returned check must be added back to the patient's account balance, along with any applicable fees charged by the practice's bank for the returned check.

Overpayment

Occasionally, a patient will overpay (pay more than the balance) on his or her account. This shows as a credit, or negative balance, on the ledger card because it is money owed to the patient. To avoid confusion the credit balance should be circled or placed in parentheses. If a refund is sent to the patient, the amount sent is debited to the account to bring the account balance to zero. Refunds should be made promptly.

Collection Process

Payment at the time of service allows the medical practice to control collection costs. Zero-balance accounts (patient accounts that are paid in full) do not have statements sent out monthly, which saves the practice the cost of preparing and mailing statements. Most often, however, full payment is not received at the time of service. A patient may make a co-payment, but the practice relies heavily on third-party payers. To be successful, a medical office should have written policies on payment, payment plans, and collection of overdue accounts.

The accounts receivable report details the age (length of time a patient's bill is left unpaid) of each account. When an account is not kept up to date, even after several statements have been mailed requesting payment, the medical practice must attempt to collect the overdue amounts in a professional manner. The office can make a call to the patient, mail a collection letter, or turn the account over to a professional collection agency. The longer the bill is unpaid, the harder it is to collect.

Payment Plans

One of the most sensitive areas in the medical office is following up with patients on an overdue account. Patients may face unexpected financial problems (e.g., loss of job, death of spouse, divorce) and may need a plan to help them complete their financial obligation.

Payment plans allow the patient to pay the outstanding balance in two or three payments. If more time is needed, the office may include a finance charge. Finance charges may be applied if four or more payments are needed. As required by the **Federal Truth in Lending Act**, a "Truth in Lending" form should be completed in duplicate, with a copy in the patient's record and a copy to the patient (Fig. 5-18). This document acts as a disclosure statement and includes the terms of the agreement, start and ending dates, financial charges, rate of interest, total payment due, and the patient's

```
                  JOHN L. SMITH
                  6100 Front Street
                  St. Louis, MO 62953

                  Telephone 351-5400


        FEDERAL TRUTH IN LENDING STATEMENT
             For professional services rendered

Patient _____ Samuel Wilson _____
Address _____ 25 Taylor Avenue _____
               St. Louis, MO 63155
Parent _____

   1. Cash Price (fee for service)       $ _____ 1200.00
   2. Cash Down Payment                   $ _____  200.00
   3. Unpaid Balance of Cash Price        $ _____ 1000.00
   4. Amount Financed                     $ _____ 1000.00
   5. FINANCE CHARGE                       $ _____   –0–
   6. Finance Charge Expressed As
      Annual Percentage Rate                 _____   –0–
   7. Total of Payments (4 plus 5)        $ _____ 1000.00
   8. Deferred Payment Price (1 plus 5)   $ _____ 1200.00

"Total payment due" (7 above) is payable to __Dr. John L.__
_Smith_  at above office address in _five_ monthly installments
of $ _200.00_ . The first installment is payable on __July 1__
20 _XX_ , and each subsequent payment is due on the same
day of each consecutive month until paid in full.

_6-10-20XX_    _____
   Date        Signature of Patient; Parent if Patient is a Minor
```

Fig. 5-18 Disclosure statement: example of document for compliance with Federal Truth in Lending Act.

signature. This form is required for accounts requiring more than four payments, even if a finance charge is not added to the account and must be kept on file for 3 years.

Procedure 5-7 explains how to establish a payment plan to assist a patient in paying for services on a large or overdue account.

Procedure 5-8 outlines how to explain the statement of account so that patients understand their obligations.

Telephone

When the medical assistant needs to contact the person responsible for an overdue account, good communication skills must be used. Even though the goal is to collect the money owed, goodwill must always be maintained. The Fair Debt Collection Act of 1977 specifies guidelines for collecting money owed. When contacting people to collect money owed to the medical office, you may not harass them with threats or abusive language. Also, contact must be made only during reasonable hours (e.g., 9 a.m. to 9 p.m.), and you may call only once a week. An office policy defining the correct approach is helpful (Box 5-1).

BOX 5-1 Sample Office Policy for the Collection of Debts

1. Calls can be made only between 9:00 a.m. and 9:00 p.m. (considered normal waking hours).
2. When telephone contact has been made, no more than one call per week is allowed.
   a. Failure to reach the patient or other party does not allow for daily callbacks.
   b. Threats or other forms of harassment are always unacceptable.
3. If an employer requests that calls not be made to the patient's place of employment, calling the patient at work must be stopped.
4. Never threaten a patient.

The following example of a medical office policy outlines what to do and say while on the phone with a patient who has a past-due account:

1. Listen to the patient's explanation as to why the account is overdue.
   a. Identify if the patient was unhappy about the treatment provided. Notify the physician if this occurs.
   b. Identify financial problems (e.g., loss of job) that the patient may be having.
2. Agree on a payment plan.
3. Maintain the goodwill of the patient. A patient who is treated rudely will speak badly of the practice and may seek legal action.

Documentation should be provided concerning the agreement made by the patient. These notes may be attached to the ledger card or filed in a "collections folder" but should never be included in the patient's medical record.

Collection Letter

If the person responsible for the account does not respond to notices on the statements or telephone messages to call the physician's office, a collection letter should be sent. The message in a collection letter needs to be clearly understood by the receiver (the patient). The wording needs to be firm but positive. Every effort to give the **debtor** (person owing money) an opportunity to pay should be offered. Provide the debtor with adequate time to respond. State the consequences of not following up on the request for payment. Box 5-2 provides suggestions on composing collection letters.

Collection Agency

The physician must make the decision to send an account to a collection agency after all other

Procedure 5-7 Establish Payment Arrangements on a Patient Account

TASK: Establish a payment plan to assist a patient in paying for services on a large ("high-dollar") or overdue account.

EQUIPMENT AND SUPPLIES
- Patient's billing statement (ledger card and account information)
- Calendar
- "Truth in Lending" form
- Paper
- Private area for discussion

SKILLS/RATIONALE

1. **Procedural Step. Determine that all information on the billing statement is correct.**
2. **Procedural Step. Discuss possible payment arrangements that are acceptable to the practice.**
   Encourage the person responsible for the account to decide which option is most appropriate for his or her budget.
   Rationale. Better compliance can be expected when the person responsible for making the payment has contributed to the discussion and agreed to the best option.
3. **Procedural Step. Determine when the first payment will be made.**
4. **Procedural Step. Prepare the "Truth in Lending" form, and have the person responsible for** the account sign the form if the agreement requires more than four installments (see Fig. 5-18).
   Rationale. A "Truth in Lending" form must be completed to be in compliance with federal regulations (Regulation Z).
5. **Procedural Step. Explain any finance charges that will accrue on the account.**
6. **Procedural Step. Document the agreement by making notes attached to the ledger card.**
   Rationale. Credit information is highly confidential and is not kept in the patient file. Attach information to the ledger card, or keep separate files for patients' financial and credit information.

---

attempts have failed. If an account is sent to a collection agency, the medical practice can no longer send statements to the patient. The patient is to pay the collection agency directly once the physician has sent the account for collection. The collection agency will keep its share per an arranged percentage (usually 50% to 60%) and will forward the remaining amount to the physician's office on a contracted basis, usually either monthly or as payments are received from the patient.

The medical assistant may have to gather all data needed by the collection agency to proceed with a collection. If a debtor contacts the medical office about the process, the debtor must be instructed to contact the agency directly. If the debtor pays the medical office instead of the agency, the office needs to contact the agency. Care should be taken in choosing a collection agency, being sure the agency has the same ethical and business attitudes as the physician. Remember that the collection agency represents the physician's office to the patient.

Procedure 5-9 explains the process of collecting delinquent accounts.

PATIENT-CENTERED PROFESSIONALISM

- Why must the medical assistant be aware of the entire billing process to be effective in patient care?

PAYROLL PROCESSING

The **payroll** is the financial record of employees' salaries, wages, bonuses, net pay, and deductions. There are two main reasons for maintaining accurate payroll records. First, complete information is needed to compute the wages for each employee for a payroll period. Second, the data provide information for the government reports (e.g., Forms 8109 and 940) that all employers are required to

Procedure 5-8 Explain a Statement of Account to a Patient

TASK: Explain a statement of account to a patient who has questions so that the patient understands his or her obligations.

EQUIPMENT AND SUPPLIES
- Patient statement
- Patient information form
- Encounter form(s)
- Physician's fee schedule
- Private area for discussion

SKILLS/RATIONALE

1. **Procedural Step. Determine that the patient has the correct statement and ask the patient what seems to be the problem.**
   Rationale. It is possible that a patient has received the wrong statement. You therefore need to make sure the statement belongs to the patient and that the insurance numbers, patient address, and patient telephone numbers that appear on the statement are all correct.

2. **Procedural Step. Examine the statement for any possible errors.**
   a. Compare the statement with the encounter form(s).
   b. Compare the statement to the fee schedule.
   Rationale. It is possible that an error has been made on the statement. For example, an incorrect charge may have been billed, or a mathematical error may have occurred. Taking this step also demonstrates to the patient that his or her concerns are important to you as well and that you are willing to make adjustments should an error be found.

3. **Procedural Step. Review with the patient each of the items that appears on the statement.**

   a. The date of the service
   b. The type of service rendered
   c. The fee charged for the service

4. **Procedural Step. If an error is located, correct it immediately and apologize to the patient.**
   Rationale. This assures the patient that you are a professional and promotes continued open communication.

5. **Procedural Step. If there was no error and your discussions do not resolve the patient's concerns, make arrangements for a discussion between the physician and patient for further explanation to resolve the problem.**
   Rationale. It is important to recognize when a conversation between the patient and physician is necessary to resolve the situation.

6. **Procedural Step. If there was no error and the patient understands the statement, it is beneficial at this time to determine whether the patient has specific concerns that may hinder payment.**
   Rationale. This provides an opportunity for making special arrangements, if needed.

---

complete. An employer is required by law to withhold certain amounts from an employee's check to pay for taxes. Payroll information is highly confidential and is handled only by authorized personnel.

Earnings and Withholding Laws

Federal laws and many state laws require the employer to deduct and collect specified amounts from employees' gross earnings (before deductions). Other laws address working conditions, hours, and earnings. Others relate to taxes that must be paid by the employer to provide specific employee ben-

efits. The employer is responsible for sending required withholdings to the appropriate government agencies, along with reports verifying the figures, on a timely basis.

Fair Labor Standards Act

The **Fair Labor Standards Act**, or the Wage and Hour Law, specifies that employers engaged in interstate commerce (the exchange of goods or services between buyers and sellers in two or more states) must pay their hourly employees (employees paid by the hour) overtime at a rate of 1½ times the regular rate (time-and-a-half) for hours worked in excess of 40 per workweek. The Fair Labor Standards

BOX 5-2   Suggestions for Composing a Collection Letter

1. Your account has always been paid promptly in the past, so this must be an oversight. Please accept this note as a friendly reminder of your account due in the amount of $ _____.

2. Since your care in this office in [March], we have had no word from you in regard to how you are feeling or regarding your account due. If it is impossible for you to pay the full amount of $ _____ at this time, please call this office before [June 15] so that satisfactory arrangements can be worked out.

3. Medical bills are payable at the time of service unless special credit arrangements are made. Please send your check in full or call this office before [June 30].

4. If you have some question about your statement, we will be happy to answer it for you. If not, may we have a payment before the end of this month?

5. Unless some definite arrangement is made to reduce your balance of $ _____, we can no longer carry your account on our books. Delinquent accounts are turned over to our collection agency on the 25th of the month.

6. **Once established, a payment plan can be reinforced by recognizing the first remittance with a letter of acknowledgment:**
   Thank you for the recent payment of $ _____ on your account. We are glad to cooperate with you in this arrangement for clearing your account. We will look for your next check at about the same time next month and your final payment the following month.

7. **When arranged by a telephone call, a payment schedule can be confirmed by a letter.**
   As agreed on in our telephone conversation today, we will expect you to mail a payment of $50 on [February 10]; $50 on [March 10]; and the balance on [April 10]. If some emergency should prevent your making one of these payments on time, please notify us immediately by telephone.

"DO"S AND "DON'T"S

Do:
1. Individualize letters to suit the situation.
2. Design your early letters as mere reminders of debt.
3. Always imply that the patient has good intentions to pay, until lack of response over time proves otherwise.
4. Send letters with a firmer tone only after you have sent one or two friendly reminders.

Don't:
1. Use the same collection letter for a patient with good paying habits as for a patient known to neglect financial obligations.
2. Place any type of overdue notice on a postcard or on the outside of an envelope. This is an invasion of privacy.

Modified from Young AP, Kennedy DB: *Kinn's the medical assistant,* ed 9, Philadelphia, 2003, Saunders.

Act provides that management and supervisory employees are exempt from this regulation. These employees are referred to as "salaried" personnel. Provisions for the minimum wage (the minimum hourly amount an employee can be paid) and a normal workweek (e.g., "full time" equals 40 hours) are also included in this act. The minimum wage rate is adjusted periodically by Congress.

Social Security Tax

The federal Social Security law, or **Federal Insurance Contributions Act (FICA)**, provides funds to support benefits for employees and their families. The FICA tax pays for retirement benefits for workers age 62 and older, dependents of the retired worker, and disability benefits. Both the employer and the employee pay the FICA tax. FICA tax requires withholding 6.2% of wages (first $87,900 of wages as of 2004, then Social Security tax not deducted for rest of year). FICA tax is a combination of the 6.2% Social Security tax and a 1.45% Medicare tax, both of which are also paid by the employer. These amounts may be periodically adjusted by the U.S. Congress.

Medicare Tax

The **Medicare tax** is collected to support Medicare, a federal health insurance program for people who have reached age 65. The tax rate is 1.45%, and this tax is withheld from the employee's pay earned all during the year. The employer matches the 1.45% of the tax collected from the employee.

Federal Income Tax

The **Tax Payment Act** requires employers not only to withhold income tax and then pay it to the Internal Revenue Service (IRS) but also to keep accurate records of the names, addresses, and Social

Procedure 5-9 Prepare Billing Statements and Collect Past-Due Accounts

TASK: Process monthly statements and evaluate accounts for collection procedures.

EQUIPMENT AND SUPPLIES
- Patient ledger card
- Patient information form
- Collection form letters
- Computer
- Stationery and envelopes
- Collection agency commission requirements

SKILLS/RATIONALE

Preparing Billing Statements
1. **Procedural Step. Determine the billing schedule for the medical practice.**
   Rationale. Initially, consider the timing of when statements are prepared and sent out. Different offices send statements according to different schedules, including monthly billing and cycle billing.
2. **Procedural Step. Assemble all the accounts that have outstanding balances (e.g., owe payment to the medical office).**
   a. Review the new balance column on the patient's ledger card.
   b. Pull each one that shows an amount owed.
3. **Procedural Step. Separate the accounts into two groups:**
   a. Routine billing accounts.
   b. Past-due accounts.

Performing Routine Billing
1. **Procedural Step. Prepare ledger cards to serve as billing statements.**
   Many medical practices use a photocopy of the patient's ledger card as the billing statement. Care is taken throughout the month in making entries on the ledger card so that when monthly statements are prepared, photocopying it for use as a statement is a quick process.
2. **Procedural Step. Photocopy each ledger card and place in an envelope.**
   The design of the patient ledger card for use as a statement allows for it to be used in a "window" envelope, thus saving the time needed to type the patient's mailing address.
   NOTE: The envelope used should be the "security" style to protect confidentiality of patient information.
3. **Procedural Step. Print out computer-generated statements, if applicable.**
   Medical practices that use computer software for management of patient accounts can easily print patient statements. The software provides a "report" function that allows for all accounts with outstanding balances to print out as individual statements. These statements are then folded and placed in a "window" envelope in the same manner as a photocopied ledger card.

Collecting Past-Due Accounts
1. **Procedural Step. Gather all patient ledger cards with past-due balances.**
   Patient ledger cards should be "flagged" when the patient's account reaches a past-due status of 30, 60, 90, or 120 days. Accounts can be placed in "tickler" files, or color-coded tabs can be placed directly on the ledger card to indicate the past-due statement.
2. **Procedural Step. Separate accounts according to the action required:**
   a. 30 days: friendly reminder.
   b. 60 days: stern letter.
   c. 90 days: letter stating that the account will be turned over to a collection agency if not paid by a specified date.
   Rationale. Sorting the ledger cards into stacks of like accounts allows you to create form letters for each category. Once form letters are created and saved on the computer, patient names, dates, and amounts can be entered specific to each patient.
3. **Procedural Step. Create the appropriate form letter for each account using company stationery, and mail to the patient.**
   a. The "friendly reminder" letter can be included with a patient's statement on company letterhead and in a company envelope.
   b. The "stern letter" should be sent on company letterhead and sent in a plain envelope without the office's return address.
   c. The third and final letter should be sent on company letterhead in a company envelope and should be sent certified mail with return receipt requested.
4. **Procedural Step. Turn the account over to the collection agency at the time specified.**
   When the patient's account reaches 120 days (or the number of days determined by the practice), and the third and final letter has been sent and return receipt received, you must turn the account over to a collection agency, as stated in the final letter. This is required by law. All monies paid once the account has been sent to collection will be received by the collection agency and are subject to the

Procedure 5-9 Prepare Billing Statements and Collect Past-Due Accounts—cont'd

commission agreement. You may not receive further payments by the patient. Any such payments made to the medical office must be immediately sent to the collection agency. If a patient calls the office wanting to discuss payment arrangements, you must refer these questions directly to the collection agency. The collection agency will send the office a statement of accounts paid and a check for monies collected, typically once a month or as contracted with the agency.

5. **Procedural Step. Post payments received from the collection agency to the patient ledger card and daysheet.**
   Any balances that are left owing may be adjusted off the account (see Procedure 5-3). This is the physician's or office manager's decision, unless mandated by bankruptcy.

Other Collection Circumstances

1. **On the death of a patient, collect any outstanding balances from the patient's estate.**

   a. A statement is sent to the patient's address by certified mail, return receipt requested.
   b. If you do not receive a response, you may contact the county probate clerk's office and file a claim against the estate.

2. **For a patient filing for bankruptcy, stop all collection efforts immediately (depending on the classification filed).**
   The medical office will be notified when a patient has filed for Chapter 11 bankruptcy. A representative from the office must attend the bankruptcy hearing or file a written proof of claim for payment. No further collection actions may be taken with Chapter 11. Medical bills are often the last claims to be paid. Most likely, no reimbursement will be paid, and any remaining balances must be adjusted off the patient's account.

   Chapter 13 bankruptcy requires that the patient pay a fixed amount that is divided between all creditors. No other collection actions may be taken.

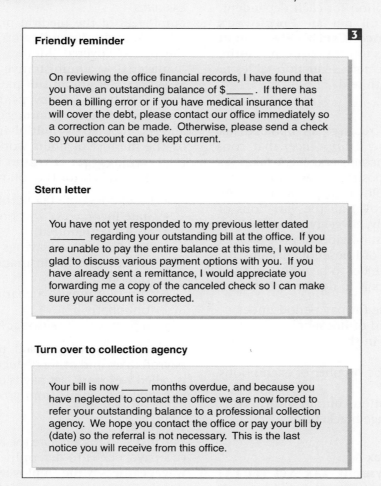

Friendly reminder

On reviewing the office financial records, I have found that you have an outstanding balance of $_____ . If there has been a billing error or if you have medical insurance that will cover the debt, please contact our office immediately so a correction can be made. Otherwise, please send a check so your account can be kept current.

Stern letter

You have not yet responded to my previous letter dated _____ regarding your outstanding bill at the office. If you are unable to pay the entire balance at this time, I would be glad to discuss various payment options with you. If you have already sent a remittance, I would appreciate you forwarding me a copy of the canceled check so I can make sure your account is corrected.

Turn over to collection agency

Your bill is now _____ months overdue, and because you have neglected to contact the office we are now forced to refer your outstanding balance to a professional collection agency. We hope you contact the office or pay your bill by (date) so the referral is not necessary. This is the last notice you will receive from this office.

Figure modified from Chester GA: *Modern medical assisting,* Philadelphia, 1998, Saunders.

Security numbers of persons employed. Records also need to be kept of the date of employment, gross earnings and withholdings, and the amounts and dates of payment for each employee.

REQUIRED FORMS

Two forms used to report employee pay must be generated regularly, as follows:

1. The employer must submit quarterly reports (Form 941) to the IRS.
2. A yearly report must be sent to the employee (W-2 form). The W-2 form reflecting the previous year's activity must be sent to employees by the end of January of the following year or within 1 month of termination. Employees use W-2 forms to file their federal and state income taxes.

The amount of federal income tax withheld from an employee's wages depends on amount of total gross earnings and number of exemptions claimed. An **exemption** is the amount of an individual's earnings that is exempt from income taxes (non-taxable) based on the number of **dependents.** An employee is entitled to one personal exemption, plus an additional exemption for each dependent. Each employee has to fill out an **Employee's Withholding Allowance Certificate (Form W-4).** If an employee fails to turn in the W-4 form, the employer will use the zero-deduction tables to calculate money to be withheld.

TAX GUIDE

Each year the employer receives an updated tax guide *(Circular E, Employer's Tax Guide)* that contains tables for federal income and FICA taxes, as well as the rules for depositing these taxes. This publication is also available at the IRS website. The wage tax-bracket tables cover all the variations of payroll periods (e.g., weekly, biweekly, semimonthly, monthly). The tables are subdivided on the basis of married, single, and head-of-household persons. An easy way to determine the tax to be withheld from an employee's gross wages is to do the following:

1. Locate the correct table for pay period under married, single, or head-of-household.
2. Find the wage bracket in the first two columns of the table.
3. Find the column for the number of exemptions claimed.
4. Read down the exemption column until you see the appropriate wage-bracket line.

Federal Unemployment Tax Act

The **Federal Unemployment Tax Act (FUTA)** requires employers to pay 6.2% tax based on each employee's earnings. This tax benefits employees who become unemployed. The taxable wage base is the first $7000. This means that for the purpose of computing tax, only the first $7000 of a worker's wages for a calendar year are counted. The **State Unemployment Tax Act (SUTA)** is tied directly to FUTA; the amount of SUTA taxes paid may be offset (credited) against what the employer owes for the FUTA taxes. Not all states have state unemployment taxes, and the tax may be determined by the number of employees.

Workers' Compensation Insurance

Workers' compensation laws require employers to pay insurance that will reimburse employees for wage losses resulting from job-related injuries or reimburse families if work-related death occurs. Employers may be required to carry workers' compensation insurance, which they can purchase through a commercial insurance company. The **Federal Employees' Compensation Act** covers only federal government workers, but it sets the standard for workers' compensation laws in most states.

EARNINGS

Employees of the medical practice may be paid a salary or wage, depending on the type of work and the period covered. Money paid to a person for managerial or administrative services is referred to as **salary** (set amount of pay for a certain period, such as 1 year). Money paid for either skilled or unskilled (no formal training) labor is called **wages** and is computed by multiplying the hourly pay rate by the number of hours worked. Deductions from total earnings (**gross wages** from either salaries or wages) are taken for the following reasons:

- Federal income tax withholding (required)
- State income tax withholding (required)
- FICA tax (required)
- Purchase of U.S. savings bonds (optional)
- Medical and life insurance premiums (optional)
- Contributions to a charitable organization (optional)
- Repayment of personal loans (optional)

The total earnings paid to an employee after payroll taxes and other deductions have been taken is called **net pay.** Net pay is calculated by subtracting total deductions from gross earnings.

Gross Pay

The first step to calculate the amount of an employee's paycheck is to determine the gross amount of wages earned by the employee. Using an hourly rate as a basis, it is necessary to know the rate of pay and the number of hours the employee has worked during the payroll period. The hours worked by an employee must be accurately maintained. If an hourly employee works overtime, the number of hours over 40 hours in a given week is calculated at time-and-a-half (if the practice falls under the Wage/Hour law).

For example, Lisa Fisher, a medical assistant, makes $10 an hour for a 40-hour workweek. Last week she worked 44 hours for Mediplace Clinic. Remembering that overtime for her is calculated at time-and-a-half, her gross pay can be calculated as follows:

Regular time hours: 40 × 10 = $400
Overtime earnings: 4 × 15 = $60
Gross pay: $460
    or
Total time × Regular rate of pay: 44 × 10 = $440
Overtime fee: 4 × 5 = 20
(The 4 overtime hours are worth an additional $5 an hour at time-and-a-half = $15 an hour.)
Gross pay: $460

Withholdings Required By Law

Federal law requires three principal deductions from the employee's gross pay, as follows:

1. The amount of *Social Security tax* deducted can be calculated either by multiplying the taxable wages by the Social Security rate (6.2%) or by referring to tax tables found in the IRS's *Circular E, Employer's Tax Guide.*
2. The *Medicare tax* is applied to the same taxable wages at a rate of 1.45%.
3. A large portion of the federal government's revenue comes from the *federal income tax* that is withheld from the employee's gross pay. The rules and regulations change often. The best practice is to use a current edition of *Circular E.*

For example, using the percentage method, the taxes for medical assistant Lisa Fisher can be computed as follows:

$460 × 6.2% (Social Security) = Tax of $28.52
$460 × 1.45% (Medicare) = Tax of $6.67
When multiplying by a percentage, remember to convert it to a decimal first. To multiply $460 by 6.2%, you must first convert 6.2% to a decimal by multiplying by 100 (6.2 × 100 = 0.062):
$460 × 0.062 = $28.52

Other Deductions

Many different types of deductions are made by agreement between the employee and the employer. Employee contributions to a retirement plan are based on total wages earned. Often a deduction is made to share part of the cost of health insurance with the employer. In situations when an employee receives advances from the employer, the employee often repays the debt through payroll deductions.

Payroll Register

Employers are required to retain all payroll records showing payments and deductions. The **payroll register** shows information about the earnings and deductions of each employee for the pay period (Fig. 5-19). It acts as a summary sheet showing all the data for each employee on a separate line. Regular, overtime, and total earnings are recorded in a payroll register from information on time cards. Amounts deducted for payroll taxes, health insurance, and other deductions are calculated and recorded in a payroll register, as are the total amount to be paid to each employee and the check number of each payroll check. Before checks are written for an employee's net pay, the calculations should be checked for accuracy.

Payroll Checks

The information used to prepare payroll checks is taken from the payroll register. A payroll check usually has a detachable stub to provide a summary of the earnings and deductions. Employees keep the pay stubs for their records of deductions and net pay received (Fig. 5-20).

Employee Earnings Records

The details affecting payments made to an employee are recorded in the **employee earnings record.** This information is recorded each pay period. The record includes earnings, deductions, net pay, and accumulated earnings for the calendar year. Employee earnings records are used to complete the required tax forms at the end of the year.

Fig. 5-21 summarizes the payroll process from calculation of earnings through generation of the employee earnings record.

PATIENT-CENTERED PROFESSIONALISM

- Why is it important for an employee to understand the regulations designed for the record keeping of payroll earnings?

CONCLUSION

Accurate and complete financial records help the medical practice stay in business and be successful. Medical assistants may be involved with some or all

```
PAYROLL - PR9972                        QRTLY / ANNUAL PAYROLL REGISTER              6:05 PM  07/06/XX
Langer Medical Office                        04/01/XX - 06/30/XX                              PAGE 1
```

	HOURS	GROSS	FICA WAGE	MEDI WAGE	FED TAX	FICA	MEDICARE	STATE TAX	DED AMT	NET AMT	CHECK NO.
0001 Anderson, Rhonda											
	80.00	692.00	692.00	692.00	41.52	42.90	10.34	21.34	14.36	561.54	4367
	80.00 @ 8.65000 = 692.00		REGULAR								
0002 Dunbar, Mario											
	80.00	2000.00	2000.00	2000.00	246.77	124.00	29.00	65.13	45.00	1490.10	4368
	80.00 @ 25.0000 = 2000.00		REGULAR								
0003 Ruiz, Selena											
	60.00	720.00	0.00	720.00	34.02	0.00	10.44	1.08	7.20	667.26	4369
	60.00 @ 12.0000 = 720.00		REGULAR								
0004 Nadich, Denise											
	80.00	1500.00	0.00	1500.00	222.69	0.00	21.75	28.23	15.00	1212.33	4370
	80.00 @ 18.7500 = 1500.00		REGULAR								

```
PAYROLL - PR9972                        QRTLY / ANNUAL PAYROLL REGISTER              6:05 PM  07/06/XX
Langer Medical Office                        04/01/XX - 06/30/XX                              PAGE 2
```

	HOURS	GROSS	FICA WAGE	MEDI WAGE	FED TAX	FICA	MEDICARE	STATE TAX	DED AMT	NET AMT	CHECK NO.
CURRENT PAYROLL TOTALS											

```
TOTAL HOURS        300.00
GROSS WAGES       4912.00
FICA WAGES        2692.00      MEDICARE WAGES   4912.00
FEDERAL TAX        545.00
FICA               166.90      MEDICARE           71.53
STATE TAX          115.78
DEDUCTION AMT       81.56

NET AMOUNT        3931.23
```

Fig. 5-19   Payroll register printed from a computerized payroll system.

of the management of the practice's finances. Regardless of what financial responsibilities you may have in the medical practice, it is important that you understand the basic accounting and bookkeeping principles and procedures needed to manage the finances.

SUMMARY

Reinforce your understanding of the material in this chapter by reviewing the curriculum objectives and key content points below.

1. Define, appropriately use, and spell all the Key Terms for this chapter.
   - Review the Key Terms if necessary.
2. State the accounting equation.
   - Assets = Liabilities + Owner's equity.

3. Explain the differences among assets, liabilities, and owner's equity.
   - An asset is anything of value owned by the medical practice.
   - A liability is an amount owed by the medical practice.
   - The owner's equity is the amount remaining after liabilities are subtracted from assets.
4. Explain the difference between a debit and a credit.
   - A debit is a charge to an account and is recorded on the left side of the T-account.
   - A credit is a payment to an account and is recorded on the right side of the T-account.
5. List three types of assets in a medical office.
   - Cash, accounts receivable, and miscellaneous assets (e.g., property, supplies,

PERIOD ENDING	EARNINGS			DEDUCTIONS									NET PAY
October 12	Regular	Overtime or Comm.	Total	Federal Inc. Tax	FICA Tax	State Inc. Tax	SDI Tax	Health Ins.	Savings	Medicare Tax	Total deduct.		Amount
HOURS WORKED Reg. 40 O.T. 5	400 00	50 00	450 00	52 00	30 00	15 80	6 80	13 40	12 00	3 99	134 59		315 41

Statement of Earnings and Deductions   Detach and retain for your records.

- -

101650

BLACKBURN PRIMARY CARE ASSOCIATES, PC
1990 Turquoise Drive
Blackburn, WI 54937
608-555-8857

94-72/1224

DATE _October 16, 20XX_

PAY TO THE
ORDER OF _Sinda Lane_ .... $ _315.41/100_

Three Hundred Fifteen and 41/100 _____ DOLLARS

DERBYSHIRE SAVINGS
Member FDIC
P.O. BOX 8923
Blackburn, WI 54937

FOR

Howard Lawler, MD

⑈055003⑈ ⑊4467820ll⑈ 678800470

Fig. 5-20 Paycheck with attached stub for employee to keep as a record. *(From Hunt SA: Saunders fundamentals of medical assisting, Philadelphia, 2002, Saunders.)*

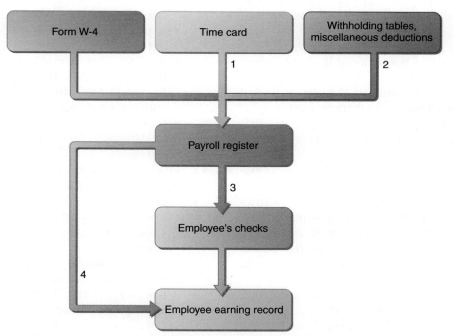

Fig. 5-21 *1,* A time card is used to record all employee hours worked and to calculate regular, overtime, and total earnings. *2,* Payroll taxes are calculated using withholding tables and information on employee's W-4 form. Other deductions are taken as well. *3,* Payroll checks are written for the net pay for each employee. *4,* Information from the payroll register is recorded on each employee's earnings record.

equipment, furniture) are all assets in a medical office.

6. Demonstrate the correct procedure for establishing a petty cash fund, maintaining an accurate record of expenditures, and replenishing the fund as necessary.
   • Review Procedure 5-1.

7. Explain what an accounts receivable "aging" report shows.
   • An accounts receivable aging report shows how long debt owed to the practice has gone unpaid. It is usually categorized as 30, 60, 90, or 120 days overdue.

8. Differentiate among the following financial statements: income statement, statement of owner's equity, and balance sheet.
   • An income statement shows the results of income and expenses over time, usually a month.
   • A statement of owner's equity reports changes in the owner's financial interest in the practice during a reporting period and why the investment has changed.
   • A balance sheet reports the financial condition of a medical practice on a given date, usually at the end of each month. It shows what the medical practice owns and owes, as well as the amount of the owner's equity.
   • An income statement is prepared first, then the statement of owner's equity, and finally the balance sheet.

9. List three types of forms used on a pegboard system to record the daily transactions.
   • Daysheets, charge forms, and ledger cards are used on a pegboard system to record daily transactions.

10. List two advantages of using a pegboard bookkeeping system.
    • When a pegboard system is used, information needs to be written only once on the top sheet, and the special paper allows the information to be transferred to the sheets below. The pegs keep all the forms in alignment.
    • The pegboard provides a hard, flat surface on which to write forms by hand.

11. Demonstrate the correct procedure for posting service charges and payments using the pegboard system.
    • Review Procedure 5-2.

12. List four advantages of using a computerized bookkeeping system.
    • Computerized bookkeeping systems allow for single, electronic entry, as well as ease in storing data, printing reports, and submitting claims electronically.

13. List the five requirements of banks for checks being deposited, and explain the importance of confirming these five items when accepting checks from patients.
    • Correct payee: The check must be made out to the health provider depositing the check.
    • Current date: Postdated checks are not acceptable.
    • Correct amount: The word and number amount must agree on the face of the check.
    • Current address and phone number: The payer's information must agree with the office account information.
    • Affixed signature: The payer's signature should agree with the payer's name as it appears on the check.
    • The medical assistant should verify all information on the check before accepting it; otherwise, it may be refused by the bank for deposit.

14. Define "third-party" check, "postdated" check, and check "paid in full."
    • A third-party check is endorsed over to a third party (the doctor) who is not the original payee (such as the patient on an insurance check).
    • A postdated check is made out for a future date, not the current date.
    • A check that is marked *paid in full* signifies that the payee will make no further attempt to collect any funds and that the account is considered closed ("paid in full").
    • Medical offices should have written policies to establish how these types of checks are handled.

15. List seven security tips for check writing.
    • Only authorized personnel should sign the check.
    • The record portion of the end-stub style should be filled in before the check is completed.
    • All lines should be filled in close to the left end of the line to prevent additions to the line. When the item written is completed, a long line should be added to fill out the line.
    • Check amounts are written with numbers and words, and the amounts should agree.
    • Write the number amount close to the dollar sign to reduce the chance of an additional number being added.
    • Enter the cents as "amount over 100" (e.g., 10 cents = 10/100).
    • Write the amount in words on the line under the "Pay to the Order of" space.

16. Differentiate between restrictive en-dorsement and blank endorsement.
    • A restrictive endorsement limits what can be done with the check (e.g., who can cash it, whether funds can be withdrawn, whether entire amount must be deposited).
    • A blank endorsement occurs when the payee (person to whom the check is written) signs only his or her name on the back of the check. When this is done, the check may be signed over to a third party.
17. Demonstrate the correct procedure for preparing a bank deposit.
    • Review Procedure 5-4.
18. List four methods of making deposits and briefly explain each.
    • Deposits can be made in person by presenting the deposit to a teller at the bank.
    • Deposits can be made by mail, with the bank returning the deposit receipt by mail.
    • Deposits can be made electronically, such as wire transfer of funds from one account to another, or one bank to another.
    • Deposits can be made by using the night deposit if the bank is closed for business when a deposit is made.
19. Demonstrate the correct procedure for reconciling a bank statement.
    • Review Procedure 5-5.
20. List four ways in which a patient statement can be prepared.
    • A patient statement can be prepared using a photocopy of the ledger card, a manually prepared statement, an outside billing service, or done with computerized billing.
21. Demonstrate the correct procedure for explaining professional fees before providing services.
    • Review Procedure 5-6.
22. Explain how an adjustment affects the balance of a patient's account, and list four reasons why an adjustment might be made.
    • An adjustment can provide a debit or a credit to a patient account balance.
    • Professional discounts, write-offs for bankruptcy or insurance adjustments, returned checks, and overpayments are reasons for adjustments to patient accounts. Occasionally, accounts may also be adjusted because of an error in coding or documentation that results in an incorrect charge.
23. Describe the collection process, including the role of third-party payers.
    • When a patient receives services, a co-payment may be made, or the fee may be paid in full if the patient has no insurance.
    • If the patient is covered by insurance, the insurance company will pay its portion of the charges after a claim for the service is submitted. Depending on the insurance, the balance of the bill may then be collected from the patient, submitted to a secondary policy, or written off according to contractual agreements.
    • If an account remains unpaid over time, an attempt must be made to collect the fee.
24. Demonstrate the correct procedure for establishing payment arrangements on a patient's account.
    • Review Procedure 5-7.
25. List four guidelines for making telephone calls to collect debts.
    • Calls can be made only during normal waking hours, usually 9 a.m. to 9 p.m.
    • Only one call may be made per week.
    • If an employer requests that calls not be made to the employee's workplace, such calls must be stopped.
    • Threatening or harassing patients is not permitted.
26. Demonstrate the correct procedure for explaining a statement of account to a patient.
    • Review Procedure 5-8.
27. Demonstrate the correct procedure for collecting delinquent accounts.
    • Review Procedure 5-9.
28. List six laws that affect earnings and withholdings and briefly explain each.
    • Fair Labor Standards Act: overtime for hourly employees set at time-and-a-half; minimum wage established; normal workweek of 40 hours.
    • Social Security tax: withheld to provide funds to retirement/support benefits for employees and their families.
    • Medicare tax: collected to support Medicare, the federal health insurance program for older people.
    • Tax Payment Act (federal income tax): employer withholds tax and pays it to the Internal Revenue Service.
    • Federal Unemployment Tax Act (FUTA): requires employers to pay tax based on each employee's earnings; to benefit employees who become unemployed.
    • Workers' compensation: requires employers to pay insurance that will reimburse employees for wage losses from job-related injuries or their families if death occurs on the job.
    • Employers must keep accurate records of deductions and withholdings from employee paychecks.
29. Differentiate between gross wages and net pay.

- Gross wages are the earnings before any deductions have been taken.
- Net pay is what an employee receives after deductions have been taken from gross earnings.
- Net pay is calculated by subtracting total deductions from gross earnings.

30. List the three principal deductions from the employee's gross pay that are required by federal law.
   - Withholdings required by federal law include Social Security (FICA) tax, Medicare tax, and federal income tax.

31. List the four types of information in the employee earnings record.
   - Employee earnings records contain the gross earnings, deductions, net pay, and accumulated earnings for the calendar year for an employee.

32. Analyze a realistic medical office situation and apply your understanding of medical office financial management to determine the best course of action.
   - Medical assistants must understand how the finances in a medical practice are managed.

33. Describe the impact on patient care when medical assistants have a solid understanding of the financial aspects of a medical office.
   - Accurate and complete financial records help ensure that patients' questions and problems can be addressed swiftly, that their claims are paid by third parties in a timely manner, and that they are aware of the charges and the expectations for payment.

FOR FURTHER EXPLORATION

To understand accounting principles better, **research the difference between cash-based accounting and the accrual method.** As you have learned, financial records provide a method for a business to monitor its financial status. Each method has advantages and different ways to record the same transaction.

Keywords: Use the following keywords in your search: cash-based accounting, accrual accounting, cash vs. accrual accounting/method.

Chapter Review

Vocabulary Review

Matching

Match each term with the correct definition.

A. accounting

B. accounts receivable

C. aging report

D. asset

E. balance sheet

F. credit

G. daysheet

H. debit

I. deposit

J. employee's withholding allowance certificate

K. endorse

L. exemption

M. financial statements

N. gross wages

O. income statement

P. liability

Q. net income

R. nonsufficient funds

S. one-write system

T. owner's equity

__DD__ 1. Amount of money not able to be collected

__I__ 2. Amount remaining after liabilities are subtracted from assets

__X__ 3. Writing a check using future date, so check can be deposited only after date on check

__Y__ 4. State of a checkbook and a bank statement being in balance

__K__ 5. To sign or place a signature on the back of a check that transfers the rights of ownership of funds

__M__ 6. Report that shows how long debt has gone unpaid

__e__ 7. Reports that indicate the financial condition of a business

__I__ 8. Money placed in an account of a financial institution

__J__ 9. Form that each new employee fills out to declare exemption from tax withholdings for earnings

__N__ 10. Recording system using a specially designed document device for the increased efficiency of recording daily transactions; also called *one-write system*

__N__ 11. Total amount of money earned by employee before deductions are taken

__ee__ 12. Financial activity of a business

__R__ 13. Indication that the payer did not have adequate funds in the bank to cover the amount of a check written

V. payable

Y. payroll

W. pegboard system

X. postdated

Y. reconciled

Z. statement of owner's equity

AA. T-account

BB. third-party check

CC. transaction

DD. write-off

___a___ 14. Numerical language of business that describes its activities

___b___ 15. Record of patient transactions showing an amount due

___v___ 16. Reports showing the results of income and expenses over time

___S___ 17. Another name for pegboard system

___A___ 18. Amount owed: debt

___V___ 19. Employees' salaries, wages, bonuses, net pay, and deductions

___F___ 20. Amount representing a payment: recorded on the right side of an accounting sheet

___E___ 21. Amount of money earned that is not taxable

___Q___ 22. Resulting figure when income is greater than expenditures

___D___ 23. Anything of value owned by a business that can be used to acquire other items

___H___ 24. Amount representing a charge or debt owed: recorded on the left side of a T-account

___U___ 25. Representing liability; accounts payable are money and funds owed to someone else

___BB___ 26. Check signed over to another party who is not the original payee

___Z___ 27. Report on the financial condition of a business on a certain date

___G___ 28. Journal for recording the day's activities

___AA___ 29. Tool used to analyze the effect of a transaction on an account

___O___ 30. Report that shows changes in the owner's financial interest over time

Theory Recall

True/False

Indicate whether the sentence or statement is true or false.

___T___ 1. A write-off is done when a portion or the entire amount of the charges cannot be collected.

___F___ 2. The statement-receipt is a charge form that lists the ICD-9 and CPT codes most frequently used in the medical practice.

___T___ 3. Checks marked paid in full should not be accepted unless the amount covers the entire current balance.

___T___ 4. Bookkeeping is the basic process of recording the financial activities of the business.

___T___ 5. The income statement reports the changes in the owner's financial interest during a reporting period and gives an explanation as to why the investment has changed.

Multiple Choice

Identify the letter of the choice that best completes the statement or answers the question.

1. The legislation requiring a disclosure statement informing a patient of a procedure's total cost, including finance charges, which is required when a patient will make more than four payments, is called ___B___.
   A. Federal Insurance Contributions Act
   B. Federal Truth in Lending Act
   C. Federal Employees' Compensation Act
   D. Federal Unemployment Act

2. A(n) ___A___ is when money is prepared and sent to a financial institution to be placed in an account.
   A. deposit
   B. ABA number
   C. endorsement
   D. debit

3. ___C___ are sometimes given to other health care professionals and their families.
   A. Adjustments
   B. Professional discounts
   C. Write-offs
   D. Exemptions

4. Payroll is the financial record of employees' ___D___.
   A. salaries
   B. wages
   C. deductions
   D. all of the above

5. A(n) ___B___ is the amount of an individual's earnings that is exempt from income taxes based on the number of dependents.
   A. deduction
   B. exemption
   C. withholding
   D. none of the above

6. The total earnings paid to an employee after payroll taxes and other deductions have been taken is called __B__.
   A. salary
   B. net pay
   C. wages
   D. all of the above

7. The legislation that provides funds to support retirement benefits, dependents of retired workers, and disability benefits is called __A__.
   A. Federal Insurance Contribution Act
   B. Federal Unemployment Tax Act
   C. Federal Employees' Compensation Act
   D. none of the above

8. __A__ acts as a journal for recording the day's activities.
   A. Daysheet
   B. Pegboard
   C. Ledger card
   D. Payroll register

9. __C__ contains demographics about the patient as well as important billing information.
   A. Daysheet
   B. Pegboard
   C. Ledger card
   D. None of the above

10. __B__ is a fixed fee that is paid by the patient at each office visit.
    A. Co-insurance
    B. Co-payment
    C. Restrictive endorsement
    D. None of the above

11. A(n) __D__ shows the results of income and expenses over time, usually a month or year.
    A. balance sheet
    B. financial statement
    C. income statement
    D. accounts payable statement

12. A(n) __B__ are reports that tell the owner the fiscal condition of the practice.
    A. balance sheet
    B. financial statement
    C. income sheet
    D. none of the above

13. A(n) __C__ fund is an amount of cash kept on hand that is used for making small payments for incidental supplies.
    A. gross wages
    B. owner's equity
    C. petty cash
    D. none of the above

14. __C__ is a document indicating the activity in an account.
    A. Statement-receipt
    B. Statement of ownership
    C. Statement
    D. Superbill

15. The __B__ is also known as the Wage and Hour Law.
   A. Social Security law
   B. Fair Labor Standards Act
   C. Tax Payment Act
   D. Federal Unemployment Act

16. The __C__ requires employers not only to withhold income tax and then pay it to the IRS but also to keep accurate records of the names, addresses, and Social Security number of person(s) employed.
   A. Social Security law
   B. Federal Labor Standards Act
   C. Tax Payment Act
   D. Federal Unemployment Act

17. Federal law requires __a__ to be deducted from the employee's gross pay.
   A. Social Security tax
   B. Medicare tax
   C. Federal income tax
   D. All of the above

18. __D__ is(are) part of the accounting equation.
   A. Assets
   B. Liabilities
   C. Owner's equity
   D. All of the above

19. In T-accounts, the left side is also known as a(n) __C__.
   A. asset
   B. credit
   C. debit
   D. equity

20. __B__ is the listing of a physician's charges for service.
   A. Balance sheet
   B. Fee schedule
   C. Ledger cards
   D. None of the above

Sentence Completion

Complete each sentence or statement.

1. ___Accounting___ is considered the "language" of business.

2. ___Bookkeeper___ reports the financial condition of a medical practice on a given date.

3. When a patient does not have enough money in his or her bank account, it will be returned for ___overdraft___.

4. ___Debtor___ is a person owing a debit.

5. ___Encounter form___ is also known as a superbill.

6. The resulting figure when income is greater than expenditures is called ___equity___.

7. ___receipt___ is a paper showing the date, amount of transaction, what was purchased, and who purchased the item.

8. ___Deposit slip___ is the listing of all cash and checks to be deposited to a certain account of a business's financial institution.

9. The amount remaining after the liabilities are subtracted from the assets is called ___equity___.

10. A(n) ___adjustments___ is an amount that is added or subtracted from the physician's fee, changing the patient's account balance.

Short Answers

1. List and explain the three important accounting principles.

Assets - Anything of value that is owned

Liabilities - are debt including what the business owes its creditors

Equity - Amount remaining after all the deductions made.

2. Explain the two major purposes for using the pegboard system.

1) Provides a solid writing base for writing on forms by hand.

2) Information is recorded on several forms at once, reducing the risk of errors.

3. List the five verifications you must make in order to accept a check.

① Correct providers name   ④ current address & phone number

② Current date   ⑤ Affixed signature.

③ Current amount

4. Explain in detail the four types of endorsements.

- Restrictive = limits what can be done in the check

Blank = payee signs only his name at the back of the check

Special = includes words that specify to whom the endorser makes the check.

Qualified = used to prevent future liability of the endorser

5. Explain the four types of billing cycles.

Daily ~ claims sent daily

Weekly - claims sent in batches on a weekly basis

Bi weekly - statement sent every 2 weeks

monthly - one time statement sent monthly.

Critical Thinking

You started working for Dr. Palmer 2 weeks ago as the administrative medical assistant. Dr. Palmer asked you this morning to create a list of all the patients with an outstanding balance on their accounts, determine which accounts are overdue, and send collection letters to all patients with an outstanding account balance over 120 days. You determine that only one account, Marjory Kreswin, has an outstanding balance over 120 days past due. Draft a collection letter stating that she has 10 days to bring the balance current or you will be required to send her account to a collection agency.

Internet Research

Keyword: "Collection regulations" in your state

Research the collection regulations in your state, and compose a list of 10 regulations. Cite your source. Be prepared to discuss your list of regulations with your classmates in an oral presentation should your instructor assign you to do so.

What Would You Do?

If you have accomplished the objectives in this chapter, you will be able to make better choices as a medical assistant. Take a look at this situation and decide what you would do.

Meredith is the office manager for a private physician. She is responsible for the financial management of the office. She is the person who tracks the assets and liabilities for the accountant and interprets "owner equity" so that the physician will know the net value of the practice. As part of her job description, Meredith also disburses petty cash. She makes sure that the vouchers, with receipts attached, and the cash on hand balance at the end of each workday. As each patient leaves the office, the payments for office visits are collected. The goal is to collect whatever is necessary from patients (co-payment, co-insurance) on the day of service. If patient receivables are current, outstanding insurance claims become the main focus for accounts receivable. Another one of Meredith's duties is to approve or disapprove of professional discounts and write-offs as fee adjustments. Finally, she generates collection letters and telephone calls for overdue and delinquent accounts.

Would you be able to perform these responsibilities in the medical office?

1. What are assets? What are liabilities?

assets - anything that the company owns

Liabilities - anything that the office owes / debts.

2. Why is it important for a physician to be aware of the owner equity before spending money for new equipment?

If there will be enough money to pay for another debt.

3. What is petty cash, and how is it used by the medical office?

Emergency funds used in the medical office; to buy small items.

4. Why is it important for Meredith to complete a petty cash voucher each time that money is removed from the petty cash fund?

To assure that all the expenses tally with the records.

5. Why is it important to keep accounts receivable at a low level?

To maintain the company profit

6. What are professional discounts?

Discounts given to specific patients directed by the doctors.

7. What is a write-off?

Is a portion or entire portion of charges cannot be collected is taken off the bill

8. How should a collection phone call be handled?

phone call like this should be done politely & is not offensive to the collected party.

Chapter Quiz

Multiple Choice

Identify the letter of the choice that best completes the statement or answers the question.

1. _b_ is an amount owed by the medical practice.
   A. Asset
   B. Liability
   C. Owner's equity
   D. None of the above

2. _C_ reports the changes in the owner's financial interest during a reporting period and why the interest has changed.
   A. Bank statement
   B. Financial statement
   C. Income statement
   D. Statement of owner's equity

3. _C_ is a special device used to write the same information on several forms at one time.
   A. Daysheet
   B. Encounter form
   C. Pegboard
   D. None of the above

4. _a_ is a charge form that lists the ICD-9 and CPT codes most frequently used in the medical practices.
   A. Receipt-charge slip
   B. Encounter form
   C. Superbill
   D. Both B and C

5. _C_ is collected to support the federal health insurance program for people aged 65 and older.
   A. FUTA
   B. FICA
   C. Medicare tax
   D. SUTA

6. The Wage and Hour Law is also known as the Fair Labor Standards Act.
   A. True
   B. False

7. _D_ records debit and credit activity of a patient in the practice.
   A. Financial statement
   B. Income statement
   C. Ledger card
   D. None of the above

8. __C__ is a numbered form used to track petty cash withdrawals.
   A. Transaction
   B. Ledger
   C. Voucher
   D. All of the above

9. The pegboard system is also known as the one-write system.
   A. True
   B. False

10. An AR report that is beneficial to the financial success of the medical practice is called the __A__ report.
   A. aging
   B. financial
   C. summary
   D. none of the above

11. __A__ is a fixed percentage of a medical cost, paid by the patient.
   A. Co-pay
   B. Co-insurance
   C. Both A and B
   D. None of the above

12. __D__ is (are) part of the accounting equation.
   A. Assets
   B. Liabilities
   C. Owner's equity
   D. All the above

13. __A__ endorsement is a type of endorsement in which only a signature is listed on the back of the check.
   A. Blank
   B. Restrictive
   C. Qualified
   D. None of the above

14. The amount recorded on the right side of the T-account is called a *debit*.
   A. True
   B. False

15. __D__ contains demographics about the patient as well as important billing information.
   A. Financial statement
   B. Ledger cards
   C. Encounter forms
   D. None of the above

16. When accepting a check for payment, you must verify __C__.
   A. current address
   B. correct provider name
   C. affixed signature
   D. All of the above

17. The ABA number __C__.
   A. helps to identify the payer's bank
   B. is located on the right corner of each check
   C. helps to identify the location of the bank
   D. all the above

18. Federal law requires _B_ to be deducted from a person's gross pay.
   A. SUTA
   B. Medicare tax
   C. medical insurance premiums
   D. none of the above

19. Total earnings paid to an employee after payroll taxes and other deductions have been taken out is called gross pay.
   A. True
   B. False

20. Accounting is considered the language of business.
   A. True
   B. False

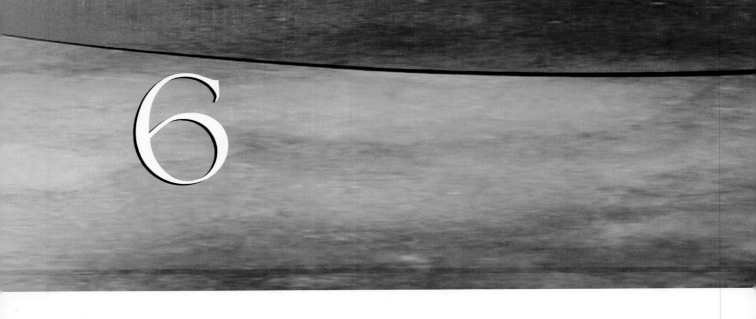

OBJECTIVES

1. Define electronic health record system (EHRS).
2. Identify the public and private organizations working toward the EHRS national initiative.
3. Discuss the history of the EHRS.
4. Understand the importance of standards in EHRs.
5. Identify the current forces and trends that are prompting the migrations to the EHRS.
6. Explain the advantages and disadvantages of the EHRS.
7. Compare the electronic health record (EHR), the hybrid, and the paper-based record.
8. Identify administrative, clinical, and billing use of data.
9. Define confidentiality, privacy, and security.
10. Discuss the Health Insurance Portability and Accountability Act (HIPAA) privacy and security requirements.
11. Understand fraud and abuse legislation.
12. Search for a patient using an EHR.
13. Identify administrative, clinical, and billing uses of the EHR.
14. Understand fraud and abuse issues with the EHR.
15. Understand how coding relates to billing.

ELECTRONIC HEALTH RECORD SYSTEM

KEY TERMS

abuse
accessibility
administrative data
administrative safeguards
alerts
Anti-Kickback Statutes
Anti-Referral Statutes
authentication
billing data
clinical data
confidentiality
covered entity

data analysis
data exchange standard
decision support
electronic health record system (EHRS)
encryption
false claims act
fraud
health care clearinghouse
HIPAA
hybrid record
interoperability
messaging standards

minimum necessary
need-to-know principle
paper-based record
personal data assistant
physical safeguards
privacy
Qui Tam Statute
security
standards
Stark Statutes
technical safeguards

THE ELECTRONIC HEALTH RECORD SYSTEM—NATIONAL INITIATIVE

The electronic health record system (EHRS) is changing the way in which health care professionals practice, especially the way in which health care professionals document, review, and provide quality care to their patients. This chapter focuses on data and information collection in the electronic health record (EHR), discussing the complex issues surrounding the way medical assistants and other health care professionals document, review, and use the EHRS.

This chapter begins with a discussion of the EHRS as a national initiative. The government, along with many national organizations, is supporting the adoption of the EHRS because it has the potential to improve documentation, aid in the coordination of care, and raise the quality of health care in our nation by eliminating or reducing the number of medical errors. In 2004, the U.S. government established the Office for the National Coordinator of Health Information Technology (ONCHIT), an office for the coordination of the EHRS under President George W. Bush. This office is responsible for leading the nation in strategic planning and the use of the EHRS in the United States. Leading, developing, and implementing the EHRS is a challenge for our country, and many organizations are working with ONCHIT to fulfill this goal (Amatayakul, 2006).

Many public and private organizations are supporting the advancement of the EHR, such as the American Health Information Management Association (AHIMA), Institute of Medicine (IOM), American Medical Informatics Association (AMIA), Healthcare Information and Management Systems Society (HIMSS), Health Level Seven (HL7), and ONCHIT. Box 6-1 is a short list of the many organizations developing and aiding in the transition to the EHR.

So, what is the EHR, and why are so many organizations working diligently toward this initiative? The EHRS is more than a computerized version of health records; therefore it is no longer called an *electronic health record (EHR)* but instead is referred to as a *system*—**electronic health record system (EHRS)**. You will find that these terms, *EHR and EHRS*, are used interchangeably in your readings. However, the bottom line is the same: The EHRS has the potential to improve documentation, aid in the coordination of care, and raise the quality of health care in our nation by eliminating or reducing the number of the medical errors. Let us review two of the common definitions given to EHRS.

BOX 6-1   Organizations

- American Health Information Management Association (AHIMA)
- American Medical Informatics Association (AMIA)
- Health Level Seven (HL7)
- Healthcare Information and Management Systems Society (HIMSS)
- Institute of Medicine (IOM)
- Office for the National Coordinator of Health Information Technology (ONCHIT)

AHIMA, one of the leading organizations, defines the EHRS as follows:

"An electronic patient record that resides in a system specifically designed to support users by providing accessibility to complete and accurate data, alerts, reminders, clinical decision support systems, link to medical knowledge and other aides." (Odom-Wesley and Brown, 2009)

The IOM is a prestigious independent organization that works to advance technology and increase the science of health. The IOM published several landmark reports defining the EHR in terms of its functionality (Dick and Steen, 1991). The IOM termed what we now know as the EHR as the *computerized patient record (CPR)*. Although the CPR is an outdated term, it remains essential to the original concept of the computerized patient record. The IOM established the concept that the patient record would not simply replace the paper-based system but would actually advance patient care. According to the IOM, the computerized record should provide the following functionalities:

Complete and accurate data
Decision support
Reminders
Alerts
Links to medical knowledge
Other aids
(Dick and Steen, 1991)

History of the Electronic Health Record to Its Current Status

The concept of a computerized health record is not new; in fact, the government has supported the adoption of the EHRS for many years. The history of the computerized patient record dates back to the 1960s and 1970s, when Stanford University experimented with products such as the clinical information system (Amatayakul, 2007). From the 1970s on, the EHR has been in various stages of development. The period from the 1990s to the present has been marked by numerous technological advancements. In fact, most industries in the United States today are electronic, so why is the health care industry lagging behind? There are many issues and challenges unique to the health care industry that must be resolved before the electronic system can fully penetrate the industry. First and foremost, the cost of the EHRS and related training of health care professionals is of great concern to the industry. As more and more offices and hospitals begin to adopt these electronic systems, the cost should lessen. Organizations such as AMIA have addressed the issue of training. AMIA is actively working on initiatives to train health care professionals using the 10 × 10 approach: training 10,000 health care workers by 2010 (http://www.amia.org/10×10).

Next and most important, the use of standards and interoperability may be viewed as the most challenging initiative facing the industry. It is important to understand this issue and what it means in terms of adopting a fully functional EHR.

Standards

It is hardly appropriate to discuss the EHR without talking about **standards**. If you plug your toaster into an electrical outlet, you feel confident that your toaster will work. If you plug that same toaster into an outlet in your neighbor's house, you will feel confident that it will work in your neighbor's house, too. If you travel to Europe with your toaster, you might need an adapter to fit the outlet, but the toaster will still work. The toaster works because there are common standards in place for this product. Health care lacks standards, and despite the advances in technology, many systems don't work together. Simply put, many computer systems don't communicate with other computer systems. Because health care has many fragmented systems, the health care industry is working with many organizations to develop a common set of standards.

Virtually every computer application that you use in the office contains information that can be shared with another computer application. The common software applications used by a medical assistant are the master patient index; registration, admission, discharge, and transfer (RADT); and transcription systems. The information that you collect in the registration process is entered into a registration system. This registration system sends the patient's information to the EHRS. Fig. 6-1 demonstrates how the information collected at the time of registration can be transferred to the EHRS. The transfer of this information is made possible by the use of **data exchange standards.**

A *standard* is a broad term used to define a common process, content, or vocabulary; for example, standards can be defined in terms of messaging standards, data content, or clinical vocabularies (Adbelhak et al., 2007). The information that you collect in the registration process or registration application is often sent to the EHRS. For proper data exchange, there must be a set of commonly accepted and agreed-upon definitions, formats, and rules. The following is a short list of standards that public and private organizations are developing. Although you may never work with standards in your career as a medical assistant, it is still important to have a basic understanding of the process behind data exchanges. As you begin to work more and more with data and systems in the office practice, you will begin to realize the importance of the EHRS and the relationship with systems.

Messaging Standards. This type of standard provides a means to exchange (communicate) patient information such as administrative and clinical data among disparate clinical systems. A messaging standard allows structure and format in exchanging data, and it is formatted in such a way that both the receiver and the sender understand the message. This standard is commonly referred to as a **data exchange standard** and is used nationally and internationally. Health Level Seven (HL7) is both a standard development organization and a messaging standard. In 1987, the HL7 organization was founded by a group of technical experts seeking information technology standards (www.HL7.org). HL7 operates at the highest level (i.e., the seventh level) of the International Standards Organization (ISO) (Quinn, 1999). A subgroup in HL7 is currently working on standards for exchange of drugs, and this group is called the *Clinical Data Interchange Standards Consortium (CDISC).* HL7 is working on many standards that support the infrastructure and use of the EHR (Adbelhak et al., 2007; Quinn, 1999).

Messaging standards are not limited to the HL7 organization, and other organizations (e.g., the American National Standard Institute [ANSI] and the National Electronic Manufacturers Association) are participating in data exchange. Take another look at the preceding diagram, and notice that the images from the radiology system can be transferred to the EHRS. Radiology images are transmitted using the DICOM and ANSI ASC X12 standards. DICOM and ANSI ASC X12 support the transfer of images and other financial information among computer systems (Adbelhak et al., 2007).

All the messaging standards are used with the computer devices commonly used by health care professionals; for example, **personal data assistants** (PDAs), computers, notebooks, and even voice recognition are supported by messaging standards.

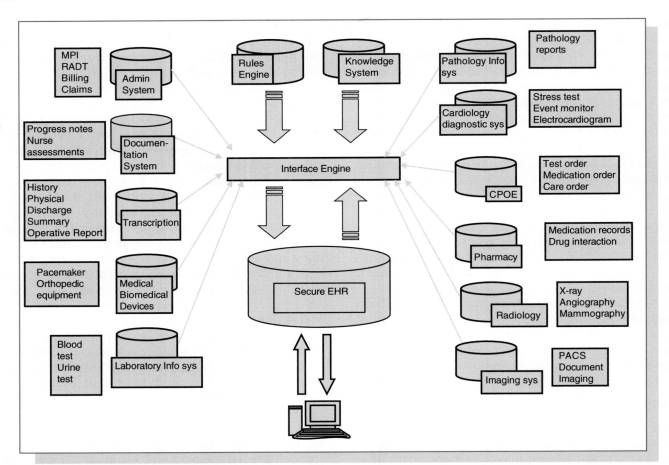

Fig. 6-1 The information collected at the time of registration can be transferred to the electronic health record system (EHRS). The transfer of this information is made possible by the use of data exchange standards. *(From Adbelhak M et al: Health information: management of a strategic resource, ed 3, St Louis, 2007, Saunders.)*

The PDA is a wireless device that allows the clinician to enter or input data at the point of care (Adbelhak et al., 2007). As a medical assistant, you may be required to enter your patient's vital signs into a PDA; this is one input device for the EHR.

Functionality. In 2003, the HL7, in collaboration with the IOM, developed standards that identified the EHRS Functional Model Standard. The functional model serves as the foundation for what *should, shall, or may be* included in EHRSs. In other words, it is an industry standard. Today, the Commission on Certification Technology (CCHIT) certifies EHRS products (software) that meet the HL7 EHRS functional model. Clinicians in the office setting should review this list before selecting an EHR product.

Vocabulary Standards. The standardization of data is another key issue for the exchange and use of data in the EHR. Data can be exchanged using the messaging standards, but the need for common terminologies and standardized data is even

greater. Shared vocabularies are important because terms must be defined in a way that everyone understands.

Forces and Trends Prompting Migration to the Electronic Health Record System

As mentioned previously, there are certainly many issues that are challenging the widespread adoption of the EHRS, but on the other hand, there are also many issues driving the transition to the EHRS. Today, the real forces behind the adoption of computerization in health care are societal trends; health care consumerism; and the government's call for efficient, safe, and high-quality health care (Gartee, 2007). First, let's take a look at the societal trends: We are surrounded by technology every day, from so-called smart phones, PDAs, and other mobile devices to automatic teller machines (ATMs). Technology works seamlessly in our lives, whether we are paying bills on-line or sending a text message. We use ATMs wherever we go, and we never stop to think about the technology behind each transaction. Today, health care consumers are becoming more knowledgeable, and they expect the seamless transactions that they experience in their daily lives to be part of their health care options. The health care industry is working toward the same goal as the banking industry did many decades ago, and that goal depends on interoperability. **Interoperability** is defined as the ability of systems to work together through common standards. Consumers want to have access to their medical files wherever they go, and they expect that their doctor's office should be able to communicate with any other health care entity that provides them with care.

Secondly, consumers recognize that the Internet is part of the fabric of their daily lives. As consumers, they want access to their individual medical records wherever they relocate or travel (Gartee, 2007). Consumers expect health data exchanges among their various health care providers, whether it is their primary care practitioner's office or the hospital in which they were treated. Today's health care environment increasingly depends on information exchanged among organizations, medical offices, and medical ancillaries such as laboratory and imaging centers. Not all organizations or offices have electronic documentation, but the transition is surely under way from the traditional paper-based system to the electronic system. Moreover, some offices are using both electronic and paper-based forms of documentation, collectively called a **hybrid record.** Regardless of the system that is currently in place, the goal is to migrate toward an EHR. This chapter focuses on the EHRS and demonstrates components of the health record that are useful in understanding the major concepts of documents.

ADVANTAGES OF THE ELECTRONIC HEALTH RECORD SYSTEM

The EHR offers clear advantages to the paper-based system; moreover, the EHRS addresses many of the deficiencies of the paper-based record. The potential benefits or advantages include the following:

1. Security
2. Accessibility to multiple users
3. Decision support
4. Alerts
5. Data analysis (Odom-Wesley and Brown, 2009)

Security

It may seem odd to say that an EHR is more secure than a paper-based record, but in many ways it is.

Software advancements in security technologies prevent unauthorized access. Many systems have security controls such authentication tools, encryption, and physical and technical controls that secure access and prevent intrusion. **Encryption** is a protection that occurs while information is being transmitted. The computer keys change the text using an algorithm to make the text unreadable before proper translation. **Authentication** is the process of identifying the author. In the EHR, the author of the document can prove authorship by using a unique identifier such as a personal identification number (PIN), password, or digital signature. Biometrics, such as retinal scans or fingerprints, can also authenticate an author (Odom-Wesley and Brown, 2009).

Security will be discussed in detail later in this chapter, in the section on the Health Insurance Portability and Accountability Act (HIPAA).

Accessibility

Unlike the paper-based record, wherein only one person can view the record at a time, the EHR permits **accessibility,** allowing multiple users to view the record from different locations. It provides fast, efficient, and secure retrieval of records. The EHR can track the user identification and identify the time and type of document reviewed with an audit trail. Security levels can establish users, allowing users access to only those portions of the record that are necessary for their job; *access is based on the* **need-to-know principle.** The level of access to the record depends on the professional responsibilities of the user.

Decision Support

There are many types of expert or clinical **decision support** tools that offer assistance when clinicians make complex decisions. A decision support tool gathers data and information from a variety of sources or computer systems and provides access to this information through a single system. For example, when a physician places an order, the decision support tool might search a variety of systems (i.e., a database) for the patient's insurance information, review the insurance formulary for approved drugs, and check for potential drug interactions (Latour and Eichenwald-Maki, 2006).

Alerts

The EHR can also provide reminders or **alerts** to clinicians. A drug interaction alert is a typical function of the clinical decision support system. Physicians can receive an automatic message or reminders of immunizations for their patients, or they may receive an alert of a potential drug interaction when ordering. These reminders can be sent direct to the clinician's e-mail account or PDA.

Data Analysis

With its wealth of data and clinical information, the EHRS is ideal for **data analysis.** The EHRS can help clinicians, researchers, and administrators analyze these data.

≋ DISADVANTAGES OF THE ELECTRONIC HEALTH RECORD SYSTEM

Although the EHR offers many clear advantages, the systems are not problem free (Box 6-2). The EHRSs present some disadvantages, including the following:

1. Cost
2. Training
3. Downtime
4. Privacy and security concerns (Gartee, 2007)

Cost

One of the most commonly cited disadvantages of EHRSs is the initial cost of the hardware and software. Most health care providers want to know that they will make a significant return on their initial investment.

Training

Both the office staff and the clinician will require training before an EHRS can be adopted. Training is time consuming, and the use of the EHRS will surely change the workflow in the physician's office. Its use in a busy practice may mean that the physician will need to perform data entry, which is quite different from entering a note in a paper-based system. Clinicians will be trained not only in data entry but also in the retrieval of data from the EHRS. The degree of training and usability depends on the

type of system selected and the software vendor. Regardless of the user's previous computer experience, employees must receive specific training related to the system. Designers of EHRSs understand the usability issues and work to make this transition as smooth as possible.

Downtime

Like any system, the EHRS requires routine maintenance, which may necessitate unscheduled downtime. The information technology (IT) professional works diligently to ensure that downtime remains at a minimal level and backup procedures and protocols are initiated so that the flow of patient care is not disrupted.

Privacy and Security Concerns

Safeguarding patient information is a primary concern for users of EHRSs. Although there are many security technologies in place, we know that no electronic system is completely immune to unauthorized intrusions, which can result in identity theft. Privacy and security concerns are paramount when selecting an EHRS. Most physician offices and organizations strive to minimize the risk of unauthorized access and inappropriate disclosures of patient information and assure the public that administrative, technical, and physical safeguards will be used to minimize this risk.

≋ ELECTRONIC, HYBRID, AND PAPER-BASED HEALTH RECORDS

Regardless of the many types of health record media, the underlying purpose is to serve as a data repository; moreover, the record is used to collect and store data about the care and treatment provided to the patient. The EHR is used for data collection and retrieval in much the same way as the paper record; however, the EHR offers many features that are not available in the paper-based record, such as data analysis, decision support, and alerts. The EHR can store many forms of data, such as images or text. Digital images from radiology or other departments can be stored in the EHR.

The electronic, paper, and hybrid records are the three basic methods for data collection and storage commonly found in the health care context. The **paper-based record** is the traditional method used in the collection of medical information and, as the name implies, relies on a strictly paper format. This type of record uses many paper forms. The forms are generated by health care practitioners and departments; for example, the laboratory depart-

BOX 6-2	Advantages and Disadvantages of EHRS

Advantages	**Disadvantages**
Availability	Cost
Decision Support	Training
Alerts	Downtime
Data Analysis	Privacy and security

TABLE 6-1	Defining Hybrid Records—Paper to Source Systems Illustrated	
Patient Record Report	**Media**	**Source Systems**
Admission history and physical examination	Paper	Transcription
Physician orders	Paper	Paper record
Clinical laboratory results	Electronic	Laboratory information system
Radiology reports	Electronic	Radiology information system
Medication records	Electronic	Bedside documentation system
Preoperative progress notes	Paper	Paper record
Progress notes	Paper	Paper record
Consents	Electronic	Optical scanning system

From Adbelhak M et al: *Health information: management of a strategic resource,* ed 3, St Louis, 2007, Saunders.

ment may generate test results (e.g., a complete blood count), the physician may report clinical findings on a progress note, and the physical therapist may use a physical therapy assessment form to document pertinent findings. The paper-based medical record has been the standard method for years, and clinicians are familiar with the ease and efficiency of this format. Regardless of these advantages, however, it has many deficiencies, including a major problem with record access. Access to the record is granted to one person at a time, in contrast to the computerized patient record, which allows anyone with access and a computer to view the record simultaneously; obviously, this cannot take place with the paper version. Members of the office staff spend many hours copying, faxing, and transporting the record to various locations. Furthermore, because the record cannot be easily updated, forms must be attached to it. Finally, the paper-based record can become fragile over the course of time and subject to many environment hazards (Odom-Wesley and Brown, 2009).

The paper-based record is generally housed in the health information management department at larger facilities that use complex filing systems. In a physician's office, the record is generally filed alphabetically. Regardless of the site, clerical staff members spend a great deal of time sorting papers and assembling the record before placing it in a file folder. Generally, the clerical staff will receive loose documents or single documents that need to be filed in the medical record. Another widely discussed deficiency is the legibility of the documentation. The Joint Commission, an accrediting body for many health care organizations, has advocated use of EHRs to reduce the errors in patient care caused by illegible writing.

As previously mentioned, the hybrid record stores records on both paper and electronic media. This type of record is commonly used in many

offices today and is considered to be a bridge to the EHRS. Many offices collect data from a variety of sources. For example, the laboratory reports may be electronic, and the patient consents or HIPAA forms may be on paper. Many clinicians use computerized physician order entry (CPOE) systems for prescribing medicine and dictating reports or notes. Dictated notes are generally transcribed and placed in the medical record. The hybrid record compiles patient information from a variety of sources. Table 6-1 is an illustration of a typical hybrid record.

USES OF THE ELECTRONIC HEALTH RECORD SYSTEM IN THE MEDICAL OFFICE

Administrative Uses

The health record contains demographic, financial, and clinical data, which serves many purposes. The primary purpose of the EHRS is the collection and storage of data that reflect the care and treatment rendered to the patient. However, the record is used for many other purposes that support patient care, including financial as well as administrative uses. First, let's begin by exploring the administrative uses of the EHRS. The EHR is closely linked to administrative systems, such as the registration process or master patient index. In the acute care setting, all hospitals have a registration process and master patient index. In the physician's office and other outpatient settings, the record serves similar purposes by identifying the patients seen and treated with a master patient index (Odom-Wesley and Brown, 2009).

The EHRS has many administrative uses in health care and contains administrative information, which includes patient-identifiable data. These data may consist of demographic or financial information (i.e., **billing data**). Whenever a patient is electively admitted into the hospital, medical office staff members generally provide the administrative data as part of the registration process. Information such as the patient's full name and address, telephone number, and Social Security number is collected by the office and entered into the registration system as **administrative data.** Patient demographic and insurance information is routinely collected, too; insurance information may be scanned (copied) as part of the data collection process.

Tracking of appointment and daily patient lists is another administrative function of the EHR in the outpatient setting.

Clinical Uses

The health record provides information for clinical use. It is a communication tool that allows clinicians to see the type of care and treatment that the patient received (i.e., **clinical data**). Depending on the setting, the clinical use may differ slightly; for example, in the context of acute care, the record is used for discharge planning and quality management. Typically, in the physician's office, clinicians document immunizations and track a problem list, and patients fill out a medical questionnaire, both of which are placed in the record. Because the physician is concerned with reducing costs for transcription, he or she may take advantage of some of the drop-down functions and report-generating capabilities of the EHRS.

The medical assistant may record the patient's medical history and vital signs in the medical record. Under the direction of a physician, the medical assistant may prepare or even administer medications. Documentation of test results is included in the medical record along with other specimens that may have been collected; all require timely documentation in the medical records. Finally, the medical record may contain copies of any instruction provided to the patient for routine or follow-up care.

Billing and Coding Uses

Reimbursement is based on the documentation provided in the patient record. The ICD-9-CM and CPT-4 codes are used for medical billing in the physician office. In a paper-based system, the medical biller reviews the records or bills for the services based on a patient encounter form. The medical biller reviews the paper-based documentation and assigns the appropriate codes for the treatment and services rendered in the paper system. In the EHRS, the codes are automatically assigned by software

that searches the physician notes and other documentation (Gartee, 2006). A coder or a medical biller is still needed to check the electronic documentation and ensure the accuracy of the codes selected by the system.

CONFIDENTIALITY, PRIVACY, AND SECURITY

The EHR highlights the need for confidentiality, privacy, and security in the collection, storage, and transfer of medical data. The words *confidentiality, privacy,* and *security* are all related but differ quite sharply in terms of definition and policy. **Confidentiality**, for the purposes of this chapter, is defined as a *practice*; it is a practice that allows or permits only authorized individuals to access medical information (Information, 2008). Patients expect that their medical information will be kept confidential and that only authorized individuals will access and share this information among other authorized users.

Privacy is an individual's right to control his or her personal health information, with the understanding that the information will not be disseminated without his or her permission (Information, 2008). Patients can learn what information has been collected in their health records; they have the right to view and copy this information and maintain control over disclosures.

Security, on the other hand, is defined as a mechanism with the protections or safeguards (administrative, technical, or physical) put in place to protect health information. HIPAA permits the Department of Health and Human Services (DHHS) to make recommendations related to the privacy of identifiable health information.

The Health Insurance Portability and Accountability Act and the Electronic Health Record System

On August 21, 1996, Congress passed **HIPAA**, Public Law 104-191. HIPAA made many sweeping changes in the effort to improve health care and reduce its cost by standardizing electronic data interchange, protecting privacy, and securing health data in electronic systems. HIPAA contains both privacy and security requirements. This chapter covers the Security Rule as it relates to the EHR.

Security Rule

The HIPAA Security Rule provides standards for electronic protected health information (EPHI). If your organization or physician practice is a covered entity, you must comply with HIPAA's Security Rule. A **covered entity** is a health care provider, plan, or clearinghouse. A **health care clearinghouse** is a company that performs billing functions. Specifically, the clearinghouse translates nonstandard data formats received from one entity (e.g., a physician office) and puts the information in an acceptable format (transferable format) so that it can be sent to another entity (e.g., an insurance company). Unlike the Privacy Rule, the Security Rule applies only to EPHI. The security standards for the protection of EPHI are cited in 45 CFR Part 160 and Part 164, Subparts A and C. You may find a copy of the full regulation at the following website: http://www.cms.hhs.gov/SecurityStandard/.

HIPAA's Security Rule was designed to be "scalable" and flexible for all organizations. According to CMS, "The security requirements were designed to be technology neutral and scalable from the very largest of health plans to the very smallest of provider practices." http://www.cms.hhs.gov/EducationMaterials/Downloads/Security101forCoveredEntities.pdf

Physician practices must review the HIPAA Security Rule and evaluate security measures in the office. Physician practices must also complete a risk analysis assessment and document any potential or possible risks that they may encounter using the EHR. A risk is a potential for harm or loss of data; for example, a physician practice may include backup procedures as part of the security plan. A security plan is unique to each physician practice and depends on the size and scale or the nature of the practice. Overall, the intent of the Security Rule is to set the standard for ensuring that those who have access to the EPHI have built-in safeguards to secure the information. The security requirements rely on administrative, physical, and technical mechanisms to provide the necessary safeguards.

Administrative safeguards are the largest portion of the security standards and, according to CMS, provide more than half of the security requirements. Administrative safeguards are defined by HIPAA as "administrative actions, and policies and procedures, to manage the selection, development, implementation and maintenance of security measures to protect electronic protected health information and to manage the conduct of the covered entity's workforce in relation to the protection of that information" (http://www.cms.hhs.gov/EducationMaterials/Downloads/SecurityStandardsAdministrativeSafeguards.pdf). Examples of administrative safeguards include a security plan, contingency plan, training programs, risk assessment, and all of the policies and procedures that the covered entity chooses to put in place.

Physical safeguards are those mechanisms put in place to protect the systems, equipment, and data from threats, intrusions, or even environmental hazards. Physical plant safety requirements may include fire alarms, fire extinguishers, smoke detectors, and other equipment used to detect or eliminate fire. Fire is not the only environmental hazard that should be addressed; physical safeguards involve any physical measure that is used to protect the environment in a case of disaster.

Technical safeguards can be viewed as the processes used to protect data and control entry into the system. Technical safeguards primarily control access to data; they include using authentication controls to verify that the person signing onto a computer is authorized to access that EPHI and encrypting and decrypting data as it is being stored and/or transmitted (Latour and Eichenwald-Maki, 2006).

Major Differences Between the HIPAA Privacy Rule and Security Rule

The intent of the Privacy Rule is to set the standard for those who have access to protected health information, whereas the Security Rule is designed to ensure that only those individuals who have the right to access the EPHI will have access. Another point of distinction between the rules is that the Security Rule pertains only to EPHI, whereas the Privacy Rule pertains to all protected health information (oral, written, or electronic). Another point of difference between the rules pertains to oversight: The Office of Civil Rights (OCR) is responsible for implementing and enforcing the Privacy Rule, whereas the Centers for Medicare and Medicaid Services (CMS) preside over the Security Rule (http://www.hhs.gov/ocr/hipaa/).

Violation of the HIPAA Privacy rule carries both civil and criminal penalties. HHS may impose civil money penalties on a covered entity for failure to comply with the requirements. This failure may result in a fine of $100 per failure but may not exceed $25,000 for the same type of violation. The OCR and the Department of Justice may also invoke criminal penalties for a person who knowingly discloses personal health information with a fine of $50,000 and up to 1 year in prison. There are harsher penalties for wrongful conduct that could involve penalties up to $250,000 and 10 years of imprisonment (OCR Privacy Rule Summary, 2003).

It is important to note that enforcement by the OCR is complaint driven; in recent years, the office has tracked the types of complaints filed by individuals and found that the top five issues were as follows:

- Impermissible uses and disclosures
- Safeguards
- Access
- Minimum necessary*
- Failure to provide notice

Protecting Patient Information

One of the greatest challenges for most covered entities and particularly the physician's office is the protection of patient information in the electronic environment. Privacy and security issues surrounding the patient's information are paramount to the consumer, and the medical office should ensure that the information meets all federal, state, and regulatory agency standards.

FRAUD AND ABUSE

Odom-Wesley and Brown (2009) list four areas of concern in the EHR environment for fraud and abuse: authorship, auditing integrity, documentation integrity, and patient identification and demographic accuracy. Authorship is subject to fraud when a clinician uses the cut and paste function, copies, or borrows information from another chart. For example:

> "A nurse sits down at the computer to document in the patient's (EHR). To complete her SOAP note, she copies the text of another nurse's entry to capture the patient's subjective complaints and symptoms. She then goes to the lab system and intake-output records to copy and paste the objective data from these sources into her documentation. Next she enters her assessment of the patient during her shift, and finally copies and pastes a plan from the patient's electronic care plan" (Amatayakul, Brandt, and Dougherty, 2003).

The EHR must have auditing integrity; in other words, the EHRS must have the ability to track users and provide an audit trail identifying when users enter information in the record and when they view the record. It is important that you understand that the record is a legal business document. You must be able to defend the integrity of this record in court using audit trails or another form of auditing.

---

*Please note: **Minimum necessary** refers to the Privacy Rule, whereas you may only release the necessary amount of information needed to fulfill a request. The Security Rule applies to the electronic health record system whereby you have the ability to assign access to the system based on the user's role. As part of Administrative Safeguard your physician office may write a policy on who has access to the EPHI. Thereby, allowing the user access to the electronic health information that they need to know in order to perform their job duties.

TABLE 6-2	Examples of Fraud and Abuse	
Provider	**Member**
Billing for services not rendered	Medical identity theft (using another person's insurance)
Misrepresenting the service	Adding or not removing individuals not in the household to or from the insurance plan
Billing an uncovered service as covered	
Upcoding (assigning higher codes for diagnostic or procedural services than were actually received)	Using multiple physicians for the same condition (drug-seeking behavior)
Unbundling (billing for a bundled service separately)	Billing the insurance company for an item or service that was never received
Double billing	

Odom-Wesley and Brown contend that electronic records have the tendency to use templates as a time saver for documentation. Use caution with templates, and make sure that you correctly indicate all services provided because if you accidentally select the wrong service, the EHRS may automatically bill for this service. In essence, you will be sending out a bill to the insurance company for services not received, which could easily be viewed as fraud (Odom-Wesley and Brown, 2009).

The federal government is the largest purchaser of health care and therefore is concerned with fraud and abuse. Moreover, the federal government recognizes that the person performing the fraud and/or abuse could be a health care provider, insurance beneficiary, or member of an insurance plan (Table 6-2). **Fraud** is an intentional act, deception, or misrepresentation for the purpose of gaining insurance benefits. **Abuse** is a practice or behavior that results from errors or inconsistencies in billing practices. Abuse occurs when a billing error causes an overpayment or cost to the insurance company.

Medicare defines fraud as "purposely billing Medicare for services that were never provided or received. Some examples of Medicare fraud include:

- Billing Medicare or another insurer for services or items you never got.
- Billing Medicare for services or equipment that is different from what you got.

- Use of another person's Medicare card to get medical care, supplies, or equipment.
- Billing Medicare for home medical equipment after it has been returned."

For more information on how to detect or report fraud, review Medicare's website at http://www.medicare.gov/fraudabuse/Overview.asp.

The federal government is not the only provider and insurer of care concerned with fraud and abuse—many private insurance companies share this concern. Review Blue Cross and Blue Shield's website at http://www.bcbsnc.com/inside/fraud/ for additional information.

Many rules and regulations govern fraud and abuse, such as the False Claims Act, Qui Tam Statute, Anti-Kickback Statutes, Anti-Referral Statutes (e.g., Stark I and II), and HIPAA (Harman, 2006).

The **False Claims Act** (31 U.S.C. §3729-3733) is a federal law that prohibits fraudulent claims to the government. Those who knowingly submit a false claim are in violation of this law. Any individual with evidence of fraud against the government may file a claim; this is commonly called a **Qui Tam Statute** or, more commonly, a *whistleblower lawsuit*. Qui Tam is a provision of the False Claims Act that allows individuals to file a claim without retaliation and receive a portion of the award. Anyone found liable can be fined up to three times the government charges and civil penalties per claim.

The **Stark Statutes** (also known as **Anti-Referral Statutes**) pertain to physician referrals under Medicare and Medicaid and state that physicians or their immediate family members cannot have a financial relationship with an entity that is referring the patient.

The **Anti-Kickback Statutes** state that it is a criminal offense to accept bribes or payment for services rendered (this includes money, gifts, gratuities, and discounts).

≋ USING THE ELECTRONIC HEALTH RECORD SYSTEM

There are many ways to use the EHR, depending on the functionality of the software. For the purposes of this chapter, we will use MediNotes. Let's begin to examine the software by navigating the menu bar.

Getting Started

At the top of the screen, you will see the menu bar, with the words *File, View, Create, Tools, Tabs,* and *Help.* You can click the words at any time, and a drop-down box will appear. Below the menu bar is the toolbar:

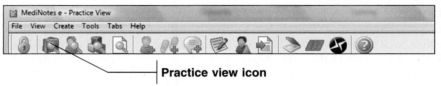

(Courtesy of MediNotes Corporation, West Des Moines, Iowa.)

The toolbar displays many icons that are commonly used in this software. The icons are buttons that allow you to access different functions in the software. For example, if you click on the practice view icon, you can locate a patient, search e-mail, complete notes, and even review notes without bills. Below is a list of items that you can select from the **practice view** icon.

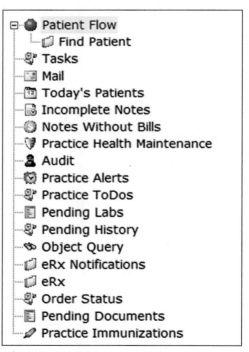

(Courtesy of MediNotes Corporation, West Des Moines, Iowa.)

Exercise 6-1

The EHR in this physician practice contains many functions. Look at the functions above. What function(s) do you think a medical assistant would use and why?

Find patient

Todays patients

Searching for a Patient

Selecting a patient is the first step in any encounter. To search for a patient in the EHR, select the Patient View icon from the toolbar.

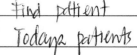

(Courtesy of MediNotes Corporation, West Des Moines, Iowa.)

You can search for a patient by his or her last name (e.g., the last name "Patient"). Such a search may find two patients, as shown below: Donald Patient and Petunia Patient. Both Donald and Petunia are existing patients at your office, both of whom have had previous encounters.

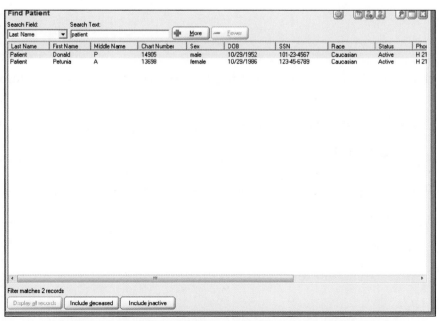

(Courtesy of MediNotes Corporation, West Des Moines, Iowa.)

Usually, there are other attributes besides first and last names that can be used to narrow your search, as shown below:

Find Patient

Search Field:

| Last Name ▼ |
| First Name ▼ |
| Chart Number ▼ |
| Birth Date ▼ |
| Sex ▼ |
| SSN ▼ |
| Race ▼ |

(Courtesy of MediNotes Corporation, West Des Moines, Iowa.)

◆ Exercise 6-2

Why is it important to use more than one attribute when searching for a patient, especially in addition to a first and/or last name?

To eliminate mistakes on common names/ proper identification of patient.

Administrative Data

To enter a new patient in your EHRS, you would use the new patient screen below:

| Common | Insurance | Ins Card | Extra | Picture |

Chart No: 13698
Status: Active

Prefix: Ms.
Nickname:

First Name: Petunia
Middle name: A
Last Name: Patient

Date of Birth: ☑ 10/29/1986
SSN: 123-45-6789
Sex: female

Home Phone: 215-707-9876
Work Phone: 215-707-2841

Cell Phone:
E-mail Address:

Primary Pharmacy:

🖳 Advance Directives   ☐ Exempt from Reporting

Address Line 1:

Address Line 2:

City: Philadelphia
State: PA
Zip Code: 19140
Country: USA

Primary Physician: DrFirst, Provider Agent
Family Physician: DrFirst, Provider
Referring Physician: <None>

Race: Caucasian
Occupation: architect

(Courtesy of MediNotes Corporation, West Des Moines, Iowa.)

◈ Exercise 6-3

Briefly describe administrative, clinical, and billing data and state whether the screen above contains any such data.

Administrative : Basic information of patient (name, bday etc.)

Clinical : patients history

Billing : Insurance provider

Busy office practices want to know the status of their patients. The EHR provides a listing of the number of patients scheduled for today, the patients who are in the waiting room, and patients' room assignments, as shown below:

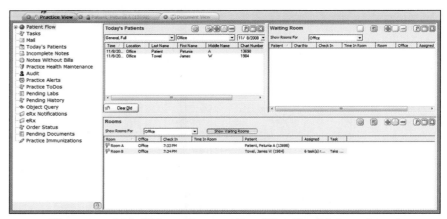

(Courtesy of MediNotes Corporation, West Des Moines, Iowa.)

Clinical Data

Entering Information on a History and Physical

After the registration process, the patient's visit begins with a comprehensive history and physical (H&P). The H&P document is used in every office and provides a summary of the patient's past and current illnesses or complaints. The medical assistant may collect information that pertains to the patient's H&P, such as the chief complaint and the patient's vital signs (Box 6-3).

The EHRS has the ability to capture data for the H&P in numerous ways. First, you can capture a Brief H&P, which is a short intake, or a lengthy review of systems. Another option provided by the EHRS is the ability to capture only negative or abnormal results. Drop-down boxes facilitate fast and easy capturing of uniform (structured) data. Unstructured data include narratives that the physician, nurse, or medical assistant enters directly into the record.

BOX 6-3 **Information Found in the History and Physical**

Chief complaint (CC): subjective statement pertaining to the reason that the patient is in the office today (e.g., "I have an earache").

Present Illness (PI): description of the current illness (e.g., ear pain began 2 days ago following a cold and persists with sharp pain and pressure when in bed).

Past Medical History (PMH): a listing of all past illness, hospitalizations, surgeries, and allergies.

Social History (SH): tobacco use, drug and alcohol use, living arrangements (e.g., patient lives alone in a three-story apartment).

Family History (FH): description of family illness (e.g., father died of lung cancer at 45).

Review of System (ROS): description of all symptoms by body system (e.g., skin; head, eyes, ears, nose, and throat [HEENT]; respiratory; cardiovascular; nervous system; genitourinary; endocrine; and gastrointestinal).

Physical Examination (PE): an objective assessment of the patient performed by the physician and recorded by the medical assistant (e.g., vital signs).

The next few displays show features in the EHR H&P that you would not have in the patient-based record. The screen below is the Chief Complaint Menu:

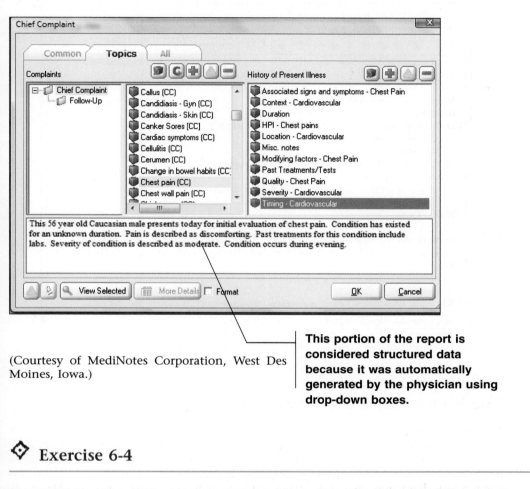

(Courtesy of MediNotes Corporation, West Des Moines, Iowa.)

This portion of the report is considered structured data because it was automatically generated by the physician using drop-down boxes.

⬥ Exercise 6-4

The EHRS has the ability to capture data using a drop-down menu. What are the advantages and disadvantages of using a drop-down menu?

Advantage = can store more details

Disadvantage = may cause confusion

⬥ Exercise 6-5

What is the patient's chief complaint on the first screen on p. 256?

Chest pain

This screen is the Chief Complaint Note:

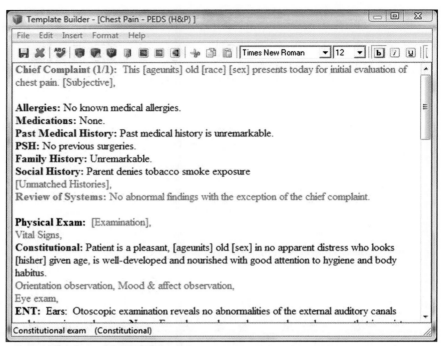

(Courtesy of MediNotes Corporation, West Des Moines, Iowa.)

Entering Vital Signs into the Electronic Health Record System

Vital signs are the functional and objective measures of the patient's blood pressure, temperature, pulse, and respirations, and they are generally recorded by the medical assistant at each visit. You can quickly record a patient's vital signs in the EHR in a number of ways. You can select the function "Vitals" from the Patient View or from within a note.

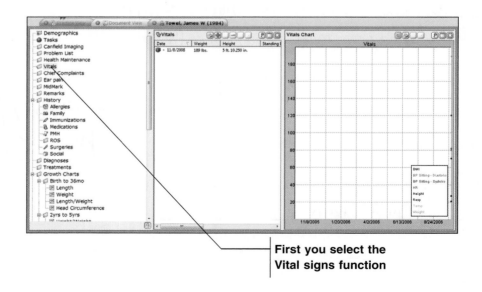

First you select the Vital signs function

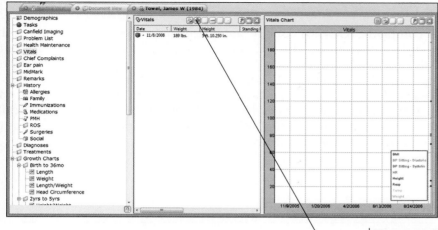

Then you click the plus sign to add the patient's vital signs

(Courtesy of MediNotes Corporation, West Des Moines, Iowa.)

MediNotes is the EHR software program used in all of the illustrations in this chapter. This software provides several data entry options to the medical assistant for vital signs charting. Look at the screen shot below. According to Medi-Notes documentation, you can "use the slider bars or type in values to add vital sign information for the patient. Writing directly into the boxes is available for users with touch screen systems with handwriting recognition. Clicking the check box to the right of each field enables or disables that field."

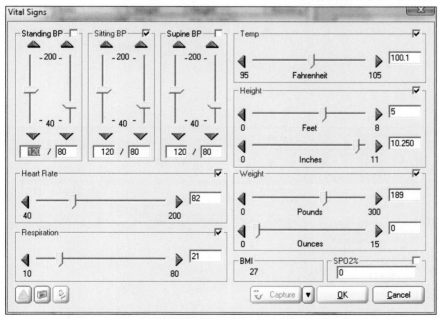

(Courtesy of MediNotes Corporation, West Des Moines, Iowa.)

Entering the Chief Complaint

The chief complaint (CC) is a concise statement that reflects the reason for the patient's visit or encounter. The CC is a subjective statement in the patient's own words describing the reason for treatment. According to the MediNotes program guide, "By adding Chief Complaint to the MediNotes Patient View, it is now possible for one person to create a chief complaint initially so that it can be pulled into a note later." The software allows the CC to be automatically incorporated into a note or the H&P. The physician can pull the CC into his or her note without retyping the information.

Step 1

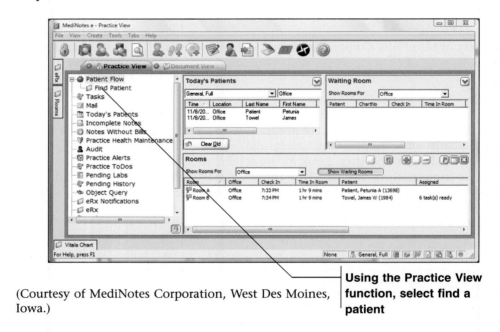

Using the Practice View function, select find a patient

(Courtesy of MediNotes Corporation, West Des Moines, Iowa.)

Step 2

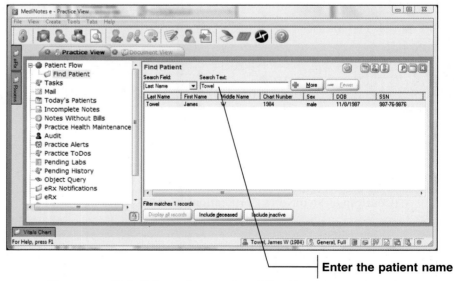

Enter the patient name

(Courtesy of MediNotes Corporation, West Des Moines, Iowa.)

Step 3

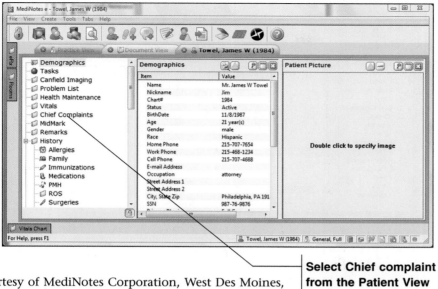

(Courtesy of MediNotes Corporation, West Des Moines, Iowa.)

Select Chief complaint from the Patient View

Step 4

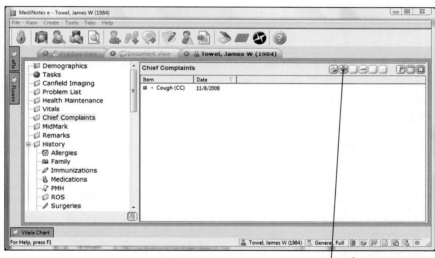

(Courtesy of MediNotes Corporation, West Des Moines, Iowa.)

Select the green plus function to add new chief complaint

Step 5

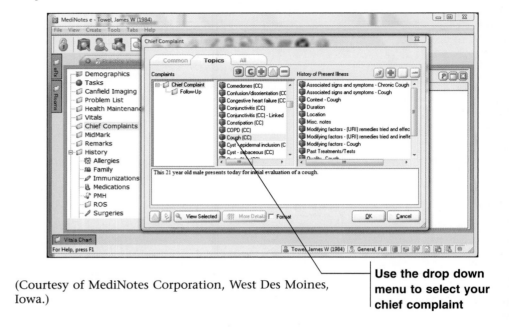

(Courtesy of MediNotes Corporation, West Des Moines, Iowa.)

Use the drop down menu to select your chief complaint

The screen above shows that the user selected "cough" as a CC. The screen also shows how technology can save time by automatically generating a note based on the information selected that reads "This 21-year-old male presents today for initial evaluation of a cough." This note can be automatically placed in the patient's H&P, visit note, or problem list.

Templates

A template is a standardized form that has a predesigned format and a limited selection of choices. Review the documentation templates found in this EHRS in the screen below:

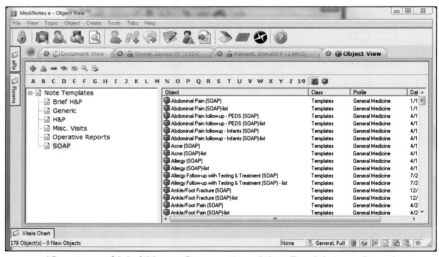

(Courtesy of MediNotes Corporation, West Des Moines, Iowa.)

A visit note (encounter note) may be formatted in a way that addresses problems; the SOAP is an example of this format, and as you can see from the example above, it is available as one of the note templates. The SOAP is divided into four parts based on the patient's problem:

S—SUBJECTIVE
O—OBJECTIVE
A—ASSESSMENT
P—PLAN

◆ Exercise 6-6

How might a SOAP note relate to the billing process in the EHRS?

Would give more detailed information on how/what to bill.

Problem List

The problem list is a summary list. It is one of the most important documents in the outpatient setting (e.g., a physician office). Generally speaking, the problem list contains the patient's diagnosis, condition, treatment, and allergies. According to The Joint Commission (an accrediting body), the problem list should be recorded in the chart by the third visit. It contains a list of both acute and chronic conditions (Odom-Wesley and Brown, 2009). The EHRS facilitates data collection and the ability to update and monitor. An example is shown below:

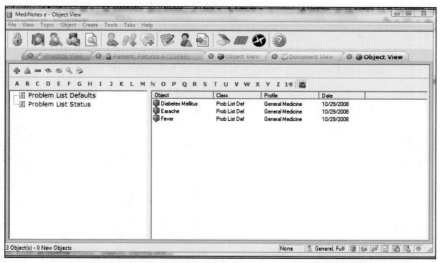

(Courtesy of MediNotes Corporation, West Des Moines, Iowa.)

 Exercise 6-7

Why is the problem list so valuable? How is this list used in the physician practice?

Medical information should be more detailed so as it will be easy to rule out illness.

 Exercise 6-8

What tools do you think the EHR can provide regarding the problem list?

Basic information of patients, contains full history of patients past or present illnesses.

Viewing Vital Signs

One of the benefits of the EHRS is the viewing capability. You can document and view vital signs in a number of ways using the EHRS's graphic display. Below you will find two screens for data entry of vital signs. Compare the views in the EHRS with those in the paper-based record.

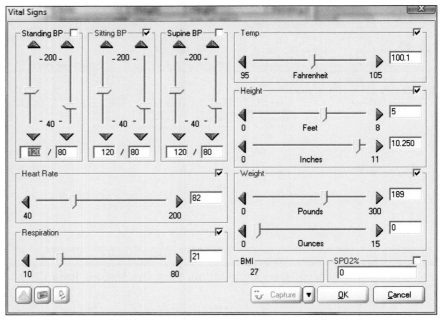

(Courtesy of MediNotes Corporation, West Des Moines, Iowa.)

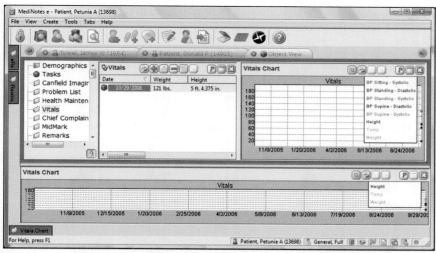

(Courtesy of MediNotes Corporation, West Des Moines, Iowa.)

Billing Use

As previously discussed, there are four areas of concern in the EHR environment pertaining to fraud and abuse: authorship, auditing, documenting, and patient identification (Odom-Wesley and Brown, 2009). You can see how easy it is to use the drop-down menu and enter a patient's vital signs or notes incorrectly. Keep in mind that the EHRS is able to automatically code the record on the basis of the documentation found in the EHRS. The software can calculate the correct code and assign the Evaluation and Management (E&M) code on the basis of the documentation; if the document is incorrect, you might bill for services that were not rendered or services that were not performed at the level at which you billed, which constitutes abuse.

ICD-9-CM codes and CPT-4 codes are used in billing. A portion of the CPT-4 codes are E&M codes, which are used in billing patient visits (encounters). The EHRS will perform the coding function by reviewing the documentation contained in the record. The following forms are critical in the billing process: the problem list, the H&P, and encounter notes.

CAUTION: Before billing, the clinician should make sure that the documentation entered into the system is correct.

Review the content in the Object Navigator and Order Requisition screens below and at the top of the next page:

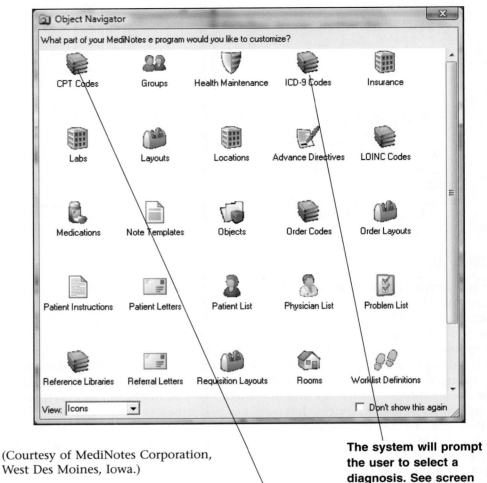

(Courtesy of MediNotes Corporation, West Des Moines, Iowa.)

The system will prompt the user to select a diagnosis. See screen below for the ICD-9 code.

CPT-4 codes are used in billing procedure(s) and treatment(s) rendered to the patient. The E&M codes are based on three components
1. History
2. Examination
3. Medical Decision

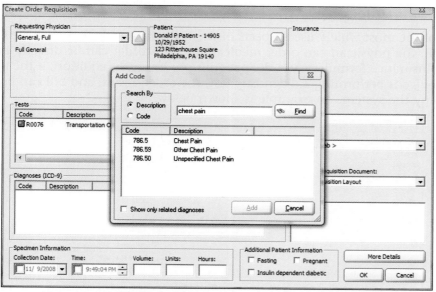

(Courtesy of MediNotes Corporation, West Des Moines, Iowa.)

 Exercise 6-9

What are the advantages and disadvantages of automated code assignment?

Advantage = simplify process

Disadvantage = error on code entered

Billing Manager

The EHRS can create a bill using CPT and ICD-9 codes. To reiterate, this billing statement is based on the documentation from the record (e.g., the patient's encounter note). After a visit note is written, you can select the appropriate diagnosis and treatment from a list and generate a bill. In MediNotes, this is called a *Billing Wizard,* as shown below:

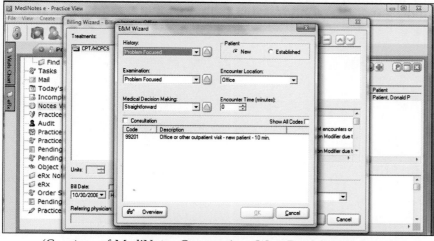

(Courtesy of MediNotes Corporation, West Des Moines, Iowa.)

Physician Orders

One of the most widely used aspects of the EHRS is the CPOE. Using the CPOE system, the physician can order medications. This order can be directly linked to an insurance formulary and the patient's pharmacy. In addition, if the physician office is performing a diagnostic test, the order, result, and bill can be captured by the system. An example is shown below.

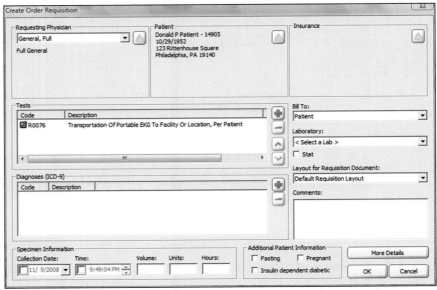

(Courtesy of MediNotes Corporation, West Des Moines, Iowa.)

CONCLUSION

This chapter contains an overview of the complex issues surrounding the EHRS and the management of patient data in the physician's office. The EHRS is both a challenge and a reality for most organizations and offices dealing with health records. For the EHR to be fully embraced and supported by health care organizations, administrators and clinicians will want to be assured that the EHRS will improve the quality of care. The challenge of making the transition to a complete EHR will continue with the support of the government and private and professional organizations. In the meantime, the EHR will be used in the collection and review of data and patient information. Because medical assistants are generally the primary users of the EHR in the office setting, it is important that they understand the administrative, clinical, and billing functions of the EHRS.

References

AHIMA e-HIM Work Group on Security of Personal Health Information (2008). Ensuring security of high-risk information in EHRS, *Journal of AHIMA* 79, no. 9 (September), 67-71.

Amatayakul M, Brandt M, Dougherty M (2003). Cut, copy, paste: EHR guidelines, *Journal of AHIMA* 74, no. 9 (October), 72, 74.

Amatayakul MK. Electronic health record. In Latour, KM, Eichenwald-Maki S, editors, *Health information management: concepts, principles, and practice,* ed 1, Chicago, 2006, AHIMA, 211-237.

Amatayakul MK. *Electronic health records: a practical guide for professionals and organizations,* Chicago, 2007, American Health Information Management Association.

CMS, retrieved from http://www.cms.hhs.gov/TransactionCodeSetsStands/.

Dick R, Steen EB. Institute of medicine. In Dick RS, Steen EB, editors, *The computer-based patient record: an essential technology for health care,* 1991, National Academy Press.

Gartee R. *Electronic health records: understanding and using computerized medical records,* Upper Saddle River, NJ, 2007, Prentice Hall.

Harman LB. *Ethical challenges in the management of health information,* ed 2, Sudbury, Md, 2006, Jones and Bartlett Publishers.

Latour KM, Eichenwald-Maki S. *Health information management: concepts, principles, and practice,* Chicago, 2006, AHIMA.

Medicare, retrieved from http://www.medicare.gov/fraudabuse/Overview.asp.

OCR Privacy Rule Summary, 2003.

Odom-Wesley B, Brown D. *Documentation for medical records.* Chicago, 2009, American Health Information Management.

Quinn J (1999). An HL7 overview, *Journal of AHIMA* 70, 32-34.

Quinsey CA (2006). Using HL7 Standards to evaluate an EHR, *Journal of AHIMA* 77, no. 4 (April), 64A-C.

OBJECTIVES

After reading this chapter and working the exercises, you should be able to do the following:

1. Explain the necessity of transcribing accurate notes on patients' progress.
2. Demonstrate the proper procedure and format for transcribing patients' medical chart notes and progress notes.
3. Use the different methods employed in transcribing entries into medical records.
4. Recognize and correct any erroneous entry made in the medical record.
5. List the basic information to be found in patient notes in emergency department, medical office, and clinic records.
6. Identify the key components of the electronic medical record and the traditional paper document.
7. Demonstrate the proper use of the metric system in medical records.
8. Discuss the importance of medical record notes to the billing cycle.

MEDICAL CHART NOTES AND PROGRESS NOTES

Note from the Author

With this chapter, you begin to work with some very interesting documents. These medical record notes are like miniature biographies that give the details of a patient's health, good or bad, which become the short story of his or her life during the present and immediate past. The details of our health significantly shape who we are, and the shape of the patient's life is acutely visible to you. Some of these stories are very sad, others are full of promise, and most are simply the day-in and day-out continuation of lives as they are being lived. I hope that you learn to feel, as I did, very privileged to share in the care of the patient even in this small way of carefully transcribing this special document.

Medical record notes (also called *chart notes* or *progress notes*) are the formal or informal notes taken by the physician when he or she meets with or examines a patient in the office, clinic, acute care center, or emergency department. These notes are a part of the patient's permanent medical record. Medical records are vital in patient care. Although medical records are used mainly to assist the physician with care of the patient, they can be reviewed by attorneys, other physicians, insurance companies, or the court. It is essential that they be neat, accurate, and complete.

"Accurate" means that they are transcribed as dictated, and "complete" requires that they be dated and signed or initialed by the dictator. It is hard to insist that the physician sign or initial the records, but you might overcome the physician's reluctance by making it easier to do so: for example, by typing a line at the end of each chart entry for the signature or initials. Then, at the end of the shift or the day, all of the reports can be stacked in a convenient area for signing. It is important that entries be reviewed and signed in a timely manner.

For a chart to be admissible as evidence in court, the party dictating or writing entries should be able to attest that they were true and correct at the time they were written. The best indication of that is the physician's signature or initials at the end of each typed note. The hospital will insist that the physician sign all dictated material and all entries he or she makes on the patient's hospital record; failure to do so could result in a loss of hospital staff privileges.

Furthermore, before copies of records leave the facility, the originals must be checked for accuracy; if the originals were not signed before, they must be signed immediately. Any liability of the transcriptionist personally is of small significance unless there are unusual circumstances, such as negligence, willfulness, or malice. A physician cannot easily shift the blame to another person because the faulty records are his or her responsibility as long as the proper procedure for release of information has been established. If a medical transcriptionist is at fault in recording improperly, the physician has the right to discharge him or her for inefficiency, and this possibility is a peril for the careless worker.

At one time, physicians handwrote daily progress entries into the patient's hospital medical record. In office or clinic situations, some physicians never dictate chart notes, preferring to enter them into the patient's record in longhand. Although it is not essential that medical records be typed, it is best to do so. Obviously, typed notes are easier to read; when more than one physician is involved in patient care, such as in a large office or clinic, it is essential that all notes be easy to read with no chance of misinterpretation. In this chapter, we are not concerned with longhand notes but rather with learning the process of taking chart notes from the equipment and transcribing the notes properly into the patient's record. In the hospital, clinic, or office setting in which notes become part of the electronic medical record, they must be typed. If written out, the notes may be copied and typed. The electronic medical record is a database that tracks vital data and *ideally* replaces paper with computer screens that are clear, easy-to-read, accurate, and accessible. It supports the entry of all patient care variables with appropriate default choices and maintains care paths. Users may enter text notes by selecting standard phrases and sentences. The notes are then fully edited to create documents that accurately record the observations of the physicians or nursing staff. Document-based electronic medical records maximize office efficiencies by managing data that make up the outdated paper. The system is fast, accurate, and easy to use. Even complex patient encounters are quickly and precisely documented. Regardless of format, text entries or templates should follow fundamental principles for the quality of the entry.

Even though the electronic age brings new variables to the recording of the most basic encounter with the patient, it does not change the foundation, which is that records must be maintained in a manner that follows applicable regulations, accreditation standards, and legal standards.

Persons dictating and those transcribing or editing records must follow established guidelines:

- Identify the patient by name and health record number when applicable on every page in the record or computerized record screen, every form, and every computerized printout.
- Make entries as soon as possible after an event or observation is made. (Entries are never made in advance.)
- Include a complete date and time on every entry.
- Use black ink for written entries. You must ensure that these are legible.
- Use specific language; avoid vague or generalized language.
- Record objective facts, not what is presumed.
- Document what can be seen, heard, touched, and/or smelled.
- Describe signs or symptoms.
- Use quotation marks when quoting the patient.
- Document the patient's response to care.
- Use only abbreviations approved by the organization.

The physician should try to dictate as soon as the patient visit is complete and the details are still fresh. Some physicians have also found it helpful to dictate the notes at the patient's bedside or with the patient present in the office or in the emergency department. This practice gives the examiner the opportunity to ask for any details that may have been overlooked in the initial history taking; it also provides an opportunity to reinstruct the patient about medication or to explain the purpose of tests and the expected results. An advantage to the patient is the ability to hear the same information repeated into the dictation equipment, reinforcing what was previously discussed. The patient also gets another opportunity to ask questions that may have been forgotten, and he or she may even provide additional pieces of information. Last, patients get a better understanding of the amount of time spent under the physician's care. Emergency department chart notes are dictated as the patient is being seen. They are usually transcribed on a STAT (immediate) basis. Some emergency departments or urgent care centers place the transcribing station within the facility or in a nearby area so that the dictator can have immediate access to the chart note. If the patient is admitted to the hospital for treatment or observation, this initial note or dictation will accompany the patient.

The items dictated into a chart note vary and may include all or only some of the following: an account of the health history of the patient and the patient's family, the findings on physical examination, the signs or symptoms occurring while the patient is under observation, and the medication and treatments the patient receives or those recommended. This information may be set off by individual topics, such as the chief complaint (CC), the reason the patient is visiting the doctor or emergency department; the history (HX) of the complaint; the physical examination (PX); the treatment (RX) recommended by the physician; and the physician's impression (IMP) or diagnosis (DX) of the problem. Abbreviations are used very freely in chart notes, and you might need to refer to a list of abbreviations. In addition, a brief general list is provided for you to refer to as you begin your assignments.

The office transcriptionist works with dictated progress notes made when the patient is seen in the office, at home, or in the specialty clinic, with reference made to admissions and discharges from the hospital or a nursing facility. Notes are also made when the physician is called in to see an established patient in the emergency department. Telephone conversations with the patient or with other physicians treating the patient may also be recorded.

GENERAL PRINCIPLES FOR COMPLETE DOCUMENTATION IN MEDICAL RECORDS

An office-based medical transcriptionist needs to be aware of the general principles for complete documentation of medical records to ensure that these notes are written or transcribed into the record, documenting services for which the provider of care expects to be paid. The following is a general outline of the principles through which payments are made. It is important to observe that these components are documented and to alert your employer when they are not mentioned. To provide documentation of services rendered, you must know what billing codes are used by the facility for the service documented. The nature and amount of physician work and documentation vary by the type of service performed, the place of the service, and the status of the patient. These general principles are applicable to all types of medical and surgical services in all settings. The billing and diagnosis codes reported on the health insurance claim form must be supported by the documentation in the record.

In addition, the following teaches you about the information that is generally found in these records and helps you set it up in a logical manner.

1. The records must be complete and legible.
2. Each patient encounter should include the following documentation:
   • date
   • reason for the encounter
   • history, physical examination, prior diagnostic test results
   • diagnosis (assessment, impression)
   • plan for care
   • name of the observer
3. Rationale for ordering diagnostic or other services should be documented or inferred.
4. Health risk factors should be identified.
5. Progress, response to treatment, changes in treatment, and revision of diagnosis should be documented.

Seven components are used when describing the level of services for evaluation and management of the patient. The level of care given determines how many of these components are used. Therefore it is important that they are documented when done. The components may be listed as separate elements of the history, or they may be included in the history of the present illness.

History

The history includes the chief complaint (CC); the history of present illness (HPI); past history, family history, and/or social history (PFSH); and the review of systems (ROS).

- The CC describes the symptom, problem, or condition that is the reason for the encounter and must be clearly described in the record.
- The HPI is the chronological description of the development of the patient's present illness from the first sign and/or symptom or from the previous encounter to the present.
- The PFSH is a review of the patient's past illnesses, operations, injuries, and treatments; a review of medical events in the patient's family, including diseases that may be hereditary; and a review of past and current activities in which the patient was or is engaged.
- A problem-pertinent ROS is an inquiry about the system directly related to the problems identified in the HPI. The patient's positive responses and pertinent negatives (i.e., all the things the patient does not have wrong) related to the problem are documented. Signs or symptoms the patient might be experiencing or has experienced are identified, including constitutional symptoms (fever, weight loss, fatigue); integumentary (skin and/or breast); eyes, ears, nose, and throat; mouth; cardiovascular; respiratory; gastrointestinal; genitourinary; musculoskeletal; neurological; psychiatric; endocrine; hematological/lymphatic; and allergic/immunological. (The ROS and PFSH may be recorded by an ancillary staff member or on a form completed by the patient.)

When directly related to the problem identified in the HPI, the time spent with the patient in history taking, care, examination, counseling, and coordination of services should also be documented.

Examination

The extent of the examination performed and documented depends on clinical judgment and the nature of the presenting problems. Examinations range from limited to complete. Depending on the level of services performed, there are four types of examinations:

1. Problem focused: a limited examination of the affected body area or system
2. Expanded: a limited examination of the affected body area or system and other symptomatic related systems
3. Detailed: an extended examination of the affected body area and other symptomatic or related systems
4. Comprehensive: a general multisystem examination or a complete examination of a single system

Medical Decision Making

There are four types of medical decision making. They are measured by the number of possible diagnoses or management options that must be considered; the complexity of medical records, tests, and other information that must be obtained, reviewed, and analyzed; the risk of significant complications associated with the problem or problems; the diagnostic procedures; and/or possible management options. They are as follows:

1. Straightforward: self-limited or minor problem
2. Low complexity
   - two or more self-limited or minor problems
   - stable chronic illness
   - acute uncomplicated illness or injury
3. Moderate complexity
   - one or more chronic illnesses with mild exacerbation, progression, or side effects of treatment
   - two or more stable chronic illnesses
   - undiagnosed new problem
   - acute illness
   - acute complicated injury
4. High complexity
   - one or more chronic illnesses with severe exacerbation, progression, or side effects of treatment
   - acute or chronic illness or injuries that pose a threat to life or bodily function

Counseling and Coordination of Care

When counseling and/or coordination of care involves more than 50% of the physician/patient/family encounter time in the office, outpatient setting, hospital, or nursing facility, the total length of time of the encounter (face-to-face) must be documented, and the record should describe the counseling and/or activities to coordinate care.

NEW PATIENT, OFFICE

When a patient comes into the office or specialty clinic for the initial visit, a chart is prepared. These charts vary, just as physicians and their medical specialties vary. Therefore we shall examine the broad methods of record preparation; you can easily apply these instructions to the method used by your employer. There really is no "best" way to keep medical records other than neat, accurate, complete, and timely (made as soon as possible after the patient is seen).

The patient completes a social data sheet during the initial visit (Fig. 7-1). These data sheets also vary according to the wishes of the individual physician medical practice, the facility, or the staff. This information is then used to prepare the accounting file for the patient, as well as to supply the initial information for the patient's medical record. Some offices transfer all of this information to the initial page of the medical record; others take the barest minimum (complete name and birth date or age). Medical consultants often wish to have the name and telephone number of the referring physician listed. It is important for you to learn exactly what information your employer wants transferred from the social data sheet to this initial chart page.

Figs. 7-2 to 7-6 illustrate a variety of chart paper styles. Some physicians have special paper printed for notes, others purchase chart paper from medical printing supply houses, but most prefer plain 8½ × 11 inch typing paper. Special paper with small illustrations of body parts printed in the margins (see Fig. 7-6) is often used in the emergency department, private medical offices, dental offices, and specialty offices (e.g., those of gynecologists, ophthalmologists, orthopedic surgeons, urologists, and medicolegal specialists). These forms are then fed into a laser printer.

After the initial information is transferred from the patient's social data sheet, the medical records administrator dates the chart paper by using a date stamp or making the entry in longhand. The date may be written out, abbreviated, or written in numerals. The paper is then placed into a labeled file folder or a clipboard and presented to the physician at the time the patient is seen.

At the conclusion of the visit, the physician writes the notes in the chart, dictates them to be

INFORMATION REQUIRED FOR CASE HISTORY FILE

Date..

Patient... Date of Birth.................. Age..............
(Mr., Mrs., Miss, Master)   First Name   Initial   Last Name

Name of Husband, Wife or Parent... Home Phone..........................

Home Address.. If Military, Serial No.
Soc. Sec. No..

Patient Employed By:...
City or Town   Zip Code

Business Address..

Occupation... Business Phone..........................

Husband or Wife Employed by:...

Business Address..
City or Town   Zip Code

Occupation... Business Phone..........................

Name of nearest relative
not named above (indicate relationship)..

Address..

Insured by:..Group No.............. Member No.....................

Recommended by:... Former Physician..................................

If patient a minor
Give name of person legally responsible:..

I hereby authorize and request the .... Insurance Company
to pay the amount due me in my pending claim for medical expense Benefits directly to
....MD

Date.. Signature..

Fig. 7-1   Example of a social data sheet.

transcribed into the chart, or dictates a separate document that takes the place of the chart entry. This document can be a formal history and physical examination report, it may be a formal report to an attorney or workers' compensation company, or it may be a consultation report to the physician who referred the patient to the office (see Fig. 7-2, entry of 2-8-0X). If the dictator prefers not to make a chart entry and dictates a document, as just discussed, to take the place of the entry, you will transcribe the document and make a note of it in the patient's record where the normal chart entry belongs. In Fig. 7-2, the medical transcriptionist (mlo) made the entry "2-8-0X See letter to Dr. Wong mlo"; thus the physician needs only to review that

letter for a summary of the February 8 office visit. This practice precludes dictating the same material twice. Another method of communication is to dictate a complete chart note and indicate that a copy of the note should be sent to the referring physician.

You may type this entry or write it in longhand. Always follow *your* personal chart entry with *your* initials written in longhand.

February 7, 200X See note to Dr. Normington mlo

(also correct)

Feb. 7, 200X See note to Dr. Normington mlo

Mary Neidgrinhaus   DOB: 06/11/XX

REF: Yuen Wong, MD
555-527-8765

12/18/20XX
HX: This 4-1/2-year-old girl has been having URIs beginning in October 200X. She
            has had several of these infections since that time and has been seen by another
            otolaryngologist who recommended that she have surgery including an
            adenotonsillectomy and bilateral myringotomies with tubes. The mother desired
            another opinion, and the family doctor referred her to me.

ALLERGIES: <u>AMPICILLIN and SEPTRA</u>

PX: Well-developed and well-nourished girl in no acute distress.
VS: Pulse: 84/min. Resp: 20/min. Temp: 98.8° axillary.
HEENT: Eyes: PERRLA. EOMs normal. Ears: The right TM was retracted and slightly
            injected. The left TM was retracted but not injected. Both canals were negative.
            Nose: The nasal septum was roughly in the midline. Mucous membrane lining
            somewhat pale and slightly swollen. Throat: Tonsils were +3 and very cryptic,
NECK: There were tonsillar nodes palpable in both anterior cervical triangles.

CHEST: Lungs: Clear to P&A. Heart: Regular rate and rhythm; no murmurs.

IMP: 1. Hypertrophy of tonsils and adenoids.
            2. Bilateral recurrent serous otitis media.

RX: Dimetapp elixir 20 mL 1 teaspoon q.i.d.

mlo   Gene M. Kasten, MD

12/28/20XX Right ear improved; no change in the left. Mother still does not want surgery.
RX: Balamine DM syrup 30 mL 1/2 teaspoon q.i.d.

mlo   Gene M. Kasten, MD

1-3-XX   *Mother telephoned: Balamine "not working." Called in
          Ceclor 4 ounces 1 teaspoon t.i.d. per Dr. Kasten. gmk*

01/14/200X No improvement in left ear. Right ear significantly the same as when last seen.
            Mother now approves surgery for removal of the tonsils and adenoids and
            bilateral myringotomies with tube insertions.

mlo   Gene M. Kasten, MD

01/15/200X *See copy of History and Physical dictated for View of the Lakes Memorial
            Outpatient Center.*

2-6-XX   *Pt. admitted to VOL outpatient 6 a.m. gmk*
2-8-XX   *See letter to Dr. Wong gmk*

Fig. 7-2 Example of a typical chart note with a variety of visits listed. Notice how the "allergy" is handled in the note of December 18.

KARL ROBRECHT, MD
INTERNAL MEDICINE
555 LAKE VIEW DRIVE
BAY VILLAGE, OHIO 44140

Name _____ | Date _____

Legal Address _____ | Tel. No. _____

Local Address _____ | Tel. No. _____

Birthplace _____ Age _____ Sex _____ | Marital Status _____

Occupation _____ Employer _____ Address _____ | Tel. No. _____

Nearest Relative, or Guardian (Relationship) _____ Address _____ | Tel. No. _____

Occupation _____ Employer _____ Address _____ | Tel. No. _____

Referred by _____ Address _____ | Tel. No. _____

Insurance Company _____ Address _____ Policy No. / Type _____

PHYSICAL EXAMINATION

Height _____ Weight _____ T _____ P _____ General Appearance _____

Eyes _____ Vision Recorded on Sight Screener _____

Ears _____ Hearing: rt _____ lt _____

Teeth _____ Nose _____

Throat _____ Thyroid _____

Skin _____ Scars _____

Heart _____ BP _____

Lungs _____

Breasts _____

Abdomen _____

Rectum _____ Hernia _____

Extremities _____

Nervous System _____

Reflexes _____

Personality _____

Hygiene _____

Remarks _____

Fig. 7-3   Example of medical office chart paper, initial visit.

EMERGENCY DEPARTMENT RECORD

Holly P. Woodsen

CHART REQUESTED

LOCATION	DATE	TIME REGISTERED	TRIAGE TIME	AM ☐ PM ☐	OUTPT ☐	INPT ☐
202	11/29/0X	11:32				

ARRIVED ▶ [X] WALKED ☐ WC ☐ AMB ☐ PARA AMB ☐ OTHER

ACCOMPANIED BY ▶ ☐ ALONE ☐ SPOUSE ☐ PARENT ☐ FRIEND ☐ RELATIVE

PATIENT'S ADDRESS

1335 11th Street
Mt. Channel, XX 54321

HOME PHONE	619 278-6489	RELATIVE TO CONTACT / PHONE	PRIMARY CARE CLINIC	PERSONAL PHYSICIAN
WORK PHONE	619 278-6489		221	W.A. Berry

AGE	SEX	TEMP	BLOOD PRESSURE	PULSE	RESP	WEIGHT (Peds)	CURRENT MEDICATIONS
027	F	99°	111/76	87	20		∅

DRUG SENSITIVITY ☐ NO [X] YES   IF YES, SPECIFY DRUG PCN   LMP   LAST TETANUS

CHIEF COMPLAINT   (IF INJURY - WHERE AND HOW DID IT OCCUR?)   ASSAULTED by boyfriend

	✓
CBC WBC	
CBC H&H	
Lytes	
Bun/Creat	
Glucose/Acet	
Amylase	
UA	
C&S	
Preg Test	
CPK	
CXR	
Abd Ser/KUB	
ABG	
Peak Flow	
Pulse Ox	
EKG	

TIME OF INITIAL EXAM   HISTORY AND EXAM

S: 27 y/o female who presents to the ER after an altercation. Pt reports that she was driving her car, her boyfriend was in the front passenger seat. The pt reported to me that she reached across and struck him on the chest, and that he responded by punching her on the right side of her face three times. Pt was driving the car and apparently did not lose consciousness and did not lose control of the car. She denies being struck in the chest or abdomen.

Incident has been reported to the police by nursing staff.

O: She is awake, alert and appropriate. Head and face appear atraumatic, no STS or ecchymosis is noted. The neck is supple. Pupils midposition and reactive, EOMs are intact. Full ROM to the mandible, no malocclusion. No chest wall or bony pelvic tenderness.

Visual Acuity OD (R)____ OS (L)____

A: Facial contusions.

P: Reassurance. Ice. ASA. Tylenol. Soft diet as needed. Re-exam for persistent pain or malocclusion.

DISABILITY ☐ NO ☐ YES   IF YES, GIVE RETURN TO WORK DATE

SPECIFY   ED PHYSICIAN

CONDITION AT DISCHARGE (CHECK ALL THAT APPLY)
☐ UNCHANGED ☐ ALERT/ORIENTED ☐ ON CRUTCHES ☐ DOA ▶
☐ ASYMPTOMATIC ☐ AMBULATORY ☐ EXPIRED ☐ OTHER ▶

INSTRUCTIONS TO PATIENT
☐ WRITTEN
☐ VERBAL   SPECIFY,

DISPOSITION (CHECK ALL THAT APPLY)   SERVICE & FLOOR   DOCTOR, DATE, LOCATION, TIME   TIME
☐ RETURN PRN ☐ WORK ☐ ADMITTED ▶   ☐ REFERRED TO ▶
☐ HOME ☐ HOLDING ☐ TRANSFERRED ▶   ☐ RETURN TO ▶

Fig. 7-4 Example of an emergency department chart note illustrating minimum heads and SOAP format.

Name _Donald Grenco_ Age _68_

Date _09-28-00_

HT _5'6"_ WT _249_ BP (R) _46/78_

T _96.5_ P _85_ R

ALLERGIES

NKA

CURRENT MEDICATIONS:

CC SOB X months "worse since stroke last year"

Dyspnea: Rest _Yes_
Exercise

Had CVA last Nov

Wt ↑ 9 lb.

Orthopnea: ⊖

Cough: ⊖

Sputum: ⊖

Wheezing: _Yes_

Fever: ⊖

Chest Pain: ⊖

Edema: _Yes_

Wt. Change: ↑ 9 lb since 7-14-00

Smoking: ⊖

Last CXR:

Last Oximetry: _today_

Last Spiro: _7-14-00_

DATE: SEP 28

TIME: 16:09:52

INVIVO MODEL 4500 PULSE OXIMETER

=====================================

OXYGEN SAT= 96%   HEART RATE= 88

OXYGEN SAT= 97%   HEART RATE= 88

OXYGEN SAT= 97%   HEART RATE= 88

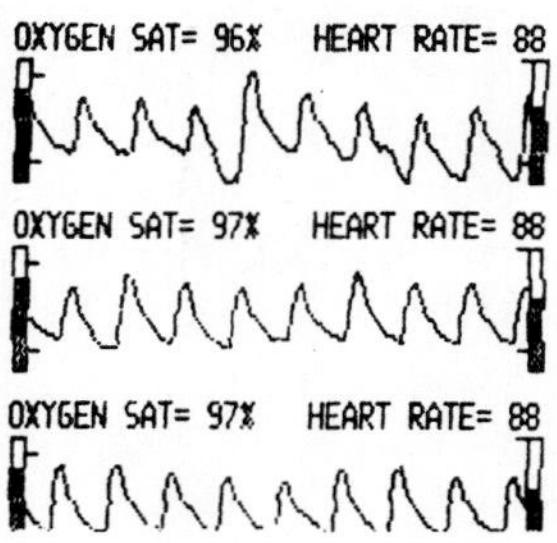

This 68-year-old patient had a CVA last November and reports that he is "weak all over." Very SOB with minimal exertion. Sleeps poorly. Very sleepy during the day.
HEENT: Negative.
Neck: Supple.
Heart: Regular rhythm.
Extremities: 2+ ankle edema.
Impression: Diabetes. Restrictive lung disease.
? Sleep disorder.
Plan: Sleep evaluation.
Get hospital records from November of last year.

WAB/lar

Fig. 7-5 Example of a chart note from a pulmonary specialist's office illustrating personalized chart paper and a combination of written notes and transcribed notes. Notice the copy of the oxygen saturation rate combined with the chart note.

Allergic to PCN

EAR NOSE & THROAT

Kingersley, Margaret O.
Patient's name

Address: 145 West Cuyamaca, Roseland Hills, XX

Tel No. 555-9743   Referred by : Dept. of Rehabilitation

Insurance   Rehab   Date: 1-9-XX

Age: 60   Sex: F

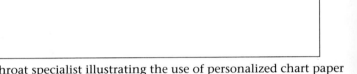

CC: This is a 60-year-old pt who was seen in the office on May 15, 200X, on referral from the Department of Rehabilitation.

HX: I obtained a history from the patient that she has been aware of hearing loss in both ears, worse in the left ear, since about 1998. She was first tested in Dr. Victor Goodhill's office at the University Clinic in 1999, and at that time showed a bilateral sensorineural deafness worse in the left ear. Because there was some asymmetry of her hearing, mastoid and middle ear tomograms were performed and these were normal. She also had a ENG, which was also normal.

Beginning in 1999, she was fitted with first, a hearing aid in her left ear, and later one in her right ear, and these are in-the-ear types. She states that she does not find them very satisfactory, in most situations, unless it is very quiet.

The pt does report some tinnitus in both ears, which has been present for a number of years. She is unable to describe this noise.

The pt has no problems with vertigo.

JHJ/ro

Fig. 7-6   Example of a chart note from an ear, nose, and throat specialist illustrating the use of personalized chart paper with diagramed body parts.

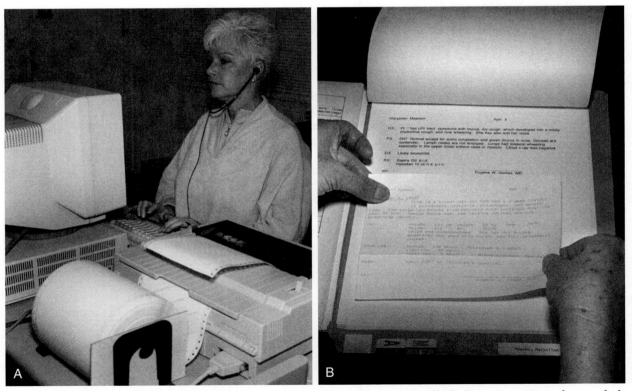

Fig. 7-7   **A**, Transcriptionist using PAT Systems pressure-sensitive paper on a roll. **B**, Demonstration of ease of placing the pressure-sensitive paper onto the existing chart note in the medical record. *(Paper courtesy PAT Systems; phone [800] 543-1911; photograph courtesy John Dixon, Grossmont College, San Diego, California.)*

ESTABLISHED PATIENT, OFFICE

Although the initial visit notes are usually lengthy, subsequent or follow-up notes may be as brief as a few lines, but they vary according to the patient's complaint and type of visit to the office. For example, an entry for an established patient being seen in the office in follow-up to a facility for a myringotomy could well read as shown in the 5-5-0X and 5-12-0X entries on the following chart note:

EXAMPLE

Tammy O. Beckley   BD: 02-15-0X

5-1-0X   Sunday, 0315 hours. Patient seen in ER complaining of pain, a.d. x 3 d. PX revealed fluid and pus. Temp. 101°.

ADVICE: Myringotomy.

DIAGNOSIS: Otitis media, right.

tat   Julian Cooke-Dieter, MD

5/2/0X Admit 0600 Mercy SurgiCenter tat
5/2/0X Right myringotomy with aspiration. Discharged 1015 hours. tat

5-5-0X   No pain right ear. Pt. Progressing. Return 1 week. Temp. 99°.

tat   Julian Cooke-Dieter, MD

5-12-0X   Temp normal; no fluid, no pus, no pain. Return p.r.n.

tat   Julian Cooke-Dieter, MD

The use of special paper in your printer makes these notes very easy to handle. Several companies manufacture pressure-sensitive paper for transcribing medical notes. This paper comes in a variety of forms, such as a continuous sheet of paper folded or on a roll. It is placed behind the pin-feed printer where the regular paper is placed or is fed into the laser printer when needed. The transcriptionist simply types the patient's name, date, and dictation, leaving a space at the end for the dictator's signature or initials. Each note is typed without removal of paper from the printer. Then, when the transcript is finished, the entire sheet is cut off and given to the dictator for signature. The use of this method makes it easier for the physician as well, because individual charts do not have to be opened and signed. This method of transcribing notes is particularly helpful when dictation is sent out of the office and the medical records do not accompany it. After approval, the notes are cut apart with a paper cutter or scissors or are separated at the perforations (Fig. 7-7, *A*). The backing is peeled off of each one, and the note is then placed on the next blank space on the progress sheet so as not to obliterate the information previously entered (Fig. 7-7, *B*). Fig. 7-8 illustrates several patient notes on a sheet of pressure-sensitive paper. After signature placement, these will be cut apart and placed in the individual records at the next available spot on the chart paper.

Again, the physician may dictate a follow-up letter to a referring physician at this point, rather than making a regular entry note. As new pages are added, be sure that the patient's name is typed on the top of the page. There is no reason why you cannot continue the notes to the back of the chart paper, and some offices do so to prevent the medical record from becoming bulky. Other physicians prefer to use only one side of the chart paper. The second and all subsequent pages of the progress notes are headed up with the patient's name. If you must continue a chart entry to the following page in the middle of an entry, be sure to type *continued* at the bottom of the beginning page and head up the following page with the date of the chart entry and the word *continued,* as well as the patient's name.

Barbara Anne Noonan
07/07/0X

The patient returns today feeling rather poorly. She was admitted to the GrandView Hospital for fluid accumulation, which came on rather suddenly last week. Fluid has been removed but the patient is still short of breath. No chest pain and no hemoptysis.

On examination, the patient looks progressively sicker than when first seen. Ankles are quite swollen. Moderately short of breath at rest. P&A of the lungs reveal probable fluid accumulation along the right base. The liver is still prominent and hard.

It would seem advisable that radiation therapy stop at this point. I am not sure what, if any, palliation we have afforded the lady, but I do not think her general situation would permit further radiation to curative doses. This was discussed with her and her husband. It was with some relief as she accepted my recommendation.
LR/do

John W. Issabel
07/07/0X

Patient's weight is up slightly at 124 pounds. Requires 4-6 Dilaudid a day, about the same as he has been taking earlier. Pain is a little better, still localized to soft tissues about 3 cm to the right of the midline at about the level of C7. His wife notices some return of night sweats, though no symptoms of this were noted by the patient and he has not measured his temperature. He is otherwise feeling well.

To exam, he looks better than he has looked on previous visits here. There are no palpable nodes. He has tan skin reaction over both ports, more so on the posterior than anterior. Chest is clear to percussion and auscultation. No distinct bone tenderness. No palpable axillary masses or liver masses. No peripheral cyanosis or edema.

PLAN: Chest x-ray with films on the right side, upper chest. Liver function test, CBC. Return here 1 month and to see Dr. Tu on 7/11/0X. I have asked that he keep track of his temperature twice a day in the interim.
LR/do

Edward Fredrickson
07/07/0X

Bilateral femur and hip films show only osteoporosis. Will consider for palliative treatment should reproducible pain persist.
LR/do

Herbert Frenay
07/07/0X

Mr. Frenay returns to be sure that his groin has healed up following significant reaction from radiation treatments.

On exam, he has no adenopathy in the area. There is some edema. The skin has healed well. There is also distal edema of the lower extremity, which is quite significant and I'm sure related to the combination of radiation and surgery. He has seen Dr. Hoffman, and Dr. Hoffman has given him a Jobst stocking for this. He will follow up with Dr. Hoffman and here only on a p.r.n. basis.
LR/do

Fig. 7-8   Chart notes on four patients transcribed onto pressure-sensitive paper. After the notes are signed by the dictator, they will be cut apart just above each patient's name and placed in the individual charts.

Figs. 7-5, 7-6, and 7-8 through 7-11 show examples of medical office progress notes.

These examples of chart entries that you have just examined are not intended to show *exactly* how to type entries but rather to indicate a variety of methods used by different transcriptionists. At this point, you will not be able to determine exactly how a chart is to be typed, because your employer may have definite guidelines for you to follow. For now, and to practice, try to achieve a readable note. Do not combine all the information, but pull out the main topics. In one style, you do not bring the line of typing back to the left margin until the third line, so that the date and topics will stand out clearly; the third and subsequent lines may be brought back to the left margin or blocked under the first two lines. (See Figs. 7-9 and 7-11 for this method.) Establish a clean, easy-to-read format for progress notes.

The following actual chart note *appears* to have a format, but the format does not contribute to ease of reading or scanning. The patient's name is not appropriately placed. Nothing is gained by having a tab setting after the date in this manner, which leaves a great deal of space that serves no purpose. The use of boldface works better when subtopics are found within text. Avoid the overuse of double-spacing, full caps, boldface, and underlining. The style selected needs a purpose: a new topic, an alert, an emphasis, an outline, and white space.

Flanaghan, Michael R.   AGE: 82

March 17, 200X

SUBJECTIVE: Patient presented complaining of insomnia, weakness, and shortness of
                     breath. Described Hx of progressive dyspnea on exertion over a 2- to
                     3-year period.

OBJECTIVE: BP 110. Pulse 120 and regular. Visible neck vein distention at
                     45 degrees elevation; rales at both lung bases. Cardiac examination
revealed an enlarged heart with PMI felt at the midclavicular line. Sounds were distant,
but a systolic murmur was described.

        ECG: Sinus tachycardia, left axis deviation, and right bundle branch block.

        ECHO: Enlarged left ventricle and calcified and stenotic aortic valve. Left
                     ventricular hypertrophy also demonstrated.

ASSESSMENT: 1. Calcified aortic stenosis.
                     2. Congestive heart failure.

PLAN: 1. Admit to hospital.
                     2. Treat with sodium restriction, digitalis, diuretic.

                     _____
mlo   Joseph D. Becquer, MD

Fig. 7-9 Sample chart note showing the SOAP method.

EXAMPLE: *Poor format*

5-4-0X   ERMA WONG returns today wearing her shoulder immobilizer. She is having difficulty sleeping at night and finds the Vicodin is quite helpful for that. Examination reveals ecchymosis of the arm, elbow, and forearm as her hematoma is resolving. She has normal neurovascular examination and normal appearance of her right hand.

X- RAYS: AP and lateral x-rays of the right shoulder were obtained. Interpretation: The x-rays show severe osteoporosis. There is impaction of the humeral head fracture. There has been slight change with further impaction since her previous x-rays. There is no displacement of the tuberosity fragment.

IMPRESSION: Satisfactory course with an unstable proximal humerus. Fracture of the right dominant upper extremity and severe osteoporosis.

RECOMMENDATIONS: The patient will remain in her shoulder immobilizer and will have her use of the right upper extremity severely limited until such time that more stability is obtained by progressive healing. Will return for follow-up examination and x-rays in 10 days. Hopefully, we will be able to start some early pendulum exercises at that time.

RFV:bmg

EXAMPLE: *Improved format*

Erma Wong

5-4-0X   Patient returns today wearing her shoulder immobilizer. She is having difficulty sleeping at night and finds the Vicodin is quite helpful for that.

PX: Ecchymosis of the arm, elbow, and forearm as her hematoma is resolving. She has normal neurovascular examination and normal appearance of her right hand.

X- RAYS: AP and lateral x-rays of the right shoulder were obtained. Interpretation: The x-rays show **severe osteoporosis**. There is impaction of the humeral head fracture. There has been slight change with further impaction since her previous x-rays. There is no displacement of the tuberosity fragment.

DX: 1. Satisfactory course with an unstable proximal humerus.
           2. Fracture of the right dominant upper extremity.
           3. Severe osteoporosis.

RX: The patient will remain in her shoulder immobilizer and will have her use of the right upper extremity severely limited until such time that more stability is obtained by progressive healing. Will return for follow-up examination and x-rays in 10 days. Hopefully, we will be able to start some early pendulum exercises at that time.

RFV:bmg

Flanaghan, Michael R.   AGE: 82

3/17/200X

HX: Patient presented complaining of insomnia, weakness, and shortness of
             breath. Described HX of progressive dyspnea on exertion over a 2- to 3-
             year period.

PX: BP: 110. Pulse120 and regular. Visible neck vein distention at
             45 degrees elevation; rales at both lung bases. Cardiac examination
             revealed an enlarged heart with PMI felt at the midclavicular line. Sounds
             were distant, but a systolic murmur was described.

ECG: Sinus tachycardia, left axis deviation, and right bundle branch block.

ECHO: Enlarged left ventricle and calcified and stenotic aortic valve. Left
             ventricular hypertrophy also demonstrated.

DX: 1. Calcified aortic stenosis.
             2. Congestive heart failure.

RX: 1. Admit to hospital.
             2. Treat with sodium restriction, digitalis, diuretic.

                              _____
                              Joseph D. Becquer, MD/gmc

Fig. 7-10   Sample chart note showing the HX (history), PX (physical examination), DX (diagnosis), and RX (treatment) method.

CHART NOTE, EMERGENCY DEPARTMENT VISIT

When patients are initially seen in the emergency department, the triage nurse determines the sequence in which patients will see a physician. Laboratory tests, radiographs, and simple tests may be ordered at this time by the triage nurse. At this point, the level of care is determined and may be described as the following:

- *Nonurgent care* involves routine care that could have taken place in a physician's office during office hours. This care is often provided for patients who have no physician. Problems include mild flu symptoms, earache, and prescription refills. Admission to the hospital is unlikely. If the emergency department is busy, these patients may be referred to a nearby urgent care center.
- *Urgent care* involves care necessitating basic emergency services. Problems include lacerations, acute flu symptoms, mild shortness of breath, broken bones, threatened abortion, and rectal bleeding. Admission to the hospital is possible.
- *Emergency care* involves care requiring immediate attention of the physician. Problems include chest pain, stroke, acute trauma, acute shortness of breath, respiratory arrest, and conditions necessitating cardiopulmonary resuscitation. Admission to the hospital is likely.

The patient, family member, or person bringing the patient to the department completes the social data information sheet (see Fig. 7-1). If the patient is brought in by emergency vehicle, the vehicle personnel generally provide some of the necessary information. Care is not withheld during the gathering of this information; often, care is begun while other personnel interview family or friends for the social history. Initial caregivers handwrite notes as the history is taken from the patient or from persons with the patient. A nurse or technician initially assesses the patient and handwrites notes or inputs data by computer. When the physician sees the patient, he or she usually handwrites a brief initial impression and orders to be carried out (i.e.,

Norman O. Brockman   Age: 4

JUL 2 6 200X   The patient is a white male, age 4, who came in to see me today
                      with a history of yellow discharge in the right ear, a fever, and a
sore throat of 2 days' duration. His oral temperature was 100. The pharynx was injected, the
tonsils inflamed, and there was crusted purulent material seen in the right ear canal. The
tympanic membrane was normal.

DIAGNOSIS: Tonsillitis and otitis externa.

Medication: Erythrocin 400 mg q.4 h.

                      _____
tr   Michael R. Stearn, MD

JUL 2 7 200X   After 24 hours of therapy, the patient was afebrile and comfortable.
                      Temperature is 99°. The throat was slightly reddened, the ear
canals were dry, and both TMs normal.

                      _____
tr   Michael R. Stearn, MD

AUG 2 200X   Follow-up exam showed him to be completely asymptomatic and
                      free of unusual physical findings. The drug was discontinued at this
                      time.

                      _____
tr   Michael R. Stearn, MD

                      Stepped on a piece of glass. Cleansed wound. Mother said Norman
OCT 1 9 200X   had tetanus booster just 6 weeks ago in Boyd Hospital ER after a
dog bite. Patient not to return unless problem develops.

                      _____
tr   Michael R. Stearn, MD

OCT 3 0 200X   Patient caught right index finger in car door 2 mrs days ago; finger
                      became inflamed, red, swollen yesterday. Today there is
seropurulent discharge present; no lymphangitis visible. Distal phalanx is involved.

Advice: Hot compress to right hand t.i.d. To return in 24 hours if no change.

DIAGNOSIS: Cellulitis, right index finger, distal phalanx.

                      _____
tr   Michael R. Stearn, MD

Fig. 7-11   Example of a chart note with two properly made corrections.

Reilly, Randa   ER D&T: 10/08/0X   DOB: 03/26/XX

CC: Head pain, post fall.

S: This 25-year-old patient presents with a HX of falling from a horse into a heavy wooden fence, breaking the fence. Patient complains primarily of head pain, neck pain, right knee pain, and some mild coccyx pain. There was a brief loss of consciousness observed by her brother and regaining of consciousness with repetitive questioning. Thereafter, she again lost consciousness for a short period of time. Patient has been slow to answer questions and has been noted to have repetitive questions since the accident.

O: Patient in no acute distress. Appears to be stable with C-collar and rigid back board.
     HEENT: Minimal tears in the occipital area. Pupils equal and reactive. EOMs full. Ears: TMs without blood.
     NECK: C-collar in place, with a tenderness over the mid C-spine bony area without obvious swelling or deformity. (C-collar left in place.)
     CHEST: Nontender to compression. Equal breath sounds. Heart regular rhythm.
     ABDOMEN: Soft. Nontender.
     EXTREMITIES: Moves all four well. There is mild tenderness on palpitation over the right patella but no instability, no limitation of ROM. Cranial nerves II-VII intact. No meds.

A: Mild concussion.

P: CT of the head after C-spine is clear. Home with head injury instructions. Recheck with private doctor in 1-2 days or return here p.r.n. with any change in mental status.

Kip I. Praycroft, MD/ref

Fig. 7-12 Example of an emergency department chart note done in the SOAP format.

medications, laboratory tests, radiographs, and treatment). At this point, dictation may begin. The dictator will indicate whether the dictation is STAT (to be transcribed immediately). This dictation may be done with a handheld recorder and the completed tape placed directly on the chart. The examiner could use equipment that transfers the dictation directly to the transcription department. Dictation for patients requiring admission or transfer must be delivered directly to the transcriptionist in some manner. (See Figs. 7-4 and 7-12 to 7-14 for examples of notes dictated from the emergency department.)

After the release of the patient, the physician writes (or dictates) a formal diagnosis and updates, appends, or completes the dictation. These notes are generally brief, and format may vary with the dictator. Some dictators ask for boldface headings for each section, whereas others may prefer the condensed story format.

The urgent care center does not triage patients but provides care in the order in which patients arrive. The center does refer the patient to the emergency department if necessary. The following hints will give you ideas for office, emergency department, and urgent care center chart notes.

TRANSCRIPTION HINTS

1. Be sure the patient's complete name is entered. Double-check the spelling of the name, and verify the ID numbers accompanying the patient's name.
2. Date every entry with the month, day, and year. These may be spelled out, abbreviated, or made with a date stamp. The time of day that the patient was examined is often required as well.
3. Single-space and keep the margins narrow (not less than ½ inch, however). Double-space between topics or major headings.
4. Condense the note to conserve space. Use phrases rather than complete sentences and use abbreviations when dictated and appropriate.

EMERGENCY DEPARTMENT RECORD

CHART REQUEST

LOCATION	DATE	TIME REGISTERED	TRIAGE TIME	OUTPT.	INPT.	NAME
202	10-08-0X	2:45 ☐AM ☒PM	☐AM ☐PM	☐	☐	REILLY, RANDA O

ARRIVED	☐WALKED	☐WC	☐AMB	☐PARA AMB	☐OTHER
ACCOMPANIED BY	☐ALONE	☐SPOUSE	☐PARENT	☐FRIEND	☐RELATIVE

PATIENT'S ADDRESS
3228 East Main, Century City, XX 12345

MED. REC. NO.

BIRTHDATE
03-26-XX

HOME TELEPHONE	WORK TELEPHONE	PRIMARY CARE CLINIC	PERSONAL PHYSICIAN
(800) 654-9863	( )		John Lambert, MD

AGE	SEX	TEMP.	B.P.	PULSE	RESP.	WEIGHT (Peds)	CHIEF COMPLAINT
25	F	98.7	120/70				Head pain, post fall

ALLERGIES

MEDICATIONS
none

S: This 25-year-old patient presents with a HX of falling from a horse into a heavy wooden fence, breaking the fence. Patient complains primarily of head pain, neck pain, right knee pain, and some mild coccyx pain. There was a brief loss of consciousness observed by her brother and regaining of consciousness with repetitive questioning. Thereafter, she again lost consciousness for a short period of time. Patient has been slow to answer questions and has been noted to have repetitive questions since the accident.

O: Patient in no acute distress. Appears to be stable with C-collar and rigid back board.
HEENT: Minimal tears in the occipital area. Pupils equal and reactive. EOMs full. Ears: TMs without blood.
NECK: C-collar in place, with a tenderness over the mid C-spine bony area without obvious swelling or deformity. (C-collar left in place.)
CHEST: Nontender to compression. Equal breath sounds. Heart regular rhythm.
ABDOMEN: Soft. Nontender.
EXTREMITIES: Moves all four well. There is mild tenderness on palpitation over the right patella but no instability, no limitation of ROM. Cranial nerves II-VII intact. No meds.

A: Mild concussion.

P: CT of the head after C-spine is clear. Home with head injury instructions. Recheck with private doctor in 1-2 days or return here p.r.n. with any change in mental status.

D: 10-08-0X
T: 10-08-0X
amd

ED PHYSICIAN	DATE
	10-08-0X

NS-7672 (9-95)

Fig. 7-13 Example of an emergency department note done in the SOAP format on special chart paper used in the emergency department. See Fig. 7-12 for the same note transcribed on plain paper.

Patient Name: Windemere, Malago
Med Rec No: 8742-A
Date of Service: 11/06/XX

EMERGENCY DEPARTMENT REPORT
County Trauma and Emergency Center, 8735 Zion Avenue, Benson, XX 99000

TIME OF EXAMINATION: 3:15 a.m.

CHIEF COMPLAINT: Left eye redness and discharge.

HISTORY OF PRESENT ILLNESS: This is a 57-year-old male who was in his usual state of health until yesterday. He began to have some sore throat. He also noted that while mowing the lawn he felt some discomfort in the left eye as if there was something in his eye. The patient was wearing wrap-around sunglasses while he was mowing his lawn and does not specifically remember anything going into his eye. He denies any changes in vision. He denies any fever, chest pain, or cough. He denies any nausea or vomiting. He does not wear contacts or glasses.

PAST MEDICAL HISTORY: None.

ALLERGIES: PENICILLIN.

MEDICATIONS: He takes no medicines.

PHYSICAL EXAMINATION
VITAL SIGNS: Temperature 97.0, blood pressure 113/73, pulse 90, and respiratory rate 18. **HEENT**: His acuity on the right is 20/20 and on the left is 20/25. The left eye is markedly injected, and there is a moderate amount of yellow purulent discharge noted. On slit-lamp examination, the discharge is again noted. No foreign bodies are noted when the eyelids are flipped. The anterior chamber is clear. On fluorescein staining, there is no ulceration or abrasion noted. The right eye is clear except for some mild conjunctival erythema. The oropharynx is clear, without exudate. **NECK**: Supple, without cervical lymphadenopathy. No stridor is noted.

DISPOSITION
1.   Nonsteroidal anti-inflammatory drugs for pain and Vicodin for more severe pain.
2.   Sulamyd drops in both eyes 4 times a day for the next 5 days.
3.   Conjunctivitis instructions.
4.   The patient should follow up with the emergency department if he does not have improvement in his symptoms in the next 36-48 hours or if he has any visual changes, vomiting, is unable to tolerate p.o., or has any other problems. He will nevertheless follow up with his primary care physician as needed.

DIAGNOSIS: Likely viral illness with viral conjunctivitis and pharyngitis; however, bacterial conjunctivitis cannot be ruled out.

EMERGENCY DEPARTMENT REPORT
Page 1 of 2

This is not an official document unless signed by physician.

8735 Zion Avenue • Benson, XX 99000 • Telephone (555) 876-9876

Fig. 7-14 Example of an emergency department chart note done in expanded format.

EXAMPLE

Dictated: Today's date is November 11, 200X, and this is a chart note on Nancy Marques, a 32-year-old female who came in today in follow-up to an upper respiratory tract infection either viral or secondary to mycoplasma. She is much better except that she has had a chronic cough now for about 10 days. The ears, nose, and throat are normal, and the sinuses are nontender. The lymph nodes are normal and the lungs are clear. The diagnosis is postviral cough. I have given her a prescription for Hycodan 5 to 10 milliliters for up to 10 days and then observation. If the cough is still present in 2 weeks, I will consider steroid trial.

Transcribed:

Nancy Marques   Age: 32
November 11, 200X

HPI: Follow-up upper respiratory tract infection, either viral or secondary to mycoplasma. She is much better except for chronic cough for 10 days.

PX: ENT: Normal. Sinuses: Nontender. Lymph nodes: Normal. Lungs: Clear.

DX: Postviral cough.

RX: Hycodan 5-10 mL for 10 days and then observation. If cough present in 2 weeks, I will consider steroid trial.

ntw
                                                 _____
                                                 Mary Laudenslayer, MD

This example is sharp looking and easy to read, and specific data can be immediately located. However, it is not that quick and simple for the transcriptionist because you cannot type exactly what is heard; instead, you must stop and analyze at the same time, being sure that all data are recorded. Practice and experience, however, make this format fast and interesting.

5. Make outline headings on all but very brief entries. These headings will vary according to the physician's style. Some physicians use the *SOAP* method or variations, described as follows (see Figs. 7-9 and 7-12):
   - S: This signifies *subjective. Subjective* means from the patient's point of view. This is the reason the patient is seeking care. It is the main problem necessitating care (also called *chief complaint*).
   - O: This refers to *objective,* or the physician's point of view, and what is found on physical examination, x-ray film, or laboratory work: the clinical evidence.
   - A: This refers to *assessment,* or what the examiner thinks may be or is wrong with the patient according to the information gathered: the diagnosis.
   - P: This refers to *plan,* or what the physician plans to do or advises the patient to do: laboratory tests, surgery, medications, referral to another practitioner, treatment, management, and so forth.

There are variations on this style. Some dictators begin with the chief complaint (CC), and others may leave out one or more of the headings. Headings are either abbreviated or spelled out. Be consistent in your choice. It is very important that the note be explicit and complete. Because the encounter with the patient is the basis for reimbursement from insurance companies, some physicians may want to include additional entries to reflect the *nature* of the presenting problem (N); the *counseling* or *coordination of care* that is involved (C), particularly when these two areas make up more than half of the time of the visit; and the *medical decision making* (M). These items are often difficult for the coder or reviewer to find in the note, and this kind of information is vital in determining the level of service performed during a patient encounter as described earlier.

Another format choice could include the following:
   - CC: This refers to the *chief complaint* (the same as *subjective* in the SOAP format).
   - PX (also PE): This refers to the *physical examination* (the same as *objective* in the SOAP format).
   - DX: This refers to the *diagnosis, impression* (IMP), or *assessment* (the same as *assessment* in the SOAP format).
   - RX: This abbreviation for *prescription* is used for the advice or plans for the patient (the same as *Plan* in the SOAP format). See Fig. 7-10.

Other titles such as LAB or X-RAY may be used as headings. Multiple-physician practices, clinics, and hospitals often use the problem-oriented medical record (POMR) format, which is a problem list with corresponding numbered progress notes. In brief, this format includes the following areas:
   - Database: The chief complaint, the history of this complaint, a review of the body

systems, physical examination, and laboratory work.

- Problem list: A numbered list of every problem that the patient has that necessitates further investigation.
- Treatment plan: Numbered list to correspond with each item on the problem list.
- Notes: Numbered progress notes to correspond with each item on the problem list.

6. Use abbreviations and symbols freely as the dictator wishes, but be sure that the abbreviations are standard and acceptable. (Remember that the records could be viewed by persons outside the office or hospital.) Abbreviations save space, and notes should be as concise as possible.

7. Insert indentations to make topics stand out. Type the main topics in full caps. Use boldface when it is helpful or requested by the dictator.

8. Underline and type drug allergies in full caps or in boldface.

9. Initial the entry just as you initial any other document that you type or transcribe. Initials may be placed at the left margin or after the dictator's name or initials.

10. Type a signature line or leave sufficient space for the dictator's signature or initials.

11. In the medical office, check daily about the previous day's house calls, emergency department calls, and hospital admissions or discharges, so that the charts can be pulled and these entries made.

Examine all the figures again for typing format. Here are some common abbreviations found frequently in office chart notes.

anPX	annual examination
BP	blood pressure
Bx	biopsy
CBC	complete blood cell count
CC	chief complaint
consult	consultation
CPX	complete physical examination
DKA	did not keep appointment
DNS	did not show (keep appointment)
DOB	date of birth
Dx (DX)	diagnosis
FUO	fever of unknown origin
Fx (FX)	fracture
H&P	history and physical examination
Hx (HX)	history
IMP	impression
inj	injection

NKA	no known allergies
PE	physical examination
?	"?" suggests a problem (for example, "?pg" is "question of being pregnant"; "?flu" is "possible flu"; "?hernia" is "possible hernia"; and so on)
PH	past history
PO	postoperative
PRE	preoperative or prepartum
pre-op	preoperative examination
pt	patient
Px (PX)	physical examination
R/O	rule out
sig.	directions
STAT	immediately
TPR	temperature, pulse, respirations
Tx (TX)	treatment
VS	vital signs

USE OF THE METRIC SYSTEM IN MEDICAL RECORDS

Here is a detailed discussion of metric abbreviations and how they are used in medical records. This section focuses on just the metric units and abbreviations that are commonly used, and so this is not a comprehensive discussion of the entire system. Notice that all the abbreviations are written in lowercase letters except for liter, for which you use a capital *L*.

Units that You Need to Know

Unit	Symbol	Measures	Replaces
meter	m	length, distance, thickness	*inch, foot, yard, mile*
gram	g	mass (weight)	*ounce, pound*
liter	L	volume	*cup, pint, quart, gallon, fluid ounce*
Celsius	C	temperature	*Fahrenheit*

Prefixes Commonly Used for More than One of a Unit

Prefix	Symbol	Relation to Unit	Example
kilo-	k	1000 of them	1 kg, 1000 g

Prefixes Commonly Used for Less than One of a Unit

Prefix	Symbol	Relation To Unit	Example
centi-	c	1/100 of a unit	1 cm
milli-	m	1/1000 of a unit	1 mL

There is more than one way of expressing a metric measurement. Usually, the less complex expression is chosen. For example, 1.5 meters (1.5 m) is also expressed as 150 centimeters (150 cm) or 1500 millimeters (1500 mm). We use the 1.5 m measurement as the least complex of the three.

Rules to Follow in Typing Metric Measurements

Symbols are abbreviated when used with numerical values. They are written out when they are not used with numerical values.

EXAMPLES

There was a bruise more than a centimeter long over the bridge of her nose. *(Correct)*
There was a bruise more than a cm long over the bridge of her nose. *(Incorrect)*

Symbols are not followed by period or other marks of punctuation unless they occur at the end of a sentence or a series of values.

EXAMPLES

25   115 kg   1000 mL *(Correct)*
25 cm.   115 kg.   1000 mL. *(Incorrect)*

Commas are not used to separate digits in large numbers.

EXAMPLES

12 640 km *(Correct)*
12,640 km *(Incorrect)*

A zero is placed in front of the decimal point in numbers less than 1.

EXAMPLES

0.5 mL   0.1 cm   0.75 mg *(Correct)*
.5 mL   .1 cm   .75 cm *(Incorrect)*

EXCEPTION: Metric description of firearms does not use the zero.

EXAMPLE

A .22-caliber slug was lodged in the wound.

A space is placed between the number and the symbol.

EXAMPLES

25 mg   1 m   *(Correct)*
25mg   1m   *(Incorrect)*

Symbols are not made plural, no matter how many units are described.

EXAMPLES

6 m   75 mg   3 L *(Correct)*
6 ms   75 mgs   3 liters *(Incorrect)*

Zeros after the decimal point are not placed after a whole number unless dictated.

EXAMPLES

The wound was 3.0 cm at its widest point. *(Incorrect)*
The wound was 3 cm at its widest point. *(Correct)*

Exceptions

- Specific gravity is expressed with four digits with a decimal point between the first and second digit.
- When the pH of a substance is given, use two numerals. If only one numeral is dictated, place a zero after the decimal point.

EXAMPLES

Dictated: specific gravity is ten twenty.
Transcribed: Specific gravity is 1.020.
Dictated: The "pee h" was seven.
Transcribed: The pH was 7.0

Common fractions are not used with the metric system.

EXAMPLES

½ cm   ¾ liter *(Incorrect)*
0.5 cm   0.75 L *(Correct)*

The derived unit for volume *cubic centimeters* and its abbreviation (cc) are not used. The abbreviation for milliliters (mL) is the proper abbreviation for this unit of measurement.

The degree symbol (°) is used with the abbreviation for Celsius (C). The word *degrees* is written out with the word *Celsius*.

EXAMPLES

Her temperature on admission was 38° C. *(Correct)*
Her temperature on admission was 38 degrees Celsius. *(Correct)*
Her temperature on admission was 38 degrees C. *(Incorrect)*

MAKING CORRECTIONS

Errors in handwritten chart notes are corrected as follows: Draw a line through the error, making sure the inaccurate information is legible and being careful not to obliterate it. Make the correct notation either above or below the error, wherever there is room, and date and initial the entry. Do not write over your error, do not erase the error, do not try to "fix" the error, and do not attempt to blot it out with heavy applications of ink or self-adhesive typing strips.

Errors that are made while the entry is being transcribed are corrected just as you would correct any other material. Errors found subsequently are corrected in longhand by following the previously described procedures. However, it is not necessary to date errors when they are made or discovered on the same day as they are entered; just correct and initial the error.

See Fig. 7-11 for an example of chart notes with entry errors properly corrected. You will notice that these corrections are not dated, which indicates that they were made on the day of the entry.

◆ Exercise 7-1: SELF-STUDY

Directions: Retype the following material into chart note format, as illustrated in Fig. 7-10.

The date is October 10, 200X. The patient is Anthony Frishman. Tony is now 12-1/2 years old. He underwent bilateral triple arthrodesis in August 200X. He is out of his splints and doing well. His foot rests are a bit long, and his feet are not touching them. He has no major complaints as far as his feet are concerned. Exam: He has a long c-curve to the right, which may be slightly increased clinically since last x-rayed in June 200X when it was twenty-five degrees. His feet are in neutral position as far as equinus. There is a slight varus inclination. X-rays: multiple views of his feet demonstrate fusion bilaterally of the triple staples. Diagnosis is limb girdle dystrophy. The plan is to return to clinic in one to two months for sitting SP spine x-ray. Also we will obtain pulmonary function test at that time. Karl T. Robrecht, MD.

◆ Exercise 7-2: PRACTICE TEST

Directions: Retype the following information as an emergency department report for Eugene W. Gomez, MD. Use the current date, minimum chart note heading, and plain (unlined) 8½ × 11 inch paper.

The patient's name is Maryellen Mawson.

Note: this is a six year old who has had a three week history of polydipsia polyuria polyphagia and weight loss. the child has become progressively more lethargic over the past twenty four hours and twelve hours ago the parents noticed she was breathing rapidly.

physical examination reveals height one hundred twenty seven centimeters weight thirty three kilograms temperature ninety nine degrees fahrenheit pulse one hundred twelve and blood pressure ninety five over seventy. the child was semicomatose. she has dry mucous membranes but good skin turgor and full peripheral pulses. a stat lab report shows sodium one hundred thirty eight milliequivalents per liter, potassium three point three milliequivalents per liter chloride ninety seven milliequivalents per liter and a total carbon dioxide of five milliequivalents per liter. blood glucose is seven hundred milligrams percent. plan is to admit stat to childrens hospital.

◆ Exercise 7-3: REVIEW TEST

Directions: *Carefully examine the examples of chart notes that have been illustrated and retype the following information as office chart notes for your employer, Laurel R. Denison, MD. You may use the minimum chart note heading, plain (unlined) 8½ × 11 inch paper, format of your choice, and standard abbreviations where applicable. Use today's date. Please notice that these are notes about several patients; therefore each patient will have a separate sheet of paper.*

1. *Gustavo deVargas.* Birthdate 3-3-34. Patient had onset of persistent vomiting five days ago. He does not appear seriously ill. The abdomen remains flat and there is no tenderness or rigidity; no masses are palpable; bowel sounds are scarce. X-ray of the abdomen yesterday revealed a four centimeter, ill-defined, round mass in the right upper quadrant and loops of small bowel containing air. Subsequent x-rays, including some taken today, revealed that this rounded mass persists, is quite well outlined on some of the x-rays, and is now in the left lower quadrant. There is small bowel distention in relation to the mass, which suggests that the mass is a loop of small bowel with gaseous distention proximal to it. It is questionable whether there is any gas in the colon. Rectal examination is negative. Impression: intestinal obstruction due to ingested foreign body. Advice: laparotomy.
2. *Mrs. Esther Conway.* Age thirty-three. Patient complains of constant dribbling, wetting at night, uses fifteen pads a day. Urinalysis: specific gravity one point zero, few bacteria, few urates. Diagnosis: urinary incontinence. Patient is to return in four days for diagnostic testing.
3. *Robin Vincenti.* Age twenty-seven. Patient complains of having had the flu and headache and of being tired. Unable to go to work today. Exam shows weakness of left hand. Hyperreflexia on the left. X-ray shows cardiomegaly and slight pulmonary congestion. Impression: post flu syndrome, transient ischemic attack; possible CVA. Patient to return in four days and may return to work in approximately one week.
4. *Marissa Weeks.* Age seventeen. CC: thrown from a horse. Px: numerous contusions, tenderness in thoracic region, x-ray ordered. Dx: compression fracture of "tee twelve." Rx: patient referred to Edward Harrison, orthopedic specialist.
5. *William Santee.* Age thirteen. (Make your entry showing a letter was dictated rather than a chart entry made. You do not type this letter; you prepare a chart note in reference to this letter. Use February 7 as your date rather than today's date.)

Exercise 7-4: REVIEW TEST

Directions: *Using the instructions you have just received, type the following information into the patients' charts that you previously prepared. Use a date 4 days from the date you used for Exercise 7-3.*

Remember that in actual practice you no longer have these records, and so you would make your transcripts one right after another, and they would be cut and pasted to the original. You may use cellophane tape to tape your entry to the appropriate document to re-enact this procedure.

1. *Gustavo deVargas.* Patient telephoned office today and agreed to laparotomy. He is to be admitted to Valley Presbyterian Hospital tomorrow afternoon at 3 for surgery the following day.
2. Secretary: Please make your own entry into the chart showing that Mr. deVargas was admitted to the hospital on the appropriate day.
3. *Robin Vincenti.* Chest clear to P&A. X-ray is clear and shows normal heart silhouette. Full use of left hand; no residual pain or weakness. Plans to return to work tomorrow.
4. *Mrs. Esther Conway.* Intravenous pyelogram and cystoscopy revealed multiple fistulae of bladder with two openings into urinary bladder and copious leakage into vagina. Continued to work. Diagnosis: multiple vesicovaginal fistulae. To be admitted to the hospital for repair.
5. Secretary: Please make your own entry into the chart for day of admission, 4 days from her last visit, into University Hospital for Mrs. Conway.

 Exercise 7-5: SELF-STUDY

Directions: *In the following chart note, the entry of "left thoracotomy" should read "right thoracotomy." You discover the error on February 1, 200X. Please correct it.*

Brad Philman   **Age: 47**

1-13-200X Pt admitted to Good Sam for bronchoscopy and possible left thoracotomy and

pleural poudrage. ⌇⌇⌇

 Exercise 7-6: REVIEW TEST

Directions: *Imagine that you are typing the following notes on pressure-sensitive paper. Do not forget to leave a little space between the notes so they can be cut apart, but do not cut your notes apart. Use today's date. Use the SOAP format for chart note 5. Your employer is Catherine R. Schultz, MD.*

1. *Lupe Morales.* Lump, right breast. Patient found this lump 4 weeks ago. It has increased in size rapidly, she says. She also has a lump under her right arm. Ordered mammograms. Diagnosis: Possible carcinoma of the breast.
2. *Adeline Pierson.* CC: pain and swelling over the right wrist. Hx: The patient states that while she was working as a waitress she was lifting and carrying a tray of dishes and it slipped, resulting in pain and swelling over the radial side of the distal radius of her right wrist. This was found to be a ganglion and was aspirated by another physician. However, it has recurred and is larger than before. She wishes this surgically removed. Her past general health has been good. She has had no serious illnesses and no surgeries. She takes no medications. Allergies: None known.
3. *Peter Barton.* PO followup. Incision looks good, some slight swelling and tenderness.
4. *Kellis McNeil.* CC: Right inguinal hernia. Hx: Patient first noticed that he had a right inguinal hernia because of pain there approximately 1 week ago. He presents with a very tender right inguinal ring.

The hernia was reduced but readily protruded. PH: The patient had an umbilical hernia repair 8 years ago. He had a hemorrhoidectomy four years ago. Drugs: Valium five milligrams t.i.d. Advice: Right herniorrhaphy.

5. *Arnott B. Weeks.* stiff finger joints. patient says more severe after sleeping or nonuse. general fatigue stopped, occurred again in last 2 weeks. stopped drinking, some weight loss. on exam there is swelling and pain around joints of fingers. symmetrical involvement. bp is one hundred forty four over eighty five pulse is sixty seven weight is one hundred seventy eight. x-ray: narrowed joint space, osteoporosis at joint. uric acid: four point two. rheumatoid arthritis. aspirin ten grains q.i.d., phenylbutazone one hundred milligrams q.i.d., number twenty eight. return 1 month.

 Exercise 7-7: REVIEW TEST

Directions: *Transcribe the following notes for the emergency department. Use the SOAP format or any variation that is appropriate and easy to read. The dictator is Marc Nielsen, MD. The date is May 1, 200X.*

Colleen Lynkins is a thirty-three-year-old female whose chief complaint is upper mid back pain. The patient woke up tonight with upper mid back pain. Patient states that she has a new mattress. There is no history of trauma or other insults. She had spontaneous pneumothorax twice in the past year. Had tubal ligation ten years ago. She states that she cannot be pregnant. Physical examination: NKA. Temperature is ninety-eight. Blood pressure is one hundred ten over eighty. The chest is clear. The heart is in regular rhythm. The abdomen is soft. Extremities were non-neurological. Central nervous system is intact. Head and neck are benign. Plan. Chest x-ray and proceed.

 Exercise 7-8: REVIEW TEST

Directions: *See 7-3 Review Test, Project 1, chart note for Gustavo deVargas. Use the SOAP method and prepare the chart note for Dr. Denison.*

 Exercise 7-9: SELF-STUDY

Directions: *Use your computer and briefly list the various components of a chart note. (Hint: Try for seven different entries.)*

Exercise 7-10: METRIC SYSTEM REVIEW

Directions: *Select the set that is incorrectly expressed in the groups that follow. Place the answer in the blank provided.*

1. _____
   a. *meter* is a basic word for distance
   b. *liter* is a basic word for volume
   c. *gram* is a basic word for liquid
   d. *Celsius* is a basic word for temperature

2. _____
   a. *g* is the abbreviation for *gram*
   b. *mL* is the abbreviation for *milliliter*
   c. *cm* is the abbreviation for *centimeter*
   d. *kilo* is the abbreviation for *kilogram*

3. _____
   a. 25 mg
   b. 0.25 mg
   c. 25 mg.
   d. 0.025 mg

4. _____
   a. 3.5 L
   b. 3 Ls
   c. 3000 mL
   d. 3 L

5. _____
   a. degree Celsius
   b. °C
   c. °Celsius
   d. degrees C

6. _____
   a. 2½ km
   b. 0.25 km
   c. 25 km
   d. 2.5 km

Student Name _____   Date _____

CHECKLIST: PERFORM PROPER HANDWASHING FOR MEDICAL ASEPSIS

TASK: Prevent the spread of pathogens by aseptically washing hands, following Standard Precautions.

CONDITIONS: Given the proper equipment and supplies, the student will be required to demonstrate the proper method of performing handwashing for medical asepsis.

EQUIPMENT AND SUPPLIES
- Liquid antibacterial soap
- Nailbrush or orange stick
- Paper towels
- Warm running water
- Regular waste container

STANDARDS: Complete the procedure within _____ minutes and achieve a minimum score of _____%.

Time began _____   Time ended _____

Steps	Possible Points	First Attempt	Second Attempt
1. Assemble all supplies and equipment.	5		
2. Remove rings and watch or push the watch up on the forearm.	5		
3. Stand close to the sink, without allowing clothing to touch the sink.	5		
4. Turn on the faucets, using a paper towel.	5		
5. Adjust the water temperature to warm—not hot or cold. Explain why proper water temperature is important.	10		
6. Discard the paper towel in the proper waste container.	5		
7. Wet hands and wrists under running water, and apply liquid antibacterial soap. Hands must be held lower than the elbows at all times. Hands must not touch the inside of the sink.	10		
8. Work soap into a lather by rubbing the palms together using a circular motion.	10		
9. Clean the fingernails with a nailbrush or an orange stick.	5		
10. Rinse hands thoroughly under running water, holding them in a downward position and allowing soap and water to run off the fingertips.	10		
11. Repeat the procedure if hands are grossly contaminated.	10		
12. Dry the hands gently and thoroughly using a clean paper towel. Discard the paper towel in proper waste container.	10		
13. Using a dry paper towel, turn the faucets off, clean the area around the sink, and discard the towel in regular waste container.	10		
Total Points Possible	100		

Comments: Total Points Earned _____   Instructor's Signature _____

Student Name _____   Date _____

CHECKLIST: APPLY AND REMOVE CLEAN, DISPOSABLE (NONSTERILE) GLOVES

TASK: Apply and remove disposable (nonsterile) gloves properly.

CONDITIONS: Given the proper equipment and supplies, the student will be required to apply and remove nonsterile disposable gloves.

EQUIPMENT AND SUPPLIES
- Alcohol-based hand rub
- Nonsterile disposable gloves
- Biohazardous waste container

STANDARDS: Complete the procedure within _____ minutes and achieve a minimum score of _____%.

Time began _____   Time ended _____

Steps	Possible Points	First Attempt	Second Attempt
Applying Gloves			
1. Assemble all supplies and equipment.	5		
2. Select the correct size and style of gloves according to office policy.	5		
3. Sanitize hands.	10		
4. Apply gloves and adjust them to ensure a proper fit.	5		
5. Inspect the gloves carefully for tears, holes, or punctures before and after application.	5		
Removing Gloves			
1. Grasp the outside of one glove with the first three fingers of the other hand, approximately 1 to 2 inches below the cuff.	10		
2. Stretch the soiled glove by pulling it away from the hand, and slowly pull the glove downward off the hand. Usually the dominant hand is ungloved first.	10		
3. After the glove is pulled free from the hand, ball it in the palm of the gloved hand.	10		
4. Remove the other glove by placing the index and middle fingers of the ungloved hand inside the glove of the gloved hand; turn the cuff downward. Be careful not to touch the outside of the soiled glove.	10		
5. Stretch the glove away from the hand and pull the cuff downward over the hand and over the balled-up glove, turning it inside out with the balled glove inside.	10		
6. Carefully dispose of the gloves in a marked biohazardous waste container.	10		
7. Sanitize hands.	10		
Total Points Possible	100		

Comments: Total Points Earned _____   Instructor's Signature _____

Student Name _____   Date _____

CHECKLIST: MEASURE ORAL BODY TEMPERATURE USING A MERCURY-FREE GLASS THERMOMETER

TASK: Accurately measure and record a patient's oral temperature.

CONDITIONS: Given the proper equipment and supplies, the student will be required to role-play with another student or an instructor the proper method for measuring an oral body temperature using a mercury-free glass thermometer.

EQUIPMENT AND SUPPLIES
- Mercury-free glass oral thermometer
- Thermometer sheath
- Disposable gloves
- Biohazardous waste container
- Pen
- Patient's medical record

STANDARDS: Complete the procedure within _____ minutes and achieve a minimum score of _____%.

Time began _____   Time ended _____

Steps	Possible Points	First Attempt	Second Attempt
1. Assemble all supplies and equipment.	5		
2. Sanitize hands.	5		
3. Greet and identify the patient.	5		
4. Explain the procedure to the patient.	5		
5. Determine if the patient has recently had a hot or cold beverage to drink or has smoked.	5		
6. Put on gloves and remove the thermometer from its holder, without touching the bulb end with your fingers.	5		
7. Inspect the thermometer for chips or cracks.	5		
8. Read the thermometer to ensure that the temperature is well below 96.0° F. Shake down thermometer as necessary.	5		
9. Cover the thermometer with a protective thermometer sheath.	5		
10. Ask the patient to open his or her mouth and place the probe tip under the tongue.	5		
11. Ask the patient to hold, not clasp, the thermometer between the teeth and to close the lips snugly around it to form an airtight seal.	5		
12. Leave the thermometer in place for a minimum of 3 minutes.	5		
13. Remove the thermometer and read the results.	10		

Steps	Possible Points	First Attempt	Second Attempt
14. Holding the thermometer by the stem, remove the protective sheath and discard in a biohazardous waste container.	5		
15. Sanitize the thermometer following the manufacturer's recommendations.	5		
16. Remove gloves and discard in biohazardous waste container.	5		
17. Return the thermometer to its storage container.	5		
18. Sanitize hands.	5		
19. Document the results in the patient's medical record.	5		
Total Points Possible	100		

Comments: Total Points Earned _____   Instructor's Signature _____

Student Name _____   Date _____

CHECKLIST: MEASURE BODY TEMPERATURE USING A DISPOSABLE ORAL THERMOMETER

TASK: Accurately measure and record a patient's oral temperature using a disposable thermometer.

CONDITIONS: Given the proper equipment and supplies, the student will be required to perform the proper method for measuring an oral temperature using a disposable oral thermometer.

EQUIPMENT AND SUPPLIES
- Disposable thermometer
- Disposable gloves
- Biohazardous waste container
- Pen
- Patient's medical record

STANDARDS: Complete the procedure within _____ minutes and achieve a minimum score of _____%.

Time began _____   Time ended _____

Steps	Possible Points	First Attempt	Second Attempt
1. Assemble all supplies and equipment.	5		
2. Sanitize hands.	5		
3. Greet and identify the patient.	5		
4. Explain the procedure to the patient.	5		
5. Determine if the patient has recently had a hot or cold beverage to drink or has smoked.	5		
6. Put on disposable gloves.	5		
7. Open the thermometer packaging.	5		
8. Place the thermometer under the patient's tongue and wait 60 seconds.	5		
9. Remove the thermometer and read the results by looking at the colored dots.	5		
10. Discard the thermometer and gloves in a biohazardous waste container.	5		
11. Sanitize hands.	5		
12. Document results in the patient's medical record.	10		
Total Points Possible	65		

Comments: Total Points Earned _____   Instructor's Signature _____

Student Name _____   Date _____

CHECKLIST: MEASURE BODY TEMPERATURE USING A TYMPANIC THERMOMETER

TASK: Accurately measure and record a patient's temperature using a tympanic thermometer.

CONDITIONS: Given the proper equipment and supplies, the student will be required to role-play with another student the proper method for measuring the tympanic temperature using a tympanic thermometer.

EQUIPMENT AND SUPPLIES
- Tympanic thermometer
- Disposable probe cover
- Pen
- Patient's medical record
- Biohazardous waste container

STANDARDS: Complete the procedure within _____ minutes and achieve a minimum score of _____%.

Time began _____   Time ended _____

Steps	Possible Points	First Attempt	Second Attempt
1. Assemble all supplies and equipment.	5		
2. Sanitize hands.	5		
3. Greet and identify the patient.	5		
4. Explain the procedure to the patient.	5		
5. Remove the thermometer from the charger.	5		
6. Check to be sure the mode for interpretation of temperature is set to "oral" mode.	10		
7. Check the lens probe to be sure it is clean and not scratched.	5		
8. Turn on the thermometer.	5		
9. Insert the probe firmly into a disposable plastic probe cover.	5		
10. Wait for a digital "READY" display.	5		
11. With the hand that is not holding the probe, pull adult patient's ear up and back to straighten the ear canal. For a small child, pull the patient's ear down and back to straighten the ear canal.	10		
12. Insert the probe into the patient's ear and tightly seal the ear canal opening.	10		
13. Position the probe.	5		
14. Depress the activation button.	5		
15. Release the activation button and wait 2 seconds.	5		
16. Remove the probe from the ear and read the temperature.	5		

Steps	Possible Points	First Attempt	Second Attempt
17. Note the reading, making sure that the screen displays "oral" as the mode of interpretation.	5		
18. Discard the probe cover in a biohazardous waste container.	5		
19. Replace the thermometer on the charger base.	5		
20. Sanitize hands.	5		
21. Document results in the patient's medical record using ⓣ to indicate a tympanic temperature was obtained.	10		
Total Points Possible	125		

Comments: Total Points Earned _____   Instructor's Signature _____

Student Name _____   Date _____

CHECKLIST: MEASURE RADIAL PULSE

TASK: Accurately measure and record the rate, rhythm, and quality of a patient's pulse.

CONDITIONS: Given the proper equipment and supplies, the student will be required to role-play with another student or an instructor the proper method for measuring a patient's radial pulse.

EQUIPMENT AND SUPPLIES
- Watch with a second hand
- Patient's medical record
- Pen

STANDARDS: Complete the procedure within _____ minutes and achieve a minimum score of _____%.

Time began _____   Time ended _____

Steps	Possible Points	First Attempt	Second Attempt
1. Assemble all supplies and equipment.	5		
2. Sanitize hands.	5		
3. Greet and identify the patient.	5		
4. Explain the procedure to the patient.	5		
5. Observe the patient for any signs that may indicate an increase or a decrease in the pulse rate due to external conditions.	5		
6. Position the patient.	5		
7. Place the index and middle fingertips over the radial artery while resting the thumb on the back of the patient's wrist.	10		
8. Apply moderate, gentle pressure directly over the site until the pulse can be felt.	10		
9. Count the pulse for 60 seconds.	10		
10. Sanitize hands.	5		
11. Document the results in the patient's chart; include the pulse rate, rhythm, and volume.	10		
Total Points Possible	75		

Comments: Total Points Earned _____   Instructor's Signature _____

Student Name _____   Date _____

CHECKLIST: MEASURE RESPIRATORY RATE

TASK: Accurately measure and record a patient's respiratory rate.

CONDITIONS: Given the proper equipment and supplies, the student will be required to role-play with another student the proper method for measuring a patient's respiratory rate.

EQUIPMENT AND SUPPLIES
- Watch with a second hand
- Patient's medical record
- Pen

STANDARDS: Complete the procedure within _____ minutes and achieve a minimum score of _____%.

Time began _____   Time ended _____

Steps	Possible Points	First Attempt	Second Attempt
1. Assemble all supplies and equipment.	5		
2. Sanitize hands.	5		
3. Greet and identify the patient.	5		
4. Explain the procedure to the patient.	5		
5. Count each respiration for 30 seconds and multiply by 2. (If breathing pattern is irregular, count for 1 full minute.)	15		
6. Sanitize hands.	5		
7. Document the results in the patient's chart; include the respiratory rate, rhythm, and depth. Document any irregularities found.	10		
Total Points Possible	50		

Comments: Total Points Earned _____   Instructor's Signature _____

Student Name _____   Date _____

CHECKLIST: MEASURE BLOOD PRESSURE

TASK: Accurately measure and record a patient's blood pressure by palpation and auscultation.

CONDITIONS: Given the proper equipment and supplies, the student will be required to role-play with another student the proper method for measuring a patient's blood pressure.

EQUIPMENT AND SUPPLIES
- Stethoscope
- Aneroid sphygmomanometer in proper size for patient
- Alcohol wipe
- Patient's medical record
- Pen

STANDARDS: Complete the procedure within _____ minutes and achieve a minimum score of _____%.

Time began _____   Time ended _____

Steps	Possible Points	First Attempt	Second Attempt
1. Assemble all supplies and equipment.	5		
2. Sanitize hands.	5		
3. Greet and identify the patient.	5		
4. Explain the procedure to the patient.	5		
5. Position the patient comfortably in a sitting or supine position.	5		
6. Palpate the brachial artery.	10		
7. Position the blood pressure cuff; wrap the cuff snugly and evenly around the patient's arm and secure the end.	10		
8. Position the aneroid gauge for direct viewing at a distance of no more than 3 feet.	10		
9. Measure the systolic pressure by palpation.	15		
10. Deflate the cuff completely and wait at least 60 seconds before re-inflating.	10		
11. Clean the stethoscope.	5		
12. Place the earpieces of the stethoscope in your ears, with the earpieces directed slightly forward.	5		
13. Position the head of the stethoscope over the brachial artery of the arm.	5		
14. Close the valve to the manometer.	5		
15. Pump the cuff at a smooth rate to approximately 20 to 30 mm Hg above the palpated systolic pressure.	10		

Steps	Possible Points	First Attempt	Second Attempt
16. Loosen the thumbscrew slightly to open the valve and release the pressure on the cuff, slowly and steadily.	10		
17. Obtain the systolic reading.	10		
18. Continue to release the air from the cuff at a moderately slow rate.	5		
19. Listen for the disappearance of the Korotkoff sounds; obtain diastolic pressure.	10		
20. Release the air remaining in the cuff quickly by loosening the thumbscrew to open the valve completely.	5		
21. Remove the earpieces of the stethoscope from your ears, and remove the cuff from the patient's arm.	5		
22. Sanitize hands.	5		
23. Document the results in the patient's chart.	10		
24. Clean the earpieces and diaphragm with an alcohol wipe, and properly store the equipment.	5		
Total Points Possible	175		

Comments: Total Points Earned _____   Instructor's Signature _____

Student Name _____   Date _____

CHECKLIST: PREPARE A PARENTERAL MEDICATION FROM A VIAL

TASK: From a vial, measure the ordered medication dosage into a 3-mL hypodermic syringe for injection.

CONDITIONS: Given the proper equipment and supplies, the student will prepare a parenteral medication from a vial in a 3-mL syringe.

EQUIPMENT AND SUPPLIES
- Vial of medication as ordered by physician
- 70% isopropyl alcohol wipes
- 3-mL syringe for ordered dose
- Needle with safety device appropriate for site of injection
- 2 × 2-inch gauze squares
- Biohazardous waste container
- Patient's medical record

STANDARDS: Complete the procedure within _____ minutes and achieve a minimum score of _____%.

Time began _____   Time ended _____

Steps	Possible Points	First Attempt	Second Attempt
1. Sanitize hands.	5		
2. Verify the order, and assemble equipment and supplies.	5		
3. Check expiration date of the medication.	10		
4. Follow the "seven rights" of medication administration.	10		
5. Check the medication against the physician's order three times before administration.	10		
6. Check the patient's medical record for drug allergies or conditions that may contraindicate the injection.	10		
7. Calculate the correct dose to be given, as necessary.	10		
8. Prepare the vial, needle, and syringe.	5		
9. Draw the amount of air into the syringe for the amount of medication to be administered.	5		
10. Remove the cover from the needle and insert the needle into the vial.	10		
11. Inject the air into vial and fill the syringe with the medication.	10		
12. Remove any air bubbles and recap the needle as necessary.	10		
13. Compare the medication to the vial label, and return the medication to its proper storage.	5		
14. Sanitize hands.	10		
Total Points Possible	115		

Comments: Total Points Earned _____   Instructor's Signature _____

Student Name _____   Date _____

CHECKLIST: ADMINISTER AN INTRADERMAL INJECTION

TASK
- Identify the correct syringe, needle gauge, and length for an intradermal injection.
- Select and prepare an appropriate site for an intradermal injection.
- Demonstrate the correct technique to administer an intradermal injection.
- Document an intradermal injection correctly in the medical record.

CONDITIONS: Given the proper equipment and supplies, the student will prepare and administer an intradermal injection.

EQUIPMENT AND SUPPLIES
- Nonsterile disposable gloves
- Medication as ordered by physician
- Tuberculin syringe for ordered dose
- Needle with safety device (26 or 27 gauge, ⅜ inch to ½ inch)
- 2 × 2-inch sterile gauze
- 70% isopropyl alcohol wipes
- Written patient instructions for post testing as appropriate
- Sharps container
- Biohazardous waste container
- Patient's medical record

STANDARDS: Complete the procedure within _____ minutes and achieve a minimum score of _____%.

Time began _____   Time ended _____

Steps	Possible Points	First Attempt	Second Attempt
1. Sanitize hands.	5		
2. Verify the order, and assemble equipment and supplies.	5		
3. Check expiration date of the medication.	10		
4. Follow the "seven rights" of medication administration.	10		
5. Check the medication against the physician's order three times before administration.	10		
6. Check the patient's medical record for drug allergies or conditions that may contraindicate the injection.	10		
7. Calculate the dose to be given, if necessary.	15		
8. Follow the correct procedure for drawing the medication into syringe.	10		
9. Greet and identify the patient, and explain the procedure to the patient.	10		
10. Select an appropriate injection site and properly position the patient as necessary to expose the site adequately.	10		
11. Apply gloves.	5		

Steps	Possible Points	First Attempt	Second Attempt
12. Prepare the injection site.	10		
13. While the prepared site is drying, remove the cover from the needle.	10		
14. Pull the skin taut at the injection site.	10		
15. Inject the medication between the dermis and epidermis. Create a wheal.	10		
16. Withdraw the needle from the injection site at the same angle as it was inserted, and activate the safety device immediately.	10		
17. Dab the area with the gauze. Do not rub.	5		
18. Discard in the syringe sharps container. Remove gloves and discard in a biohazardous container.	5		
19. Sanitize the hands.	5		
20. Check the patient.	5		
21. Read or discuss with the patient the test results.	10		
22. Sanitize hands.	5		
23. Document the procedure.	10		
Mantoux Test			
24. Check to be sure test was given 48 to 72 hours earlier.	10		
25. After sanitizing the hands and applying nonsterile gloves, gently rub the test site with a finger and lightly palpate for induration.	10		
26. Using the tape that comes with the medication, measure the diameter of the area of induration from edge to edge.	10		
27. Record the area of induration and notify the health care provider of the measurement if not within the negative range.	10		
28. Record the reading in the medical record.	10		
Total Points Possible	245		

Comments: Total Points Earned _____   Instructor's Signature _____

Student Name _____   Date _____

CHECKLIST: ADMINISTER A SUBCUTANEOUS INJECTION

TASK
- Identify the correct syringe, needle gauge, and length for a subcutaneous injection.
- Select and prepare an appropriate site for a subcutaneous injection.
- Demonstrate the correct technique to administer a subcutaneous injection.
- Document a subcutaneous injection correctly in the medical record.

CONDITIONS: Given the proper equipment and supplies, the student will prepare and administer a subcutaneous injection.

EQUIPMENT AND SUPPLIES
- Nonsterile disposable gloves
- Medication as ordered by physician
- Appropriate syringe for ordered dose of medication
- Appropriate needle with safety device
- 2 × 2-inch sterile gauze
- 70% Isopropyl alcohol wipes
- Sharps container
- Biohazardous waste container
- Patient's medical record

STANDARDS: Complete the procedure within _____ minutes and achieve a minimum score of _____%.

Time began _____   Time ended _____

Steps	Possible Points	First Attempt	Second Attempt
1. Sanitize hands.	5		
2. Verify the order, and assemble equipment and supplies.	5		
3. Check expiration date of the medication.	10		
4. Follow the "seven rights" of medication administration.	10		
5. Check the medication against the physician's order three times before administration.	10		
6. Check the patient's medical record for drug allergies or conditions that may contraindicate the injection.	10		
7. Calculate the correct dose to be given, if necessary.	15		
8. Follow the procedure for drawing the medication into the syringe.	5		
9. Greet and identify the patient, and explain the procedure.	10		
10. Select an appropriate injection site and properly position the patient as necessary to expose the site.	10		
11. Apply gloves.	5		
12. Prepare the injection site.	10		

Steps	Possible Points	First Attempt	Second Attempt
13. While the prepared site is drying, remove the cover from the needle.	5		
14. Pinch the skin at the injection site and puncture the skin quickly and smoothly, making sure the needle is kept at a 45-degree angle.	10		
15. Aspirate the syringe to check for blood. If no blood is present, inject the medication.	10		
16. Place a gauze pad over the injection site and quickly withdraw the needle from the injection site at the same angle at which it was inserted.	10		
17. Massage the injection site, if appropriate.	5		
18. Discard the syringe and needle into a rigid biohazardous container.	5		
19. Remove gloves and discard in a biohazardous waste container.	5		
20. Sanitize the hands.	5		
21. Check on the patient.	5		
22. Document procedure.	10		
Total Points Possible	175		

Comments: Total Points Earned _____   Instructor's Signature _____

Student Name _____   Date _____

CHECKLIST: ADMINISTER AN INTRAMUSCULAR INJECTION TO AN ADULT

TASK
- Identify the correct syringe, needle gauge, and length for an adult intramuscular injection.
- Select and prepare an appropriate site for a pediatric intramuscular injection.
- Demonstrate the correct technique to administer an intramuscular injection.
- Document an intramuscular injection correctly in the medical record.

CONDITIONS: Given the proper equipment and supplies, the student will prepare and administer an intramuscular injection to an adult patient.

EQUIPMENT AND SUPPLIES
- Nonsterile disposable gloves
- Medication as ordered by physician
- Appropriate syringe for ordered medication dose
- Appropriate needle with safety device (21 or 25 gauge, 1 inch to 1½ inch)
- 2 × 2-inch sterile gauze
- 70% isopropyl alcohol wipes
- Sharps container
- Biohazardous waste container
- Patient's medical record

STANDARDS: Complete the procedure within _____ minutes and achieve a minimum score of _____%.

Time began _____   Time ended _____

Steps	Possible Points	First Attempt	Second Attempt
1. Sanitize hands.	5		
2. Verify the order, and assemble equipment and supplies.	5		
3. Follow the "seven rights" of medication administration.	10		
4. Check the medication against the physician's order three times before administration.	10		
5. Check the patient's medical record for drug allergies or conditions that may contraindicate the injection.	10		
6. Check expiration date of the medication.	10		
7. Calculate the correct dose to be given.	20		
8. Greet and identify the patient, and explain the procedure.	10		
9. Select an appropriate injection site by amount and density of medication. Properly position the patient as necessary to expose the site adequately.	10		
10. Apply gloves.	5		
11. Prepare the injection site.	10		
12. While the prepared site is drying, remove the cover from the needle.	10		

Steps	Possible Points	First Attempt	Second Attempt
13. Secure the skin at the injection site.	10		
14. Puncture the skin quickly and smoothly, making sure the needle is kept at a 90-degree angle.	10		
15. Aspirate the syringe.	10		
16. Inject medication using proper technique for density of medication.	10		
17. Place a gauze pad over the injection site and quickly withdraw the needle from the injection site at the same angle at which it was inserted. Activate the safety shield over the needle.	10		
18. Massage the injection site if appropriate for medication.	10		
19. Discard the syringe and needle into a sharps container.	5		
20. Remove gloves and discard in a biohazardous waste container.	5		
21. Sanitize the hands.	5		
22. Check on the patient.	10		
23. Document procedure.	10		
Total Points Possible	210		

Comments: Total Points Earned _____   Instructor's Signature _____

Student Name _____   Date _____

CHECKLIST: ADMINISTER AN INTRAMUSCULAR INJECTION USING THE Z-TRACK TECHNIQUE

TASK: Demonstrate the correct technique to administer an intramuscular injection using the Z-track technique.

CONDITIONS: Given the proper equipment and supplies, the student will prepare and administer an intramuscular injection using the Z-track technique.

EQUIPMENT AND SUPPLIES
- Nonsterile disposable gloves
- Medication order by physician
- Appropriate syringe for ordered dose
- Appropriate needle with safety device
- 2 × 2-inch sterile gauze
- 70% isopropyl alcohol wipes
- Biohazardous waste container
- Patient's medical record

STANDARDS: Complete the procedure within _____ minutes and achieve a minimum score of _____%.

Time began _____   Time ended _____

Steps	Possible Points	First Attempt	Second Attempt
1. Sanitize hands.	5		
2. Verify the order, and assemble equipment and supplies.	5		
3. Follow the "seven rights" of medication administration.	10		
4. Check the medication against the physician's order three times before administration.	10		
5. Check the patient's medical record for drug allergies or conditions that may contraindicate the injection.	10		
6. Check expiration date of the medication.	10		
7. Calculate the correct dose to be given.	20		
8. Follow the correct procedure for drawing the medication into syringe.	10		
9. Greet and identify the patient, and explain the procedure to the patient.	15		
10. Select an appropriate injection site and properly position the patient.	5		
11. Apply disposable gloves.	5		
12. Prepare the injection site.	5		
13. While the prepared site is drying, remove the cover from the needle.	5		

Steps	Possible Points	First Attempt	Second Attempt
14. Secure the skin at the injection site by pushing the skin away from the injection site.	10		
15. Puncture the skin quickly and smoothly, making sure the needle is kept at a 90-degree angle.	10		
16. Continue to hold the tissue in place while aspirating and injecting the medication.	15		
17. Inject the medication.	10		
18. Withdraw the needle.	10		
19. Release the traction on the skin to seal the track as the needle is being removed. Activate safety shield over needle.	10		
20. Discard the syringe and needle into a rigid biohazardous container.	5		
21. Remove gloves and discard in a biohazardous waste container.	5		
22. Sanitize the hands.	5		
23. Check on the patient.	5		
24. Document the procedure.	5		
25. Clean the equipment and examination room.	10		
Total Points Possible	215		

Comments: Total Points Earned _____   Instructor's Signature _____

Student Name _____   Date _____

CHECKLIST: PERFORM VENIPUNCTURE USING THE EVACUATED-TUBE METHOD (COLLECTION OF MULTIPLE TUBES)

TASK: Obtain a venous blood specimen acceptable for testing using the evacuated-tube system.

CONDITIONS: Given the proper equipment and supplies, the student will be required to perform a venipuncture using the evacuated-tube system method of collection.

EQUIPMENT AND SUPPLIES
- Nonsterile disposable gloves
- Personal protective equipment (PPE) as required
- Tourniquet (latex-free)
- Evacuated tube holder
- Evacuated tube multidraw needle (21 or 22 gauge, 1 or 1½ inch) with safety guards
- Evacuated blood tubes for requested tests with labels (correct nonadditive or additive required for ordered test)
- Alcohol wipe
- Sterile 2 × 2-inch gauze pads
- Bandage (latex-free) or nonallergenic tape
- Sharps container
- Biohazardous waste container
- Laboratory requisition form
- Patient's medical record

STANDARDS: Complete the procedure within _____ minutes and achieve a minimum score of _____%.

Time began _____   Time ended _____

Steps	Possible Points	First Attempt	Second Attempt
1. Sanitize hands.	5		
2. Verify the order, and assemble equipment and supplies.	5		
3. Greet the patient, identify yourself, and confirm the patient's identity. Escort the patient to the proper room. Ask the patient to sit in phlebotomy chair.	5		
4. Confirm that the patient has followed the needed preparation (e.g., fasting).	10		
5. Explain the procedure to the patient.	5		
6. Prepare the evacuated tube system.	5		
7. Open the sterile gauze packet and place the gauze pad on the inside of its wrapper, or obtain sterile gauze pads from a bulk package.	10		
8. Position the remaining needed supplies for ease of reaching with nondominant hand. Place tube loosely in holder with label facing downward.	10		
9. Position and examine the arm to be used in the venipuncture.	10		
10. Apply the tourniquet.	10		
11. Apply gloves and PPE.	5		

Steps	Possible Points	First Attempt	Second Attempt
12. Thoroughly palpate the selected vein.	5		
13. Release the tourniquet.	5		
14. Prepare the puncture site using alcohol swabs.	10		
15. Reapply the tourniquet.	10		
16. Position the holder while keeping the needle covered, being certain to have control of holder. Uncover the needle.	10		
17. Position the needle so that it follows the line of the vein.	5		
18. Perform the venipuncture.	5		
19. Secure the holder. Push the bottom of the tube with the thumb of your nondominant hand so that the needle inside the holder pierces the rubber stopper of the tube. Follow the direction of the vein.	10		
20. Change tubes (minimum of two tubes) as required by test orders.	10		
21. Gently invert tubes that contain additives to be mixed with the specimen.	10		
22. While the blood is filling the last tube, release the tourniquet and withdraw the needle. Cover the needle with the safety shield.	10		
23. Apply direct pressure on the venipuncture site, and instruct the patient to raise the arm straight above the head and maintain pressure on the site for 1 to 2 minutes.	10		
24. Discard the contaminated needle and holder into the sharps container.	10		
25. Label the tubes as appropriate for lab.	10		
26. Place the tube into the biohazard transport bag.	5		
27. Check for bleeding at puncture site and apply a pressure dressing.	5		
28. Remove and discard the alcohol wipe and gloves.	5		
29. Sanitize the hands.	5		
30. Record the collection date and time on the laboratory requisition form, and place the requisition in the proper place in the biohazard transport bag.	10		
31. Ask and observe how the patient feels.	5		
32. Clean the work area using Standard Precautions.	5		
33. Document the procedure, indicating tests for which blood was drawn and the labs to which blood will be sent.	10		
Total Points Possible	250		

Comments: Total Points Earned _____   Instructor's Signature _____

Student Name _____   Date _____

CHECKLIST: PERFORM VENIPUNCTURE USING THE SYRINGE METHOD

TASK: Obtain a venous blood specimen acceptable for testing using the syringe method.

CONDITIONS: Given the proper equipment and supplies, the student will be required to perform a venipuncture using the syringe method of collection.

EQUIPMENT AND SUPPLIES
* Nonsterile disposable gloves
* Personal protective equipment (PPE) as required
* Tourniquet (latex-free)
* Test tube rack
* 10-cc (10-mL) syringe with 21- or 22-gauge needle and safety guards
* Proper evacuated blood tubes for tests ordered
* Alcohol wipe
* Sterile 2 × 2-inch gauze pads
* Bandage (latex-free) or nonallergenic tape
* Sharps container
* Biohazardous waste container
* Laboratory requisition form
* Patient's medical record

STANDARDS: Complete the procedure within _____ minutes and achieve a minimum score of _____%.

Time began _____   Time ended _____

Steps	Possible Points	First Attempt	Second Attempt
1. Sanitize hands.	5		
2. Verify the order. Assemble equipment and supplies.	5		
3. Greet the patient, identify yourself, and confirm the patient's identity. Escort the patient to the room for the blood draw. Position the patient in phlebotomy chair or on examination table.	5		
4. Confirm any necessary preparation has been accomplished (e.g., fasting). Explain the procedure to the patient.	5		
5. Prepare the needle and syringe, maintaining syringe sterility. Break the seal on the syringe by moving the plunger back and forth several times. Loosen the cap on the needle and check to make sure that the hub is screwed tightly onto the syringe.	15		
6. Place the evacuated tubes to be filled in a test tube rack on a work surface in order of fill.	15		
7. Open the sterile gauze packet and place the gauze pad on the inside of its wrapper, or obtain sterile gauze pads from a bulk package.	5		
8. Position and examine the arm to be used in the venipuncture.	10		
9. Apply gloves and PPE.	5		

Steps	Possible Points	First Attempt	Second Attempt
10. Thoroughly palpate the selected vein.	10		
11. Release the tourniquet.	10		
12. Prepare the puncture site and reapply tourniquet.	10		
13. If drawing from the hand, ask the patient to make a fist or bend the fingers downward. Pull the skin taut with your thumb over the top of the patient's knuckles.	15		
14. Position the syringe and grasp the syringe firmly between the thumb and the underlying fingers.	10		
15. Follow the direction of the vein and insert the needle in one quick motion at about a 45-degree angle.	10		
16. If drawing from AC vein, with your nondominant hand pull the skin taut beneath the intended puncture site to anchor the vein. Thumb should be 1 to 2 inches below and to the side of the vein.	15		
17. Position the syringe and grasp the syringe firmly between the thumb and the underlying fingers.	10		
18. Follow the direction of the vein and insert the needle in one quick motion at about a 15-degree angle.	10		
19. Perform the venipuncture. If flash does not occur, gently pull back on the plunger. Do not move the needle. If blood still does not enter the syringe, slowly withdraw the needle, secure new supplies, and retry the draw.	10		
20. Anchor the syringe, and gently continue pulling back on the plunger until the required amount of blood is in the syringe.	10		
21. Release the tourniquet.	5		
22. Remove the needle and cover the needle with safety shield without locking.	10		
23. Apply direct pressure on the venipuncture site, and instruct the patient to raise the arm straight above the head. Instruct the patient to maintain pressure on the site for 1 to 2 minutes.	5		
24. Transfer the blood to the evacuated tubes as soon as possible.	10		
25. Properly dispose of the syringe and needle.	10		
26. Label the tubes and place into biohazard transport bag.	10		
27. Check for bleeding at venipuncture site and place a pressure dressing.	10		
28. Remove and discard the alcohol wipe and gloves.	5		
29. Sanitize the hands.	5		
30. Record the collection date and time on the laboratory requisition form, and place the requisition in the biohazard transport bag.	10		

Steps	Possible Points	First Attempt	Second Attempt
31. Ask and observe how the patient feels.	5		
32. Clean the work area using Standard Precautions.	5		
33. Document the procedure.	10		
Total Points Possible NOTE: Awards points for Steps 13-14-15 OR 16-17-18, not both	255		

Comments: Total Points Earned _____   Instructor's Signature _____

Student Name _____   Date _____

CHECKLIST: PERFORM VENIPUNCTURE USING THE BUTTERFLY METHOD (COLLECTION OF MULTIPLE EVACUATED TUBES)

TASK: Obtain a venous blood specimen acceptable for testing using the butterfly method.

CONDITIONS: Given the proper equipment and supplies, the student will perform a venipuncture using the butterfly method of collection.

EQUIPMENT AND SUPPLIES
- Nonsterile disposable gloves
- Personal protective equipment (PPE) as required
- Tourniquet (latex-free)
- Test tube rack
- Winged-infusion set with Luer adapter and safety guard
- Multidraw needle (22 to 25 gauge) and tube holder, or 10-cc (10-mL) syringe
- Evacuated blood tubes for requested tests with labels (correct nonadditive or additive required for ordered tests)
- Alcohol wipe
- Sterile 2 × 2-inch gauze pads
- Bandage (latex-free) or nonallergenic tape
- Sharps container
- Biohazardous waste container
- Laboratory requisition form
- Patient's medical record

STANDARDS: Complete the procedure within _____ minutes and achieve a minimum score of _____%.

Time began _____   Time ended _____

Steps	Possible Points	First Attempt	Second Attempt
1. Sanitize hands.	5		
2. Verify the order. Assemble equipment and supplies.	5		
3. Greet the patient, identify yourself, and confirm the patient's identity. Escort the patient to the proper room for venipuncture.	5		
4. Ask the patient to have a seat in the phlebotomy chair or on the examination table.	5		
5. Confirm any necessary preparation has been followed (e.g., fasting). Explain the procedure to the patient.	10		
6. Prepare the winged infusion set. Attach the winged infusion set to either a syringe or an evacuated tube holder.	15		
7. Open the sterile gauze packet and place the gauze pad on the inside of its wrapper, or obtain sterile gauze pads from a bulk package.	5		
8. Position and examine the arm to be used in the venipuncture.	10		
9. Apply the tourniquet.	10		
10. Apply gloves and PPE.	5		
11. Thoroughly palpate the selected vein.	10		

Steps	Possible Points	First Attempt	Second Attempt
12. Release the tourniquet.	10		
13. Prepare the puncture site and reapply the tourniquet.	5		
14. If drawing from the hand, ask the patient to make a fist or bend the fingers downward. Pull the skin taut with your thumb over the top of the patient's knuckles.	10		
15. Remove the protective shield from the needle of the infusion set, being sure the bevel is facing up. Position needle over vein to be punctured.	10		
16. Perform the venipuncture. With your nondominant hand, pull the skin taut beneath the intended puncture site to anchor the vein. Thumb should be 1 to 2 inches below and to the side of the vein. Follow the direction of the vein and insert the needle in one quick motion at about a 15-degree angle.	20		
17. After penetrating the vein, decrease the angle of the needle to 5 degrees until a "flash" of blood appears in the tubing.	5		
18. Secure the needle for blood collection.	10		
19. Insert the evacuated tube into the tube holder or gently pull back on the plunger of the syringe. Change tubes as required by the test ordered.	10		
20. Release the tourniquet and remove the needle.	10		
21. Apply direct pressure on the venipuncture site, and instruct the patient to raise the arm straight above the head. Maintain pressure on the site for 1 to 2 minutes, with the arm raised straight above the head.	10		
22. If a syringe was used, transfer the blood to the evacuated tubes as soon as possible.	10		
23. Dispose of the winged infusion set.	5		
24. Label the tubes and place the tube into the biohazard transport bag.	5		
25. Check for bleeding and place a bandage over the gauze to create a pressure dressing.	5		
26. Remove and discard the alcohol wipe and gloves.	5		
27. Sanitize the hands.	5		
28. Record the collection date and time on the laboratory requisition form, and place the requisition in the biohazard transport bag.	10		
29. Ask and observe how the patient feels.	5		
30. Clean the work area using Standard Precautions.	5		
31. Document the procedure.	10		
Total Points Possible	250		

Comments: Total Points Earned _____   Instructor's Signature _____

Student Name _____   Date _____

CHECKLIST: CHARTING

TASK: Create new medical records, organize contents, interview patients, and document subjective and objective data.

CONDITIONS: Given the proper equipment and supplies, the students will be required to create new medical records by labeling them correctly and organizing sample forms and/or reports within each appropriately. The student will then role-play with another student or an instructor to demonstrate how to interview a patient. Finally, using the list of common charting abbreviations (as directed) from the student handbook, the student will record the "patient's" chief complaint (subjective data) as well as every procedure in this module using the sample documentation provided on the procedure competency checklists (objective data).

EQUIPMENT AND SUPPLIES

- File folders
- Blank file labels
- Color-coded year labels
- Alphabetical labels
- Medical alert labels
- Other labels as appropriate
- Sample forms and/or reports
- Sample documentation (on procedure competency checklists)

STANDARDS: Complete the procedure within _____ minutes and achieve a minimum score of _____%.

Time began _____   Time ended _____

Steps	Possible Points	First Attempt	Second Attempt
1. Assemble all equipment and supplies.	5		
2. Create a file label (patient name).	5		
3. Attach other labels as appropriate (year, initials, medical alert).	5		
4. Organize preprinted forms appropriately within the folder.	10		
5. Review medical history form with the patient (subjective data).	10		
6. Record chief complaint (in patient's own words/subjective data).	10		
7. Document all procedures on appropriate forms using correct terminology and abbreviations (objective data).	10		
8. Record all information legibly.	10		
9. Maintain HIPAA privacy guidelines.	10		
10. Maintain professional qualities as defined.	10		
11. Clean area when finished.	5		
Total Points Possible	90		

Comments: Total Points Earned _____   Instructor's Signature _____

Student Name _____   Date _____

CHECKLIST: DIAGNOSTIC CODING

TASK: Assign the proper *International Classification of Diseases (ICD-9-CM)* code based on medical documentation to the highest degree of specificity.

CONDITIONS: Given the proper equipment and supplies, the student will assign the proper *ICD-9-CM* code based on medical documentation to the highest degree of specificity.

EQUIPMENT AND SUPPLIES
- Current *ICD-9-CM* codebook
- Medical dictionary
- Patient's medical records
- Pen or pencil
- Work product (see next pages)

STANDARDS: Complete the procedure within _____ minutes and achieve a minimum score of _____%.

Time began _____   Time ended _____

Steps	Possible Points	First Attempt	Second Attempt
1. Assemble all supplies and equipment.	5		
2. Identify the key term in the diagnostic statement.	10		
3. Locate the diagnosis in the Alphabetic Index (Volume 2, Section 1) of the *ICD-9-CM* codebook.	20		
4. Read and use footnotes, symbols, or instructions.	15		
5. Locate the diagnosis in the Tabular List (Volume 1).	10		
6. Read and use the inclusions and exclusions noted in the Tabular List.	10		
7. Assign the code to the highest degree of specificity appropriate.	20		
8. Document in the medical record.	10		
9. Ask yourself these final questions (NO points awarded for this section).	0		
a. Have you coded to the highest degree of specificity?			
b. Are there any secondary diagnoses or conditions addressed during the encounter that need to be coded?			
Total Points Possible	100		

Comments: Total Points Earned _____   Instructor's Signature _____

Student Name _____   Date _____

CHECKLIST: PROCEDURAL CODING

TASK: Assign the proper *Current Procedural Terminology* (CPT) code to the highest degree of specificity based on medical documentation for auditing and billing purposes.

CONDITIONS: Given the proper equipment and supplies, the student will assign the proper (CPT) code to the highest degree of specificity based on medical documentation for auditing and billing purposes.

EQUIPMENT AND SUPPLIES
- Current *CPT* codebook
- Medical dictionary
- Patient's medical records
- Pen or pencil
- Work product (see next pages)

STANDARDS: Complete the procedure within _____ minutes and achieve a minimum score of _____%.

Time began _____   Time ended _____

Steps	Possible Points	First Attempt	Second Attempt
1. Assemble all supplies and equipment.	5		
2. Read the introduction, guidelines, and notes of a current *CPT* codebook.	10		
3. Review all service and procedures performed on the day of the encounter; include all medications administered and trays and equipment used.	20		
4. Identify the main term in the procedure.	15		
5. Locate the main term in the alphabetical index. Review any subterms listed alphabetically under the main term.	10		
6. Verify the code sets in the tabular (numerical) list. Select the code with the greatest specificity.	10		
7. Determine if a modifier is required.	20		
8. Assign the code using all necessary steps for proper code determination.	10		
9. Ask yourself these final questions (NO points awarded for this section).	0		
a. Have you coded to the highest degree of specificity?			
b. Are there any secondary diagnoses or conditions addressed during the encounter that need to be coded?			
Total Points Possible	100		

Comments: Total Points Earned _____   Instructor's Signature _____

Student Name _____   Date _____

CHECKLIST: USE *PHYSICIAN'S DESK REFERENCE*

TASK: Demonstrate understanding of *Physician's Desk Reference's* organization by creating a fact sheet for each drug listed on a prepared document.

CONDITIONS: Given proper equipment and supplies, the student will be required to identify the trade and generic names for each listed drug, its classification, one indication for its use, one contraindication for its use, its usual dosage and administration, and any possible side effects.

EQUIPMENT AND SUPPLIES
- *Physician's Desk Reference*
- List of drugs (on following pages)
- Pen or pencil

STANDARDS: Complete the procedure within _____ minutes and achieve a minimum score of _____%.

Time began _____   Time ended _____

Steps	Possible Points	First Attempt	Second Attempt
1. Assemble all equipment and supplies.	5		
2. Create a fact sheet for each medication listed on the prepared drug list (see next page) to include the following:			
• Trade name, generic name, and drug classification	10		
• Identify indications for assigned medications	10		
• Identify contraindications for assigned medications	10		
• Identify dosage and administration of assigned medications	10		
• Identify side effects of assigned medications	10		
3. Display professional abilities through penmanship.	10		
4. Clean area.	5		
5. Proofread and correct your work and submit to your instructor. Demonstrate professionalism throughout procedure and accept constructive feedback with a problem-solving attitude.	10		
Total Points Possible	80		

Comments: Total Points Earned _____   Instructor's Signature _____